002017469
D1589293

An Introduction to African

An Introduction to African Politics is an ideal textbook for those new to the study of this vast and fascinating continent. It makes sense of the diverse political systems that are a feature of Africa by using familiar concepts, chapter by chapter, to examine the continent as a whole. The result is a textbook that identifies the essential features of African politics, allowing students to grasp the recurring political patterns that have dominated this part of the world since independence.

Features and benefits of *An Introduction to African Politics*:

- It is thematically organised, with individual chapters exploring issues such as colonialism, ethnicity, nationalism, social class, ideology, legitimacy, sovereignty, and democracy.
- It identifies key recurrent themes such as the competitive relationships between the African state, its civil society, and external interests.
- It contains useful boxed case studies at the end of each chapter, including: Kenya; Tanzania; Nigeria; Botswana; Côte d'Ivoire; Uganda; Somalia; Ghana; Zaire; and Algeria.
- Each chapter concludes with key terms and definitions as well as questions, advice on further reading, and useful notes and references.
- It is clearly and accessibly written by an experienced teacher of the subject.

Students seeking a comprehensive survey and useful resource to help in their understanding of the complex theories and events that characterise Africa will find this textbook essential reading.

Alex Thomson is a Senior Lecturer in Politics and Government at the University of Central Lancashire.

An Introduction to African Politics

Alex Thomson

London and New York

First published 2000
by Routledge
11 New Fetter Lane, London EC4P 4EE

Simultaneously published in the USA and Canada
by Routledge
29 West 35th Street, New York, NY 10001

Routledge is an imprint of the Taylor & Francis Group

Reprinted 2001

. © 2000 Alex Thomson

Typeset in Goudy by Taylor & Francis Books Ltd
Printed and bound in Great Britain by MPG Books Ltd, Bodmin

All rights reserved. No part of this book may be reprinted or
reproduced or utilised in any form or by any electronic,
mechanical, or other means, now known or hereafter
invented, including photocopying and recording, or in any
information storage or retrieval system, without permission
in writing from the publishers.

British Library Cataloguing in Publication Data
A catalogue record for this book is available
from the British Library

Library of Congress Cataloging in Publication Data
Thomson, Alex.
  An introduction to African politics / Alex Thomson.
  p. cm.
  Includes bibliographical references and index.
  1. Africa–Politics and government. I. Title.
  DT31 .T5157 2000
  320.96–dc21   99-054692

ISBN 0–415–18198–4 (pbk)
ISBN 0–415–18197–6 (hbk)

Contents

List of tables   viii
Acknowledgements   ix

1 Introduction: state, civil society and external interests   1

2 History: Africa's pre-colonial and colonial inheritance   7
  The pre-colonial inheritance 7
  The colonial inheritance 9
  State and civil society 20
  Case study: Kenya's historical inheritance 21

3 Ideology: nationalism, socialism, populism and state capitalism   30
  Decolonisation in Africa 31
  Nationalism 33
  African nationalism 34
  The differing ideological shades of African nationalism 36
  State and civil society 44
  Case study: socialism and ujamaa in Tanzania 48

4 Ethnicity: ethnic groups, 'tribes', and political identity   57
  Definitions of ethnicity 58
  The creation of 'tribes' 58
  Ethnicity as a method of modern political mobilisation 62
  State and civil society 64
  Case study: ethnicity and the nation-state in Nigeria 65

5 **Social class: the search for class politics in Africa**   **74**
Marx on social class 74
The problems of exporting Marx to Africa 76
The African mode of production 77
A more flexible look at social class in Africa 79
Identifiable social groups within African society 79
The value of class analysis in explaining African politics 89
State and civil society 91
Case study: social class in Botswana 92

6 **Legitimacy: neo-patrimonialism, personal rule and the
centralisation of the African state**   **99**
Centralisation of the African state 100
Personal rule 107
The search for legitimacy 110
Clientelism 111
State and civil society 112
Case study: personal rule in Côte d'Ivoire 114

7 **Coercion: military intervention in African politics**   **121**
African military coups d'état 122
Why has Africa experienced so many military coups? 125
Problems facing military rulers 129
The outcomes of military rule in Africa 131
State and civil society 133
Case study: Uganda's 1971 military coup 133

8 **Sovereignty: external influences on African politics**   **141**
Inter-African international relations 142
Superpowers, the Cold War and Africa 143
The impact of the Cold War on African politics 149
Africa and the New World Order 150
State, civil society and external interests 154
Case study: Somalia's international relations 156

9 **Sovereignty again: neo-colonialism, structural adjustment, and Africa's political economy** **165**
Burdens of the international economy 168
The African debt crisis 170
The era of structural adjustment 173
The economic, social and political ramifications of structural adjustment 175
State, civil society and external interests 179
Case study: Ghana's structural adjustment 181

10 **Authority: the crises of accumulation, governance and state collapse 189**
The growing crisis of state legitimacy 190
The loss of state authority 195
The state's own survival strategies 200
State and civil society 203
Case study: Zaire – Mobutu's vampire state 205

11 **Democracy: re-legitimising the African state?** **215**
Democracy 216
Explaining the emergence of multi-party democracy 218
The obstacles to democratic consolidation 222
State and civil society 231
Case study: the search for democracy in Algeria 232

12 **Conclusions: state and civil society in post-colonial Africa** **242**

Appendix: multi-party legislative and presidential elections in Africa, independence to 1999 **247**

Notes **255**
Index **268**

Tables

2.1	Potential problems created by the colonial inheritance	19
3.1	Decolonisation in Africa	32
3.2	Africa's nationalist ideologies	43
5.1	African social groups	88
7.1	African military coups since independence	124
9.1	Comparative global economic and social indicators	166
9.2	African export concentration, 1982–6	169
9.3	Index of international trade, 1960–95	170
11.1	Comparative African political systems, 1988 and 1999	216
11.2	African democratic transitions, 1990–9	231

Acknowledgements

To write any academic book alone is almost an impossible task, not to say foolish. In this particular instance, no one person could possibly formulate enough theories or collect enough empirical evidence to help them explain the politics of a whole continent. My first acknowledgement must therefore go the authors of all the many books and papers that I have examined over the last two years. The most rewarding of these can be found in the suggested further reading at the end of each chapter, while other works are cited in the notes. I can only hope that this book reflects these authors' arguments accurately, and that my own ideas follow in the laudable tradition of Africanist scholarship that these individuals have established.

I would also like to acknowledge the assistance of my editor at Routledge, Mark Kavanagh. His management of this project, and, above all, his patience, have ensured that *An Introduction to African Politics* has reached the shelves in good order.

It is to friends and family, however, that I owe the most. They have collectively ensured that this project has been completed without too much embarrassment. Keith Faulks put me right on my use of political science (even if we still cannot agree on the concept of authority); Nick James ensured that I looked beyond the end of my political nose (introducing geographical approaches to Africa); while Jake Hollyfield and Pat Thomson looked after my dubious comprehensive school grammar. Between us, I hope we have ironed out all my original errors. Of course, if any mistakes remain, these are, alas, all my own.

A.R.T.
Manchester, 1999

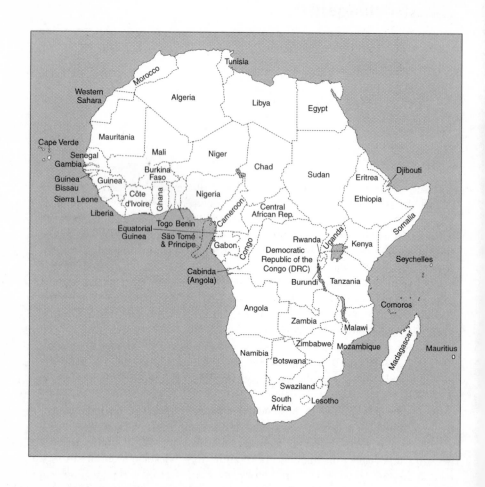

1 Introduction

State, civil society and external interests

Africa has a lot to offer the student of politics. It has it all. Autocrats vie with democrats; governments espousing socialism neighbour those bound by liberal constitutions; some states are a model of stability, while others are near the point of total collapse; multi-party systems jostle with one-party states; and social divisions based on ethnicity, religion, class and race all challenge political leaders in their attempts to maintain order. The politics that these realities create make Africa a stimulating and rewarding place to study.

Yet, it could be asked, 'why should Westerners spend valuable time analysing the politics of Africa?' Should they not concentrate on countries closer to home? Indeed, what is it precisely that this continent has to offer? Well, apart from the reward of investigating Africa's fascinating political nuances for their own sake, the continent is also invaluable as a source for the study of comparative politics. Africa's variety of political processes and institutions provide an abundance of alternative case studies for the student of politics to investigate. After all, studying political phenomena outside familiar (Western) settings can add a new dimension of understanding. As many travellers have learnt, experiencing foreign cultures not only helps with an appreciation of the country visited, it also forces the traveller to view their own country in a different light. This is what comparative politics is all about.

However, to benefit from what Africa has to offer, new scholars of this continent first need to abandon their preconceptions. Average Western views of Africa tend to be rather selective and not always accurate. The most common exposure the continent receives in the West is via broadcast journalism, and if individuals rely solely on this source, then Africa is a continent of famines, disasters and civil war. All these factors do exist on the continent from time to time, but to see such events as the sum of African politics is to be profoundly misled. Journalistic selectivity and ignorance based on the images of Tarzan, mud huts and warring tribes, all have to be left behind before the real essence of Africa can be grasped. Newcomers to the continent should approach this part of the world with an open mind.

George Alagiah, a former Africa correspondent for the BBC, highlights this problem of perception. Assessing his stint on the continent, he was well aware of the 'bad press' that this part of the world received during his watch. Despite his efforts to inform, he conceded that Western television pictures painted Africa as 'a faraway place where good people go hungry, bad people run government, and chaos and anarchy are the norm'. He regretted that rarely do viewers get to see Africa 'in full flower'. Illustrating this point, Alagiah recounts an instance towards the end of his stint. While covering the 1998 famine in southern Sudan, he filed two reports. These were broadcast on the UK's national news on consecutive nights. The first described the situation on the ground, and the second made a conscious effort to explain why this famine had occurred. It was the first film that had most impact. Letters from correspondents reflected people's feeling of genuine sorrow 'for the poor souls of southern Sudan', but few recalled being told why this tragedy had actually happened. As Alagiah puts it, 'To get people in British living rooms to identify with the frazzled aid worker as she tries to cope with a humanitarian disaster is easy. To get people to see that the crisis is part of the convulsive process of post-colonial political realignment is more difficult.'[1]

This is precisely the problem that new students of Africa have to overcome. The difficulty is that many Westerners, when it comes to African politics, simply see cause and effect as the same thing. Why is there a civil war in Liberia? Why was there genocide in Rwanda? Why has the Somali state collapsed? All these questions are satisfactorily dealt with in people's minds by the answer 'because it is Africa': these things happen 'naturally' on the continent; it is an *inherently* unstable region. This is the central myth that *An Introduction to African Politics* aims to destroy.

Africans are innately no more violent, no more corrupt, no more greedy, and no more stupid than any other human beings that populate the world. They are no less capable of governing themselves. Not to believe this is to revive the racism that underpinned the ethos of slavery and colonialism. In this sense, African political structures are as irrational as any other systems of government. If there have been more military coups in Africa than in the United States, then there has to be a *reason* for this. An explanation also exists for why the continent's political systems are more susceptible to corruption than those of the United Kingdom. By applying reason, the worst excesses of African politics (the famines and the civil wars) can be accounted for, as can the more common, more mundane, day-to-day features of conflict resolution on the continent. This book uncovers the genuine underlying post-colonial political processes that have been at work, and, as such, asks its readers to abandon any preconceived explanations they may harbour which involve Africans being seen as inferior, irrational, volatile and artless victims of their own political environment.

A second preliminary piece of advice that this book offers is for newcomers not to regard Africa as homogeneous. It is a massive land mass, home to many different cultures and societies. There is no such thing as a typical African polity. There are 53 separate independent states. Each is unique, and each has its own system of politics. The Gambia is a tiny country of just 11,000 sq km, while the Sudan's territory is 250 times larger than this; Nigeria has a population of over 108 million, while Lesotho has just two million inhabitants;

Botswana is largely an arid state, but Congo-Kinshasa is lush in vegetation; Ethiopia is racially homogeneous, while South Africa is home to several racial communities. The north of the continent is predominantly Muslim and the south Christian, not to mention the mixture of indigenous spiritual traditions found throughout. No one political system would be capable of serving all these states, as local demands necessarily produce different and individual polities.

To cope with this diversity, there is certainly no substitute for studying each African country in its entirety. Each state deserves to be examined in as much detail as possible. A vast literature on the politics of the continent exists in an attempt to do just this. Yet apprentice Africanists often find it difficult to digest this detailed and sometimes complex body of work without investing first in some more general preparatory reading. The present book was written with this fact in mind.

An Introduction to African Politics offers a comparative approach to the whole of Africa. The book will make a general sweep across the continent, identifying common elements within these societies. What is lost in detail by this broad introduction is made up for by the grounding that such an approach gives with respect to the basics of African politics. It allows newcomers to ease themselves into the politics of the continent, identifying the essentials rather than grappling with the minute detail found in the literature addressing individual states. The book thus acts as a starting point for those interested in African politics.

Having established that the politics of Africa are rational and worthy of study, and that the continent in not homogeneous, it would be wise now to outline this book's methodology. As indicated earlier, the practice of politics on the African continent is not so different from political processes found elsewhere in the world. It is still about power, resource distribution and conflict resolution, as well as the governments that oversee these processes. In this sense, Africa may be a unique stage on which political transactions are carried out, but the actual processes themselves have more similarities than differences with other continents. Note, for example, how socialism, issues of ethnicity and class, military *coups d'état*, state collapse, newly formed democracies and one-party states have all been features within European politics during the same post-colonial period.

In this respect, new scholars of African politics should not be unduly daunted. The knowledge readers already have of (Western) political processes and concepts can be applied to the African continent. And this, indeed, is how the book will be structured. Each chapter takes a familiar political concept, and then examines how this concept relates specifically to the African environment. Chapters tackle issues such as ideology, nationalism, social class, legitimacy, coercion, sovereignty, authority and democracy, among others. Not only does this thematic approach introduce the nature of the African polity, giving a knowledge of what has actually happened in African politics since decolonisation, but it also reinforces an understanding of these important basic political concepts themselves.

If the book deconstructs the 'whole' of African politics chapter by chapter, dividing it into its various conceptual component parts, in addition it also needs methodological 'cement' to help the reader then reconstruct these separate parts. This methodological cement comes in the form of the relationship among three actors: the state, civil society, and external interests. Each twist in the path of Africa's political development since independence can be traced back to a realignment of the relationship among these three groups.

A minimalist definition of the modern state would identify *a set of political institutions that govern within a delimited territory*. But a modern state cannot be seen just as a geographic entity and a body of institutions. A more useful definition of the state also has to take into account the political authority that these structures generate. After all, it is to the institutions and officials of the state that citizens look for leadership and government, as well as being the sovereign body that foreign states recognise. In this respect, the state has immense power. Max Weber, in his definition of the state, pointed to the fact that deference of citizens is generated by the reality that the state claims a monopoly of legal violence within a territory.[2] Given that the state is the only authority able to establish and upkeep a society's laws, it starts from a position of strength. The state is therefore the dominant political authority within a society, and it will protect this position if need be by using this monopoly of legitimate violence. The danger is, of course, that individuals or groups with access to state structures may use this power to serve their own, or their class's, interests, rather than ensuring that these institutions increase the welfare of all the territory's citizens. Consequently, whether it is an autocracy or a democracy, this concentration of power ensures that the most visible political competition found within a country will be focused within these state institutions.

This is not to say that all politics happens as 'high politics'. Conflict resolution is not confined to the level of parliaments, presidential palaces and bureaucracies. Political (and, indeed, economic and social) exchange can be found throughout society, at a 'deeper' level than that of the state. This is why the idea of civil society is so important in explaining African politics.

In the context of this book, civil society can be defined as *the organisations that arise out of voluntary association within society, found between the extended family and the state*. Examples of these include professional organisations, labour unions, trade associations, women's groups, church assemblies, businesses, special interest lobbies, community groups, and so on, right down to sports and social clubs. In this respect, any group organised beyond the family, but not part of the state apparatus, can be defined as part of civil society.

Political activity within civil society is diverse. Groups representing numerous different interests, naturally enough, are not united in their demands. Politics within civil society is competitive, just as it is in the 'high politics' of the state. These different interests also influence how civic associations relate to the state. Some groups will cooperate with the government, others will voice their opposition. If a large gap develops between the interests of civil society and the state then this may lead to citizens actually challenging the authority of the state.

The third party within this competitive relationship is that of 'external interests'. African countries are identical to others around the world in that their fates are not decided totally within the domestic political arena. International relations are also influential. Historic and economic factors conspire to ensure that the states of Africa are influenced by external events perhaps even more than their neighbours on other continents. Indeed, imperialism or 'neo-colonialism' has been cited by many Africanists as the major governing force behind Africa's poor economic and political performance in the post-colonial era. The ways in which foreign governments, international organisations and transnational companies have interacted with African states and civil society groups have certainly been influential. They have played a major part in Africa's post-colonial political development. Whether this has been an entirely negative contribution, or not, is a debate taken up in the main text of this book.

An Introduction to African Politics is all about exploring the interaction among these three actors. On the whole, it is a story of how the state and civil society have failed to engage one another productively. The state, starved of resources (partially due to the nature of the international economy), became somewhat introverted, excluding civil society from the political process. This resulted in the under-representation of citizens by their governments. Indeed, it was often the case that state actors were only concerned about their own private welfare. Consequently, most services or resources passed down to ordinary citizens were channelled through inefficient patronage networks based on inequality. Civil society, for its part, never really engaged the state. Where it was possible, and advantageous to do so, citizens by-passed state authority. In many instances, this avoidance became a survival strategy of necessity. It may be, however, that the wave of multi-party elections that swept the continent during the 1990s has initiated a process whereby state and civil society will build a more profitable relationship.

Government in Africa today is far removed from Weber's model state, where politicians and bureaucrats clearly separate their private and public interests, and the 'national good' is served through neutral, legal/rational institutions. This is not to say that all societies ought to adopt these foundations of liberal democracy. Africans may find a different model of government more appropriate for their continent. Yet there can be little doubt that the post-colonial disharmony found between state and civil society has cost Africa dear. In many cases, and for long periods, social and economic development on the continent stalled, or even regressed. Using the political concepts mentioned above, alongside a state/civil society framework, this book seeks to introduce the political events and processes that have underpinned this disharmony. Chapter by chapter, the intricate mechanism that drives African politics will be revealed.

Glossary of key terms

Civil society	The organisations that arise out of voluntary association within society, found between the extended family and the state.
External interests	Foreign governments, international organisations and transnational corporations that interact with African states and civic associations.
The state	A set of political institutions that govern within a delimited territory.

2 History

Africa's pre-colonial and colonial inheritance

The world does not radically reinvent itself on a continuous basis. It evolves. There are no total revolutions where all that has gone before is laid to rest, and a new polity is born enjoying a completely clean slate. Traditions, customs, institutions and social relationships will survive and adapt from one era to another.

This is why the study of history is so useful to the political scientist. A scholar who wishes to understand the present must know something of the past. Some would say, for example, that modern French politics are still steeped in a republican tradition that stretches all the way back to the revolution of 1789. Similarly, those interested in the contemporary politics of the United States would be wise to familiarise themselves with the ideas of that country's 'founding fathers'. The same goes for Africa. As it will be seen, there are lines of continuity that run from the pre-colonial period, through the colonial era, right into the modern age.

This chapter searches out the continent's historical trajectories. These will form an excellent foundation, helping to explain the political events and processes of the post-independence years. First the influences on modern day politics that have their roots in the pre-colonial era will be identified. The chapter then goes on to investigate Africa's colonial legacy.

The pre-colonial inheritance

Until recent years, historians interested in Africa concentrated largely on the era of colonialism. They were concerned with the 'European' impact on Africa. These scholars of imperialism have produced enlightening work, but their collective yield falls far short of revealing the continent's complete historical trajectory. This is bound to be the case, given that formal European rule usually represented just 70 or 80 years out of centuries of African history. Humanity, after all, originated in Africa, some two to three million years ago. Before investigating the colonial legacy, therefore, it would be wise first to consider what modern African states have inherited from this earlier, pre-colonial period.

Pre-colonial Africa was as varied as the continent itself. Different circumstances produced different societies with different traditions, customs and politics, and these societies rose, fell, adapted and changed as the centuries passed. Despite this variety, however, it is possible to divide political organisations among these communities into two broad categories: states and stateless societies.

Low population densities, and the production of relatively small economic surpluses, hindered the formation of states in many parts of pre-colonial Africa. This was particularly the case in central and southern regions of the continent. These stateless societies, however, did not lack political organisation. Westerners, steeped as they are in state traditions, often regard the lack of state institutions as a sign of backwardness. This simply was not the case. The political systems that these stateless societies developed were well adapted to the environment they served. Considerable evidence of sophisticated forms of representation, justice and accountability among these communities has been unearthed. In several cases, confederations of villages provided security and a community for many thousands of Africans.

Several of these larger stateless societies developed institutions and hierarchies that evolved, over time, into states. This occurred most commonly, though certainly not exclusively, in West Africa. The stimulus for state formation was often the production of an economic surplus. This wealth enabled communities to sustain leadership groups, as well as administrative structures to support these governors. The states of Ghana and Mali, for example, were built on the profits from trans-Saharan trade. Further east, it was agricultural surpluses, from the fertile lands of the Nile River and central Great Lakes, that helped establish ancient Egypt and the kingdom of Buganda. Elsewhere, the empires of Ashanti and Benin were founded on mining and metalwork skills. States could also be built around monarchical authority, religious affiliation or military prowess (the Zulu nation providing an excellent example of this last category).

Some of these grand civilisations were in advance, technically and socially, of their European contemporaries, but the fascinating details of these states, given the particular focus of this book, will have be left to the historians. The task of this chapter is to extract relevant aspects of history that help to explain African politics today. The factor of continuity that stands out above all the others, in this respect, is the issue of lineage.

Lineage and kinship dominated pre-colonial social relationships. This is the idea of the extended family. A lineage kinship group can theoretically trace its past back to the same ancestor, and these bonds of origin bind communities together. Consequently, ancestor worship is at the heart of many African spiritualist traditions. In reality, actual genealogical links are sometimes tenuous, with membership of the group usually being relatively flexible. Outsiders may be brought into the clan, individuals will marry into families of different lineages, and groups as a whole interlink and disperse over time (commonly as a result of migration and war). Even the most instrumental lineage associations, however, construct powerful social bonds. As a member of the group, individuals will obey life-determining customs regarding marriage, inheritance, justice and the allocation of land. This gives the leader of a clan, village or ethnic group a great deal of political power. Lineage groups, in return, provide solidarity, offering security and welfare to their members. There is thus a reciprocal relationship between those who respect the authority of ethnic leaders and the chiefs who are obliged to look after their followers. Even today this results in Africans seeing themselves more as members of a community, rather than adopting the degrees of individuality widespread in the West.

In Chapter 3, tracing the historical trajectory of these pre-colonial lineage traditions, the book explores how this sense of community influenced the state ideologies of post-colonial Africa (notably 'African socialism'). Similarly, Chapter 4 investigates just how these powerful ethnic ties helped shape political exchange in the modern era.

The colonial inheritance

Africa did not evolve in isolation prior to European colonisation. The continent, like other parts of the world, had to adapt to invasions and imperial rule as history unfolded. Just as Britain experienced eras dominated by Roman and Norman occupation, North Africa played host to Persian, Greek, Roman and Ottoman empires over time. Africa was also subject to religious influences. Islam spread across the north, reaching the Atlantic Ocean in the first years of the eighth century, while Christianity had gained a permanent foothold in Ethiopia earlier in the fourth century. Further south, to some extent, the barrier of the Sahara desert limited cultural exchange between the rest of the world and tropical Africa, but sub-Saharan Africans, by the fifteenth century, had built strong land and maritime trading links with both Arabs and Europeans. The whole continent, in this respect, participated in the international economy prior to colonialism.

In 1415, the Portuguese established a garrison on Africa's Mediterranean coast at Ceuta. They then went on to build a number of trading posts on both the west and east coasts of the continent. Later, in 1652, the Dutch established Cape Town on the southern tip of Africa, which under British control developed into modern-day South Africa. By the eighteenth and nineteenth centuries, numerous trading posts could be found along Africa's coastline, with Europeans busy buying gold, ivory and slaves, among other products. Christian missionaries were also establishing themselves on the continent by this time. All this was achieved without direct political control. This situation was to change dramatically, however, in the second half of the nineteenth century.

Again, it is best to leave the details and motivations behind the 'Scramble for Africa' to the historians, but the results of this imperial competition are obvious.[1] Whether it was for economic, strategic or cultural reasons, agreements confirmed at the 1884–5 Berlin Conference (and after) saw Africa carved up between the European powers. Only the empire of Ethiopia and the territory of Liberia (a country established for freed slaves) escaped this partition.

France favoured North, West and Central Africa; Britain claimed great chunks of West, East, Central and Southern Africa; Portugal took the territories of Angola, Mozambique and Guinea-Bissau; King Léopold of Belgium was awarded the Congo; Italy established control in Libya, Eritrea and part of Somalia; Spain did likewise in north Morocco, the Spanish Sahara and Spanish Guinea; while Germany gained areas in the south-west and the east of the continent, as well as the Cameroons and Togoland. Germany, however, was to lose these possessions with its defeat in the First World War (the League of Nations distributing these territories among the other colonial powers; see Map 2.1).

Despite the absence of 'true' colonialism in much of Africa, with only South Africa, Southern Rhodesia, Kenya, South West Africa and Algeria having significant numbers of white settlers, European imperial rule had become firmly established by the first decade of the twentieth century. This colonial era may have been relatively short in duration (in most cases from the 1880s or 1890s to the 1960s), but its impact on the subsequent political environment was considerable. Once more, lines of continuity can be traced between the past and the present. Six elements within this colonial inheritance of particular importance (summarised in Table 2.1 at the end of this section) are: the incorporation of Africa into the international modern state structure; the imposition of arbitrary boundaries; the failure to develop links between the state and society; the promotion of an African state elite; the building of specialist export economies; and the absence of strong political institutions. Each of these elements will now be examined in turn.

Modern states

The most obvious legacy of colonial rule was the division of Africa into modern states. European rule resulted in Africa being fully integrated within the international jigsaw puzzle of sovereign territories. This meant that worldwide (Antarctica excepted) states now accounted for the entire land surface of the globe. All of these had clearly delineated and fixed boundaries, and all legal political interaction was now channelled through, or at least held accountable to, state institutions.

As already indicated, pre-colonial Africa hosted many stateless societies, and even where there were states, these were considerably less well defined than their modern descendants. Boundaries would fluctuate as power at the centre ebbed and flowed. Indeed, many communities, even if they did recognise a higher authority, also enjoyed considerable autonomy. In this respect, few Africans had previously experienced the reality of a hegemonic state. The post-colonial consequences of being incorporated into this international political system feature prominently in all the chapters of this book.

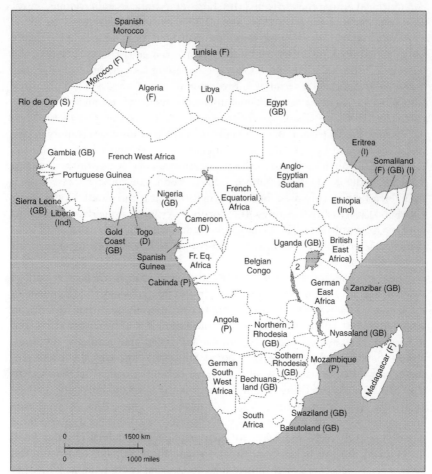

Map 2.1 Africa at the outbreak of the First World War
Notes:
D=Germany, F=France, GB=Britain, I=Italy, Ind=Independent, P=Portugal, S=Spain

Changes after First World War
1   German South West Africa: to Britain
2   German East Africa: to Britain (Tanganyika), except Ruanda Urundi to Belgium
3   Cameroon: part to France, part to Britain
4   Togo: part to France, part to Britain
5   Jubaland: ceded from Britain to Italy (joins Italian Somaliland)

Arbitrary boundaries

The imperial powers' imposition of state borders on African territory had major
ramifications. The problem lies with the fact that, when they were delineated,
these state boundaries rarely matched existing pre-colonial political, social or
economic divisions. They were 'arbitrary'. Not arbitrary in the sense of random,

but arbitrary because they reflected the short-term strategic and economic interests of the imperial powers, and not the interests of the Africans they housed.[2]

A quick glance at the contemporary map of Africa, for example, clearly shows an external, rather than internal, logic to the units chosen. Many of the boundaries are ruler-straight, following lines of longitude and latitude. Historically determined social divisions rarely do this. Other oddities also stick out. Why was German South West Africa (Namibia), for example, awarded a narrow tract of land (the Caprivi Strip) to its north-east; and why does West Africa host the tiny state of The Gambia? In the first instance, Namibia's odd shape was created by the strategic requirements of Germany's foreign minister, Count von Caprivi. He insisted that this territory have access to the Zambezi River, in order to deploy a gunboat. The second case arose because British commercial interests had established a trading post at the mouth of the River Gambia. Despite French cajoling, the British government refused to give up this territory. Consequently, The Gambia, is a micro-state, no more than fifty kilometres wide at any one point, and entirely engulfed by Senegal (except for its short coast line).

Then there is the curiosity of Cabinda. This oil-rich enclave is part of Angola. Yet, it is separated from greater Angola by the Democratic Republic of the Congo. This is because King Léopold of Belgium insisted that his African kingdom should adjoin the Atlantic Ocean. Again, it is important to stress that if African state borders had reflected 'natural' social and economic divisions, rather than these having been imposed arbitrarily and virtually overnight, these, and other, anomalies would not have become a reality on the modern map of Africa. As the British Prime Minister of the day, Lord Salisbury, quipped at a 1890 Anglo-French conference: 'we have been engaged in drawing lines upon maps where no white man's foot ever trod; we have been giving away mountains and rivers and lakes to each other, only hindered by the small impediment that we never knew exactly where the mountains and rivers and lakes were.'[3] Salisbury's after-dinner joke loses some of its humour when put into the context of the problems that these 'arbitrary' borders created for post-colonial governments.

Many of these borders do not make economic sense. As well as the initial disruption to lines of communication and trade, colonial boundaries also created longer-term problems for African states. Decisions made in the capitals of Europe in the late eighteenth century, for example, have resulted in fourteen African countries being landlocked. In terms of trade, this puts a state at a serious disadvantage. They have to rely on their neighbours' willingness and ability to transport the bulk of their imports and exports. No other region is home to so many landlocked states.

Imperially imposed borders also left several states without significant resources from which to build their economies. Whether this is a shortage of agricultural land, minerals, other raw materials or people, no country can secure its future without an economic base. Polities that grow into states 'organically' do this just because they can command resources. There was no such imperative in the formation of African states. Niger, for example, has little land within its borders suitable for agriculture, and only minor mineral deposits. Consequently this state, like many others on the continent, has struggled to prosper.

Alongside economic obstacles, Africa's artificial boundaries have also precipitated political and social problems. Colonial borders ran though existing political and social units, resulting in many communities finding themselves split between different states (and even different imperial powers). Some pre-colonial political entities did survive. Rwanda, Burundi, Lesotho and Swaziland have boundaries acknowledging pre-colonial realities, but such an acknowledgement was very rare. Imperial partition scattered the Somali people, for example, among five sovereign states. Fellow Somalis were now to be found in British Somaliland, Italian Somaliland, French Somaliland, Ethiopia and Kenya. Similarly, the present-day borders of Burkina Faso cut across the traditional territory of 21 cultural and linguistic groups.[4] In this sense, colonial rule 'dehumanised' Africa's borders.[5]

This failure of the imposed boundaries to recognise existing divisions was at the root of two major problems for post-colonial governments. First, there was the possibility of irredentism. Irredentism is *the desire to unite under one flag a community that is currently divided.* If a pre-colonial political unit found itself split between two states, then there was always a danger that, after independence, violence would be used to re-unite this community. Somalia went to war with Ethiopia in the 1970s, for example, to try to win the Ogaden, an area populated by ethnic Somalis. The government in Mogadishu wanted to house all the Somali people within the boundaries of just one sovereign state.

The second potential problem was the possibility of internal ethnic conflict within a state. Imperial boundaries not only split social groups, they also caged them together within these new nation states. There are over two hundred ethnic groups residing within the boundaries of Tanzania, for instance. Post-colonial states were thus forced to find institutions and political procedures that ensured that any conflict among their divided populations could be resolved peacefully. Just how successful governments have been at managing the legacies of these arbitrary boundaries is the focus of Chapters 3 and 4, respectively examining nationalism and ethnicity in post-colonial Africa.

Weak links between state and society

As well as arbitrary boundaries, independent Africa also inherited weak links between state and society. Colonial political authority had been gained on the continent through conquest, and political institutions imposed. Coercion acted as a substitute for legitimacy. The state, in this sense, never rested on a social contract between government and people. Indeed, colonial administrators were not even accountable to the Africans they ruled. Instead, they obeyed orders emanating from their superiors back in the capitals of Europe. Government was therefore about maintaining order, balancing budgets and overseeing the extraction of raw materials for export. It was never about the provision of public services for citizens. This is why Crawford Young describes the colonial state as 'alien to its core'.[6]

By comparison, stronger links between state and society had developed within the modern European state. Here, the state had both grown out of, and been shaped by, its own society. Over centuries, elements of civil society had competed with monarchs and emperors, resulting in, first, the middle class, and then the working class, gaining empowerment. Each group eventually succeeded in shaping state institutions to reflect their demands. Today, notions of democracy underpin this relationship between state and society, and a complex provision of public services has resulted.

This contrasts strongly with Africa, where the modern state arrived almost overnight, and its nature owed little to existing indigenous civil society. Africans were simply left out of any representative relationship between government and people. Consequently, trust and shared political values never developed between the rulers and the ruled. State institutions never sought or gained the respect of the people.

This was a situation that did not bode well for a successful interaction between the state and society in post-colonial Africa. Chapter 6 will show how the independent governments followed the example of their imperial forebears, also restricting political activity within civil society. Legitimacy continued to be substituted by coercion. By comparison, Chapter 10 examines this state/civil society relationship from a different angle. It explores how, during the 1980s and 1990s, civil society took its 'revenge' by disengaging from these authoritarian and exploitative states.

The formation of state elites

Although, by and large, colonial states were content to distance themselves from their African subjects, some contact was needed. After all, the 'thin white lines' of imperial administrators could not keep the state going all by themselves.[7] A number of Africans were required to sustain the imperial administration's authority among the masses. And this led to the creation of small indigenous elites within the colonies. These elites, having benefited from their access to state institutions, would then go on to manage the liberation campaigns, and form the first governments after independence.

Initially, colonial administrators selected traditional leaders to be the intermediaries of imperialism. Chiefs or monarchs, who already commanded authority among their people, were charged with raising taxes, supplying labour and ensuring that colonial laws and regulations were respected. In return, these intermediaries could expect the power of the state to back their leadership, with considerable benefits in terms of 'tribute'. Administrators, for example, fully expected chiefs to take a percentage of the tax revenue they raised or the fines they imposed. These traditional leaders were also left to run their jurisdiction largely as they saw fit, as long as colonial interests were not compromised. This relationship between access to state power and personal opportunities for accumulation is an issue returned to throughout the book.

The state elite was not just composed of traditional leaders, however. As time progressed, a younger African elite began to emerge. These individuals also gained their position from their proximity to state power, but their source of social mobility was not necessarily traditional authority. The main currency was now education. Access to an education (usually from a mission school) brought access to the state. This 'proto-elite' was often employed in the lower ranks of the government, as clerks, teachers or court interpreters, or became professionals such as lawyers and doctors. As such, they received relative prosperity from their salary, and they engaged in the 'Western' society of the towns and cities. As with the traditional leaders, there was also an opportunity to extract personal wealth from their privileged position in the state apparatus (through 'corrupt' practices). Towards the end of colonial rule, most colonial governments attempted to 'Africanise' their civil service. As a consequence, the numbers of this bureaucratic class swelled, as did the numbers of professionals employed by the state.

In effect, imperial rule had created its own executioners. By the 1950s, nearly all the colonial states were being challenged by the forces of nationalism, and these movements were led by those who had prospered most under colonial rule. Nationalist politics flourished among the educated urban elite. To take the example of the Uganda National Congress, its Central Committee consisted in 1952 of five shopkeepers, four journalists, three full-time politicians, two clerks, two lawyers, two schoolteachers, and a student studying abroad.[8]

Nationalism certainly had considerable support among the peasantry in the countryside, but it was not a case of society, as a whole, demanding independence. Instead, it was about the colonial governments handing over power to African educated elites. The very element of African society that had been most closely associated with the colonial state ousted its former employers. The clerks, teachers and lawyers captured state institutions for themselves. Chapter 5, investigating social class within African politics, assesses the consequences of this elite inheriting the state.

The economic inheritance

Of all the elements of Africa's colonial inheritance, it has been the economic legacy that has been most widely debated among Africanists. This is because the most obvious feature of modern African history has been the continent's poor economic performance. Ignoring widely supported contemporary predictions, economies simply failed to 'take off' after independence. In several cases, despite economic development being the priority of governments, African states were no better off at the end of the twentieth century than they were during the 1960s at decolonisation.

A dominant school of thought, at its height in the 1970s and early 1980s, directly blamed the colonial inheritance for this lack of development. Its followers maintained that the continent had been systematically *under-developed* by imperial interests, and this now left the new independent states in a highly vulnerable 'dependent' position. As such, colonial administrators had failed to provide Africa with the basic economic foundations governments now needed if their countries were to flourish.

The arguments of the underdevelopment school are well worth investigating. They clearly reveal present-day structural problems that can be attributed to colonial rule. More recent academic work, however, broadens the blame for this economic failure. Although Africans were certainly exploited in the past, and left with relatively weak economies at independence, this position was not insurmountable, and economic failure was not inevitable. Just as much as their imperial predecessors, policies and practices adopted by governments in the post-colonial period have also contributed to Africa's economic malaise.

Central to the idea of underdevelopment is that all states operate in a single, global system. This has increasingly been the case over the last four centuries, with capitalism gradually coming to influence all societies around the world as the dominant method of economic exchange and production. Not all states are equal within this single international system, however. They are divided into two groups. There are those developed states at the centre or core (Western countries), and the less developed countries on the periphery (largely the Third World).

The differences in wealth between core and periphery have not resulted from the West and the Third World embarking on two historically different economic paths. They are the product of the same process, with the core developing at the periphery's expense. The prosperity the West enjoys today has been founded on exploitation of the periphery's resources. Development and under-development, therefore, are two sides of the same coin. Economic activity, which could have helped African economies, has instead advanced the position of the West. Imperial rule was the formal political authority that enhanced this process of exploitation.

Numerous examples of underdevelopment were put forward in support of this thesis. The more convincing of these included the exploitation of labour, the drain of capital from the periphery to the core states, and the failure of colonial states to diversify local economies.

Examining the issue of labour exploitation first, the West began to take advantage of African workers even before formal colonial rule was established. The Atlantic slave trade transported up to fifteen million people from Africa to work on the plantations of the Caribbean and the Americas, and more died in the process of capture, or during transit. Portuguese and Arab merchants organised a similar trade in human beings from the east coast of the continent. The results were far reaching. Populations in parts of Africa were devastated. Also destroyed were local political and social formations. People whose labour could have advanced the development of African economies and societies were, instead, forced to contribute to capital accumulation elsewhere. Europeans (and Arabs) had underdeveloped Africa by literally stealing its labour force.

Exploitation of labour also continued into the formal colonial era. Once imperial authorities realised that the bulk of Africa (South Africa excluded) was not going to be a new Eldorado, as gold-rich South America had been for the Spanish empire earlier, they set about exploiting other resources that could be found on the continent. African labour was an obvious target. Colonial laws and tax systems were devised to force peasants from their subsistence farming, pushing them into employment in mines, on the commercial plantations, or growing cash crops to be exported to the West. The colonial authorities, however, did not pay African labour the wages enjoyed by European workers. Even taking into account the vast gap in standards of living, a worker on the African continent was still paid below the level of his or her subsistence needs. This forced workers to supplement their cash income from sources elsewhere (usually additional subsistence farming). In parts of Africa, if a labour force could not be raised voluntarily, forced labour was introduced. Africans in the Congo and Mozambique, for example, were legally compelled to work for the state for part of the year, or face prosecution. Had African workers been paid more for their labour during the colonial era, enough capital may have been accumulated locally to ensure that post-colonial governments inherited a much healthier economic situation.

Underdevelopment also resulted from the export of surplus. Instead of African economies benefiting from new economic activity on the continent, raw materials extracted, and profits raised, by African labour were simply whisked away from the periphery in order to develop the economies of the West. For economic advancement to occur anywhere in the world, not only does a surplus have to be produced, it also has to be used productively. Reinvestment of profits into the economies of Africa could have stimulated growth locally. Instead, the West expropriated this surplus for its own use. It is no coincidence that the economies of the core expanded at a previously unprecedented rate during the years of colonialism.

Underdevelopment also stunted African advancement by only developing primary production on the continent (mining and agriculture). Colonial rule ensured peripheral economies became predominantly export economies (minerals, coffee, tea, cocoa, vegetable oil, groundnuts, cotton, sisal, etc.). As a result, at independence, many African states were faced with the problem of a 'monocrop' economy. In Zambia, for example, the economy is overwhelmingly dominated by copper extraction, while in Ghana it is cocoa production. If the price of this commodity falls on the world market, then there is no other economic sector that the country can fall back on. A balance of payments crisis ensues. If the colonial authorities had developed economic sectors such as food production and secondary manufacturing industry, then post-colonial African economies would have been less specialised, and consequently less vulnerable. Imperial administrators, however, were only concerned about the needs of

Western industry (the demand for raw materials). They had no interest in building strong integrated economies in the periphery.

The external imperatives of African economies are also very apparent with respect to investments the colonial authorities did make in their territories. Transport infrastructure, for instance, only revolved around moving goods from the point of extraction to a port (allowing export to the West). By comparison, few lines of communication were built to enhance internal or regional trading links. This is why African commerce today remains more engaged with Western, rather than local, markets. The Côte d'Ivoire (Ivory Coast), for example, trades more with France than it does with its neighbour, Ghana.

Similarly, little investment was made in African human resources. As David Lamb observes, after 300 years of Portuguese rule in Guinea-Bissau, imperialism left just fourteen university graduates, an illiteracy rate of 97 per cent, only 265 miles of paved road, and a single factory (a brewery that served the Portuguese troops). A greater proportion of the profits generated in Africa, reinvested locally, would have produced a much healthier economic inheritance for post-colonial African governments.

More recent academic thought, however, considers the underdevelopment thesis too polemic. Although most scholars agree that exploitation and expropriation held back potential African development to a degree, they argue that the colonial economic experience was not entirely negative for Third World countries.

The African continent prior to imperial rule, for example, was not on the brink of economic 'take-off'. Population densities were relatively stable, and there were no major technological breakthroughs imminent. The plough and the wheel were not utilised, wind and water power remained largely absent, nor was irrigation extensive. Indeed, Bill Warren argues that colonialism, as the pioneer of capitalism, was necessary to close the development gap between the West and the Third World.[9] Imperial rule may have brought great hardship to Africa, but it also brought improved economic techniques, better health and wider experience of education to the continent. Warren argues that, in this respect, there is no better indicator of development than infant mortality rates and life expectancy. Both of these improved dramatically under colonialism. Smallpox, diphtheria and tuberculosis were reduced considerably with Western medicines, and better health enhanced productive forces across the entire continent.

Similarly, it could be argued that, although the imperial authorities only really concentrated on developing the primary sector within their colonies, at least this was one area of the economy that had the potential to provide a platform for later diversification. Zimbabwe, for example, was left with coal mines to produce power for any post-independence industrial development, while Algeria had a small steel industry to build upon.

How, then, should we judge Africa's economic inheritance? Did colonial exploitation destroy Africa's potential, or did minor (admittedly self-interested) investments leave these territories at least the substructure of a modern economy? Well, there is no doubt that the imperial powers extracted a great deal of wealth from their colonial possessions via labour exploitation, and raw material and profit export. This capital could have been used to benefit Africa rather than the West, and may have resulted in a more prosperous continent today. The colonial era did, however, leave Africa with economic foundations based on the primary sector. These economies may not have been particularly diverse, but nor were they condemned to permanent poverty as some under-development theorists have suggested. Political independence brought at least the potential for more rapid economic growth. The flow of profit export to the core could now be stemmed by political means, and this capital reinvested locally. The successful diversification of several ex-colonial economies in the Far East (the Asian 'Tiger' economies) would seem to support this view. The book returns to these issues of underdevelopment (and charges of continued exploitation in the post-colonial era) in Chapter 8.

Table 2.1 Potential problems created by the colonial inheritance

Arbitrary boundaries	*Potential problems:* Illogical territorial units Divided communities Irredentist movements Internal ethnic competition Inappropriate economic units (landlocked, under-resourced)
Weak links between state and society	*Potential problems:* No shared political culture between state and society A deficit of legitimacy Unaccountable states Distant civil societies Society disengaging from the state
Formation of a state elite	*Potential problems:* Strong associations between political office and personal wealth Social mobility dominated by access to the state Corruption An exploitative 'bureaucratic bourgeoisie'
The economic inheritance	*Potential problems:* Disadvantage in the international economy Underdevelopment of human resources Lack of public services Economies over-reliant on primary sector Over-reliance on exports Bias towards European, not local or regional, markets
Weak political institutions	*Potential problems:* Fragile liberal democratic institutions without historical moorings Return to colonial-style authoritarian and bureaucratic state after independence

Weak political institutions

The final element of Africa's colonial inheritance to be examined are the weak political institutions left by the imperial powers. As decolonisation approached, nationalist movements began to mobilise, leading the colonial authorities to look for ways of transferring power to indigenous governments. In the majority of cases, negotiation proved to be the key to independence.[10]

The result of this negotiation was usually the (eventual) agreement of the imperial authorities to oversee multi-party elections, with the victor of this poll taking up the reins of power under a new independence constitution. All these constitutions guaranteed pluralist democracy and the rule of law.

This was the ultimate irony of colonial rule. Imperial powers sought to leave a legacy of constitutional liberal democracy. These were the liberties and political representation that imperial administrators had consciously withheld from Africans during their own rule. After all, colonial structures were about control and expropriation at the lowest possible cost. Imperialism did not have as its goal the creation of legal-rational institutions on foreign soil. In this respect, colonial states had been highly bureaucratic and authoritarian. They never sought legitimacy from their subjects; they were highly interventionist; they had few pretensions about representing the views of their subjects; and they ruled through domination, supported by coercion. The political culture that these realities underpinned was hardly an appropriate midwife to oversee the birth of new liberal democratic states. Indeed, despite the last-minute installation of democratic trappings, many of the elements of the colonial authoritarianism listed above would simply resurface in the post-colonial era. Bureaucratic authoritarianism, as it will be seen in Chapters 6 and 10, would be the true institutional legacy left to the former colonies.

State and civil society

Having identified the most relevant elements of Africa's past which would have an influence on post-colonial politics, this chapter can now conclude by briefly considering this historical inheritance in the light of the book's underlying theme: the relationship between state and civil society.

There were certainly major obstacles to be overcome if Africa was to achieve economic and political development after independence. States, for example, were in a vulnerable position. They had to manage divided communities created by arbitrary colonial boundaries. Institutional mechanisms and ideologies of solidarity, for example, would have to be found to reduce ethnic tensions, while 'good neighbourliness' would also have to emerge to prevent the threat of irredentism. Similarly, the newly independent economies had to be diversified and expanded. This was the only way to reduce their monocrop insecurity and provide the capital for previously absent basic public services (such as health and education).

Civil society also had to overcome major challenges in the post-colonial era.

The danger was that these voluntary associations would become dominated by the state. This would damage opportunities for pluralist competition, and thus limit society's influence over state policies. After all, modern states in Africa had no track record of either representation or accountability. The colonial example had been one of bureaucratic authoritarianism. It was now possible that the educated elite that had inherited these states would simply adopt the same style of rule practised by their imperial predecessors. If state domination returned, of course, it would be civil society that would suffer.

This is not to say, however, that the pre-colonial and colonial inheritance predestined the continent to fail economically and politically. It was never inevitable that this legacy would get the better of African politicians. Independence had been won. The nationalists who took over the state had gained the trust and support of civil society though their liberation leadership and independence election campaigns. Consequently, a degree of legitimacy had been generated between the governors and the governed. There was also an economic base to work on, however fragile this was. And, what is more, democracy had been proven to work once, with multi-party elections successfully selecting the successors to colonial governments. Indeed, at the time, there was great hope in Africa, as well as abroad, that the continent was poised to enter a prosperous new epoch.

Building on the historical trajectories explored in this chapter, the rest of the book will seek to explain why, at the start of the twenty-first century, Africa is still yet to enter into this more affluent era.

Case study: Kenya's historical inheritance

Kenya straddles the equator on the east coast of Africa, and has a number of climatic zones. Much of the country is arid or semi-arid, only supporting low-density subsistence farming. Other areas, however, are suitable for intensive agriculture. The coastal strip along the Indian Ocean is one such region, but it is the highlands either side of the Great Rift Valley, and the shores of Lake Victoria, that have proved to be especially productive. Kenya can also boast the bustling cities of Nairobi, Mombasa and Kisumu.

Archaeological evidence shows present-day Kenya to have been one of the first hosts to human life. Human remains have been found near Lake Turkana dating back two to three million years. An equally significant event in the peopling of Africa was the Bantu migrations. These Bantu people, originating in West Africa, over centuries would eventually inhabit all of Tropical Africa, pushing down into what is now South Africa. As they travelled south and east, they colonised many of the societies they came across. The Kikuyu, Embu, Mbere,

Kamba, Tharaka, Luhya and Gusii of present-day Kenya are the descendants of these Bantu migrants. Their ancestors reached the Rift Valley approximately one thousand years ago.

Another significant migration arrived later, in the fifteenth century. Niolitic and Cushitic groups came from the north, and produced lines of descent that formed today's Masai, Kalenjin, Luo and Somali ethnic groups. In addition to these African peoples, Arab traders have also been visiting Kenya since the seventh century, while Europeans settled here from the end of the nineteenth century onwards. Adding to this diverse population, Asians originating from the Indian subcontinent have been a significant part of Kenya's civil society in the twentieth century.

Political organisation in pre-colonial Kenya rested largely on state-less societies. The most sophisticated of these could be found in the highlands, and westwards towards Lake Victoria. Although each of the African groups mentioned in the previous paragraph had its own iden-tity, social, economic and cultural boundaries were permeable, and co-existence (as well as war) existed between these various parties. The 'Lords of the Rift', the Masai, for example, were the 'bankers of the highlands'.[11] They were a purely pastoral people, but benefited from residing close to other, mixed farming, ethnic groups. This was so that they could profit from providing cattle to their neighbours – cattle being the primary form of currency and exchange among these communities (used for trade and paying social debts, such as the marriage bride-price).

This region was also well connected with both the rest of Africa and the wider world. Coastal trade existed from early times, while Arab caravans entered the interior regularly throughout the nineteenth century. Largely trading for ivory and slaves, these caravans operated between Mombasa (on the Indian Ocean coast) and Lake Victoria. This commercial activity was controlled from the island of Zanzibar, where Omani Arabs exerted authority over the whole region.

The British gained influence in this part of Africa towards the end of the nineteenth century. In 1888, a royal charter for what would become Kenya was granted to the commercial Imperial British East Africa Company. Company rule, however, proved something of a disaster. London had to take control itself when the company became bankrupt. The British government established its East African Protectorate in 1895. Kenya became a formal crown colony 25 years later, when white settlement in the territory was firmly entrenched. In the space of these 25 years, Kenya had been transformed from a region that provided a home for numerous stateless societies into a single modern colonial state. The territory now had powerful central administrative structures and a significant white settler community.

Kenya reflects the rest of Africa in that it inherited arbitrary state boundaries from its colonial age. To the south, for example, Kenya's ruler-straight border with Tanzania suddenly changes course at Moshi. It is as if a mistake has been made, and the map-maker's pen has slipped temporarily, before continuing its geometrically correct journey to the Indian Ocean. Queen Victoria wished to make a gift of Mount Kilimanjaro to her grandson, the future Kaiser Wilhelm II. The border between German and British East Africa was moved accordingly. In this respect, and illustrating the irrational nature of African borders, the outcome of whether thousands of Africans are today citizens of Kenya or Tanzania was decided by the bestowing of a birthday present.

Although this is an extreme case, it is obvious that African states were not created with local necessities in mind. Instead, they were shaped to meet the demands of imperialism and the interests of its managers. This is a fact also reflected in Kenya's western border with Uganda. This boundary, despite being moved in 1926, still cuts across the territory of ten cultural groups.[12]

It is Kenya's north-eastern boundary, however, that has created most problems in the post-colonial era. As we have seen, the Somali people were divided among five colonial states as a result of imperial partition. Consequently, north-eastern Kenya has a large ethnic Somali population, many of whom wish to be part of a greater Somaliland. The Somali Republic, itself, certainly wishes to see this part of Kenya become Somali sovereign territory. During the First World War, the British government came to a secret agreement with Italy to transfer 94,050 square kilometres of its East African protectorate to Italian Somaliland. This was Italy's reward for allying with Britain during its war with Germany. The treaty was honoured, and Jubaland was ceded in 1924. Many ethnic Somalis, however, were still left living on Kenyan territory, even after this boundary change.

The issue was revisited just before independence, in 1963. Britain negotiated with Somalia, and was apparently willing to give up further territory. Somalia demanded the whole of Kenya's Northern Province, however. This was much more than Britain would cede, and the talks ended in stalemate. Kenya's independent government inherited this boundary dispute, and an irredentist guerrilla war was fought in this province. Relations improved between Kenya and Somalia from 1967, however, and the war faded out. The fact remains, though, that there are still many Somalis living in Kenya who owe their political loyalties more to kin across the border than to the Kenyan government.

Kenya's economic inheritance from its colonial rulers was equally problematic. Evidence supporting the underdevelopment thesis can certainly be found. Land was alienated in the most fertile areas (the 'white highlands') from Africans and used to settle European farmers; labour was also exploited, with Africans being taxed, forcing them into the cash economy; and economic development concentrated largely on cash crops (tea and coffee) denied the Kenyan economy the chance to diversify. Even in 1995, Kenya's trading links remained much stronger with the old metropolitan economy of Britain than with local markets in East Africa. The result of this 'underdevelopment' would be that post-colonial administrations would inherit a land problem (how should the land owned by European settlers be returned to the farmers it was taken from?). There was also the difficulty of producing development from an economy based primarily on agricultural exports. The Kenyan economy would indeed suffer each time the price of coffee or tea fell.

The economy was not completely underdeveloped, however. Kenya inherited a good communications infrastructure from the colonial state, a basic health service, and an education system. What is more, by comparison with the rest of Africa, Kenya had a significant industrial sector. Based on a nucleus that developed to serve white settlers, manufacturing grew during the post-colonial period. Kenya has consequently profited from sales to the rest of East Africa and beyond. Although it still relies heavily on its cash-crop farming, the Kenyan economy is also active in the chemical industry, in producing cement, manufacturing consumer goods, and is particularly successful in refining petroleum products (from imported oil). Tourism also attracts considerable sums of foreign exchange each year. Although Kenyan labour and resources had been exploited by imperial interests before independence, and it had inherited an economy seriously skewed towards the export of primary produce, it would seem that the economy was not 'underdeveloped' beyond hope. The present-day economy still has massive obstacles to overcome, but it has reaped limited successes through diversification.

Organised opposition to colonial rule in Kenya, especially among the Kikuyu, can be traced back to the 1920s. It was the so-called Mau Mau uprisings, however, that finally forced the British into the negotiations which led to Kenya's independence. Some 13,000 Africans and 1,000 Europeans died in this unrest that centred on land rights in the highlands. The Kikuyu wanted access to their land, and threatened to take this by force. Over 80,000 Africans were detained in 're-education' camps. When the level of violence rose sharply in 1952, a state of emergency was declared. Nationalist leaders were imprisoned (including future president Jomo Kenyatta), and British troop re-inforcements deployed to quell the rebellion. Once this had been achieved, the colonial authorities sought to foster a political class with which it could build a collaborative partnership of government.

The nationalist leaders that the imperial authorities sought to engage certainly did not represent a cross-section of African society in Kenya. They were an urban educated elite, who often already had close associations with the state (as employees or business partners). When, for example, Africans were allowed to sit alongside European representatives in the Legislative Council for the first time in 1957, the employment of the candidates standing was revealing. Most were teachers, others included veterinarians, journalists, businessmen, civil service union leaders, an army warrant officer, a social worker, and a lawyer. The vast majority of these had a secondary school education; a sizeable proportion were university graduates; and several had studied or worked abroad.[13] They shared few social characteristics with the peasants who sustained the Mau Mau rebellion. It would be this elite that would inherit the Kenyan state from the imperial authorities with decolonisation. As will be shown later in the book, it can be argued that this elite subsequently formed an exploitative 'bureaucratic bourgeoisie'.

Kenya's independence came in 1963, rather more quickly than Britain had planned. Nationalists were looking for complete independence and self-rule, rather than just a junior partnership with the imperial administration. Power sharing formulae were swept aside, and with this, colonial rule perished. Before departing, however, the British government did leave Kenya with a liberal democratic constitution, drawn up during pre-independence negotiations.

With the benefit of hindsight, it was obvious that the political institutions created by this constitution would be incredibly weak. Like the colonial state itself, they were imposed. They had not grown, over time, out of society, and they had been ushered in overnight. For example, the new constitution instigated multi-party democracy for Kenya. In reality, such pluralism had never previously existed in this territory. There had not been a single African national political party established prior to the Second World War; and after the war, organisations of this nature were often banned. Nor had their been a representative parliament in Kenya under colonial rule. In short, liberal democracy had no historical foundations in Africa. Yet this was the legacy that imperial rule left. Kenya was expected instantly to create a political culture that could support this system of politics.

The Westminster constitutional model of politics soon broke down in post-colonial Kenya. Within a year of decolonisation, the smaller of two parties that had contested the independence elections, the Kenya African Democratic Union, merged with the victor, the ruling Kenya African National Union (KANU). KANU governed Kenya without an opposition from this point in 1964, right through until electoral reforms were forced upon the state in the early 1990s. The most serious challenge to the ruling party came in 1966, when the Kenya People's Union was formed. President Kenyatta promptly banned this organisation.

Other moves to centralise state power were also undertaken by KANU. In 1964, for example, the Office of the Prime Minister was abolished, with a more powerful and centralised presidential office being established instead. Similarly, in 1966, Kenya's second chamber was dissolved, creating a unicameral system, further centralising the state. Also in that year, the Preventative Detention Act became law, by-passing the independence constitution's Bill of Rights (by permitting detention without trial in the interests of 'public security'). Power was systematically being taken away from Parliament, and given to Kenyatta's Office of the President, and his allies in the civil service and army. Kenya was reverting to a style of bureaucratic authoritarianism familiar in the colonial era.

The accession to the presidency of Daniel arap Moi in 1978, following Kenyatta's death, promised a programme of political liberalisation. Moi did indeed release a number of political prisoners and start to tackle issues of corruption, but this did not last. Consolidating his own position of power after an attempted air force coup in 1982, Kenya became a formal one-party state. The last vestiges of liberal democracy were thus removed. The independence constitution that ushered in pluralist, multi-party competition, but had been built on the shaky historical foundations of colonial bureaucratic autocracy, was now itself history.

It was only in the 1990s that Moi came under serious pressure to reform his government. Multi-party politics returned to Kenya during this decade (events which will be examined in Chapter 11). The president himself managed to deploy his wily political skills to survive two General Elections during this period, although it may be that with these democratic moves the legacy of weak political institutions is now seriously being addressed. The fact remains, however, that elements of the colonial inheritance are still at work. Historically embedded social, economic and political problems still have to be overcome if Kenya is to prosper in the future.

Kenya[14]

Territory:	583,000 sq km	Population:	32.7 million
Colonial power:	Britain	Independence:	1963
Major cities:	Nairobi (capital)	Ethnic groups:	Kikuyu
	Mombasa		Luhya
	Kisumu		Luo
Urban pop.:	29.3%		Kamba
Languages:	Kiswahili		Kalenjin
	English		Masai
Currency:	Kenyan shilling	Life expectancy:	54 years
Infant mortality:	65 deaths/thousand births	Adult literacy:	78.1%
Religion:	Traditional	Exports:	Tea
	Christian		Coffee
	Islam		Petroleum products
	Hindu		Vegetables and fruit
GDP per capita:	US$315	External debt:	US$6,893 million

Glossary of key terms

Arbitrary borders	State boundaries reflecting imperial interests, rather than local economic, social or political realities.
Bureaucratic autocracy	A system of government that relies on coercion rather than legitimacy, and seeks to administer a territory avoiding public representation and accountability.
Cash crop	Agricultural produce grown for export (e.g. coffee, tea, cocoa, sisal, and other commodities), not produce for personal or domestic consumption (e.g. food).
Core and peripheral states	The notion that the international system consists of wealthy states (the West), which have enhanced their economic position by exploiting and 'underdeveloping' those territories on the periphery of the international system (the Third World).

Export of surplus	The export of profits denying investment opportunities in the colony of origin.
Indirect rule	A system of colonial administration favouring the use of intermediaries, and offering a degree of devolution, rather than full-scale central government intervention.
Irredentism	The desire to unite a people or territory previously divided.
Lineage and kinship ties	Social bonds based on ties of family, clan and descent.
Monocrop economy	A national economy that is over-reliant on one or two products.
Primary sector	Economic activity other than secondary manufacturing industry or the service sector (e.g. mining and agriculture).
Scramble for Africa	Late nineteenth and early twentieth century partition of Africa among European imperial powers.
State elite	An educated and urban class which owes its privileges to its access to state institutions.
Stateless society	A society whose political organisation does not rely on strictly defined territory and centralised political institutions.
Underdevelopment	The systematic holding back of a state's economic potential to serve an imperial power's interests instead.

Questions raised by this chapter

1   What elements of pre-colonial African society continue to influence African politics today?
2   How have Africa's imperially imposed borders affected the continent politically, economically and socially?
3   To what extent did the state and civil society engage in colonial Africa?
4   What role did the African educated elite play in colonial rule and national liberation?
5   Does the evidence from Africa support the thesis of underdevelopment?
6   How appropriate were the political institutions left to Africa at independence?

Further reading

Basil Davidson's book provides an excellent place to start learning about pre-colonial Africa, while John Iliffe's historical survey covers more of the continent, over a wider time span. For a more specialist text on the state, Crawford Young's look at colonial

Africa is invaluable. For those interested in Africa's boundary politics, although dated, Saadia Touval's book is still the best introduction to this subject.

Underdevelopment theory commands a vast literature. For an introduction to this school of thought from one of its strongest advocates, it is well worth reading Andre Gunder Frank's *Capitalism and Underdevelopment*. To see how this thesis was applied specifically to Africa, a combination of Samir Amin's article and Walter Rodney's book prove useful. These should be balanced by criticisms of underdevelopment theory, of which Bill Warren's *Imperialism: the Pioneer of Capitalism* stands out.

A particularly profitable and accessible book that covers many of the issues tackled in this chapter has been written by Ieuan Ll Griffiths.

Amin, Samir (1972) 'Underdevelopment and dependency in Black Africa', *Journal of Modern African Studies* 10(4), 503–24.

Davidson, Basil (1998) *West Africa before the colonial era: a history to 1850*, London: Longman.

Frank, Andre Gunder (1971) *Capitalism and underdevelopment in Latin America*, London: Penguin.

Griffiths, Ieuan Ll (1995) *The African inheritance*, London: Routledge.

Iliffe, John (1995) *Africans: the history of a continent*, Cambridge: Cambridge University Press.

Rodney, Walter (1989) *How Europe underdeveloped Africa*, Nairobi: East African Educational Publishers.

Touval, Saadia (1972) *The boundary politics of independent Africa*, Cambridge, MA: Harvard University Press.

Warren, Bill (1980) *Imperialism: the pioneer of capitalism*, London: Verso.

Young, Crawford (1994) *The African colonial state in comparative perspective*, New Haven, CT: Yale University Press.

3 Ideology

Nationalism, socialism, populism and state capitalism

Robert Putnam describes an ideology as *a lifeguiding system of beliefs, values and goals affecting political style and action*.[1] In this sense, individuals use ideologies to help them understand and explain the world. They provide a way for human beings to synthesise the mass of information around them into something more logical and meaningful; giving them a 'world view'. Catholicism, Islam, socialism, liberalism and anarchism, for example, all serve as guides to their disciples. They provide interpretations of history, and explanations of present events, as well as supplying an accompanying set of values to which followers can adhere.

The study of politics is furthered by analysing the key characteristics of these ideologies, as well as examining their impact upon the process of governing. Ideology, in this respect, acts as a socialising force. People with similar world views will cooperate to further mutual interests, and defend this lifestyle against competitors. Consequently, most societies have a dominant ideology that provides the basis of social order. Liberal democracy, for example, prospers in western Europe and North America, permeating right though society. It is an ideology that binds state and civil society together, and it provides governments with their mission, coherence and, most importantly, their legitimacy.

If the study of ideology helps political scientists to understand the politics of the West, then the same should also be true for post-colonial Africa. Any book seeking to explain the politics of this continent therefore needs to identify and explore the dominant ideologies that are at work in this environment. This is precisely the task of the current chapter. The ideologies investigated will reveal the very foundations of African political systems.

As the following paragraphs will show, it has been nationalism that has dominated modern African politics. This can be explained by the shared struggle against imperialism, and the desire to build cohesive nation-states after independence. This is not to say, however, that all African countries share a common ideology. Numerous, distinct shades of nationalism have emerged. The chapter groups these different nuances into four general categories: African socialism, scientific socialism, populism and state capitalism. Each of these ideologies is examined in turn, followed by some concluding thoughts on how nationalism has helped shape the relationship between state and civil society in the post-colonial period.

Decolonisation in Africa

Nationalism was the mobilising force that saw Africans liberate themselves from imperial rule. Libya (1951), Morocco (1956), the Sudan (1956), Tunisia (1956), Ghana (1957), and Guinea (1958) were the initial countries to expel their colonial masters in the 1950s. Most African states, however, gained their independence during the 1960s (see Table 3.1).

The majority of Francophone colonies in Sub-Saharan Africa secured their political sovereignty, more or less *en masse*, in 1960. Three other French territories had to wait longer. Algeria won its independence in 1962; the Indian Ocean state of the Comoros (minus one of its islands) did likewise in 1975; while Djibouti, a tiny state on the Red Sea, completed France's mainland decolonisation in 1977. Algeria proved to be the most problematic case of French withdrawal. Only a bitter war of independence, and the collapse of the Fourth Republic back in France itself, brought this country its political freedom.

By contrast, London opted for a steadier programme of decolonisation. Pressures from within Africa ensured that there were regular Union Jack flag-lowering ceremonies throughout the 1960s. All but the Seychelles (decolonised in 1976) and Zimbabwe (Rhodesia) had become independent by the end of this decade. Britain only formally relinquished control of Zimbabwe in 1980. The delay was created by Ian Smith's rebel minority white settler government, which had unilaterally declared independence from London in 1965. Smith's administration only submitted to negotiations, and majority rule, after a protracted insurgency war.

Portugal put up most resistance to the 'winds of change' sweeping through Africa. Lisbon held on desperately to its colonies of Angola, Mozambique and Guinea-Bissau until the mid-1970s. It was at this point that strains created by the guerrilla wars fought in these territories precipitated a military coup in Portugal itself. On taking power, Lisbon's new military government withdrew its forces from Africa, and independence followed for the three colonies in 1975.

Since Zimbabwe's independence in 1980, two remaining loose ends of imperialism have been tidied up. Namibia gained its independence from South African occupation in 1990, while majority rule came to South Africa itself in 1994. This leaves just two externally governed territories remaining on the African mainland (Spain's pair of Mediterranean enclaves at Ceuta and Melilla). There are also several sets of islands in both the Atlantic and Indian Oceans still under European sovereignty.

A number of factors combined to produce this tidal wave of decolonisation. In most cases, the imperial powers recognised that (eventually) they would have to grant all peoples the self-determination and democracy that they had demanded for themselves and their allies during the Second World War. Arguments that only civilised (for 'civilised', read 'white') human beings could cope with liberty and political autonomy were beginning to wear thin. The United States, in particular, was pushing for its version of liberalism and capitalism to spread across the globe. Also there was the issue of cost. Empire, now

Table 3.1 Decolonisation in Africa

Country (former name)	Imperial power	Independence
Algeria	France	1962
Angola	Portugal	1975
Benin (Dahomey)	France	1960
Botswana (Bechuanaland)	Britain	1966
Burkina Faso (Upper Volta)	France	1960
Burundi (Urundi)	German, then Belgium from 1916	1962
Cameroon	German, then Britain and France from 1918	1960
Cape Verde	Portugal	1975
Central African Republic (Ubangi Chari)	France	1960
Chad	France	1960
The Comoros	France	1975 (except Mayotte island, which remained a French 'territorial community')
Congo, Republic of (French Congo, Congo-Brazzaville)	France	1960
Congo, Democratic Rep. of (DRC)(Belgian Congo, Congo-Kinshasa)	Belgium	1960
Côte d'Ivoire (Ivory Coast)	France	1960
Djibouti (French Somaliland, Afars and Issas)	France	1977
Egypt	Britain	1922
Equatorial Guinea (Fernando Po and Rio Muni)	Spain	1968
Eritrea	Italy	Federated to Ethiopia 1952 Independent 1993
Ethiopia	None	–
Gabon	France	1960
The Gambia	Britain	1965
Ghana (Gold Coast)	Britain	1957
Guinea	France	1958
Guinea-Bissau	Portugal	1974
Kenya	Britain	1963
Lesotho (Basutoland)	Britain	1966
Liberia	None	1847
Libya	Italy	1951
Madagascar	France	1960
Malawi (Nyasaland)	Britain	1964
Mali (Soudan)	France	1960
Mauritania	France	1960
Mauritius	Britain	1968
Morocco	Spain and France	1956
Mozambique	Portugal	1975
Namibia (South West Africa)	Germany, then South African mandate from 1920	1990
Niger	France	1960
Nigeria	Britain	1960

Rwanda (Ruanda)	Germany, then Belgium from 1916	1962
Sahrawi Arab Republic (Western Sahara)	Spain	Occupied on Spanish withdrawal by Morocco, 1976
São Tomé and Principe	Portugal	1975
Senegal	France	1960
Seychelles	Britain	1976
Sierra Leone	Britain	1961
Somalia	Britain and Italy	1960
South Africa	Union of British colonies and Boer republics	1910 (majority rule 1994)
Sudan	Britain (Anglo-Egyptian Condominium)	1956
Swaziland	Britain	1968
Tanzania (Union of Tanganyika and Zanzibar)	1 Germany, then Britain from 1919 2 Britain	1 Tanganyika 1961 2 Zanzibar 1963 Tanzania united in 1964
Togo	Germany, then Britain and France from 1919	1960 (British Togoland ceded to Ghana)
Tunisia	France	1956
Uganda	Britain	1962
Zambia (Northern Rhodesia)	Britain	1964
Zimbabwe (Southern Rhodesia)	Britain	1980 (UDI 1965)

that it involved responsibilities and not just exploitation, proved to be a heavy burden on the metropolitan powers' treasuries. In this respect, there were financial, as well as moral, motivations for political withdrawal. Above all, however, it was pressures created from within the colonies themselves that secured independence. 'Africa for the Africans' was now the demand. African nationalism had come of age, and, indeed, would remain at the centre of the nation-building project for the entire post-colonial period.

Nationalism

Nationalism is relatively simple to define. It is *the desire that the nation should be housed in its own sovereign state*. The problem with this definition is that the inquirer first has to know what a nation is.

A nation is not so much a physical entity as a sentiment. It is *a collection of people bound together by common values and traditions, often sharing the same language, history and an affiliation to a geographical area*. Individuals within the group will identify with fellow members of the nation, and define themselves in contrast to outsiders belonging to other nations. Benedict Anderson talks of nations as 'imagined communities'. This is because the members of even 'the smallest nation will never know most of their fellow-members, meet them, or even hear of them, yet in the minds of each lives the image of their communion'.[2] Using interpretations of the past and symbols such as flags, anthems and ceremonies, the people of the nation generate social cohesion based on their shared national values and way of life. In this sense, individuals gain psychological and material protection from a sense of belonging. What is more, this security can be greatly enhanced if the nation is united with political power. This is where the idea of nationalism comes to the fore.

Nationalism occurs when members of a nation desire to be united as one political unit. This gives the nation political organisation and power. Only then is it likely that a nation can enjoy self-determination, with tailor-made state institutions serving its interests and controlling its destiny. State power can protect the nation from the unwanted influences of other nations, as well as guarding national values internally.[3]

A classic example of nationalism giving birth to a new state can be found with the formation of Italy in the mid-nineteenth century. Prior to 1861, the Italian people were divided among several territories. However, diplomatic activity and a guerrilla war assisted these previously divided people to unite and form the single sovereign state of Italy. The Italian nation had secured itself the prize of statehood, which in turn brought self-government and dedicated political institutions to serve the Italian nation's interests. Germany emerged from a similar process ten years later, in 1871. In both cases, a nation demanded a state, and then it was up to the new state to sustain and develop the nation that had created it.

African nationalism

The nature of African nationalism is slightly different to its European cousin. In terms of origins, for example, modern African states were not created by the demands of indigenous social forces. They were not the product of local nationalist appeals. Instead, Africa states were externally imposed. As we saw in the previous chapter, imperial powers drew political boundaries that meant very little to the Africans they enclosed. This meant that groups with diverse, or even conflicting, identities were gathered together within these 'alien' states. A lack of unity or common culture meant these communities could not be described as nations. Instead, Africans retained and developed ideas of community at a more local, sub-state level (lineage groups, clans and 'tribes'). Imperial administrators encouraged these divisions, contributing to the absence of a national identity emerging within the colonial states. In short, modern states arrived in Africa well before any nation considered these states their own. It was not until the mid-twentieth century that political activists began successfully to arouse widespread nationalist sentiments on the continent.

African nationalism began seriously to challenge imperial rule in the 1950s. It emerged as a reaction to colonialism, and its immediate aim was to rid the continent of foreign rule. In this respect, African nationalism was a classic expression of the demand for self-determination. The leaders of these liberation movements, however, only rejected imperial rule. Unlike the European nationalists before them, they were not seeking to establish a new state to house their nation. Instead, they aimed to capture the existing colonial states themselves to govern. As such, the retention of the 'alien' state . wholesale, including the recognition of its associated 'arbitrary' boundaries mission was to build new African nations within the prefabricated structures the already existing colonial states. This, the nationalists argued, would bring Africans into the modern era of nation-states.

National unity was at the heart of African nationalism. The objective was to transform multi-ethnic, multi-cultural, multi-religious, and even multi-racial societies into single unitary nations. A new nation would be built to fill the political space delineated by the borders of the already existing (colonial) state. In this respect, cultural pluralism was frowned upon by nationalist leaders. Where previously Africans had rooted their identities in descent and ethnicity, rather than territory, now they were called upon to join the community of the nation-state. As President Hastings Banda of Malawi declared, 'So far as I am concerned, there is no Yao in this country; no Lomwe; no Sena; no Chewa; no Ngoni; no Nyakyusa; no Tonga; there are only 'Malawians'. That is all.'[4] President Samora Machel of Mozambique was more succinct. He stated, 'For the nation to live, the tribe must die.'[5]

In striving to build nations such as Malawi and Mozambique, nationalists (politicians and academics alike) regarded Africa's complex ethnic relationships as a hindrance. 'Tribes' were the antithesis of a nation. They were portrayed as retrogressive, part of the past, and an obstacle to progress. In this respect, 'tribalism' was regarded as a sin against the post-colonial state, and the freedoms that had been won. The nation was now the priority, not outdated 'tribal' associations, and state power would be used to promote this process of nation-building.

For these reasons, nationalism lost none of its urgency after independence. It became the dominant component within the ideologies of all Africa's new states. Added to this theme of unity was the related goal of economic growth. These words of President Julius Nyerere, written just after Tanganyika's independence in 1961, captured the mood of nationalist thinking at this time. He described his state's work as 'a patriotic struggle that leaves no room for differences and unites all elements of the country; the nationalists who led them to freedom must inevitably form the first governments of the new States. Once the first free government is formed, its supreme task lies in building up the economy.... This, no less than the struggle against colonialism, calls for the maximum united effort by the whole country if it is to succeed. *There can be no room for difference or division.*'[6]

As a consequence, after independence, political activity was often channelled through just one state-sanctioned party, with opposition groups banned. Similarly, organisations that had previously been active within civil society, such as trade unions, youth movements and women's groups, were co-opted by the state, restricting their autonomy. Ethnic associations were also often banned, and even the numerous indigenous languages spoken within each African state were disregarded. Usually just one official 'national' language was chosen, generally that of the departing colonial power. In short, pluralist competition was sacrificed to the higher goals of national unity and economic development in the post-colonial period. Nationalism, fostered by the state, became the dominant ideology.

The differing ideological shades of African nationalism

Although all the newly independent African states were clearly anti-imperial and nationalist in approach, this did not result in these countries adopting identical ideologies. Each state followed its own unique ideological path in its attempt to secure national unity and economic development. Indeed, most nationalist leaders had their own personal political philosophies, which were often placed at the heart of all state activity. Senghor, for example, preached *négritude*; Kaunda *humanism*; Nyerere *ujamaa*; and Mobutu *Mobutism*. Despite this diversity, however, it is possible to gather these nationalist ideologies into four general categories (African socialism, scientific socialism, populism and state capitalism – summarised in Table 3.2 at the end of this section). By looking at each of these categories in turn, it is possible to analyse in more detail the ideological foundations underpinning Africa's post-colonial political systems.

African socialism

It is not surprising that most states on the continent adopted a socialist outlook after independence. Having rid their countries of colonial rule, the task was now to reduce dependence on the West, and to restructure economies to ensure that local development needs were prioritised. Only in this manner could poverty be reduced and social welfare provided for all.

Few African leaders considered capitalism and liberalism appropriate methods to achieve these goals. These had been the ideologies of their former colonial oppressors, and still remained the philosophy behind the international system that continued to disadvantage African economies. Instead, the more egalitarian approach of socialism was adopted. Socialism represented a 'free good', a 'political amulet', that many thought could offset neo-colonial threats, bringing progress and material gains to the continent.[7] As Aristide Zolberg wrote at the time, 'for those who are faced with the overwhelming burdens of government in Africa, socialism is more than a scientific method. It is a modern gnosis which promises to unveil to its initiates the secrets of economic development'.[8]

This is not to say that African leaders adopted socialism as prescribed by the Soviet Union. Although fraternal links were extended, African states were careful to keep their distance. As Ahmed Sékou Touré, the President of Guinea, warned, 'trying to "Westernise or Easternise" Africa leads to denying the African personality'.[9] Instead, true to their nationalist roots, politicians on the continent promoted their own specific version of socialism, that of *African socialism*.

The new President of Senegal, Léopold Senghor, outlined the problem of adopting orthodox European socialism. He argued, 'It is evident that African socialism can no longer be that of Marx and Engels, which was designed in the nineteenth century according to European scientific methods and realities. Now it must take into consideration African realities.'[10] Classical theories of socialism, for example, saw the proletariat as the revolutionary class that would defeat the bourgeoisie. In Africa, with its small industrial base, there was no real working class to talk of, nor were there societies marked by massive inequalities. African states needed guiding ideologies more relevant to their own experiences.

This is why African socialism stressed the continent's traditional values. African leaders portrayed their communities as having been classless, communal and egalitarian prior to colonial rule. There had been no landowners in these societies, it was argued, and the interests of the community had always been put above those of the individual. In this respect, Senghor believed Africans had 'already realized socialism before the coming of the Europeans'.[11]

African socialism was therefore an attempt to recover these traditional values, and to marry them with new technology and the modern nation-state. It was about combining the equality, cooperation and humanism of the village community with the wealth and organisation potential that could be generated by modern production methods and state institutions respectively. African socialism, in this manner, sought to skip the capitalist stage of development outlined in classical Marxist analysis. Neither would an alternative Soviet-style 'dictatorship of the proletariat' have to be constructed. African leaders believed this self-reliant, non-capitalist path to socialism would create a new social order where poverty could be reduced, welfare improved and human dignity maximised.

Practically, the pursuit of African socialism cast the state in a central role not only politically, but also economically and socially. The state would be the engine of development. Public enterprise came to dominate these centrally planned economies; large elements of the private sector were nationalised (including foreign capital); and the state itself embarked on grand development projects of infrastructure and industrialisation. Similarly, harvests were bought by state marketing board monopolies; consumer goods were sold largely in state-run shops; prices were set by government agencies; and imports and exports controlled centrally. In short, the free market was curtailed, with the state itself controlling both production and distribution.

The state, in a similar vein, also came to dominate politically (as will be seen in Chapter 6). Most African countries became one-party states led from the centre, with little leeway given to opposition movements or local politics. This curtailment of pluralism was justified in the name of national unity and the need for the government to deliver a coherent and consistent development strategy.

Whether political or economic in nature, these practical characteristics of African socialism dovetailed neatly into those aims of nationalism already mentioned (anti-imperialism, self-reliance, national unity and the promotion of economic development). African leaders were convinced they had found a non-capitalist path to future prosperity.

All African states struggled in their nationalist ambitions, however, and those espousing African socialism proved no exception. Like other ideologies, this particular strain of socialism was hampered by a number of realities: the nature of the international economy (explored in more detail in Chapter 9); an inability to mobilise the peasantry in this project (see the case study at the end of the chapter); internal social division (see Chapter 4); and the tendency of state elites to serve their own, and not the wider community's, interests (Chapters 5 and 10). Consequently, many of these experiments perished with the onset of the military coups from the mid-1960s onwards.

African socialism also came under attack intellectually. Many regarded it as merely a convenient justification for the repression of alternative viewpoints and the suppression of civil liberties. Others, on the Left, criticised these states for not following a classical (European) Marxist-Leninist path to socialism. They judged the radical rhetoric of Africa's nationalist leaders not to be matched by their public policy. The Soviet Union itself, in this respect, regarded many of these governments as merely 'reformist'. They saw fault in the independent nature of African socialism, with its strong traditional and humanist, rather than scientific socialist, values.

Scientific socialism

'Our socialism cannot be called Somali socialism, African socialism, or Islamic socialism.... Our socialism is scientific socialism founded by the great Marx and Engels.'[12] These words of President Mohamed Siad Barré acknowledged a change in the ideological approach undertaken by Somalia and several other African states from 1969 onwards. Marien Ngouabi's military regime in Congo-Brazzaville was the first government to declare its allegiance to scientific socialism. Somalia followed suit a year later, and the mid-1970s brought a further wave of ideological change. The Portuguese coup of April 1974 saw Marxist-Leninist-inspired guerrilla movements take power in both Mozambique and Angola; in September of that year Emperor Haile Selassie of Ethiopia was deposed, making way for a regime advocating scientific socialism; two months later, Lieutenant-Colonel Mathieu Kérékou launched a 'revolution within a revolution' in Benin; while Madagascar's military government moved to Marxism-Leninism in June 1975. Given that the liberation movements of Zimbabwe, Namibia and South Africa also expressed sympathies with this ideology, events had provided scientific socialism with a firm foothold on the African continent by the late 1970s.

Marxism-Leninism began to prosper on the continent after the first wave of (African) socialism began to be criticised. African socialism had failed to break the shackles of economic dependence, and many of the governments it inspired soon degenerated into corrupt dictatorships vulnerable to military coups.

Marxist-Leninists considered this inevitable. They thought African socialism too amorphous and shapeless. Romantic notions of inherent African communalism masked the reality of underlying class antagonisms. Indeed, in many cases it was argued that a petty-bourgeois state elite was simply disguising its exploitation of the masses with a false socialist rhetoric. In this respect, the Marxist-Leninists declared there to be only one true socialism, that based on the science of class analysis. This demanded that petty-bourgeois state elites should immediately commit class suicide, and in their place working class governments should be established. These would then rule, allied to the peasant masses. Only after these revolutionary changes were undertaken could a true socialist society be built.

Ethiopia provides an excellent case study of what actually happened to an African state after a Marxist-Leninist regime came to power. In 1975, Colonel Mariam Mengistu's new government nationalised all major domestic industrial, financial and commercial enterprises without compensation. The role of private capital was severely restricted, as decreed by the 'Government Ownership and Control of the Means of Production Proclamation'. The state itself was now to command the economy. Similarly, the small amount of foreign investment present in Ethiopia was also nationalised (with compensation). Land ownership, too, now came directly under government control (previously, Ethiopian society was unique in Africa in hosting a landlord class). In terms of economic development, the government concentrated its efforts on industrialisation, promoting state factories, and the socialisation of agriculture with the establishment of state farms. The working class and peasantry, after all, were to be the leaders of the revolution. The regime also eventually established the Workers' Party of Ethiopia to act as the vanguard of the revolution.[13]

In terms of public policy, it is often difficult to distinguish between these Marxist-Leninist governments and their African socialist neighbours. Scientific socialist states may have been more systematic about their socialism, and may have avoided the personalisation of this ideology, yet it cannot be said that scientific socialist regimes were any less nationalistic than their African socialist predecessors. There was no 'proletarian internationalisation', for example, with African states joining the global ideological block led by the Soviet Union. Just as President Samora Machel of Mozambique declared, 'We do not intend to become another Bulgaria', Moscow reciprocated by only regarding these Afro-Marxist regimes 'socialist in orientation'.[14] Indeed, the Afro-Marxist regimes took a very pragmatic approach to Marxism-Leninism. Tell-tale signs, such as the absence of antagonism towards organised religion and government cooperation with transnational corporations, were obvious. Indeed, Africa's Marxist-Leninist regimes consistently traded more with the West than they did with the Soviet Union or Eastern Europe. This independent interpretation of scientific socialism led Kenneth Jowitt to conclude, 'The most striking feature [of Afro-Marxist regimes] is the absence of ideological commitments, developmental strategies, and institutional developments consistent with their identity.'[15] Nationalist demands of unity and development, more often than not, gained priority over considerations of the class struggle.

Despite the rhetoric, the reality remained that there was an absence in Africa of the material conditions that Marx himself predicted would bring about a socialist revolution. In Barry Munslow's words, there was no 'strong, self-conscious working class which could lead the revolutionary take-over and construct socialism on a strong technological base, a socialism with such high levels of production and productivity that the power of the world capitalist economy would be incapable of bringing it to heel'.[16] Even the Soviet Union, with its strong foundation of heavy industry, technological innovation, military might and an abundance of natural resources, failed to do this. African states whose security forces had difficulty subduing internal conflict (most Afro-Marxist states had to contend with ongoing civil wars), and whose economies remained dependent on the international economy for their very survival, were never going to make the transition to scientific socialism. However committed to Marxism-Leninism these states' leaders were, post-colonial Africa was not to be a utopia of worker and peasant power.

Compromised by the harsh economic realities of the 1980s, scientific socialist regimes, along with all other African states, began to liberalise their public policy. Governments had little choice but to accept structural adjustment programmes imposed by the international financial institutions (IFIs) of the World Bank and International Monetary Fund (see Chapter 9). The continent's socialist experiments were now at an end. Ironically, it was the IFIs, found at the very heart of the international capitalist economy, which had succeeded in reeling in both African socialist and Marxist-Leninist states.

Populism

A third group of states sharing a similar nuance of nationalism can be termed populist regimes. Although populism is not usually considered a true ideology, given that it is found right across the political spectrum (as indeed is nationalism), these governments did have similar belief-systems influencing their decision-making.

Populism involves putting the 'ordinary person' in society to the fore. It is the idea that individuals should be involved in the political process, and that state institutions should be more responsive to their needs. Populist movements often evolve where existing governments have become too self-interested, and they have as their goal the return of power to the masses.

On the African continent, populism is often associated with military governments. Officers instigate a *coup d'état*, removing the previous dictatorial and corrupt regime. The military government then attempts to consolidate its legitimacy by reconstructing or building new public institutions that close the gap between the state and civil society. Ideas of morality, probity and accountability

University
of Ulster
LIBRARY

are stressed, and new levels of democracy and participation are encouraged within the political process.

The governments of Captain Thomas Sankara and Flight-Lieutenant Jerry Rawlings, in Burkina Faso and Ghana respectively, provide two excellent examples of African populist regimes. Sankara's leadership lasted from 1983 to 1987, while Rawlings has governed Ghana since New Year's Eve 1981. Other candidates to be included in this populist category include Colonel Muammar Gaddafi's Libya (since 1969), and possibly the government of Yoweri Museveni in Uganda (which since the rebellion of 1986 has sought to build a 'no-party state').

Many African regimes have been described as populist, given that welfare issues are often prominent within African public policy. Yet it is the institutions introduced by the governments mentioned above that set these states aside as a separate populist category.

In Ghana, for example, the Rawlings regime established Peoples' Defence Committees (PDCs) after the 'revolution'. These were designed to bring the masses directly into the governmental process. These committees oversaw the work of state officials, and PDC members theoretically had the power to hire and fire administrators at the local level, as well as overrule any decisions they made. As the *Worker's Banner* newspaper read, 'power will not be concentrated at the top anymore'.[17]

In Burkina Faso, Sankara's government built 'revolutionary committees' in villages, urban areas and work places right across the country. This was combined with anti-corruption drives and a tighter control of state salaries. In Libya, Colonel Gaddafi's brand of populism attempted to blend Islam with notions of Greek direct democracy. Changing the name of his country to the Socialist People's Libyan Arab Jamahiriyya (state of the masses), workers took over businesses, students replaced diplomats, and non-professionals moved in to run government departments in Tripoli.

All these populist governments, however, faced an identical problem. Those commanding the state's core executive were reluctant to devolve too much power to local committees. They feared the consequences of losing control. Nationalist demands of building tight central authority, in order to maintain national unity and coherent economic development, overruled populist demands of letting the masses truly administer themselves. Devolution would only go so far. This is why Pearl Robinson talks of the state trying to 'overcontrol' politics in Burkina Faso, and the 'façade of quasi-democratic institutions.' She concluded that 'the objective function of grassroots participation was subversive of the rulers' intent'.[18] The state president and members of the core executive, as in all other African political systems, remained very much in control. In reality, the African populist experiment proved to be more useful as a method for the state to penetrate civil society than it was for civil society to penetrate the state.

State capitalism

The final ideological category that this chapter seeks to highlight is that of 'state capitalism'. Although most African countries followed socialist paths of political and economic development after independence, a number adopted a more liberal approach. Countries such as Côte d'Ivoire, Kenya, Malawi, Nigeria, Cameroon, Morocco and Gabon all left their economies, to varying degrees, open to free market activity.

Instead of presiding over a command economy, where the state directly controls economic production, distribution and exchange, state capitalist regimes encouraged private enterprise. Indigenous activity of this nature occurred most frequently in the agricultural, transport and trading sectors of these countries' economies. As such, independent commercial farmers and import/export entrepreneurs, for example, could go about their business.

There was also a more benign attitude towards foreign investment forthcoming from these state capitalist regimes. Notions of 'self-reliance' were relatively absent, as long as the transnational corporation concerned was not perceived as exploitative. Nationalist sentiments, however, still determined that joint ventures (involving a mixture of local and foreign capital) were the most popular form of investment, rather than wholly foreign owned enterprises.

Even the most liberal of these state capitalist regimes, however, could not be regarded as truly *laissez-faire* in outlook. The state, rather than civil society, was still very much the senior partner in any economic or political activity. Crawford Young, in this respect, considered these regimes to practise 'a highly nationalist version of capitalism'. The development and unity goals of African nationalism were still paramount, making it impossible, in leaders' minds, for the economy to be left entirely to 'the beneficient workings of the invisible hand' of the free market.[19]

This resulted in heavy state intervention in the economy. State enterprises competed with smaller private concerns; prices, imports and exports were still largely controlled centrally; the government dominated the marketing of cash crops; and there was considerable public spending on welfare programmes. This intervention, however, can be regarded as more pragmatic, rather than ideologically motivated. The state considered itself as acting in the interest of strategic economic development, rather than following the principles of socialism or populism.

Similarly, the (tempered) liberalism found within these economies rarely spread to their countries' political systems. State capitalist countries were not necessarily more democratic than their neighbours, nor were they any less exempt from being dominated by a self-interested political èlite. And in terms of economic performance, despite better records in the first two decades after independence, capitalist-oriented countries still floundered, like the others, in the 1980s. Consequently, just like their neighbours, they were forced to succumb to the demands of international financial institutions. Structural adjustment programmes, for example, required state capitalist regimes to sell many of their public enterprises to the private sector.

Table 3.2 Africa's nationalist ideologies

African nationalism	*Characteristics:* Anti-imperialist – initial goal of decolonisation Autonomy – removing state's economic and political dependency on the West Unity – the desire to build a nation within inherited boundaries Economic development – restructured economies to serve Africans, not the West State-led – nation building project defined and controlled by government Against 'tribalism' – state discourages sub-national identities and mobilisation Strong executive – controlling activity within civil society *Examples:* All African states
African socialism	*Characteristics:* Independent – building upon, not dogmatically reproducing, Marxism Importance of tradition – African sense of community, classlessness and cooperation Modern – combining tradition with technology and modern production methods Skipping the capitalist stage of development – non-capitalist path to socialism Nationalisation – private capital taken into state control State marketing monopolies – farmers have to sell cash crops to state agencies State distribution – goods sold in state shops, at state-determined prices State control of imports and exports State control of banking and finance Curtailment of political pluralism – legally, only one party allowed to mobilise *Examples:* Senghor's Senegal, Nyerere's Tanzania, Kaunda's Zambia and Touré's Guinea
Scientific socialism	*Characteristics:* Marxist-Leninist – following the class analysis of orthodox Marxism Importance of working class/peasant alliance At its height in the 1970s and early 1980s Fraternal links with the Soviet Union – but still independent of the Soviet bloc Still an African version of socialism – tolerant of religion, economic links with West Nationalisation – private capital taken into state control State marketing monopolies – farmers have to sell cash crops to state agencies State distribution – goods sold in state shops, at state-determined prices State control of imports and exports State control of banking and finance Curtailment of political pluralism – only one legal party *Examples:* Machel's Mozambique, Neto's Angola and Mengistu's Ethiopia.

Populism	*Characteristics:* Advocates people's representation Participation – formation of people's committees Probity – anti-corruption drives Often formed in the wake ôf military coups – regimes trying to build legitimacy *Examples:* Sankara's Burkina Faso, (earlier) Rawlings' Ghana and Gaddafi's Libya.
State capitalism	*Characteristics:* Tolerant of private capital – both domestic and foreign Lively small-scale capitalism – farmers, transport and export/import entrepreneurs Still heavy state intervention – marketing monopolies, price setting, large parastatals State still the largest producer and distributor within economy Curtailment of political pluralism – often only one legal party permitted *Examples:* Houphouët-Boigny's Côte d'Ivoire, Kenyatta's Kenya, and Nigeria.

State and civil society

The final section of this chapter looks at the impact of ideology on the relationship between the state and civil society in post-colonial Africa. The ideologies adopted, particularly dominant sentiments of nationalism, have in some respects been a positive force on the continent; they have contributed to the maintenance of a basic nation-state system. Without this mutual respect for international borders, political instability in Africa could have been far worse than it actually was during this period. This stability, however, came at a price. The ideologies adopted tended to favour the interests of state elites, hampering political and economic expression in civil society. Nationalism, in all its guises, may have brought stability internationally but, in the long run, the myopic crusade for unity (or perhaps, more accurately, state conformity) generated conflict internally.

Despite the problems of 'non-organic' states and international borders cutting across cultural boundaries, there have only been two occasions when the map of Africa has been re-drawn during the post-colonial period. This was to accommodate Tanganyika and Zanzibar merging soon after independence to form the new state of Tanzania in 1964, and to recognise Eritrea's secession from Ethiopia in 1993. In all other cases, colonial boundaries have endured. This reflects a remarkable victory for African nationalism and its ability to protect the concept of the inherited nation-state.

When the Organization of African Unity (OAU) was established in 1963, its members soon agreed that colonial boundaries should be regarded as inviolable. Although Africans certainly considered these borders to be problematic, there was general agreement that any alterations to the colonial frontiers would only create even greater conflict. Only Morocco and Somalia refused to agree to this principle. As a result of this OAU doctrine, post-colonial Africa has avoided a scale of international warfare found elsewhere in the world during periods of nation-building. There has been no Third Reich attempting to expand its borders, for example, nor has there been an African Lebanon where sovereign territory has been consistently violated by neighbouring states. Indeed, the only instance of full-scale international conflict (where one state totally defeats another) came in 1979, when the Tanzanian army occupied Uganda. Even here, Tanzania withdrew its forces once the irritant of Idi Amin had been removed from power.

This is not to say that international clashes have been entirely absent on the continent. South Africa in the 1980s persistently destabilised its neighbours in its attempts to defend apartheid; Morocco continues to occupy Western Sahara claiming it (and parts of Algeria and Mauritania) as part of the historic Moroccan empire; while Libya and Chad have battled over the Aouzou Strip. Other minor international skirmishes have occurred elsewhere on the continent.

It is the irredentist state of Somalia, and the separatist movements in Katanga, Biafra and Eritrea, however, that have proved the to be the greatest threats to Africa's nation-state boundaries. It is worth investigating these conflicts briefly, as they prove to be exceptions to the rule, and show what could happen in Africa should political support for the inherited boundaries disappear.

Irredentism is a desire to unite a cultural community under one flag that is currently located in more than one state. Donald Horowitz defines it as a 'movement by members of an ethnic group in one state to retrieve ethnically kindred people and their territory across borders'.[20] Of all the African states, it is Somalia which has pursued irredentism to the greatest extent. The Somali people were divided among five separate states during the era of colonialism: French Somaliland (Djibouti), British Somaliland, Italian Somaliland, Ethiopia and Kenya. At independence in 1960, only British Somaliland and Italian Somaliland were united. This left ethnic Somalis living across international boundaries in the three remaining states. By refusing to agree to the OAU principle of inviolable boundaries, Somalia served notice that it wished to provide a nation-state for all the Somali people. Soon after independence, the Mogadishu government supplied rebels in north-east Kenya with arms to fight the irredentist cause. Support was also given to Somali groups in the Ogaden region of Ethiopia. This latter conflict escalated, and the Somali army eventually invaded the Ogaden in 1977. Only foreign intervention by the Soviet Union ensured that this Somali invasion was unsuccessful.

Nationalism also triumphed in defending Africa's new nations from separatist threats. Only one such movement, the Eritrean Peoples' Liberation Front (EPLF), has secured its demands in post-colonial Africa.

The motivation for separatism usually stems from the sentiment that a community is suffering internal colonialism; the government at the centre, and the state in general, is not serving the interests of the local community. As a reaction, rather than trying to establish a more favourable balance of power in central state institutions, the oppressed community demands territory for itself, and independence.

In Congo-Kinshasa (later Zaire, and then the Democratic Republic of the Congo), the region of Katanga tried to gain autonomy when the Belgian imperial authorities withdrew in 1960. Although the secessionists had the advantage that Katanga was rich in mineral resources, enjoying close contacts with foreign corporations, they failed to build enough support to resist the power of the central state (though not before this crisis had precipitated a military *coup d'état* at the centre, and involved the intervention of the United Nations). Nigeria also went through a secessionist crisis in the 1960s, as will be explored in greater depth in the case study at the end of Chapter 4. It is worth noting at this point, however, that neither of these conflicts resulted in a permanent re-drawing of Africa's international boundaries. The nation-state system remained intact.

The reason why Eritrean separatists succeeded where the Katangans and Biafrans failed relates to the level of power at the centre, and Eritrea's historic claim to autonomy. Eritrea, formerly a separate Italian colony, was federated with Ethiopia in 1952. After over 20 years of guerrilla war, this territory finally gained its independence in 1993. This was because the Ethiopian state had imploded. A coalition of opposition movements from all over Ethiopia joined forces and marched on Addis Ababa. The resulting fall of Haile Mariam Mengistu's regime created a power vacuum at the centre. No authority remained to enforce the unity of the nation. Consequently, in the talks between the opposition movements that followed Mengistu's fall, Eritrean representatives were successfully able to negotiate independence for their region.

Eritrea, however, it has to be stressed, was the exception to the rule. Elsewhere the colonial boundaries remain intact. There seems to be little evidence to support the idea that artificial historical boundaries have set up 'crippling' *international* tensions on the continent.[21] Indeed, most African states have gone out of their way to respect existing borders. It is precisely because these boundaries are so artificial that no state finds itself able to make a claim against another's territory. States struggling for cohesion themselves are too vulnerable to mount irredentist claims of their own.[22] If Zambia was to take land from across the border in the Democratic Republic of the Congo (DRC), for example, this could only invite Malawi to demand land from Zambia based on the same precedent. Instead, most African leaders are willing to except the *status quo* and back the OAU agreement on borders. In this way, international tensions are reduced, stability increases, and each state receives a welcome recognition of legitimacy from other African states, as well as the wider international political system.

It may be, however, that Eritrea's independence in 1993 has marked a watershed. The inherited borders are perhaps becoming less sacred. Concurrent with diminished state power in the 1990s has been an increase in the number of international clashes on the continent. In the Great Lakes region of Central Africa, for example, the continent experienced its first regional war. Events, starting with Rwanda's genocide in 1994, first led to Uganda assisting rebels to topple the government in Kigali, and then saw Rwandan and Ugandan forces involved in DRC's (formerly Zaire's) civil war. Eventually this war would draw military support from a number of regional powers. Zimbabwe, Angola, Namibia, Sudan and Chad, as well as Rwanda and Uganda, had all dispatched troops to fight in this conflict by 1999. This war, added to other eruptions of international violence, such as the border clash between Ethiopia and Eritrea in the late 1990s, may have put the OAU agreement, or at least respect for territorial sovereignty, in danger. Yet there can be no doubt that, when the post-colonial period is taken as a whole, recognition of the inherited boundaries (in effect, respect for each other's nationalist ideology) has produced a degree of peace many would not have predicted at independence.

The continent's international stability, however, came at a price. It is one thing to gain mutual respect for nations externally; it is another to suppress political competition internally in the name of national unity. Nation-building was accompanied by many states trying to dictate to, and exploit, civil society. Authoritarian edicts were common, proclaiming exactly what the people had to do in the name of national unity. Any dissent from this official nationalist line was deemed subversive by the political leadership, and dealt with accordingly.

Pluralist systems of conflict resolution had difficulty surviving in this environment. There was little room for alternative views to be aired. If a challenge to a state's nationalist programme was channelled through ethnic mobilisation then it was dismissed as 'tribalism'. If this opposition stemmed from a particular part of the country, then this region was condemned as separatist. If just a minority within the population was involved, then the dissenters were told (or forced) to desist and pull together with the rest of the nation. Members of the political elite, in this respect, controlled the state as they saw fit, becoming the self-proclaimed guardians of national unity.[23] In this sense, African nationalism was very much a state-defined and state-led phenomenon. Civil society, rather than actively participating in the nation-building project, became instead merely its passive recipients.

The addition of a socialist dimension to this basic nationalist creed similarly failed to improve things for civil society. The 'revolution', after all, was usually instigated from above. Having selected an ideology that justified the centralisation of power, and the suppression of private economic activity, the state elite was firmly in control. Indeed, whether socialism, populism or state capitalism was promoted, all these ideologies had the same result: the centralisation of power in the hands of a bureaucratic and political elite. Although many African leaders were sincere about their commitment to their chosen ideology, the inequality that grew between state and civil society left these leaders open to the charge that they were merely attempting to hide exploitative behaviour through the creation of a 'false consciousness' among the masses.

This recurrent split between the interests of the state and those of civil society has, in many parts of Africa, been the downfall of the nation-building project itself. Amílcar Cabral, the leader of Guinea-Bissau's liberation movement, warned his guerrilla forces that 'the people are not fighting for ideas, nor what is in a man's mind. The people fight and accept the sacrifices demanded by the struggle in order to gain material advantages, to live better and in peace, to benefit from progress, and for a better future for their children.'[24] If the state and its ideology do not serve civil society's interests, then the masses tend to disengage from the state. As Chapter 10 will show, this is exactly what happened in a number of African countries during the 1990s. The result was a slide towards state collapse.

However attractive an ideology, if it is not used to serve civil society's interests, then in the long run it will be discredited. Ideology has to be accepted by, and not imposed upon, the masses. Nationalism, in this respect, may have helped maintain a degree of international stability on the African continent in the post-colonial years, but the way it was applied to domestic public policy only resulted in a growing internal distrust between the governors and the governed. This political disharmony had the effect of endangering the very nation-building project itself.

Case study: socialism and ujamaa in Tanzania

Tanzania is located on the east coast of Africa just below the equator. It came into existence in 1964, when mainland Tanganyika and the Indian Ocean islands of Zanzibar came together to form the United Republic of Tanzania. The country has a varied topology: much of the mainland consists of a dry central plateau, but there is also a humid coastal strip, grassland (including the Serengeti), and even areas of semi-desert. The great Rift Valley, and ancient volcanic activity on Tanganyika's borders, have produced some of the country's more spectacular features. There is the permanently ice-capped Mount Kilimanjaro, and the massive lakes of Victoria, Tanganyika and Malawi. By contrast, Zanzibar is a group of low-lying islands approximately 50 kilometres from the mainland, which boasts a hot and humid tropical climate (ideal for growing spices and fruit).

The nationalism pursued by the Tanzanian government had at its heart similar goals to other brands of nationalism found elsewhere on the African continent. At the centre of these ideologies were the twin desires to build national unity and to foster economic development. Unity was very important for the stability of Tanzania, as over 120 ethnic groups can be found on the country's mainland. Similarly, there are 'racial' divisions among Tanzania's people. Alongside its African inhabitants, there are Asian Tanzanians, Arab Tanzanians and a smaller community of white Tanzanians. The population practises Islam, several denominations of Christianity and numerous traditional beliefs. Added to these differing social identities are potential clashes of interest between the residents of Zanzibar and those on the mainland.

Given these social divisions, the government's first task was to set about building a single nation within the inherited state boundaries. The aim was to enhance the unity generated by the independence campaign, and Julius Nyerere, Tanzania's first president, continued to urge his people to regard themselves primarily as Tanzanians, and only after this as Chagga, Arab, Asian or Shirazi. And this unity, indeed, has been Tanzania's post-colonial success story. There has been very little ethnic conflict in the years since independence. Tanzania has been a model of political and social stability on the African continent.

Tanzanian nationalism, however, was less successful with respect to its second goal of economic development. With few natural resources to exploit, Tanzania has always relied heavily on agricultural production to generate wealth. At independence, the country was self-sufficient in food, but this production was largely confined to smallholdings farmed by peasants. There were relatively few large commercial enterprises feeding the economy. The task of the state's economic planners in the post-colonial period was therefore to increase production. This, in turn, would generate greater surpluses, which could then be re-invested to develop the economy further. Like most African leaders, Nyerere considered capitalism to be an inappropriate method of generating this economic expansion. Instead, he advocated socialism as the correct ideology to follow. This would secure growth that could be shared by all Tanzanians.

Like many African leaders at this time, Nyerere formulated his own genus of African socialism. Termed *ujamaa* (familyhood), this ideology was very much associated with the president personally. Like all other breeds of socialism, ujamaa was critical of individualism and capitalism. Instead, it advocated the public ownership of the means of production; it gave a special status to workers and peasants; and it had as its goal the creation of social equality. In this respect, it followed closely the classical socialist mantra, 'from each according to their ability; to each according to their need'. As Nyerere himself put it, 'Socialism, as a system, is in fact the organisation of men's inequalities to serve their equality.... Its concern is to see that those who sow reap a fair share of what they sow.'[25]

Nyerere, however, did not believe Tanzania would benefit from a dogmatic application of Soviet-style socialism. He pointed out that 'Africa's conditions are very different from those of the Europe in which Marx and Lenin wrote and worked. To talk as if these thinkers provide all the answers to our problems, or as if Marx invented socialism, is to reject the humanity of Africa and the universality of socialism. Marx did contribute a great deal to socialist thought. But socialism did not begin with him, nor can it end in constant reinterpretations of his writings.' Continuing on this theme, Nyerere stated that if Marx 'had lived in Sukumaland, Masailand or Revuma, he would have written a different book than *Das Kapital*, but he could have been just as scientific and just as socialist.'[26] In short, ujamaa was not an imported ideology, it was a social blueprint that aimed specifically to address both African conditions and African needs.

Nyerere argued that Tanzanians 'have no more need of being "converted" to socialism than we have of being "taught" democracy. Both are rooted in our own past – in the traditional society that produced us.'[27] Instead of seeing socialism as being born out of class conflict, as it was in Europe, many African leaders considered that their predecessors had already practised socialism prior to the onset of colonial rule. African socialism was inherent in the notion of the extended family and the mutual cooperative nature of village communities. A member of these classless societies 'saw no struggle between his own interests and those of his community.... We took care of the community, and the community took care of us.'[28]

Put simply, Nyerere saw ujamaa's mission in the post-colonial era as the neutralisation of the vestiges of capitalism (and the embryonic class conflict) that colonialism had introduced to the continent. This involved re-capturing the socialist ideals of traditional African society and adapting them to the modern era. In this respect, Tanzania was seeking a non-capitalist path of development. Why 'create capitalism, with all the individualism, the social aggressiveness and human indignities which it involves?', Nyerere asked.[29] By using the organisational capacity of the modern nation-state, and by harnessing new technology and production methods, Nyerere argued that ujamaa would produce a more harmonious path towards socialism.

Tanzania's commitment to ujamaa was confirmed with the Arusha Declaration of 1967. At a time when, elsewhere, a number of African socialist regimes were beginning to lose their way, and several others had fallen prey to military coups, Nyerere moved to reinforce Tanzania's ideological foundations. The Arusha Declaration aimed 'to create a society based on cooperation and mutual respect and responsibility, in which all members have equal rights and equal opportunities, where there is no exploitation of one person by another, and where all have gradually increasing levels of material welfare…'[30] To assist this transition to socialism, the Declaration highlighted four specific problems that had to be overcome: the potential inequalities between state employees and civil society; that capital development may come at the expense of human-centred development; that private capital was making profits that could be invested in development for all; and that there was an urban–rural imbalance evolving in favour of towns and cities.

Legislation was enacted to address all four of these issues. Tanzania's public servants and political elite have been more disciplined than most in the post-colonial era. The Declaration prevented government leaders from undertaking additional employment, holding shares or renting out property. Salaries were also restricted. This prevented a 'bureaucratic bourgeoisie' emerging in Tanzania on the scale that occurred in other African states. Nyerere himself even went to the extent of living and working in a village commune for a period of time, in order to stress that *all* Tanzanians had to work to secure economic development.

Similarly, the government kept to the Arusha Declaration's promise that human-centred development would be prioritised. Universal primary education was introduced, literacy campaigns undertaken, and village health centres built. As for the issue of nationalisation, most private capital in Tanzania (both indigenous and foreign) was taken into public ownership almost immediately. The aim was to make these enterprises serve the needs of the people collectively, rather than just let them generate profits for private gain.

With respect to the fourth area highlighted by the Arusha Declaration, it is with its experiment in rural development that ujamaa is most associated. As this is the case, the remainder of this case study will concentrate solely on this specific programme.

Tanzania has one of the least urbanised populations in the world. Ujamaa therefore had to find a way of increasing national production by developing rural sectors of the economy. Yet Nyerere, in his desire to do this, came up against the same realities that the German and British colonial administrators had faced before him. Tanzania's future prosperity relied upon disparate and scattered peasant smallholders, whose priorities lay chiefly in their own subsistence and not necessarily in the wider development of the national economy. Nor could these peasants be classed as a modern agricultural workforce, employing modern methods of production. Nyerere responded to this problem by attempting to house the majority of rural Tanzanians in model villages that would act as collectivist units of production.

The central idea behind the 'villagisation' programme was to combine tradition (village life of mutual assistance) with modern production methods (larger collective farms with access to technology). Economies of scale could be gained with the whole village combining to farm common land rather than their own separate plots. Rural Tanzanians would work together for the community, to provide both its subsistence and a surplus enabling the village to develop. The villages would also act as a point of contact for government officials to teach peasants modern agricultural techniques, and for them to supply technology (machinery and fertilisers). There was also the opportunity for the state to invest in the country's human resources. The majority of Tanzania's new schools and health centres, for example, were built in these *ujamaa vijijini*. Similarly, the villages served as centres of local democracy, with community members, aided by state administrators, making decisions for themselves. As Paul Kaiser observed, 'The process of villagisation was intended to integrate the logic of economic efficiency with the goal of social equality.'[31]

By 1977, over 13 million Tanzanians lived in ujamaa villages. This represented almost all the country's rural population. Some were attracted by the nationalist and socialist aims of the project. More were enticed by the government waiving its poll tax for these communities, the provision of schooling and basic facilities, and the access to subsidised seeds and fertilisers. State coercion, however, was needed in later years to resettle more reluctant communities. Yet, despite this massive undertaking of social engineering, the ujamaa experiment failed to produce the levels of rural development required to keep Tanzania's economic expansion ahead of its population growth.

Goran Hyden argues that the *ujamaa vijijini* failed to meet their production targets because the state, and its ideology, failed to 'capture' the Tanzanian peasantry.[32] Members of these village communities certainly respected many of the social goals of ujamaa (living as a community, and having access to government-supplied technology and welfare), but they never really adopted the modern agricultural production methods advocated. This was because, even in their traditional societies, Africans were never collectivist farmers. They would certainly cooperate as a community to clear land, and offer mutual assistance at times of harvest or need, but the tradition was never to farm together, sharing the product of this labour. This 'peasant mode of production' continued in the ujamaa villages. Common land was farmed collectively, but only after villagers had attended to their own individual plots first. In other words, subsistence gained from the individual plots was the main activity; collective work was only undertaken to raise additional income above this. Hyden concluded that, 'To the peasants, work on the communal farm was never considered an end in itself. To them it remained a supplementary activity, to which attention was given when circumstance in the household permitted.'[33]

The villages, given their retention of the peasant mode of production, did not produce the efficiency of modern agricultural enterprises. 'It was not laziness as much as a different set of priorities and limited capacity that explain *ujamaa* shortfalls in rural areas. The peasants did not have a capitalist orientation and were thus unconcerned with the need for a surplus as an end in itself.'[34] With the peasantry largely content in producing their subsistence, the wider national economy failed to 'take off'. This left the nationalist leadership without the economic development it promised, and, in many cases, not even with the funds to cover the initial costs of establishing these villages. Nyerere, in his review of Tanzania's progress to socialism written ten years after the Arusha Declaration, candidly admitted 'the truth is that the agricultural results have been very disappointing.'[35]

Ujamaa's lack of success in terms of rural production, however, cannot be blamed entirely on the peasantry remaining 'uncaptured'. The state itself must accept some of the blame. Administrative errors were made. People were occasionally settled in unproductive areas, inappropriate crops grown, and there was generally a lack of transport infrastructure preventing the efficient movement of harvests. Mistakes of this kind are almost inevitable in a development project of this scale. It was in the interaction between the peasantry and local administrators, however, where the state let its ujamaa ideology down the most. Faced with a peasantry reluctant to farm collectively, bureaucrats often returned to the same authoritarian and managerial styles of public administration experienced during the colonial years. What is more, in order to shore up their legitimacy under these circumstances, local administrators began to build patron–client relationships with their villages. Development funds were therefore now being absorbed in bureaucratic empire building, rather than being fully utilised in expanding production. With an uncaptured peasantry managed by patrimonial administrators, it is not surprising that most 'collectivist' ujamaa villages failed, by some degree, to reach the production levels attained by Tanzania's few remaining private (capitalist) farms.

The problem remained that Tanzania's economy was expanding at a rate slower than its population growth. The development envisaged at independence failed to emerge. Adaptations were made to the ujamaa ideology in an attempt to rectify these problems, and, indeed, Tanzania was one of the last countries in Africa to retain public policy based on the ideals of African socialism and self-reliance. The non-capitalist path of development was still being advocated even during the early 1980s when neighbouring states were turning to international financial institutions (IFIs) to shore up their crumbling economies. Eventually, however, Tanzania succumbed too. Forced by its crippling external debts, it agreed in 1986 to an IFI structural adjustment programme involving the liberalisation of the Tanzanian economy. Yet, before critics judge the ujamaa experiment as a total failure, they should acknowledge that Nyerere and his government administered a remarkably stable and equitable society. Tanzania was a country where levels of education and health care improved remarkably in the years after independence. Some of this work has now been undone with the application of 'market ideals' to the provision of public services. It remains to be seen if structural adjustment, in the longer term, will produce a level of economic growth that will compensate for this cut in human investment.

Tanzania[36]

Territory:	939,760 sq km	Population:	32 million
Colonial power:	(Germany) Britain	Formation:	1964
Major cities:	Dar es Salaam	Ethnic groups:	Ewe
	Mwanza		Kabare
	Tabora		Masai
Urban pop.:	29.3%		Among many
Languages:	Kiswahili		others
	English	Birth rate:	41 per thousand
Currency:	Tanzanian shilling	Life expectancy:	52 years
Infant mortality:	80 deaths/thousand births	Adult literacy:	67.8%
Religion:	Traditional	Exports:	Coffee
	Christian		Cotton
	Islam		Cashew nuts
	Hindu		Tobacco
GDP per capita:	US$234	External debt:	US$7,412 million

Glossary of key terms

African socialism	A strain of socialism built more on African 'traditional values' (village communalism and cooperation) than the class struggle of classical Marxism-Leninism.
Ideology	A lifeguiding system of beliefs, values and goals affecting political style and action (R D Putnam).
Irredentism	A movement by members of one ethnic group to retrieve people and their territory across borders (Horowitz).
Nation	A collection of people bound together by common values and traditions, often sharing the same language, history and an affiliation to a geographical area.
Nationalism	The desire that the nation should be housed in its own sovereign state.
Nation-building	The post-independence attempts to unite peoples, and develop economies, within Africa's inherited colonial boundaries.
OAU inviolable borders	The agreement among most OAU members in 1963 that the inherited colonial boundaries should remain, and be respected.
Populism	A political movement favouring the wishes and interests of 'ordinary people'.
Scientific socialism	A strain of socialism based on the class analysis of Karl Marx, later developed by V I Lenin.
Separatism	The desire for a region within a state to secede, forming its own (or joining another) sovereign state.
State capitalism	A policy that assists (local and foreign) free market activity, but still involves heavy state intervention in the economy.
Structural adjustment	Loan programmes that require borrowing countries to liberalise both their economies and public policy.
'Tribalism'	The charge that groups continue to hold divisive 'outdated' ethnic allegiances counter to the state's goal of national unity.

Questions raised by this chapter

1 What role does ideology play in the practice of politics?
2 How does African nationalism differ from other nationalisms found elsewhere in the world?
3 How successful have African nationalists been in defending the inherited nation-state structure on the African continent?
4 To what extent did African socialist and Afro-Marxist regimes conform to the principles of 'classical' socialism as developed in Europe?

5   Were populist and state capitalist administrations more successful at
    governing African states than their socialist-oriented counterparts?
6   To what extent has African civil society suffered in the post-colonial period
    as a result of state-sponsored ideologies?

Further reading

Ernest Gellner's general work on nationalism is an excellent place to start any further
reading. This could be complemented by Basil Davidson's book, which concentrates
specifically on the African continent, and Crawford Young's article, which explores
how Africanists have used the concept of nationalism in their studies. Sources that
could be consulted to develop a deeper knowledge of African socialism include
Chapter 4 of Harvey Sindima's book, Thomas Callaghy's article, and the introduction
to Julius Nyerere's collection of speeches and writings. Those interested in scientific
socialist African regimes should read Kenneth Jowitt's chapter in Rosberg and
Callaghy (1979).

All the above suggestions can be read in conjunction with case studies. Christopher Clapham provides a good account of the Marxist-Leninist revolution in
Ethiopia; Adotey Bing looks at populist participation in Ghana; Goran Hyden has
analysed the ujamaa experiment in Tanzania; while Crawford Young's book addresses
several post-colonial African ideologies, illustrating his arguments with numerous
examples taken from the entire continent.

Bing, Adotey (1984) 'Popular participation versus people's power: notes on politics and
    power struggles in Ghana', *Review of African Political Economy* 31, 91–104.
Callaghy, Thomas M (1979) 'The difficulties of implementing socialist strategies of
    development in Africa: the "first wave"', in Carl G Rosberg and Thomas M Callaghy,
    eds, *Socialism in Sub-Saharan Africa: a new assessment*, Berkeley: Institute of Interna-
    tional Studies, University of California.
Clapham, Christopher (1987) 'Revolutionary socialist development in Ethiopia', *African
    Affairs* 86(343), 151–65.
Davidson, Basil (1992) *The black man's burden: Africans and the curse of the nation-state*,
    London: James Currey.
Gellner, Ernest (1983) *Nations and nationalism*, Oxford: Blackwell.
Hyden, Goran (1980) *Beyond Ujamaa in Tanzania: underdevelopment and an uncaptured
    peasantry*, London: Heinemann.
Jowitt, Kenneth (1979) 'Scientific socialist regimes in Africa: political differentiation,
    avoidance, and unawareness', in Carl G Rosberg and Thomas M Callaghy, eds,
    Socialism in Sub-Saharan Africa: a new assessment, Berkeley: Institute of International
    Studies, University of California.
Nyerere, Julius K (1970) *Freedom and socialism: a selection from writings and speeches,
    1965–1967*, Oxford: Oxford University Press.
Sindima, Harvey J (1995) *Africa's agenda: the legacy of liberalism and colonialism in the crisis
    of African values* (Chapter 4), Westport, CT: Greenwood.
Young, Crawford (1982) *Ideology and development in Africa*, New Haven, CT: Yale University Press.
Young, Crawford (1994) 'Evolving modes of consciousness and ideology: nationalism and
    ethnicity', in David E Apter and Carl G Rosberg, eds, *Political development and the new
    realism in Sub-Saharan Africa*, Charlottesville: University Press of Virginia.

4 Ethnicity

Ethnic groups, 'tribes', and political identity

Ethnic mobilisation can often be found at the heart of political competition. No state is devoid of its influence. Notions of ethnicity and nationalism during the Second World War, for example, tore Europe apart in the middle of the twentieth century. More recently, in the 1990s, similar sentiments have brought devastation to the Balkans. Even within the European Union, ethnic tensions are common. The populations of Northern Ireland and Spain's Basque country, for example, know well enough the tragedy that such 'clannish' competition can generate. Similarly, the United States is also no stranger to communal violence. Isolated instances of rioting over the last few decades have made it quite clear that minority ethnic groups are discontented with the inequality they suffer within US society.

This is not to say that expressions of ethnicity always result in violence. Such desires and demands are usually channelled peacefully through political institutions, just like other clashes of interest within society. Scotland in 1997, for example, voted for its own parliament. Ethnic groups in the United States are also adept at constitutionally promoting their interests.

As in the West, political interactions on the African continent are also influenced by considerations of ethnicity. Indeed, given that these states are relatively young, sentiments of ethnicity are often as powerful as notions of nationalism. As such, when making decisions, political leaders in Africa not only have to think of the national interest, they also have to consider the reactions of the various ethnic constituencies housed within their country. The key for these political leaders is to keep this competition peaceful, and help channel it through constitutional institutions.

This chapter explains the influence that ethnic mobilisation has had on African politics during the post-colonial era. First it examines how social scientists define ethnicity in general. Then the chapter moves on to look at ethnic identity, specifically within the African context. Throughout, the chapter argues that ethnicity is not a primordial 'tribal' force, a leftover from times gone by. Instead, it is a modern social identity, constantly adapting.

Definitions of ethnicity

A basic definition of an ethnic group would be *a community of people who have the conviction that they have a common identity and common fate based on issues of origin, kinship ties, traditions, cultural uniqueness, a shared history and possibly a shared language.* In this sense, an ethnic group is much like the 'imagined community' of the nation. Ethnicity, however, focuses more on sentiments of origin and descent, rather than the geographical considerations of a nation.

Notions of ethnicity become pronounced when they are used to distinguish one social group from another within a specific territory.[1] As such, this 'contested' ethnicity is of particular interest to political scientists. They can learn a great deal from studying how ethnic groups relate to each other, and their interactions with broader social organisations such as the nation and the state. This is especially relevant in situations where more than one ethnic group resides within a country.

The popular view is that an ethnic group is a smaller community found within a larger society. More recent immigrant communities within the United Kingdom, for example, have become known as 'ethnic minorities'. United States minority groups are also often defined in terms of ancestral origins (Irish-Americans, African-Americans, and so on). These interpretations of ethnicity are misleading, however. All individuals will have ethnic allegiances, whether they are from a minority of a state's population or part of the majority. To be 'English' or 'Scottish' is just as much being part of an ethnic group as is being a member of the smaller British 'Afro-Caribbean' or 'Asian' communities. Ethnicity is therefore a sentiment expressed by both majority and minority populations, and political scientists have to monitor these expressions (just as they do with other sources of social cleavage). Social pluralism of this sort, after all, will result in differences of interest, which is the very stuff of politics itself.

The creation of 'tribes'

Ethnicity, or 'tribalism', is frequently used as an auto-explanation of political events in Africa. The media will often report that there has been violence on the continent because tribe 'A' has clashed with tribe 'B'. No further exploration of the cause of this violence is offered, or apparently needed. It is only natural, it is presumed, that ancient ethnic rivalries will result in conflict from time to time, as Africans are inherently 'tribalistic' and will therefore act in a 'tribalistic' manner.

This *primordialist* explanation sees African 'tribes' as something left over from the pre-colonial past. The argument states that historical loyalties, often demonstrated in a primitively savage fashion, have been brought into present-day politics. This will continue to be the case until the forces of modernisation make tribal associations redundant. They will disappear only when Africans develop a national consciousness, working together to enjoy the fruits of modern-day civilisation (as Westerners do in their nation-states). In the meantime, it is only normal that tribes will clash, sometimes violently.

These 'tribalistic' interpretations of African politics, however, are worthless. A good political scientist has to go beyond such simplistic, not to mention racist, approaches to social pluralism on the continent. They should find out *why* tribe 'A' has entered into conflict with tribe 'B'. Conflict, after all, is not an unprompted phenomenon. What was the specific cause of the dispute? Why has the clash happened at this time? Why was the altercation not contained by peaceful political bargaining, in the manner of most differences? These are the sort of questions that should be asked. The simple answer, 'tribalism', satisfies none of these inquiries. Ethnicity may often be the agent of political mobilisation in Africa, but it is rarely the primary cause of conflict.

Gérard Prunier made sure he asked such questions in his efforts to understand the 1994 genocide in Rwanda. Television viewers around the world simply could not grasp the fact that 800,000 people died over a three-month period in a series of massacres. It was difficult for them to remember who was killing whom, let alone *why* it was happening. It was easier to ignore the details and put it all down to African 'tribalism'. Yet Prunier is adamant: 'What we have witnessed in Rwanda is a historical product, not a biological fatality or 'spontaneous' bestial outburst. Tutsi and Hutu have not been created by God as cats and dogs, predestined from all eternity to disembowel each other...'[2] There had to be a motive for these killings. The Rwandan genocide was no more 'tribalistic' than the extermination of Jews by Nazi Germany or North American natives by the US army. All these events had specific historical introductions and immediate political imperatives. Conflict in Africa needs to be explained in the same manner as conflict elsewhere in the world. It cannot just be put down to 'tribalism'. As Prunier pleaded, to allow the Rwanda killings to be 'misunderstood through simplified clichés would in fact bring the last touch to the killers' work, in completing their victims' dehumanisation.... To deny a man the social meaning of his death is to kill him twice, first in the flesh, then in the spirit.'[3]

The primordial 'tribal' argument is clearly wrong, as African ethnic groups are not simply ghosts from the past, or a residue left from history. Ethnic groups remain an important form of social organisation today because they continue to serve contemporary political and economic needs. It is also a fact that African 'tribes' are *modern* social constructions. Indeed, largely having been formed no earlier than the late nineteenth century, African 'tribes' have actually gained in importance over the last 150 years (and not retreated in the face of modernisation, as the primordial argument runs).

Few communities could be defined as 'tribes' prior to colonialism in Africa. Traditionally, ethnic associations were much more fluid than their modern regimented equivalents. In this sense, Aidan Southall talks of 'interlocking, overlapping, multiple identities'.[4] There were certainly lineage groups, clans and kinship communities, but these were not, as yet, consolidated into larger 'tribes'. Neither was the membership of these groups necessarily set in stone.

Loyalties changed over time (through migration, enslavement, military conquest or marriage, for example). The ancestors of the Ghanaian citizens who today regard themselves as Akan, for instance, would have categorised themselves variously as Asante, Fante, Brong, Akim or Nzima in the past. Being described as part of a larger Akan 'tribe' would have meant very little to these people prior to the twentieth century.

This is why many Africanists refuse to use the term 'tribe', and most others put this word in inverted commas. It is more accurate to talk about ethnic groups. In this manner, stereotypes of primordial, rather than socially constructed, communities can be avoided (as well as the many racist associations that are attached to the word 'tribe'). Why are Africans and not the Welsh or Texans referred to as tribes, for example? The images that are conjured up by this word obscure more than they illuminate. The more universal concept of 'ethnicity', therefore, is more useful.

Why, then, did tribes form in the late nineteenth, and throughout the twentieth, centuries? Why were more fluid ethnic associations abandoned at this point? Well, it is no coincidence that the process of 'tribalisation' emerged concurrently with the era of colonial rule in Africa. The continent's people gathered into tribes for two specific reasons. First, the administrative imperatives of imperial rule demanded this, and second, Africans themselves found these new ethnic identities to be advantages within the new colonial political environment.

Once they had established their authority on the continent, Europeans had to make sense of the societies they now ruled. In the typically arrogant manner of the age, imperialism never really got to grips with the nature of existing kinship communities in Africa. Instead, colonial rulers attempted to mould reality to their own administrative requirements. As Crawford Young puts it: 'In the construction of its hegemony, the colonial state soon acquired a compulsion to classify. Particularly for the British and Belgians, administrative organization was rooted in a "tribal" image of Africa. The task of the ruler was to identify, rationalize, and streamline ethnic cartography.'[5]

Communities were therefore gathered together into regional blocs ('tribes') in order to make their political and economic management easier. Where conveniently distributed 'tribes' did not exist, the colonial authorities did their best to create them. Acting as amateur anthropologists, colonial officials assigned all their subjects to a 'tribe', often based on very dubious historical or ethnological research. After this, a suitable chief would be appointed to act as an intermediary between this new ethnic group and the colonial state. Sometimes this would be an existing African leader, on other occasions a more pliant candidate was promoted.

The Fulbe of northern Cameroon, for instance, were categorised as a single tribe by the imperial authorities. This enabled these people to be slotted neatly into the administrative mechanisms of the colonial state. In reality, a closer examination of this 'tribe' reveals extensive internal fault lines. Contained within this group are the Kirdi, a community the Fulbe had subjugated some hundred years earlier. Separate identities between these two peoples, however, still existed. The Fulbe, for example, had largely converted to Islam, while the Kirdi continued to practise animist beliefs. Even within the Kirdi, there were distinct groups such as the Mundang, Tupuri, Guisiga, Massa, Mbum and Duru. Yet, for administrative purposes, all were now regarded by the colonial authorities as members of the single Fulbe 'tribe'.[6] Gone was the flexibility of pre-colonial identities, and, consequently, ethnic boundaries became less porous as the twentieth century progressed.

However, it was not just a case of tribes being imposed on Africa. Many Africans themselves willingly took on these new identities to further their own interests and those of their communities. This was particularly so for those who strove to be the intermediaries between the state and the 'tribe'. These individuals benefited from becoming leaders of larger communities, as well as gaining a degree of access to state institutions (and the spoils that this position produced). Chiefs often became richer and more influential as a result of colonial rule. Under these circumstances, it is not surprising that these intermediaries had an overriding interest in building the myth of the tribe.

Similarly, many of the individuals who made up these 'tribes' also adopted the myth. To belong to a tribe enabled members to share the resources that their ethnic intermediaries extracted from the colonial authorities. This, after all, was the key conduit along which state-allocated goods were distributed. Conversely, not to belong to a tribe resulted in an automatic exclusion from the competition for state spoils. States wanted to deal with 'tribes', so Africans responded by constructing the larger ethno-regional groups required. Leaders and followers alike involved themselves in inventing traditions and symbols to bind these 'imagined' communities together. History was manipulated to give the 'tribe' a long and honourable past. In this manner, while the colonial authorities were busy assigning Africans to 'tribes', Africans were busy building 'tribes' to belong to.

The above evidence suggests that African 'tribes' should be seen as *instrumental* social constructions, and not 'natural' or 'primordial' phenomena. Africans identify themselves as belonging to an ethnic group because it is in their interests to do so. Cultural solidarity has become a method of securing tangible political power and economic advantage. In this sense, Robert Bates talks of ethnic groups being 'a form of minimum winning coalition, large enough to secure benefits in the competition for spoils but also small enough to maximise the per-capita value of these benefits'.[7]

Despite their cultural make-up, therefore, ethnic groups are little different from interest groups that can be found working within other political systems. Their representatives lobby the state, seeking resources for the group and public policy measures that serve their interests. Individuals will identify themselves as belonging to this group, supporting it, because this is a method of securing new wells, medical centres, schools and roads, or a new factory for their community and region. This reality requires Africanists not to regard ethnic conflict as an exotic clash of cultures, but more simply as the perennial clash over scarce resources. It is not irrational primordial rivalry, in this respect, it is simply political competition. Tribalism in Africa has become the most efficient way for individuals to mobilise politically in order to serve their interests within the modern state structure. As such, ethnic mobilisation represents the familiar politics of the 'pork barrel' with an African twist.

Ethnicity as a method of modern political mobilisation

Ethnicity is frequently portrayed as having been a hindrance to Africa's political and economic development in the post-colonial period. This has become the popular view, fuelled by nationalist arguments. Such a condemnation of ethnicity, however, is not necessarily warranted. Operating in the right political environment, ethnicity can be as progressive a force as any type of social organi-sation. Indeed, in the harsh arena of Africa's authoritarian one-party governments, ethnicity provided a rare degree of pluralism and representation.

No state is socially homogeneous. Social cleavage produces conflicting inter-ests everywhere. In each country, different issues act as the primary point of mobilisation. Nationalism, class, religion and ideology are all favoured rallying cries gathering individuals together, enabling them to make their political demands to the state, and to society as a whole. Ethnicity, too, could be a common tool enabling groups to aggregate demands. So why should not African societies mobilise on the basis of ethnicity? Ethnicity, after all, is the most obvious social divide on the continent.

Ethnicity made a positive contribution to many post-colonial African coun-tries in that it managed to serve both state and civil society to some degree. Even in the most repressive of African societies, state elites were forced to acknowledge ethno-regional power. Although these leaders gave scant public recognition to this rival source of political strength (given that it grated against their nationalist credo and their own elite interests), tacit concessions were nevertheless consistently made to sub-state groups. Cabinets, for example, were often a fine balancing act. Most ethnic groups had their own cultural brokers within this state institution. The failure to include leading members of each ethnic group within the executive would risk provoking a challenge to the regime from each absent region. Similarly, ethnic quotas were also exercised in bureaucratic appointments (the military, civil service, police, and public agen-cies), as well as in the allocation of local budgets, and the allotment of state resources in general. Of course, there was not automatically an equal distribu-tion of these resources, but the state elite knew that they would have to pay a political price if any group perceived itself to have been left out of these ethnic calculations.

In this sense, the state had to acknowledge ethnic demands, which resulted in it bargaining with each group, as well acting as a mediator between them all. This, in turn, made the state, however grudgingly and limited, responsive to, and representative of, civil society. Donald Rothchild describes this state–ethnic relationship in terms of a 'hegemonial exchange'. This is where African states do not have enough power to impose themselves totally on civil society, as they cannot unilaterally impose their will on powerfully mobilised ethno-regional groups. As a result, the state has to win a degree of legitimacy from these ethnic groups to avoid full scale regional challenges to its authority. This legitimacy is bought through the distribution of state controlled resources. As Rothchild put it, 'as an ideal type, hegemonial exchange is a form of state-facilitated co-ordination in which a somewhat autonomous central state and a number of considerably less autonomous ethnoregional (and other) interests engage in a process of mutual accommodation on the basis of commonly accepted procedural norms, rules, or understandings.'[8] In other words, because the state cannot extend its hegemony over powerful ethnic groups, it negotiates with them instead (albeit from a position of strength). Ethnic groups, in return, relinquish any overt challenge to the state, as long as they feel enough resources are flowing into their region.

This, of course, to Western eyes, is an arrangement far removed from the ideals of liberal democracy. Yet it does provide a measure of stability and order within divided societies. The state and civil society are bound together by these political channels, with a degree of legitimacy and compliance being traded for a degree of representation. Many African societies avoided violent confrontation for long periods of time through this 'hegemonial exchange'. Indeed, President Jomo Kenyatta of Kenya and Félix Houphouët-Boigny of Côte d'Ivoire took the art of ethnic balancing onto a different plane, and consequently managed to govern over remarkably stable societies for decades.

Three major potential problems, however, stand out in societies dominated by hegemonial exchange. The first could arise from a lack of skill, or will, to balance *all* the ethnic groups within the nation-state; the second problem relates to the massive inefficiencies that rule through hegemonial exchange generate; and the third is the reality that this basis of government only provides a limited degree of representation for those in civil society.

The first of these problems would arise if an ethnic group feels itself to be discriminated against by the state. Its members may perceive that they are being excluded from rights and resources enjoyed by other groups. The balancing act, using ethnic arithmetic, under the 'hegemonial exchange' model is difficult to maintain at the best of times, and miscalculations can often lead to conflict. There are, however, plenty of examples in post-colonial Africa where state elites *consciously* maintained an uneven ethnic balance. Where this occurred, the state became identified with one particular ethnic group (or groups). Instead of pursuing a policy of social inclusion, therefore, elites allocated a disproportionate amount of the country's resources to favoured regions. Under these circumstances, state power is needed to temper any opposition emanating from the excluded groups.

Hegemonial exchange also hinders the logical execution of public policy. It is simply not efficient for resources to be distributed according to demand, rather than need. If one ethnic group absorbs the bulk of a state's resources (simply because it is the most powerful), this results in weaker regions forfeiting their share. Site 'A', for example, in terms of raw materials and transport links, may be the most practical place to build a state factory, but it may be that site 'B' is chosen instead because of the imperatives of ethnic balancing. Political stability, in this respect, is bought at the price of policy inefficiencies. Hegemonial exchange can also result in a lack of strategic planning. Short-term deals are the order of the day, instead of long-term considerations. President Milton Obote, in the 1960s, complained of Ugandan politicians that they did not act as if they were members of a national parliament. Instead, they resembled an 'assembly of peace conference delegates' involved in some curious game of 'Tribal Development Monopoly'.[9] Parochial ethnic interests, in post-colonial Africa, continually prevented public policy measures that could have brought greater national gains, rather than limited region benefits.

Above all, however, it is in its lack of opportunity for mass public participation that the hegemonial exchange model must be most criticised. Politics within these countries was the preserve of ethnic brokers and state officials. Rarely would the 'masses' become involved. Consequently, short-term ethnic inclusiveness and political stability overrode considerations of mass participation. Legitimacy accordingly suffered in the long term. Indeed, with resources becoming increasingly scarce during the 1970s and 1980s, ethnic brokers often failed to deliver to their communities. Consequently, a split emerged between the mass of civil society on one hand, and their ethnic intermediaries (parliamentarians, local councillors and traditional leaders) and state officials (politicians and bureaucrats) on the other. What is more, one-party state structures left no other avenues open for civil society to express its grievances. The result was a wholesale crisis of legitimacy for the state in Africa. This is a theme taken up in more detail in Chapters 10 and 11, but it should be noted here that Africans during the 1990s successfully demanded greater levels of representation and a return to multi-party politics.

The dramatic move towards multi-party competition certainly highlights the flaws in the hegemonial exchange model. In itself there is no problem with Africans mobilising along ethnic lines. Long-term stability and political development can only come, however, if this ethnic mobilisation occurs within a system more responsive to civil society's demands. New opportunities for ethnic competition channelled through pluralist institutions will, hopefully, prove a more profitable model for African countries in the twenty-first century.

State and civil society

Ethnic sentiments are, of course, not the sole foundation for political relationships in Africa. They intermingle with other social considerations such as class, religion, 'race', ideology, gender and age, to mention but a few. Ethnicity has been particularly relevant, however, to the structure of African post-colonial political systems. As such, it is a concept that reveals much about the general underlying theme of this book: the competition between the state and civil society on the African continent.

Nationalism was clearly the 'ideology' favoured by state elites. This was a tool that served them well in maintaining their authority over political institutions, and over society as a whole. Central to elite ideas of government was the conviction that the nation-state was the key to the future. They talked about the opportunities arising from nation-building, and discouraged alternative 'tribalist' loyalties. The nation-state, they argued, had to beat back any subnational challenges to its authority, in order to protect modern economic and political development.

Despite the protestations of African leaders, it was not necessarily true that ethnic loyalties were counter-productive to stable political systems based on the foundation of the nation-state. Indeed, in many cases, the pluralism that ethnic mobilisation brought to an otherwise closed political system often proved beneficial. Ethnicity opened a channel of negotiation and bargaining between the nationalist state and civil society. Indeed, in a political environment of one-party states and authoritarian rule, many Africans received the bulk of their political representation through this channel, by way of membership of an ethnic group. Unlike political parties, only in a handful of cases did state elites manage completely to eradicate or neutralise this alternative source of political power.

Africans certainly came to see themselves as national citizens, Zambians or Gambians for example, but they also held on strongly to identities at a sub-state level. This was because multiple identities served their interests well. As members of civil society they were unable to put all their political faith into nation-state institutions (due to the limited representation these structures provided). Indeed, it is as well that they did not do this. The fact remains that ethnic associations brought Africans more political rewards in the post-colonial period than did any national affiliations. In this respect, if nationalism was the ideological tool of the state, then ethnicity remained the tool of civil society.

Case study: ethnicity and the nation-state in Nigeria

Nigeria is located on Africa's west coast, and is the continent's most populous state. Its topography consists of swamps and lagoons in the Niger River delta, making way for areas of tropical forest and savannah up-country. In the far north, there are arid fringes that begin to impinge on the Sahara Desert.

Nigeria ranks as one of Africa's more developed states, having benefited from the export of its oil reserves. Ongoing conflicts of interest between various social groups, however, have hindered further political and economic development. Much of this conflict has encouraged political mobilisation along ethnic lines.

Contained within Nigeria's national boundaries are over 250 ethnic groups. The largest three of these have dominated Nigerian politics since independence in 1960. They each mobilise in a distinct geographical region. The northern Hausa-Fulani consist of 30 per cent of the country's total population; the western Yoruba furnish 20 per cent of the total; and the eastern Ibo register 17 per cent. This observation, however, should not hide the fact that each of these regions is also home to numerous other, smaller ethnic groups. It should also be noted that the three dominant ethnic groups can be further divided into subgroups. Twenty-nine distinct divisions can be identified within the Hausa-Fulani community, for example, 12 within the Yoruba, and 32 within the Ibo.[10]

This last fact, of prominent sub-ethnic identities, reveals a great deal about the respective histories of the Hausa-Fulani, the Yoruba and the Ibo. Evidence from the past clearly shows these communities not to be primordial entities. They are ethnic groups that have been socially constructed in relatively modern times. Indeed, the creation of these 'tribes' is closely linked to the era of British imperial rule.

It is no coincidence, for example, that the three regions of independent Nigeria closely resemble the administrative boundaries of the colonial years. The northern region had previously been the Northern Protectorate administered through indirect rule, relying on the Fulani emirs as intermediaries. The eastern and western regions had been the Southern Protectorate, which had combined in 1906, after being run as two separate administrative areas prior to this. Despite the Northern and Southern protectorates being united to form a single Nigeria in 1914, each region retained considerable autonomy under colonial rule.

Given this distinct regional administrative pattern, it was only natural that 'tribes' would develop within, and identify with, these separate (northern, eastern and western) regions. This was a rational way to lobby the colonial authorities for resources. In other words, mobilisation along ethno-regional lines proved to be the most effective manner of building Robert Bates's 'winning coalitions'. Consequently, groups which had previously sought only loose affiliations now came together as 'tribes'. Such an instrumental consolidation of clans and lineage groups was also encouraged by the colonial authorities, who demanded larger groups for administrative purposes.

A brief examination of the creation of the western Yoruba 'tribe' illustrates this process well. The historical evidence shows how this group, far from being a primordial social formation, with its origins shrouded in the mists of time, is in fact a modern political and social construct.

Prior to colonial rule, there had been no such thing as a Yoruba political unit or identity. Indeed the word 'Yoruba' was not familiar to the people of south-west Nigeria until the nineteenth century. Instead, the individuals of this region regarded themselves as Oyo, Ketu, Egba, Ijebu, Ijesa, Ekiti, Ondo, or members of a number of other, smaller communities. Certainly, each group was aware of their neighbours, having established trading links, social contacts, and even through the waging of war, but none of these societies shared a larger 'Yoruba' identity. Similarly, although the groups may have had a common language in academic linguistic terms, different dialects meant that these languages were not always mutually intelligible.

Social relationships between the 'Yoruba' clans changed dramatically under colonial rule. The imperial authorities needed much larger communities to reduce the costs and difficulty of administration. Missionaries also desired larger communities, and for these people to speak the same language. This would aid their conversion to Christianity. In this respect, a standard Yoruba vernacular was invented by missionaries (based on the Oyo dialect, the largest clan), and a Yoruba bible was printed. From this point onwards, it was in the interests of the 'clans' to adopt this standard Yoruba language, as it became the medium of Western education. Similarly, it was also vital for individuals in this region to take on a broader Yoruba identity to be recognised by, and to gain access to, the colonial state. A failure to bargain with the imperial authorities as a united force would have resulted in all the 'clans' losing out to other, more consolidated groups, found elsewhere in Nigeria. In short, ethnic coalitions were re-forged and enlarged to meet the demands and opportunities of the new modern state. And just as the Yoruba adapted, so did the Fulani-Hausa and the Ibo. [11]

It should be no surprise, then, that, at independence, Nigeria's First Republic was dominated by these ethno-regional groupings. Indeed, the independence constitution rested firmly on this political reality. A federal system of three regions was established, which sought to recognise the needs, and balance the aspirations, of the these dominant ethnic groups. Each region had a strong, relatively autonomous government, while the central administration concentrated on 'national' issues such as defence, foreign policy and international trade.

Nigerians, naturally enough, responded to this ethno-regional constitution by voting for their respective 'cultural brokers'. They charged their chosen candidates with capturing central federal resources, bringing these back to the regional community. Consequently, no powerful nationwide political party or constituency emerged. Local considerations dominated, and issues of ethnicity became increasingly politicised. Each region was governed by a political party that squarely identified with just one ethnic group. The Fulani-Hausa governed the north, the Yoruba the west, and the Ibo the east.

The First Republic's three-legged constitution, however, failed to institutionalise this ethnic balancing act within a stable political system. Too many suspicions existed between the regions. The Christian south feared the larger-populated Muslim north, while the 'underdeveloped' north feared the better-educated south. Similarly, the west and north resented the larger presence of easterners in the federal bureaucracy. Each region saw itself in a vulnerable position. What is more, the tripartite federal constitution ignored the aspirations of minority ethnic groups which could not break this political oligopoly of the Ibo, Yoruba and Hausa-Fulani.

Perhaps the greatest constitutional danger, however, lay with the fact that it was possible for two of the regions to join forces against the third. Indeed, soon after independence, the northern party formed a coalition with the eastern party and did just this. Later, they attempted to exploit an internal split within the isolated western Yoruba party. Using their majority in the national assembly, they created a fourth federal region in order to disperse the power of the Yoruba. The instability this created, along with economic mismanagement and labour agitation, left the way open for two military coups in 1966. The military intervened, they declared, to restore order and discipline.

This military intervention, however, precipitated even more political turmoil. Ibo politicians, unhappy with the northern (Hausa-Fulani) dominance of the military government, promptly led their western region to secession. An independent state of Biafra was declared in 1967. This was the low point in Nigerian aspirations of national unity, and probably the high point of political mobilisation based on ethnicity. The country would eventually be re-united, after three years of civil war, but not before up to two million 'Biafrans' had died as a result of the federal government's siege of the west.

Nigeria's first period of military rule lasted from 1966 to 1979. The generals attempted to tame ethnic mobilisation by installing nationalist political structures instead. Government was to become more centralised, and it aimed to produce national unity and economic development for the whole country. The number of regions (now states) in the federation, for example, increased from four to twelve in

1968, and then to 19 by 1976. This was an attempt to loosen the stranglehold of the three dominant ethnic groups, and open up opportunities for smaller communities (and other interests). Military rule, in many ways, also assisted the consolidation of power among national bureaucrats. Although ethnic balancing was still a feature of government appointments, political competition gradually became channelled more through federal structures, rather than the earlier regional dominance. The military also successfully protected Nigeria's national integrity. No real attempt at secession emerged after the 1967–70 civil war. This is not to say, however, that the country enjoyed total political stability during this first period of military rule. Officers, disaffected with corruption within the bureaucracy and Nigeria's poor economic management, overthrew their superiors in 1975, forming a successor military government.

The regime of Lieutenant-General Olusegun Obasanjo returned Nigeria to civilian rule in 1979. The Second Republic had at its helm President Alhaji Shagari, leading the National Party of Nigeria (NPN). It is true to say that the lion's share of NPN power lay in the northern region, but the support this organisation enjoyed among southern voters did give credibility to its pretensions to be a national party.

This Second Republic (1979–83) was very much an age of patronage, giving a good illustration of Donald Rothchild's 'hegemonial exchange' model. The federal government at the centre looked after its own interests, but also had to acknowledge ethno-regional power. Resources were distributed accordingly. As well as material goods and local budgets, political posts were also part of this ethnic arithmetic. The NPN itself, for example, made sure that the posts of President, National Chair, Vice President and head of the Senate were rotated among party notables hailing from the north, east, west and central zones respectively. The federal cabinet was also inclusive, representing all Nigeria's major ethnic brokers. No one ethnic group could be perceived to be too dominant, nor could any of these groups be excluded.

The Shagari regime, however, was to fall to a military coup on New Year's Eve, 1983. The army's rejection of this democratic administration was not based on a failure of ethnic arithmetic, nor its nationalist sentiments. It was the inability of these civilian politicians to manage the economy (at a time when oil revenue was declining), and its failure to stem corruption.

In a system of government that relied on ethnic patronage for its survival, corruption was hard to control. Politics had become centred on the short-term winning of state resources, and gaining access to the levers of power. Little long-term strategic political or economic planning could survive in this institutionalised system of political exchange. Resource capture and distribution had become more important to politicians and bureaucrats than the actual development of the economy that produced these resources. Nigeria had hit, head-on, the problems of inefficiency and legitimacy associated with the hegemonial exchange model.

The administration of Major-General Muhammadu Buhari failed to find any immediate remedies for Nigeria's economic problems, and his regime became increasingly authoritarian as it began to lose popular support. This prompted yet another military coup in 1985 in which Major-General Ibrahim Babangida became head of state. Babangida imposed an economic structural adjustment programme, and promised a return to civilian rule by 1992. In this respect, the regime set about attempting to formulate a constitution that could manage Nigeria's social divisions more successfully than the democratic experiment of the Second Republic.

The Babangida constitution introduced a number of new ideas to Nigerian politics. First, the Armed Forces Ruling Council (AFRC) declared that former politicians, and its own members, would not be able to participate as elected officials in the Third Republic. Nor would the institutionalised ethnic balancing of the past be reproduced. Instead, Babangida opted for a two-party system, based on national, rather than regional, political competition. Both parties would have to gain support right across the country, if they were to win power.

True to its word, the Babangida regime invited political parties to form and compete to be one of the two legal political parties within the new constitution. Forty groups applied, and thirteen were deemed to meet the national credentials set by the regime. The AFRC, however, later dissolved all thirteen of these parties because, they claimed, they did not have a distinctive ideology (and were too closely linked to proscribed former politicians). Instead, the AFRC created two parties of their own, along with their accompanying manifestos. The transition to civilian rule stalled, however, when pressures from within the military led to the 1993 presidential election being annulled. The victor of this democratic poll, Moshood Abiola, was subsequently thrown into jail. Evidently, elements of the military enjoyed their taste of political power, and were not prepared to relinquish the reins of the state.

Multi-party democracy was not to return to Nigeria until 1999, when President Olusegun Obasanjo was duly elected to lead the Third Republic. That Obasanjo was a retired general, and had led the 1976–9 military government, clearly illustrates the 'veto' that the armed forces still held over Nigerian politics.

Nigeria endured a struggle that was common among most African states in the post-colonial period. Different political sentiments were mobilising forces pulling in different directions. On the one hand there was the desire to maintain the modern nation-state, and Africans are justly proud of the countries they won through decolonisation. On the other hand, the most efficient way for Africans to build political 'winning coalitions' was for them to mobilise at a sub-state, ethno-regional level. This put state structures under extreme pressures, even to the point of civil war in Nigeria's case. The ethnic balancing act of 'hegemonial exchange' may have brought these countries a degree of stability in an inherently unstable political environment, but this came at a price of inefficient and unproductive distributive politics. In this respect, Nigeria joined the bulk of African states in being remarkably successful at keeping their nation-states intact during this period; few of these territories, however, managed to find institutions that successfully channelled ethnic mobilisation into a more productive political system.

Nigeria[12]

Territory:	923,850 sq km	Population:	118.2 million
Colonial power:	Britain	Independence:	1960
Major cities:	Lagos	Ethnic groups:	Hausa
	Ibadan		Yoruba
	Ogbomosho		Ibo
Urban pop.:	41%		Fulani
Languages:	English		250+ others
	Hausa	Life expectancy:	52 years
	Yoruba	Adult literacy:	57.1%
	Ibo	Exports:	Oil
Currency:	Naira		Gas
Infant mortality:	80 deaths/thousand births		Coffee
Religion:	Traditional		Cotton
	Christian		Cashew nuts
	Islam		Tobacco
GDP per capita:	US$2567	External debt:	US$618,407 million

Glossary of key terms

Distributive politics	A style of politics where state resources are distributed according to demand, rather than to need. Political calculations override social or economic considerations.
Ethnic arithmetic	Calculations required to ensure that all ethnic groups within a society receive an appropriate share of state resources.
Ethnic brokers	Intermediaries or members of the state elite who represent the interests of, and seek resources for, their ethnic group.
Ethnic group	A community of people who have the conviction that they have a common identity and common fate based on issues of origin, kinship ties, traditions, cultural uniqueness, a shared history and possibly a shared language
Hegemonial exchange	Where the state, unable to completely assert its hegemony over ethnic groups, exchanges resources and patronage in return for political compliance.
Instrumental ethnicity	Where members seek to become part of an ethnic group because it is in their interests to do so.
Primordial ethnicity	The idea that ethnic affiliations are relatively static and loyalties pre-destined, 'tribes' having been formed in the mists of time.
'Tribalism'	A derogatory accusation used by nationalists, considering ethnic identities to be retrogressive and harmful to the development of modern nation-states.
Winning coalitions	A coalition 'large enough to secure benefits in the competition for spoils but also small enough to maximise the per-capita value of these benefits' (R. Bates).

Questions raised by this chapter

1   Why did Africans start mobilising on a 'tribal' basis in the nineteenth and twentieth centuries?
2   Do you consider African ethnic groups to be primordial or instrumental in nature?
3   Is the 'hegemonial exchange' model an appropriate form of government for African societies?
4   Have ethnic identities assisted or hindered the political process in post-colonial Africa?

Further reading

Sources that could be consulted to develop a deeper knowledge of ethnicity in Africa include Crawford Young's chapter in David Apter and Carl Rosberg's book (looking at how Africanists have studied the concept of ethnicity), as well as Louise de la Gorgendière, Kenneth King and Sarah Vaughan's edited collection which covers a remarkable amount of ground. For a detailed case study, Gérard Prunier's book on Rwanda is highly recommended, while those readers interested in how African ethnic groups consolidated as a reaction to colonial rule should consult the extremely informative book edited by Leroy Vail. The instrumentalist case of 'hegemonial exchange' is argued well in Donald Rothchild's essay, and David Welsh has written an excellent article drawing together many of the above ideas.

Gorgendière, Louise de la, Kenneth King and Sarah Vaughan, eds (1996) *Ethnicity in Africa: roots, meanings and implications*, Edinburgh: Centre of African Studies, University of Edinburgh.

Prunier, Gérard (1995) *The Rwanda crisis 1959–1994: history of genocide*, London: Hurst.

Rothchild, Donald (1985) 'State–ethnic relations in middle Africa', in: Gwendolen M Carter and Patrick O'Meara, eds, *African independence: the first twenty-five years,* Bloomington: Indiana University Press.

Vail, Leroy, ed. (1989) *The creation of tribalism in Southern Africa*, London: James Currey.

Welsh, David (1996) 'Ethnicity in Sub-Saharan Africa', *International Affairs* 72(3), 477–91.

Young, Crawford (1994) 'Evolving modes of consciousness and ideology: nationalism and ethnicity', in David E Apter and Carl G Rosberg, eds, *Political development and the new realism in Sub-Saharan Africa*, Charlottesville: University Press of Virginia.

5   Social class
The search for class politics in Africa

The next concept that this book will use to investigate post-colonial African politics is a trusty tool of all social scientists, the notion of class. This concept is invaluable to those studying politics because it is an excellent way of identifying the age-old battle between the 'haves' and 'have nots' within society. Class, in this sense, is the study of inequality. And where inequality exists, relationships between competing groups, including the exploiters and the exploited, will follow. Politics will determine how such conflict is resolved. Indeed, Marxists believe class to be the key defining feature of any society. As Marx and Engels wrote in their *Communist Manifesto*, 'The history of all hitherto existing society is the history of class struggles.'[1]

Initially, this chapter will use the ideas of Karl Marx to subject African states to class analysis. Such an analysis will certainly add to the understanding gained from the previous chapters' investigations of history, nationalism and ethnicity. Marxism, however, has its limits when it comes to the African continent. This is why other theories are presented in the second half of the chapter, giving perhaps a more accurate picture of how 'classes' have competed for power in post-colonial Africa.

Marx on social class

Karl Marx provided a model of society that was determined by class conflict. His ideas help identify competing groups within society, and the basis of the relationship between these groups. Marx, however, went beyond mere description, adding dynamism to class analysis. He argued that class formation is inherently related to the progression of history. Indeed, class conflict itself is the motor of all history.

The key to understanding Marxist class analysis, especially within the African environment, is to recognise what is meant by the *means of production*. Marx, after all, defined classes in relation to these means of production. Their owners constitute the ruling class, and are therefore in the position to exploit the rest of society.

As Friedrich Engels explained, 'the determining factor in history is, in the final instance, the production and reproduction of immediate life'.[2] In other words, all people have to produce at least their subsistence needs to survive (food, shelter and clothing). This is a basic fact of life. Achieving this goal, however, is much easier for the owners of the means of production than it is for the masses. The means of production are, therefore, the material factors such as land, tools and machinery that help human beings produce their subsistence needs, and any economic surplus beyond this.

Classes form in relation to the means of production. Under the capitalist mode of production, for example, society divides into two classes: the bourgeoisie and the proletariat. Landlords and capitalists form the ruling bourgeois class as they secure an excellent standard of living, and political power, by using their ownership of these means of production (land and machinery). From this position they exploit the mass proletariat.

The proletariat, by contrast, has a problem. Its members do not own any means of production, yet they still have to produce to meet their subsistence needs. They therefore have to gain access to productive forces, and this comes at the price of exploitation from the bourgeoisie. The proletariat is vulnerable because it only has its labour to sell.

The ruling class does not pay the full value for this labour. Capitalists pay enough to ensure that the work force can reproduce itself, ensuring the survival of a labour force, but they share little of the profit from this productive process with the proletariat. Any surplus, even though it is generated by the toil of the workers, is retained by the bourgeoisie to maintain their higher standard of living, and to re-invest in further exploitative ventures. In this manner, members of the proletariat are reduced to mere units of production, working for the ruling class in their factories and on their land.

Naturally enough, this class exploitation is reflected within the structure of the state. The bourgeoisie is hegemonic. The government always supports the interests of the bourgeoisie over those of the proletariat. As Marx himself put it, 'The executive of the modern state is but a committee for managing the common affairs of the whole bourgeoisie.'[3] The entire political system is therefore geared towards serving this ruling class.

This is how Marx, writing in the nineteenth century, saw the development of modern society. He observed: 'Our epoch, the epoch of the bourgeoisie, possesses... this distinctive feature: it has simplified the class antagonisms. Society as a whole is more and more splitting up into two hostile camps, into two great classes directly facing each other: Bourgeoisie and Proletariat.'[4]

Marx's work assists political scientists in that not only does it help identify classes, it also puts the relationship between these classes within an historical framework. Underlying all Marx's work is the idea of 'revolution'. Classes have formed, consolidated, and then fallen to new class formations throughout history. In this respect, it was Marx's belief that the process of class evolution would not end with capitalism. There was one more stage to go. Revolution would usher in socialism, defeating capitalism when this system was finally sufficiently weakened by its own internal contradictions.

The key to capitalism's downfall would be that this mode of production did indeed create a mass proletariat. Given their exploitation by the ruling class, and the reality that this working class far out numbered their oppressors, the proletariat would eventually become uncontrollable. At first, workers would protect their interests via collective action such as trade union activity, and then a revolutionary movement would develop, completing the transition from capitalism to socialism. After the revolution, socialism would create a classless society, where inequality and exploitation would be at an end. In the words of Karl Marx: 'What the bourgeoisie, therefore, produces, above all, is its own grave-diggers. Its fall and the victory of the proletariat are equally inevitable.'[5]

The problems of exporting Marx to Africa

However brilliant the work of Karl Marx is, he could not escape his own mortality. Naturally enough, Marx's work is largely a critique of nineteenth century European capitalism. This is the world he knew, and with what his work teaches about this period, and the foundation it has provided for contemporary studies in the social sciences, no other person has offered more. The modern world, however, is a different place. Even within today's European capitalist systems, Marxist analysis has hit several fundamental problems (mostly to do with a growing middle class and the absence of a revolutionary working class). Outside Europe, there is even less empirical evidence to support Marx's thesis. Africa certainly tests any belief that the Marxist paradigm of class analysis has a universal application.

Africa, at this first glance, is not open to classical Marxist interpretation because the continent has not been fully penetrated by the capitalist mode of production. Chapter 2 certainly showed how imperialism drew various sectors of the colonial economy into the capitalist world system, but capitalism did not come to dominate all economic activity within African states, and still does not do so today.

The lack of widespread industrialisation on this continent is clear evidence of this fact. South Africa apart, there have been no real industrial revolutions within African states. It is therefore not surprising that the accompanying social relations created by the capitalist mode of production are also absent. Few African states have a proletariat to speak of, while there is also a distinct lack of any classical bourgeoisie. And with no bourgeoisie and no proletariat, there is no Marxist revolutionary dynamic pushing forward the transition of history from capitalism to socialism.

Considering these facts, many have described Africa as being classless. This was certainly the view of several African nationalists who led their countries to independence. Instead of class, the communalism of traditional Africa was emphasised. Village life, based on inalienable land rights for all, community cooperation, and leaders being both responsible and accountable to their people, was portrayed as the typical form of social relationship on the continent. In this respect Tom Mboya, a Kenyan nationalist, argued: 'The sharp class divisions that once existed in Europe have no place in African socialism and no parallel in African society. No class problems arose in traditional African society and none exist today amongst Africans.'[6] Other nationalist politicians agreed with Mboya. Nyerere, Senghor and Sékou Touré all stressed that there was a common ownership of the means of production (as all had access to land), while African leaders served their people and did not exploit them.

Clearly, then, the bulk of Marx's work is not applicable to explaining post-colonial African politics. This, however, should come as no surprise. Marx died before the twentieth century began and never sought to analyse social classes on the African continent. Yet, just because African conditions cannot be shoe-horned into dominant European explanations of class, this is not to say that class and class conflict were, and are, absent in African states. Indeed, the next section of this chapter shows nationalist arguments of classlessness to be unfounded. It will show that social relationships determined by class (or, at least, by inequality) have been at the forefront of African politics since early times, and continue to play a major part in African politics today.

The African mode of production

The problem that many students have in understanding social relationships within African states arises because they have difficulty in distancing them-selves from the capitalist mode of production. This, after all, is where Marx produced his best work, and it is also the area where most apprentice political scientists cut their teeth when learning about the class dimension to politics. It is a fact, however, that Africa is still to be fully penetrated by capitalism. Africanists therefore have to look beyond just this one, capitalist, mode of production.

This is not to say that capitalism is totally absent on the African continent. It has penetrated and captured strategic sectors of all African economies. Yet today, many Africans still undertake the same economic activities that their forebears practised for generations. Many peasant farmers, for example, only have limited contact with the capitalist market, as they own their means of production (land and basic farming tools). Consequently, they produce largely for themselves, avoiding the exploitation of a bourgeois class. In this sense, class relations on the continent are not only a product of the capitalist mode of production, but are also still influenced by *pre*-capitalist modes of production.

African historians, especially in the 1960s and 1970s, spent a great deal of time trying to identify the nature of these pre-capitalist modes of production. This was undertaken to reveal a better understanding of the social forces that were still operating in tandem with capitalism. The starting point for these historians were the supplementary writings that Karl Marx had penned consid-ering modes of production other than capitalism.

In Europe for example, Marx argued, feudalism had preceded capitalism. Africanists, however, found little evidence of this type of class relationship ever existing in Africa. Feudalism was based on relationships between landlords who extracted a surplus from the serfs farming their land. In Ethiopia, something akin to feudalism existed, as an 'aristocracy' did own land, but in most African societies land was held in common. Each family within a community had an inalienable right to land, and without landlords feudalism cannot exist.

Undaunted, historians of the continent sought to identify an alternative, and a unique, 'African mode of production'. Some Africanists, for example, pointed to 'tribute' or 'lineage' modes of production fostering class formation. In these societies, certain families received gifts and tribute as a result of their status. Consequently, these families came to form the ruling elites, holding positions of political power over their followers. Other historians highlighted external commerce as sources of surplus accumulation. Complex social formations were created in West Africa, for example, by the trans-Saharan trade routes. The surplus that this exchange of goods brought created merchant classes, who then went on to translate this economic power into political power. Similarly, conquest could produce a surplus, and thus a ruling class. Instead of exploiting domestic societies, military raids against neighbouring societies generated wealth that was then transformed into political power back at home.

Presumably there are an infinite number of modes of production that have existed in African (and world) history. Different modes have been created by different local conditions. This, of course, makes class analysis much more complex. Gone is Marx's relatively simple model of two capitalist classes, a bourgeoisie versus a proletariat. Yet, this search for the African mode of production has been extremely useful for those interested in African politics. These scholars have shown that pre-colonial Africa did not abound with utopian classless societies. Historical African ruling elites were just as adept at exploiting the masses as their European contemporaries. Perhaps what is more important, however, is that there is now a better understanding of pre-capitalist modes of production themselves. This knowledge is extremely important, because it is these modes that are still interacting with the capitalist mode today.

Africa, in this respect, currently straddles both pre-capitalist and capitalist modes of production. Uneven development means that capitalism has a great deal of influence but it is still yet to completely replace its predecessor. A great deal can therefore be explained about African politics by the interaction, or the *articulation*, between these two modes of production. African class formation is therefore a complex mixture of the traditional and modern. Notions of 'tribute', for example, are as much a reality as capitalist-induced 'wage-labour'. Similarly, Africa is still home to the spectacle of economically powerful urban business people (theoretically the owners of the means of production) returning home in their Mercedes Benz to respect the authority of their village chief. As Marx put it, 'No social order is ever destroyed before all the productive forces for which it is sufficient have been developed, and new superior relations of production never replace older ones before the material conditions for their existence have matured within the framework of the old society.'[7] African states today have highly complex class structures as they represent the articulation between pre-capitalist and capitalist modes of production, and (unfortunately for the political analysts) complex class structures result in complex systems of class politics.

A more flexible look at social class in Africa

Africanists have been left with the task of trying to analyse the intersection of two modes of production. Much illuminating work has been produced on this issue. Yet, despite all this academic activity, basic questions still remain. What, for example, does all this Marxist theory actually reveal about the day-to-day realities of political interaction in post-colonial Africa? It is, no doubt, essential to know that African societies do not have simple class conflicts between a bourgeoisie class and a proletariat, but what exactly is the nature of class conflict on the African continent? The answers to these questions are best sought, in the remainder of this chapter, by identifying common social groups found in African states, and then by assessing the consequences of the competition between these groups.

In this respect, it is now time to move beyond rigid Marxist doctrine. Marx's ideas have to be adapted and built upon. It is certainly wise to use the foundations explored in the paragraphs above, but even Marxists concede that, given that classes are still forming in Africa (due to the transitory articulation between modes of production), class alliances and class consciousness are bound to be complex. Even more sceptical are the non-Marxists. Many consider grand European-constructed models of class analysis to be more of a hindrance than a help in the African case. They seek other explanations of social interaction, and talk of 'elites' and 'groups' rather than 'classes'.

Whoever is correct, there is no doubt that Marx's unyielding economic determinism loses some of its precision in such a complicated social environment. A more flexible conceptual framework is needed to identify African social groups. In a sense, something more descriptive and less dynamic than Marx's ideas works best under African conditions.

Identifiable social groups within African society

Here Max Weber's notion of status as a determinant of social class is useful. This approach distances the scholar from myopic economics and associated modes of production. Instead, issues of power and social position come to the fore. Structural functionalist ideas of tying class definitions to occupation and income can also help. Indeed, anything concrete and empirically based is most welcome when trying to identify social groups within Africa's complex societies. Discussed below (and summarised in Table 5.1 on p. 88) are the continent's more recognisable social classes.

At independence, broadly similar social groups could be found in most African states. At the top of the hierarchy was an elite of educated bureaucrats and professionals. These were the Africans who had benefited most from the days of colonial rule, and were set to profit yet again as those most closely associated with the institutions of the post-colonial state. Independent African states also often had a small merchant class of entrepreneurs who had found a niche within the capitalist market that, up to this point, had been dominated by the imperial authorities. Then there were the traditional leaders who had either weathered the storm of having their authority tempered by the colonial state, or had actually benefited from imperial rule. Further down the social hierarchy was usually a small proletariat working in the continent's mines, limited manufacturing industry or in its transport sector. The vast majority of Africans at independence, however, were peasants, whose central economic activity involved farming smallholdings. Events that determined the nature of post-colonial African politics, in part, would be defined by how these social groups interacted. This being the case, each of these classes needs to be investigated in greater depth.

The peasantry

It is the peasantry, rather than a proletariat, that can be described as 'the masses' in African societies. Teodor Shanin describes peasants as '*small agricultural producers, who, with the help of simple equipment and the labour of their families, produce mostly for their own consumption, direct or indirect, and for the fulfilment of obligations to holders of political and economic power*'.[8] The peasantry is thus a class of individuals whose main economic activity is providing their own subsistence from small-scale farming, whose social focus is that of the village community. African tradition and custom usually dictate that these people have free access to land. In this sense, they control their own means of production, and can therefore limit their need to interact with the capitalist market. Peasants, however, will become involved with this market to secure products that cannot be produced on their own smallholdings (cooking oil, kerosene, consumer goods and school fees, for example), or to meet the demands of political authority (taxation or tribute).

Self-sufficiency certainly reduces this class's potential of being exploited by other classes, but since peasants make up the vast bulk of Africa's population, they are the main target for exploitation by those above them in the social hierarchy. Peasants are particularly vulnerable because they are the individuals furthest away from the state. They have little access to government institutions and the power that these institutions bring.

Yet, despite being the most exploited social group, their isolation and traditional beliefs make the African peasantry a rather conservative class. There is little evidence in the post-colonial period of peasants mobilising, as a class, to challenge their oppressors. The liberation struggles in Mozambique and Zimbabwe may be the exception, but there certainly has not been a revolutionary peasant movement similar to those found in China or Vietnam during this same period. As Colin Leys observes, 'it really requires a rare combination of tyranny and misery to produce a peasant revolt, let alone a peasant revolution'.[9]

The most common way for the African peasantry to retaliate against its exploiters is simply to try to keep out of harm's way. As the peasantry controls its own basic means of production, through having access to land, it can withdraw from the capitalist market. If state-imposed taxes on income from labour, or on consumer goods, become too high, for example, or a derisory price is being offered for cash crops grown for the market, then peasants simply disengage. They revert to subsistence farming, relying on their self-sufficiency to survive, or seek profits from 'informal' economies instead. Indeed, as will be discussed in Chapter 10, the 1980s and 1990s saw mass peasant disengagement (alongside urban dwellers) in many African countries, resulting in state structures coming close to collapse.

There are, however, opportunities created by the capitalist mode of production. Peasants do often supplement their smallholding income with external sources of revenue. Indeed, both colonial and post-colonial governments encouraged this, often *forcing* peasants out of their subsistence way of life. Taxes, for example, were imposed by state authorities to coerce peasant farmers into the capitalist market. To pay these taxes, peasants had to sell their labour as migrant workers, or use some of their land to grow cash crops. Where there was still resistance to entering the capitalist economy, further pressure was exerted. During colonial times in the Belgian Congo and Mozambique, for example, forced labour was introduced. Peasants were compelled to leave their smallholdings for a period of time each year to undertake employment determined by the state. Post-colonial methods of creating a labour force were less harsh. Several states did, however, oblige smallholders to use a proportion of their land to produce cash crops for the market. In academic terms, peasants were being partially drawn out of their pre-capitalist mode of production, and being exposed to the modern economy of the capitalist mode of production.

Indeed, it is in the interest of the ruling class to keep the peasantry trapped between the old and the new modes of production. This allows capitalists to pay migrant labourers' wages below the level of reproduction. In other words, mine owners and farm managers rely on the fact that peasants are also producing for themselves back on their smallholdings (farmed in their absence by their families). As workers have this additional source of subsistence, wages can be kept low. If they were a classical working class, with only their labour to sell, and no other means of production, higher wages would have been essential. This, however, was not the case. In the 1950s, African migrant workers were earning half the income of more permanent labourers in private industry, and a quarter of that of public service employees.[10] A disparity between the wages of this temporary labour force and their fully proletarianised colleagues still exists today.

In sum, peasants can be defined by their reliance on smallholding farming. Yet members of the family will often seek additional income and goods from the market by selling their labour and growing cash crops. Many peasants therefore have one foot in the traditional subsistence economy and one foot in the modern capitalist economy, forming what could be termed a 'peasantariat'.[11]

The proletariat

As we have seen, the absence of a mass proletariat is the key difference between European and African class formations. Levels of industrialisation are simply not enough to produce a majority working class.

Africa can, however, provide examples of isolated pockets of working class consciousness. Organised labour can be found with the miners of Zambia's Copperbelt, for instance, amid the dockers of Dar es Salaam, and among railway workers in Ghana; but this is not a common form of class expression. Indeed, these workers' privileged position makes them almost an 'aristocracy of labour', rather than a proletariat. They enjoy the security of relatively stable employment, and income levels above those of their peasant compatriots. These benefits make African proletarians less likely to challenge the *status quo*, as they are not to be found at the bottom of the social hierarchy.

Only in South Africa, where the trade union movement played a major role in the fight against apartheid, has a proletariat emerged that is in any way akin to the Marxist model. This was a result of an industrial revolution in South Africa, absent elsewhere on the continent. Yet, even here, many of the workers are still migrants, relying on their families back in the homelands to produce part of their subsistence.

The capitalist mode of production will have to penetrate African societies much deeper before a widespread classical proletariat will form.

The commercial bourgeoisie

The African commercial bourgeoisie is the closest social group this continent has to offer by way of Marx's notion of a (classical) bourgeoisie. They are predominantly merchant groups that developed despite the trading constraints imposed by colonial and post-colonial governments. Capitalists involved in small-scale commercial farming and manufacturing industry can also be found on the continent, but these are generally not so numerous as their merchant colleagues.

These traders, small manufacturers and farmers do indeed own their means of production, but have not yet developed into a full-scale bourgeoisie. In this sense, many within this class could be described as petty bourgeois. They are only minor owners of productive property, whose exploitation of other classes is limited. Usually this exploitation amounts just to the mark-up they can place on commodities sold in their shops. Economic power is limited because most goods first have to be obtained from foreign suppliers.

In many African states, this commercial bourgeoisie often has a large non-African ethnic contingent. Lebanese traders are prominent in West Africa, for example, while Asian merchants dominate East Africa. Elsewhere, a 1980 survey of Kisangani revealed that nearly half of the locally owned businesses in this Congo-Kinshasa town were run by Greeks and Asians.[12] In former settler societies, South African and Zimbabwe for example, the pattern is similar. The

big commercial farms will be owned by 'Europeans', as will the few large industrial concerns.

Throughout the continent, there are also numerous 'indigenous' African
entrepreneurs, notably larger-scale peasant farmers, but, even when added to
their Asian and European colleagues, they do not constitute a bourgeoisie with
enough economic power to be regarded as the dominant class. This commercial
bourgeoisie may form part of a ruling class, but its relatively weak position
ensures that Africanists have to look further to find truly powerful groups
within African societies.

The bureaucratic bourgeoisie

Given that Africanists have to approach the concept of class with flexibility,
they would do well to take the advice of Max Weber. He stated, ' "Economically
conditioned" power is not, of course, identical with "power" as such. On the
contrary, the emergence of economic power may be the consequence of power
existing on other grounds.'[13] This has been a theme taken up by neo-Marxists
and liberals ever since Marx laid the foundations for the modern era of class
analysis.

These scholars argue that Marx's work is too reductionist. As Nicos
Poulantzas put it, classical Marxist analysis suffers from 'economism'. The
complete subordination of class formation to economic determinants obscures
too many political factors that are also important. Indeed, Poulantzas went on
to argue that these political factors could produce periods in history when the
dominant economic class actually fails to control the state. The owners of the
means of production are, therefore, not necessarily the ruling class. Instead, a
political elite may be dominant.[14] Presumably the chances of this occurring are
increased in the more confused periods of articulation, when class formations
are immature or decadent respectively, and are consequently less influential.

In the search for African ruling classes, then, it is wise still to lean heavily on
Marx's work. After all, the dominant group will still use its position to exploit
the masses, accumulating capital at their expense. The point is, however, that it
may be that this ruling elite uses *political* strength, more than *economic* power, to
achieve and maintain its position of dominance.

In this respect, Stanislaw Ossowski considered not only the means of production as a defining feature of class, but also the means of consumption and the
means of compulsion.[15] Richard Sklar built on Ossowski's work, applying it
directly to African states. The ruling class on this continent, Sklar argues, is
more usefully identified in relation to the political realm rather than to the
economic realm.[16] The dominant elite is not necessarily the group that *owns*
the means of production, but is more likely to be the group that *controls* the
means of production. In other words, a politically advantaged class has the
power to take economic surplus from wherever it finds it within the country.
This class has little part in producing a surplus itself, but still has the ability to
appropriate capital for its own members' accumulation.

Not surprisingly, if political power is so important in identifying ruling classes in Africa, then this class is going to have the state itself as its main conduit of power. Indeed, as early as 1962, Dumont was talking of 'a "bourgeoisie" of a new type, that Karl Marx could hardly have foreseen: a bourgeoisie of the public service'.[17] The African state became a tool for accumulation, offering possibilities of social mobility. Instead of the state merely being the executive committee of the bourgeoisie, assisting this class in its exploitation via private commercial activities, it is the state itself that becomes the central tool of accumulation for the bourgeoisie. Individuals in Africa, therefore, gain more power the closer they are associated to state institutions. Political power brings economic rewards. Hence the ruling class found in Africa is a political *bureaucratic bourgeoisie* (also termed a state, organisational or managerial bourgeoisie), not an economic, commercial or industrial bourgeoisie.

This bureaucratic bourgeoisie is predominantly an urban coalition consisting of ministers, party officials, members of parliament, bureaucrats, military officers, the managers of public industries and, indeed, anyone who exploits their command over state institutions. As a class, this group has its historical roots within the colonial administration. As was seen in Chapter 2, an educated African elite was employed by the colonial service to act as junior administrators and professionals. As the group consolidated, this petty bourgeoisie of bureaucrats, doctors and teachers formed the backbone of the nationalist movements that won Africa's independence. Their reward at liberation was accession into their former colonial masters' jobs.

This bureaucratic bourgeoisie has proved very proficient in converting political power into economic gain. Not only do its members profit from their state salary, but also from the trappings of office (such as cars, expense accounts, education for children, health care, and access to cheap – even non-repayable – loans). Then there are the prebends (stipends of office) that state employment provides. These benefits include simple corruption: the pocketing of a proportion of the money handed over in payment for government services (such as export licences, legal fines, passports, or even the simple registration of births and deaths. Indeed, anything that needs an official stamp or signature). Alternatively, there are opportunities for collecting commission for services rendered (a 'gift', maybe, for awarding a state contract to the right person). In many cases, bureaucrats make much more money from 'backhanders' than they do from their official salaries. Indeed, state salaries are artificially low, as employees know they can use their position of power as a springboard for accumulation. Association with state institutions has therefore become the key to a higher standard of living in post-colonial Africa. Ndiva Kofele-Kale, for example, has calculated that the bureaucratic bourgeoisie makes up about 2 per cent of Cameroon's population, yet it grosses a massive one-third of this state's national income.[18]

With the state being at the heart of the bureaucratic bourgeoisie's power, the most common expression of class consciousness from this group relates to the defence of its command over state structures. This leads to conflicts between the bureaucratic bourgeoisie and other classes. The bureaucratic bourgeoisie may clash with the commercial bourgeoisie, for instance. In the Democratic Republic of Congo (Congo-Kinshasa/Zaire), the state neutralised the threat of an independent commercial bourgeoisie in one dramatic act. On 30 November 1973, Mobuto Sese Seko nationalised nearly all of the private sector within this country, and confiscated all foreign-owned businesses. The control of these concerns then passed directly to the state and its clients. Indeed, all over Africa, the bureaucratic bourgeoisie attempted to keep as much economic activity as possible within the public sector where it could be controlled and utilised by the state elite (rather than give away power to a commercial bourgeoisie within the private sector). Just how this bureaucratic bourgeoisie has hampered Africa's development, by siphoning off economic surplus for its own interests, is discussed in Chapter 10. For now it is sufficient to note that the bureaucratic bourgeoisie is the group that has wielded most power in post-colonial African politics.

Traditional leaders

The emergence of a bureaucratic bourgeoisie as the dominant group within African societies has not totally eclipsed sources of traditional authority. Old elites still have a role to play in the modern African state. Swaziland, for example, has retained a monarchy whose ancestors ruled this territory in pre-colonial times. Many other states have also seen traditional leaders use their historic authority as a springboard to occupy positions of power within modern political systems.

These traditional leaders do not necessarily always refer to history. They may rely on custom to gain part of their authority, but to rely solely on the past would find these individuals rapidly sidelined. Just as chiefs and monarchs adapted to colonial rule, gaining what they could from imposed imperial administrative structures, the following generation modernised themselves to retain power within post-colonial societies. Many of the old 'aristocracy', for example, played prominent roles in the nationalist movements that ended European rule. Nelson Mandela, in this respect, was not only the leader of the African National Congress of South Africa, but he also hailed from a leading family in the Transkei. In the post-independence era, chiefs often became local party dignitaries, local members of parliament, or heads of regional government. Many state presidents also have powerful family connections. In this manner there is a strong continuity of authority running from pre-colonial times, through the years of imperial rule, right into the modern era.

Informal sector entrepreneurs

Another group found within African societies that defies classical Marxist analysis are what can be termed 'informal sector entrepreneurs'. These individuals make a living from petty trading, often straddling the line between legal and illegal activities. The closest category to this group that Marx wrote of was a 'lumpenproletariat'.[19] He used this word to identify an 'underclass' of society: thieves, prostitutes, vagabonds, beggars and the like (who were far from gaining class consciousness).

A lumpenproletariat is too inaccurate and insulting a term to use, but there is a large social group in most African societies that occupies this underclass position, especially if the continent's large mass of unemployed is added to this category. These people attempt to produce their subsistence from casual work and small-scale entrepreneurial activities. Urban women, for example, many of whom have rejected their 'rural yoke', can be found in African cities in occupations such as small wholesalers running markets, as beer brewers, or as vendors of food or handicrafts on the streets.[20]

Such entrepreneurial activities frequently involve breaking the law. Street traders, for instance, rarely pay taxes or obtain the appropriate commercial licences from the state. Indeed, with the growth of the informal sector generally in African countries, numerous smugglers, 'black market' money changers and 'hawkers' of all descriptions can be added to this social category. Although lacking class consciousness and organisation, due to their fragile and nefarious position, these individuals have played an important role in post-colonial political activity. These vulnerable people, especially in urban areas, often made up the foot-soldiers of any 'bread riots' directed against state authority. Allied to students and workers, these groups, in the bluntest of manner, can deliver considerable political clout.

An international bourgeoisie

So far, this social survey has focused on the domestic arena. Peasants and a small proletariat are exploited by a bourgeoisie that largely derives its power through the mechanism of state institutions. Operating at the fringes of society are 'informal sector entrepreneurs', and also present is a commercial bourgeoisie, although this latter group is overshadowed by the bureaucrats, as they have failed to muster enough political power to compete with the ruling class.

Together, the bureaucratic and commercial bourgeoisie can be termed a *national bourgeoisie*. Yet, the problem remains that neither of these groups owns the means of production to any great extent. As such ownership is paramount to Marxist class analysis, academics of this school have continued the search for Africa's true ruling class. Many consider they have found this dominant group by linking their analysis to theories of underdevelopment and dependency. This paradigm locates the real bourgeoisie outside Africa.

Dependency theorists argue that it is the owners of international capital that form the true ruling class, not only in Africa, but all over the world. Transnational corporations and international financial institutions are hegemonic. In this respect, members of indigenous national bourgeoisies in the Third World are just agents or lackeys of this *international bourgeoisie*. They are merely collaborators, or *compradors*, to use the terminology of the dependency theorists.[21]

Officials within African states, therefore, act as debt-collectors for external agencies, receiving international backing and taking a minor share of the profits for their services. These compradors are in the business of facilitating foreign capital, often at the expense of the national interest. In other words, state officials will look after the needs both of international capital and of themselves before they consider what course of action is suitable for their people. This line of reasoning explains why the national bourgeoisie holds power despite not owning the means of production. The true bourgeoisie operates from the Western capitalist countries, exploiting the masses of the Third World, while the local, national, bourgeoisie only occupies an intermediary position in this world economy. Compradors therefore gain their power from being agents of, rather than owners of, the means of production.

This dependency school of thought dominated studies of class in Africa throughout the 1970s and 1980s, and still holds great sway today. In recent years, however, many Africanists have been seeking to revise this paradigm. They argue that dismissing the national bourgeoisie as a mere comprador class is too reductionist.

A more subtle analysis of Africa's local dominant groups is required. Using a model of a world capitalist economy explains a great deal, but relegating Africa to just a footnote of the wider international political system diverts scholars from explaining African realities. What about political events generated by internal class conflict? What about the divisions within the national bourgeoisie (the battle between the commercial and the bureaucratic wings, for example)? There is also a question about the level of autonomy these 'compradors' enjoy.

The reality is that, in the post-colonial period, peripheral states have selected different economic development strategies; groups within them have accumulated capital creating internal politics of inequality; governments have changed trading partners; and local leaders have selected different public policy options. There is a considerable degree of autonomy for locally dominant state elites to exercise. Indeed, the national bourgeoisie may even act against the interests of international capital. Several states in the post-colonial period, for example, have nationalised the assets of foreign companies operating within their territory. In this respect, African bourgeoisies are as keen as any other bourgeoisie to make a profit and protect their position of power. They are quite willing to tap into sources of international capital if this is beneficial, especially as sources of indigenous capital are limited, but they will also use their autonomy to protect their interests against international capital should this be necessary. They may have to work within the constraints of the international economy, but this does not make the national bourgeoisie a passive, subservient and powerless class. To think this is to profoundly misunderstand the national bourgeoisie's role within African politics.

Table 5.1 African social groups

Social Group	Characteristics
Peasants (Small agricultural producers, producing largely for their own consumption)	Majority of the population Based in small rural communities Involved primarily in subsistence agriculture Family is the main unit of production Limited contact with the capitalist economy Occupies an 'underdog' position in society
Proletariat (Wage-earners within capitalist societies who rely on selling their labour)	Small proportion of the population Landless rural labourers Urban labourers (industry, mining, transport, etc.)
Informal sector entrepreneurs (Individuals making a living from petty trading, often involving illegal activities)	Not permanently employed in formal economy Often irregular/insecure work Often unlicensed/illegal Street vendors Money changers/lenders (including foreign currency) Smugglers Petty thieves Prostitutes
Petty bourgeoisie (Minor owners of productive property whose exploitation of labour is limited, or the lower ranks of the salaried state bureaucracy)	Predominantly male Self-employed artisans Small farmers employing labour Small traders Teachers Soldiers Lower ranks of public service
Bourgeoisie	The ruling class
National bourgeoisie (The indigenous ruling class)	Predominantly male A small proportion of the population
a. *Commercial Bourgeoisie* (The classical bourgeoisie as defined by Marx in his studies of Western capitalist societies)	Largely in the trading and agricultural sector (rather than manufacturing) Entrepreneurs Business interests Commercial farmers Land owners
b. *Bureaucratic Bourgeoisie* (Those who 'control' rather than 'own' the means of production, exploiting their command over the institutions of the state to accumulate capital)	Largely urban Educated State decision makers Political class (MPs, ministers, party officials, etc.) Higher rank bureaucrats Military officers Public managers (e.g. in nationalised industries) Professionals (public sector)

c. Comprador Bourgeoisie	Any section of the national bourgeoisie which acts as an agent for the international bourgeoisie
International bourgeoisie (International capitalists based in the 'North' who exploit the peripheral economies of Africa, and other areas of the 'South')	The ultimate ruling class according to underdevelopment dependency theorists Transnational corporations International financial institutions
Traditional rulers (Those whose authority is based mainly on tradition and custom)	Clan heads Chiefs Paramount chiefs Emirs Monarchs, etc.

The value of class analysis in explaining African politics

These, then, are the social groups that can be identified within African states. But how useful is class analysis under African conditions? To what degree do the preceding paragraphs really contribute to an explanation of African politics? For the political scientist whose knowledge is based mainly on studying Western societies, the above exercise is invaluable. Western-formulated models of class, particularly Marxism, are almost as useful in how they fail to conceptualise African class formations as they are in providing an understanding of African politics. These models highlight the significant differences between Western classes and those found on the African continent. It is not all negative, however. An adaptation of classical class theories do help identify the main groups within African societies, and they also put these classes in an historic framework, pointing to the articulation between pre-capitalist and capitalist modes of production.

Yet the fact remains that Africa is not willing to be shoehorned into the models most used by social scientists elsewhere. Class analysis is meant to simplify things. Academic work is easier if a society only has two classes, a competing bourgeoisie and proletariat. Of course, reality itself is never this simple, even in mature capitalist countries, but in Africa things remain complex even after conceptual short-cuts have been taken. The articulation between modes of production ensures this. Instead of two classes, the African masses are divided into peasants and proletarians, while the bourgeoisie comes in at least three parts (commercial, bureaucratic and international), of which the dominant African branch is an administrative class that has its social base in the state itself, rather than civil society as Marx himself argued. And somewhere among this mix, a place has to be found for traditional leaders and informal sector entrepreneurs. Add notions of what Marxists call 'false consciousness' (ethnic or religious loyalties, for example), and the picture gets even more confused. A point has to be reached where Africanists have made so many adaptations to classical models of class that the whole exercise should be abandoned and new ideas of social groups put forward.

One such alternative approach is based on the fact that ruling groups are rarely homogeneous in Africa. The elite holding power is perhaps more usefully seen as a coalition of competing factions, rather than a single consolidated class. At the most basic level, for example, the national bourgeoisie is part commercial and part bureaucratic. Within the bureaucracy itself there are splits between the military and civilian wings. Factions mobilising around ethnic identities are also prominent within African political systems. As a result, there is internal competition within the ruling group. Many state elites simply represent too many interests for the coalition to survive long. The various factions want different things, and hold little class solidarity with their allies. Consequently, many African governments are particularly vulnerable to shifting alliances within the ruling group. Witness the number of military *coups d'état* experienced by certain African states in the post-colonial period.

This reality of power is why some scholars talk of African politics being underwritten by a 'hegemonic drive'.[22] No longer is class conflict solely between the bourgeoisie and the proletariat, or corresponding pre-colonial economic groups, it is more about groups and individuals cooperating and competing in order to capture the power of the state. Social alliances are not therefore based on class solidarity, but on the willingness to cooperate with strategic allies in order to receive more of the spoils associated with the state. Under these circumstances, social leaders will search each other out, to see if their corresponding factions can, indeed, do business together, and further their hold on the state.

Jean-François Bayart, in this respect, talks of the 'assimilation of elites'.[23] Powerful groups within society will respect each other's position, forming an uneasy ruling coalition: a 'hegemonic bloc'. The members of this coalition, and their position within it, will constantly change, but all realise to compete too hard risks political turmoil and the possibility of losing access to the state altogether. Nobody wishes to give up this opportunity to accumulate, so the elites have to cooperate to some degree. Bayart therefore argues that classical class categorisations are misleading, as they artificially obscure the component parts of this hegemonic bloc.

Links are forged between the different factions, weakening group boundaries. Note for example how, once the bureaucratic bourgeoisie has accumulated wealth via its control over state structures, not all this wealth is spent on ostentatious consumption. Members of the bureaucratic bourgeoisie will also invest in commercial projects. They set up businesses and buy property, often using their position within the state to facilitate this. A bureaucrat, for example, may allocate himself or herself a plot of government land, usher through planning permission, and negotiate a loan from the state bank to build property for renting. Many state managers, in this respect, accumulate significant private commercial empires during their term of office. State assistance is also extended to the family, friends and clients of the bureaucrats. Such entrepreneurial activity by state officials closes the gap between themselves and the members of the commercial bourgeoisie also found within the ruling hegemonic bloc.

Links between other elites also form: between traditional leaders and the state executive, for example; or among trade union leaders and the Department of Labour. Indeed, the ruling coalition tends to co-opt the leaders of all the important factions within society. Hence the term 'assimilation of elites'. As Bayart puts it, these are the people, after all, who 'drive the same Mercedes, drink the same champagne, smoke the same cigars and meet in the same VIP lounges at airports'.[24] Having a similar level of power and the same desire to consolidate their hold on state institutions, it is not surprising that these leaders, even if they do not share cognate class backgrounds, join to form an hegemonic bloc. This is how as diverse a collection of leaders, such as business people, bureaucrats, soldiers, chiefs, trade union activists, ethnic brokers and women's representatives, assimilate themselves into a state's ruling elite.

State and civil society

The above evidence confirms that social class is an important factor influencing the central theme of this book: the relationship between state and civil society. Scholars may differ on how to identify these groups, and also disagree on the nature of these social formations, but what is certain is that African societies cannot be described as classless. Inequality does exist.

Unfortunately, class politics in Africa cannot be reduced to a simple competition between bourgeoisie and proletariat. This, of course, reduces the attractiveness of using class as an analytical tool. Yet the fact that the continent is host to numerous complex societies, harbouring varied group dynamics, should come as no surprise. Even Europe no longer easily reflects Marx's model of capitalist relations. Perseverance, however, does allow Africanists to identify various common social groups within African societies, and, as will be seen later in the book, the interaction between these groups has determined much of the continent's post-colonial political history.

Indeed, it is still possible to apply a simplistic model to African social relations, avoiding the complications of Marxist analysis. Since independence, the continent has staged a battle between two separate parties. It is the age-old conflict between the haves and the have-nots to which we referred at the beginning of this chapter; in this case, between state and civil society. As the Ghanaians put it, Africa's post-colonial political environment has been dominated by a divide between the 'big men' and the 'small men'.[25]

The big men, inevitably, are those individuals who have access to state institutions. Association with the state, after all, has been the key to social advancement on the continent in modern times. Once this access had been achieved, individuals commanded a share of the means of compulsion, bringing both opportunities for accumulation and political power. Class in Africa is therefore more to do with access to political power than it is to do with owning the economic means of production. The result has been the building of hegemonic coalitions across the continent, where leading members of society have been assimilated into state elites. It is these sometimes fragile hegemonic blocs that have been at the heart of African politics in the post-colonial period. Just how these big men have used their power, and engaged the small men within civil society, is the subject of the next chapter, addressing the issue of legitimacy.

Case study: social class in Botswana

Botswana is a landlocked country of just 1.5 million people located in Southern Africa. Most of this territory is consumed by the Kalahari Desert, and, at independence, it was one of the poorest countries in the world. Yet, today, Botswana is often cited as Africa's 'success story'.

What this country has achieved in the post-colonial period is remarkable. From independence in 1966, Botswana enjoyed sustained economic growth. Indeed, it was one of the world's fastest growing economies during these years. Per capita GNP expanded from less than US$100 dollars in 1966 to over US$3,000 by the 1990s. What is more, Botswana is the only mainland African state to have retained an unbroken record of liberal democracy since independence. The country's first multi-party election was held in 1965, and similar polls have been repeated every five years since that date. This political stability is all the more striking when one considers Botswana's location on the doorstep of the potentially disruptive influence of apartheid South Africa.

Initial post-colonial development strategies were based on cattle and the export of meat. This, after all, was Botswana's only significant commercial activity prior to independence. Diamonds, and to a lesser extent other minerals, however, became the key to Botswana's relative prosperity. As the former British protectorate of Bechuanaland, mining contributed nothing to Botswana's GNP. By contrast, in 1990, this sector of the economy accounted for 60 per cent of national income.

A state's politics, however, are influenced by factors beyond just macro-economic indicators and regular elections. This case study seeks to introduce Botswana by analysing another important political deter-minant: the issue of class.

Like all societies, Botswana has been host to social groups competing for power, and one of these can certainly be identified as a ruling elite. Originally this group relied on its ownership of the main economic commodity, cattle, as its basis of power (land, the *means* of production, after all, was held in common). Traditional elites in this part of Africa had been a cattle-owning class for centuries. This commodity provided the surplus wealth that underpinned their political authority. Even with the arrival of colonialism, traditional leaders managed to maintain their position as a ruling class. Following the path of indirect rule, British administrators relied on these leaders as their intermediaries of government. Then, as Africa entered the era of decolonisation, many members of this traditional cattle-owning elite went on to play a significant role in the nationalist movement. They consequently gained influence within the structures of the post-colonial state.

As was the case with other African states, however, elites whose authority was rooted in tradition or commerce did not rule alone. It was a bureaucratic bourgeoisie that expanded most, both in size and power, during the modern era. As the economy grew, so did the state apparatus managing it. New social provision – education and health, for example – also required a bigger bureaucracy. More individuals were being employed to run state institutions, which provided these officials with opportunities to enhance political power and economic wealth.

Indeed, a trend developed where bureaucrats ran directly for political office, resulting, in time, with them taking over from the older generation of nationalist leaders. Civil servants thus crossed the divide and became politicians. In short, a 'bureaucratic' bourgeoisie formed and came to dominate Botswanan politics, a fact determining that, despite the holding of free and competitive elections, only one party, the Botswana Democratic Party (BDP), held office in the independence period.

A thumbnail biography of Botswana's first president illustrates the nature of this ruling elite. Seretse Khama led Botswana from independence in 1966 until his death in 1980. He was a hereditary chief of the Bamangwato, and a direct descendent of Khama III (a hero who had united the Tswana people and negotiated wisely with the European authorities in the nineteenth century). Seretse Khama was well educated. He studied in South Africa, and completed his schooling at Oxford University. Khama, in this sense, was fully in touch with European society, and would eventually marry a British woman. His hereditary and educational credentials brought him to the head of Botswana's nationalist movement, and he helped form the BDP in 1962. Khama was also a relatively wealthy individual, having purchased land in the new freehold areas of the country and farmed cattle. In this respect, Seretse Khama was almost an 'assimilation of elites' or a 'hegemonic bloc' by himself. He had strong links with traditional society, the modern political elite, the bureaucracy and the commercial sector. Khama was a natural candidate for state president, as he could represent all the elites that came together to form the post-colonial ruling coalition.

The Botswanan ruling elite, like many of its counterparts elsewhere on the continent, also sought to prosper through contacts with international capital. Dependency theorists would define this group as a comprador class, acting as agents for foreign capitalists rather than serving their own people. The Botswanan government, indeed, went out of its way to encouraged transnational corporation (TNC) mining of the country's resources. DeBeers, for example, developed the diamond mines that are at the heart of the country's economy, and with DeBeers having been given a monopoly over the extraction of Botswana's diamonds, the government certainly opened itself up to charges that it was assisting acts of neo-colonialism, merely overseeing the stripping of Botswana's assets by these TNCs. It cannot be denied, however, that foreign management of the mines, using foreign capital and foreign technology, produced vast sums of money available for public spending. The government also cultivated a good relationship with international aid donors. Attracted by its stability and good human rights record, donors gave generously to Botswana in the post-colonial period.

Class analysis, however, is not just about the 'haves' within society. Outside the hegemonic bloc, the masses in Botswana, as they do all over Africa, bore the brunt of elite exploitation. Although class conflict is perhaps more muted in Botswana than elsewhere on the continent because of the democratic links between state and civil society, there is certainly still evidence of class relationships influencing political actions.

With the structure of labour, for example, it is in an elite's interests to keep wage earners as migrant labourers, rather than encouraging them to develop into a more stable proletariat. A more permanent proletariat, after all, would find it easier to organise and challenge these elite interests.

Bechuanaland was established as a protectorate in 1885, essentially to act as a vast labour reserve for South Africa. As occurred all over Southern Africa, peasants were taxed and had their land rights curtailed in order to force them into the wage economy. For the majority, this meant seeking work in South African mines. By 1943, half of all Botswanan males aged 15 to 44 were supplementing production on their smallholdings by working as miners for part of the year.[26] They were a 'peasantariat'. Independence, and the development of mining in Botswana itself, has seen the 'nationalisation' of this work-force. Yet peasants are still employed as migrant labour, not as a more skilled permanent workforce. In this way, the demands of modern capital are met, but the costs of labour are minimised.

Reflecting its alliance with the domestic commercial bourgeoisie and the TNCs, the Botswanan government (the bureaucratic bour-geoisie) also tended to favour the interests of capital, rather than labour, in the post-colonial period. Labour organisations were tightly controlled to create a more advantageous environment for TNCs. In 1991, for example, 50,000 workers went on strike in Botswana. The government responded by dismissing 18,000 public employees, only agreeing to re-instate them on less favourable contracts. Botswana is also still to adopt several key standards drawn up by the International Labour Organization.[27]

As well as its coalition partners, the Botswanan bureaucratic bour-geoisie is also adept at serving its own interests. In 1992–3, for example, 10 per cent of Botswana's budget was spent on defence. In particular, vast sums of money have been allocated to the building of a military airbase outside Molepolole during the 1990s. Such non-productive defence investments, in terms of sustainable development, are questionable in such a fragile economy, especially since the demise of apartheid has removed any major military threat to Botswana. Instead of putting this capital into rural development, the bureaucratic bourgeoisie is spending money on itself.[28] The state contracts and state employment involved in the Molepolole airbase, after all, create far more opportunities for corruption and patronage than would numerous small-scale community projects. Bureaucrats are thinking more of what public programmes will bring for themselves in short-term, rather than economic development that would benefit the whole population.

Given these examples, there is little doubt that there is inequality in Botswana, laying the foundations for class politics. Not everybody has benefited equally from the country's impressive economic growth in the post-colonial period. Less than a quarter of the population, for example, is involved in the wage economy, while most do not own enough cattle to benefit from the decision to develop this industry. Indeed, arguments that Botswana has experienced economic growth, but without an accompanying income redistribution, are backed by the fact that most Batswana cannot even produce their own subsistence. They rely on relatives in the urban areas to supplement their income.

Statistics show that 40 per cent of the population shares just 10 per cent of the national wealth, while the top 20 per cent owns 61.5 per cent of this sum.[29]

There is no doubt, however, that the citizens of Botswana are better off than most Africans. Besides the self-interested non-productive bureaucratic investments, considerable sums of money are spent on projects that benefit the whole population. From scant social provision at independence, Botswana now has an extensive primary health care network, and most Batswana enjoy free schooling for a 10-year period. Given that these people live in a country with a good human rights record, and that they have an opportunity to remove the ruling party via democratic channels if they so wish, most Batswana are content to continue to vote for the ruling BDP (thus maintaining the bureaucratic bourgeoisie's position of power). As Jack Parson put it, participatory politics and the ruling elite's not-inconsiderable attention to the welfare of the masses, on a continent where these are usually conspicuously absent, have blunted the otherwise 'sharp edge of class politics' in Botswana.[30]

Botswana[31]

Territory:	575,000 sq km	Population:	1.5 million
Colonial power:	Britain	Independence:	1966
Major cities:	Gaborone (capital)	Ethnic groups:	Batswana
	Francistown		San
	Selebi-Phikwe	Life expectancy:	44 years
Urban pop.:	30.7%	Adult literacy:	69.8%
Languages:	Setswana	Exports:	Diamonds
	English		Vehicles and parts
Currency:	Pula		Copper-nickel
Infant mortality:	59 deaths/thousand births		Meat
Religion:	Traditional	External debt:	US$576 million
	Christian	GDP per capita:	US$2,907

Glossary of key terms

African mode of production	A pre-capitalist mode of production sought by Marxists, akin to feudalism preceding capitalism in European societies.
Aristocracy of labour	Where the proletariat is not socially disadvantaged within society.
Articulation between modes of production	A time when remnants of the passing mode of production are operating alongside social

relations generated by the ascendant mode of production.

Assimilation of elites — The formation of a ruling coalition consisting of leading representatives from the most powerful groups within society.

Bourgeoisie — The ruling class in the capitalist era of history, whose power is based on their ownership of the means of production.

Bureaucratic bourgeoisie — Those who 'control' rather than 'own' the means of production, exploiting their command over the institutions of the state to accumulate capital.

Commercial bourgeoisie — The classical bourgeoisie as defined by Marx in his studies of Western capitalist societies.

Comprador — Any section of the national bourgeoisie which acts as an agent for the international bourgeoisie.

Hegemonic bloc — A political coalition seeking the capture of state power.

Informal sector entrepreneurs — Individuals gaining their subsistence from (often illegal) petty trading.

International bourgeoisie — International capitalists based in the 'North' who exploit the 'peripheral' economies of Africa, and other regions of the 'South'.

Means of production — The materials needed to produce human subsistence and economic surplus (land, machinery, etc.).

National bourgeoisie — The indigenous ruling class.

Peasants — Small agricultural producers, producing largely for their own consumption.

Petty bourgeoisie — Minor owners of productive property whose exploitation of labour is limited.

Proletariat — Wage earners within capitalist societies who rely on selling their labour.

Traditional leader — Those whose authority is based mainly on tradition and custom.

Questions raised by this chapter

1 To what extent can Karl Marx's model of class be applied to African societies?
2 Is there a pre-capitalist 'African' mode of production'?
3 How does the articulation between modes of production affect African class formations?

4   Can African classes be defined solely by the means of production, or do political considerations also play a prominent role?
5   Should the ruling elite in African states be termed a 'class', or is it more a coalition of elites forming a 'hegemonic bloc'?

Further reading

For anybody interested in a classical Marxist explanation of class formation and conflict, there is no better starting point than Marx and Engels's *Communist Manifesto*. With respect to social class specifically in Africa, Crawford Young's look at how Africanists have tackled this issue would be a valuable read. Catherine Coquery-Vidrovitch's work on the African mode of production was at the centre of this particular debate in the 1970s, and her chapter in the book edited by Gutkind and Wallerstein is particularly useful. On the idea that political power, not only economic production, has an important role to play in African class analysis, see Richard Sklar's article. Similarly, Immanuel Wallerstein's paper puts African class formations into the context of a broader international economy. For a more recent look at how Africanists view class analysis, Chapters 6 and 7 of Jean-François Bayart's seminal book *The State in Africa* introduces the idea of the ruling class in Africa being an assimilation of elites, forming an hegemonic bloc. Catherine Boone's chapter in Migdal, Kohli and Shue's collection provides an excellent general discussion of the ideas raised in this chapter.

Bayart, Jean-François (1993) *The state in Africa: the politics of the belly*, London: Longman.
Boone, Catherine (1994) 'States and ruling classes in post-colonial Africa', in Joel S Migdal, Atul Kohli and Vivienne Shue, eds, *State power and social forces: domination and transformation in the Third World*, Cambridge: Cambridge University Press.
Coquery-Vidrovitch, Catherine (1976) 'The political economy of the African peasantry and modes of production', in Peter C W Gutkind and Immanuel Wallerstein, eds, *The political economy of contemporary Africa*, Beverly Hills: Sage.
Marx, Karl and Friedrich Engels (1967) *Communist manifesto*, London: Penguin.
Sklar, Richard (1979) 'The nature of class domination in Africa', *Journal of Modern African Studies* 17(4), 531–52.
Wallerstein, Immanuel (1973) 'Class and class-conflict in contemporary Africa', *Canadian Journal of African Studies* 7(3), 375–80.
Young, M C (1986) 'Nationalism, ethnicity and class in Africa: a retrospective', *Cahier d'Etudes Africaines* 26(3), 421–95.

6 Legitimacy

Neo-patrimonialism, personal rule and the centralisation of the African state

Legitimacy should be at the heart of any government. Without it, coercive measures have to be deployed, and it is far more productive to keep a society content by providing for its needs than it is for a self-interested ruling elite to seek compliance through violence. The social contract between the rulers and the ruled should therefore be one based on trust and respect, not on fear and coercion. In this respect, legitimacy can be defined as *a psychological relationship between the governed and their governors, which engenders a belief that the state's leaders and institutions have a right to exercise political authority over the rest of society*. Legitimacy will convince, rather than force, citizens to obey the state.

Max Weber identified three pure sources of legitimacy: tradition, charisma and legal-rational authority.[1] Traditional legitimacy rests on a society's culture and history. Few subjects in medieval Europe, for example, questioned the right of monarchs to rule over them, given that hereditary succession (the divine right of kings) was well established by this time. Most believed that this was how God chose to order their societies, and consequently they bowed to this type of government.

With charisma, Weber's second source of legitimacy, individuals choose to follow and obey simply because of their leader's personality or the ideals the leader imparts. Warlords, or religious teachers, for example, rely on charisma to generate legitimacy among their constituency.

It was legitimacy based on legal-rational government, however, that was meant to underlie state authority in post-colonial Africa. This was to be provided by the liberal democratic institutions left by imperial powers as part of the colonial inheritance. Legal-rational government, in this respect, is government based on a social contract. Citizens obey the state because state institutions have been specifically constituted to serve their interests. Governments rule on the citizen's behalf, formulating, executing and enforcing laws designed to advance collective welfare. In doing this, those within the state officiate impersonally, putting society's interests above their own. A bureaucratic culture of public service obscures any ideas officials may harbour about using state institutions for their own private gain. In return for this beneficial and rational system of government, citizens are obliged to obey state laws.

It is legal-rational legitimacy that underpins the relationship between state and society in the current democracies of Western Europe and North America.

Yet Africa's inheritance of weak legal-rational institutions did not prosper in the post-colonial era. Liberal democracy was soon abandoned. At first glance, institutions such as parliaments and presidents may seem familiar, but a closer examination reveals these governments to be very different from those found in the West. The façade of modern institutions may remain, but behind this lies a completely different political environment. As will be seen, 'personal rule' superseded any notions of 'legal-rationalism', and this was achieved by centralising political activity. Power was removed from civil society and peripheral institutions of the state, and hoarded instead within the core executive, often with just one individual being dominant. And with legal-rational legitimacy lost through this 'centralisation of the state', alternative representative links had to be forged between state and society. Patronage, based on the distribution of state resources, became the main bond between the governors and the governed in post-colonial Africa. In short, the continent's leaders took the inherited modern states, adapted liberal democratic institutions to their own interests, and then 'patrimonialised' the whole system. The current chapter is designed to explain further these two phenomena of the *centralisation of the African state* and the accompanying *neo-patrimonialisation of government*.

Centralisation of the African state

Representative, accountable and efficient government usually requires political power to be distributed right across society. No one area should become hegemonic. Within the state itself, for example, there should be a number of branches of government acting as a check and balance upon each other. Such a 'separation of powers' deters a dangerous accumulation of authority within a single area of government. Similarly, power should also be dispersed between the state and civil society. State institutions should not come to monopolise the political process. Political parties must be able to compete fairly for control over the state, and interest groups should be able to influence the making of public policy. The absence of such pluralism risks the state becoming 'inverted', turning in on itself, and concentrating more on serving its own interests rather than the collective good.

Along with a separation of powers, and links between state and civil society, a representative state should also in the final analysis be accountable to the people. Multi-party elections, involving a universal franchise, are perhaps the best way of assuring this accountability. These polls diminish the opportunities of state power being abused by either state officials alone, or in an exploitative alliance accommodating elites within civil society. Only if power is diffused evenly among these three elements of society (the state, civil society and the people as a whole) can representation and accountability be guaranteed.

In a centralised state, by contrast, there is a dangerous concentration of power. Dispersal is limited. A centralised state can be found where centrifugal

University
of Ulster
LIBRARY

forces have resulted in political power shifting away from those within civil society and 'peripheral' state institutions. Instead, power accumulates in specific core offices of the state, usually within the executive branch. A monopoly over all formal political power is sought by these leaders.

The key to maintaining this concentration of power at the core is the limitation of opportunities for organised opposition. No rival source of power can be endorsed or tolerated by the political elite. Opposition political parties, for example, are often outlawed. Only the official party of the state is permitted to campaign, creating one-party states, and even here the one party is usually tightly controlled by the ruling elite.

Indeed, the elite does not confine the protection of its political monopoly to neutralising challenges through formal government channels. It also restricts rival political activity emanating from within civil society. Labour unions, professional groups and other voluntary associations are commonly heavily influenced or co-opted by the government of a centralised state. Co-option usually involves civil society leaders being offered positions within the state structure, giving them a stake in the *status quo*. Potential sources of opposition thus become decapitated, as these social movements lose their leaders to the state elite. As they say in Cameroon, 'the mouth that eats does not speak'.[2] Voluntary associations that resist this pressure and continue to maintain their independence from the state will be harassed or banned out of existence. Nigeria's execution in 1995 of Ken Saro-Wiwa, and eight other campaigners for Ogoni rights, is a single example among tens of thousands that demonstrate the lengths leaders will go to protect their monopoly of political power.

Similarly, economic functions, which are largely located within civil society in the West (private sector activities such as the production, distribution and sale of goods) are also dominated by government institutions in a centralised state. To leave these economic activities to the free market would risk empowering individuals operating outside state institutions. It is almost as if the state, or at least those at its core, have no limit to their ambition over what they should control. When the centralisation process is complete, no potential source of opposition remains, either inside or outside state structures.

Ghana in the 1960s illustrated this phenomenon of state centralisation well. In 1957, Kwame Nkrumah's Convention People's Party (CPP) won Ghana's multi-party independence elections, and formed a government under the inherited Westminster-style constitution. Although the CPP had won considerable electoral support, it did face organised opposition in several regions of the country. In particular, the Ashanti were seeking a degree of autonomy. Nkrumah refused, however, to tolerate any such 'separatism'. The CPP's first step, therefore, was to use its parliamentary majority to outlaw ethnically based organisations with the 1957 Avoidance of Discrimination Act. With this one piece of legislation an important area of civil society mobilisation was stifled. Regional assemblies were also proscribed. A year later, Parliament passed the Preventative Detention Act. This measure, suspending *habeas corpus*, was used to detain political dissidents who continued to oppose the CPP. Leading opposition members were intimidated, imprisoned or forced into exile. Similarly, traditional leaders were stripped of their constitutional powers and sidelined into an advisory House of Chiefs, while the press was put on a short lead. Next it was the turn of Ghana's independent system of justice. The judicial branch was circumvented by establishing special courts to hear political cases of treason and sedition. These trials were overseen by judges appointed directly by Nkrumah himself. Given all these measures, it was not surprising that when it came to the 1964 referendum asking the Ghanaian people whether they wanted a one-party state, there was no organised opposition left to campaign against this final act of centralisation. The one-party state was approved by 2,773,920 votes to 2,452.

Since the centralisation of the state is such an important factor in understanding post-colonial African politics, the next two sections of this chapter concentrate on two common components of the process: the neutralisation of party political opposition, with the establishment of a one-party state; and the manipulation of power within the state itself, where the core executive by-passes 'peripheral' institutions such as parliaments, local government and judicial constraints.

The one-party state

Of course, moves towards a one-party state, in Ghana and other African countries, were not portrayed by the political elite as an exercise of naked power accumulation. African leaders put forward several arguments justifying this centralisation of the state. Kwame Nkrumah dismantled the multi-party system in Ghana because he declared this system to be socially divisive; Houphouët-Boigny did likewise in the Côte d'Ivoire on the grounds that no opposition actually existed; Sekou Touré opted for single-party structures because Guinea's socialist ideology demanded this; Julius Nyerere favoured the one-party state because he considered it the most appropriate way to build a democracy in Tanzania. The vast majority of African countries adopted this model of government, and each leader had their own set of justifications for the constitutional amendments employed.

At the time, these justifications rang true. Many Africans, and indeed many Africanists in the West, welcomed these changes. After all, they agreed, there was no reason why democracy in Africa had to mimic Western multi-party competition, especially considering that this pluralist form of democracy had no historical roots on the African continent.

In terms of justification, most leaders cited 'unity' as the main reason for curtailing multi-party activity. Given the alien nature of the colonial state in Africa, independent governments inherited ethnically divided societies, many with separatist tendencies. If these regional forces had remained unchecked, the authority of the national government, and the very integrity of the state itself, could have been threatened. In this sense, nationalist leaders argued that African countries could not yet afford multi-party structures. Africans would mobilise along ethnic lines, and political competition of this nature would simply pull the nation apart. Instead, institutions fostering unity were required, and the institution that would contribute most to the nation-building project would be the single party. Just as George Washington had warned of the 'baneful effects of the spirit of party' two hundred years earlier in the United States, African nationalist leaders such as Nyerere also argued that multi-party systems could only bring misfortune during these 'vital early years' of independence.[3]

It also has to be remembered that the governments which imposed these one-party states enjoyed considerable support from the electorate. Most gained their initial legitimacy from liberating their countries from colonial rule, and by subsequently gaining landslide victories in the independence elections. Many of these countries were practically *de facto* one-party states anyway. Tanzania, for example, had just one (independent) opposition MP sitting in its parliament before the one-party state was created in 1965. Why should Tanzania, it was argued, suffer a Westminster-style multi-party constitution when its people had selected representatives from only one party? It would be better to have a political system that reflected African realities instead.

Nationalist leaders were also quick to point out that there was no previous tradition of multi-party democracy in Africa. An adversarial political culture, it was argued, was alien to the continent. These nationalists considered it foolish to recreate political institutions that had largely evolved out of Europe's need to manage social inequality and class conflict. Africa was largely devoid of these particular social cleavages. Once again, it was proposed, that African political institutions should reflect African customs. Leaders, such as Senghor and Nyerere, invoked a romanticised interpretation of the past by describing how their forebears had traditionally met as communities, rather than as individual contestants, in order to make decisions. Under a village tree, elders would talk out an idea until consensus was reached. Consensus was thus the key to African politics, not competition. It therefore followed that a one-party model was the best method of recreating this style of consensus politics within the framework of the inherited modern state.

It was also thought that if Africa's political institutions were to reflect African needs, rather than the pluralist ideals inherited from the imperial powers, it would be sensible for governments on the continent to prioritise economic development. They maintained that, as a response to historical underdevelopment, the new independent states required strong leadership to bring about modernisation. Africa, in this respect, could not afford the 'short-termist' policies and resource bargaining that multi-party competition encourages. Strategic economic management, and strong direction from the state, were required instead. Again, this would best be achieved within a one-party system.

Unity, lack of opposition, tradition and the imperatives of economic development, then, were put forward as justifications for the creation of the one-party state. Even today, many of these arguments deserve respect. Yet it has to be said that the one-party state's performance in Africa leaves a lot to be desired. Justifications offered have not been confirmed by results. Even when it is taken into account that each single-party structure was unique, each functioning in a different political environment, several common flaws can be found regarding this political experiment. This explains why, in the 1990s, popular pressure forced the vast majority of African states to abandon their one-party structures, and return instead to multi-party elections as the basis of government (as we will see in Chapter 11).

The problem with the one-party state was that, in practice, this system reduced links between the state and civil society, and between governors and governed generally. The main function of a party in a political system is to act as an intermediary. Leaders use party institutions to remain in touch with the people, while civil society utilises party structures in order to channel their demands through to the political elite. Where leaders consistently fail to respond to the demands of society, then accountability is lost.

In the first few decades of independence, as a consequence of the lack of open political competition, many politicians and bureaucrats took their privileged position for granted. Indeed, with no rival parties threatening to replace them, these elites abused their position within the state. The previous chapter, for example, showed how single-party structures encouraged corruption and the formation of an exploitative bureaucratic bourgeoisie. Multi-party competition could have potentially broken the monopoly of this ruling elite. New ideas and new personnel could have been introduced through competitive elections. Such non-violent regime change, however, simply did not occur in post-colonial Africa. In the absence of competitive elections, political succession – if there was any – was confined to *coups d'état*. No other channels of conflict resolution were open to dissenting individuals and movements.

The arguments for one-party rule in Africa become even less convincing when it is considered how these parties actually fared in the post-colonial political environment. Instead of being key institutions at the heart of the nation-building project, binding state and civil society together, most of them atrophied after independence. Following the general trend of the centralisation of the state, the power that parties had enjoyed during the anti-colonial campaign diminished. This power was transferred from the party to the core executive, following the party leaders themselves as they took up their positions within the new independent state. In this respect, single parties rarely became central institutions of policy making in post-colonial Africa. Instead, they were manipulated from above, degenerating into political machines.

It was not just the power of parties, however, that was usurped by this political elite operating at the apex of the executive. African parliaments, local government and judicial branches also became subordinate to the executive.

The subordination of 'peripheral' state institutions to the core executive

Parliaments all around the world have lost a degree of power to their executives in the twentieth century. In post-colonial Africa, however, this power loss was extreme. Most of the continent's national assemblies became mere appendages to their executives during this period.

The restriction of the Kenyan parliament proves an interesting illustration of this process. Between independence in 1963 and constitutional amendments that made Kenya a one-party state in 1982, there were relatively competitive elections for members of parliament. This was despite the fact that the Kenya African National Union (KANU) was the sole active political party for much of this period, making Kenya a *de facto* one-party state.

KANU members would compete among themselves to have their name put forward as an official KANU candidate, and thus the uncontested MP for a particular constituency. Although KANU's Executive Committee had a final veto, and candidates had to swear allegiance to the party, its policies and the president, any Kenyan was eligible to stand for election to Parliament. These primary elections proved to be genuinely competitive. In the 1969 contest, for example, 77 incumbent MPs were defeated, including five ministers and 14 assistant ministers.[4] By comparison, fewer incumbents are removed in most US elections.

African one-party structures, however, simply did not offer the level of choice that Western electorates enjoy. Even in countries such as Kenya and Tanzania, where elections were more open, African parliamentary candidates rarely stood on issues or policies. They failed to offer choice between political alternatives. This was not possible, after all, since political decision-making only took place in the higher echelons of the executive, and not in parliament. As Goran Hyden and Colin Leys remarked in their study of the 1969 Kenyan General Election, 'It is very difficult to identify any policy decision or legislative act which is traceable to the electoral outcome.'[5] Certainly there was a greater degree of linkage where more open one-party elections were held, but even here civil society's influence on public policy was limited. Instead, voters were looking for lobbyists who could secure state resources for their constituency, keeping the resource 'tap' turned on, and 'the life chances flowing'.[6] If this candidate failed to win these resources, then the electorate would vote for an alternative candidate in the next primary election (hence the large turnover of personnel in Kenya's 1969 poll). Linkage, however, was limited to the local accountability of MPs to their constituents, judged on this ability to secure resources.

In this respect, executives retained a monopoly over political activity within their societies. On the rare occasions that MPs did challenge the executive, they often found themselves in danger. As such, it was advisable for MPs to concentrate on local resource issues, rather than wider national or international affairs. One MP who did challenge the presidential elite was Kenya's

J M Kariuki. After he died in suspicious circumstances in 1975, the Kenyan Parliament went against the wishes of the executive by mounting its own investigation into the role of the security forces in Kariuki's death. President Jomo Kenyatta responded by dismissing those junior ministers who supported the investigation, while the ringleaders of this parliamentary 'revolt' were promptly detained. Subsequently, the executive made sure the Kenyan parliament was never to exercise this level of independence again, and Kenyatta's successor, Daniel arap Moi, confirmed this position when he altered the constitution and made Kenya a *de jure* one-party state in 1982.

Of all the liberal democratic institutions that African states inherited after independence, local government structures were the most established. This was because several of the imperial powers favoured indirect rule, and as part of the decolonisation process most encouraged local democracy as a stepping-stone to full self-determination. Often, colonial administrators would grant local autonomy to nationalists in order to delay giving full independence to the territory. After independence, however, the strength of local democracy on the continent declined precipitously.

The problem with this form of governing was that it involved distributing political authority horizontally, rather than hierarchically. Given that in a centralised state leaders will not tolerate uncontrolled concentrations of political power outside core institutions, local government was doomed. Consequently, locally elected and accountable institutions were removed, substituted by officers and agencies directly controlled by the centre. In this respect, local *government* was replaced by local *administration*. Issues such as education, health, road maintenance and the collection of taxes were all now overseen by regional administrators who reported to, and took orders from, their superiors in the state capital. As a result, national rather than local initiatives came to dominate, while local communities had little influence over the policy-making process. The executive, again, was in the driving seat.

Just as parties, legislatures and local government lost power to the executive in post-colonial Africa, so did the judicial branch of government. In legal-rational states, although most courts do not have official policy-making roles, they are still powerful institutions. They gain their authority from their function of maintaining the rule of law. All within society, including the law-makers themselves, have to respect the courts' judgments. Even the judiciary, however, was sidelined by the centralised African state. In a political environment where executives were so powerful, laws became arbitrary. Politicians and bureaucrats felt disinclined to obey the constitution, if their private interests were threatened. Laws became less binding on those who ran the state, while those in civil society were still expected to conform. Indeed, some leaders blatantly took the law into their own hands, paying little heed at all to the statute book. Idi Amin's Uganda, Jean-Bédel Bokassa's Central African Republic and Macías Nguema's Equatorial Guinea were extreme examples of this, but even in states where leaders were more constitutionally minded, the executive still tended to find ways to ensure that the judicial branch did not interfere with 'political' matters.

With this centralisation of power in the hands of the core executive, in many senses independent African states had reverted to the hierarchical, centralised and autocratic model of government found earlier under imperial rule. Government was controlled from the centre, and civil society played little part in the formal political process. Yet post-colonial Africa was different from imperial rule in one vital respect: the continent was now governed by *personal* (rather than institutional) rule, combined with *clientelism* to retain legitimacy within the political system. The rest of this chapter will explain these two terms in more detail.

Personal rule

Colonialism brought 'legal-rational' *institutional* states to Africa. Within this form of political order, offices and institutions are established, based on legal authority, to carry out the functions of government. Civil society supports these institutions as they follow patterns of accepted rules. Both those in government, and those in wider society, know where they stand. Each side abides by clearly defined laws and practices, and the entire governing process gains predictability. In short, institutional norms take precedence over personal whims, and this is where legitimacy is generated.

There is also a clear distinction between private and public roles within a legal-rational system of government. It is illegal, or at least immoral, for the private interests of officials to interfere with their public duties. The public interest is paramount. In this respect, Max Weber declared this institutional legal-rational model as the most efficient form of government.[7]

Yet, as has been seen, post-colonial African states do not always follow this legal-rational pattern. The rule of law is not always guaranteed, and many public officials use their position within the state to serve their own, and not just the public, interest. In this sense, African politics more often resemble the environment described in Machiavelli's *The Prince* or Hobbes's *Leviathan*, rather than Montesquieu's *Spirit of the Laws*. This does not necessarily mean, however, that African societies are anarchic. Political order and legitimacy do still exist in Africa, it is just of a different type. Given this failure of legal-rational institutions in post-colonial Africa, Africanists have attempted to explain the continent's politics in terms of *personal rule*.

Patrimonialism is similar to personal rule. It is a form of political order where power is concentrated in the personal authority of one individual ruler. The leader gains this position from their status in society. He or she may be bound by traditions or customs, but there are no legal-rational constraints on government. The leader is above the law, and indeed often *makes* the law by personal decree. In this respect, patrimonial leaders treat all political and administrative concerns of state as their own personal affairs. The state is their private property, and the act of ruling is, consequently, quite arbitrary.

No system of government can be managed by just one person, however, but instead of building legal-rational institutions to carry out the duties of the state, patrimonial leaders distribute offices as patronage among close relatives, friends and clients. As a result, all these lesser officials have to demonstrate personal loyalty to the leader in order to maintain office. In this respect, clients are retainers tied to their benefactor, rather than salaried officials serving the government institutions in which they are employed. Loyalty to the leader brings rewards. Clients are free to exploit their position of authority, creating their own fiefdoms. Historical examples of patrimonialism include the monarchical and religious states of medieval and early modern Europe.[8]

It is true that many characteristics of patrimony can be readily identified in post-colonial Africa. Yet it cannot be said that these African regimes were purely patrimonial. Patrimony derives from tradition, and legal-rational institutions will play no part in this form of political order. By contrast, legal-rational institutions may have been weak in post-colonial Africa, but they did still exist and function (as any modern state requires). As this is the case, independent African politics should be seen as a fusion between patrimonialism and legal-rational institutions. Private interests are pursued within a political structure that has a legal-rational façade. In this sense, the modern African state is the domain of the president-monarch rather than a purely patrimonial figure. Christopher Clapham is therefore correct when he suggests that the term *neo-patrimonialism* is more accurate.[9] Robert Jackson and Carl Rosberg prefer to use a completely separate phrase, and talk of post-colonial Africa being dominated by 'personal rule'.[10]

The characteristics of personal rule

African personal rule can be characterised as authoritarian, arbitrary, ostentatious and inefficient. It has produced fragile governments, even in states where presidential-monarchs have reigned for decades. This personalised political system has also created administration that is based on factions, rather than institutions and officials working together. It is worth taking the time to look at each of these characteristics a little more closely.

The vast majority of African leaders in the period since independence have achieved high office either by being in the vanguard of their country's nationalist movement, or by leading military coups. As such, many regarded themselves as the 'father' of their nation, and such self-perception encouraged these leaders to act as if they were above the law. Authoritarianism is very much a characteristic of personal rule. Above all, to protect their own position, presidential-monarchs frequently resorted to the coercive resources of the state. Individual challengers were intimidated, or even assassinated, by the security forces, while group challenges were countered by bannings, harassment, election manipulation and the withholding of state resources from regions where dissidents drew their support.

Personal rule also brought continuity to Africa's leadership. By contrast to legal-rational systems, where leaders tend to change at regular intervals, more permanent 'Big Men' were the feature of post-colonial Africa. Presidential-monarchs often ruled for more than a decade. Skilful politicians such as Tunisia's Bourguiba, Congo-Kinshasa's Mobutu, Malawi's Banda, Côte d'Ivoire's Houphouët-Boigny, Zambia's Kaunda, Tanzania's Nyerere, Kenya's Kenyatta and Moi, Liberia's Tubman and Zimbabwe's Mugabe (the list goes on) were the key political influence within their respective countries during the first few decades of independence. Only in the late 1980s and the 1990s, when old age and the arrival of multi-party elections began to take their toll on the Big Men, was this longevity of personal rule broken.

Personal rule is also often ostentatious. In the West, attempts are made to distinguish between the individual and the office they hold. In Africa, no such effort was made. Presidential-monarchs linked their private interests and their public interests, and many sought to display the wealth they had accumulated as a result of high office. Consequently, African leaders operated in a world of private jets, motorcades, limousines, palatial residences and ceremony. In two more extreme cases, Félix Houphouët-Boigny made his home village of Yamoussoukro the capital of Côte d'Ivoire, building a US$360 million cathedral in the process, while Jean-Bédel Bokassa spent US$20 million on his own coronation as Emperor of the Central African Republic (bankrupting the state in the process). Symbols of the president are also important. As well as the leader's photograph, and a report of his movements (however inconsequential) appearing in the press on a regular basis, portraits will be displayed in prominent public places, as in well as private homes. T-shirts and posters will be produced featuring the image of the president, stadiums, schools and hospitals will be named after him, and, all in all, nobody will be left in any doubt about who actually runs the country.

Personal rule is also arbitrary. As Weber observed of patrimonial leaders, neo-patrimonial autocrats may also 'refuse to be bound by formal rules, even those that they have made themselves'.[11] The rule of law cannot be taken for granted in such political systems. Post-colonial African leaders ignored rules, bent rules, and made new rules to serve their own interests. The rules of the game were often changed overnight. In this manner, opposition forces, as well as the presidential-monarch's own followers, were kept off-balance, while the leader himself was free to satisfy his own personal whims. As a result, African politics were somewhat unpredictable. The whole of society was denied the security that alternative constitutional (legal-rational) systems produced.

Another characteristic of personal rule is that it encourages competition among intra-governmental factions. In their seminal study of personal power in Africa, Jackson and Rosberg describe how this system 'is a dynamic world of political will and action that is ordered less by institutions than by personal authorities and power; a world of stratagem and countermeasure, of action and reaction, but without the assured mediation and regulation of effective political institutions. Political power is capable of being checked and stalemated in Africa, as elsewhere, but less by institutions than by countervailing power.'[12]

This breeds a political environment of factionalism, schisms, purges and coups. Groups will jockey for position under the leader, offering support in return for resources and patronage, but if the leader is perceived to be weak, then these previously loyal lieutenants will not hesitate to challenge the president's authority. Many African states suffered when this personalised rivalry failed to be contained within the political system. Competition spilt over into instability and violence, where the military was often the beneficiary by staging a *coup d'état*. Even the longest-serving presidential-monarch is vulnerable to this factional competition, should it get out of hand.

Yet, it is often in the leaders' interests to foster controlled factional rivalry. If they are distracted by competition, the lower political ranks cannot mount a challenge for the ultimate prize, the presidency itself. President Mobutu Sese Seko of Congo-Kinshasa was the master at seeing off potential competitors and managing his 'courtiers' to his own ends. Richard Sandbrook wrote of Mobutu's reign, 'No potential challenger is permitted to gain a power base. Mobutu's officials know that their jobs depend solely on the President's discretion. Frequently, he fires cabinet ministers, often without explanation. He appoints loyal army officers and other faithfuls as provincial governors, but only to provinces outside their home areas. And he constantly reshuffles and purges his governors and high army command. Everyone is kept off balance. Everyone must vie for his patronage. Mobutu holds all the cards and the game is his.'[13] It took 22 years before Mobutu was finally deposed.

Above all, personal rule breeds inefficiency. As we saw in Chapter 4 on ethnicity, African administrations tend to allocate resources on the basis of demand, not need. Personal rule contributes to this problem. Powerful factions will receive control over the lion's share of the state's resources, leaving less-well-represented groups at a disadvantage. Similarly, public policy receives little feedback or scrutiny under a system of personal rule. There is little incentive to evaluate policy systematically in a country where success or failure is neither rewarded nor punished by an electorate. Indeed, nobody is in a position to challenge the presidential-monarch's chosen policy path anyway. To leave the final words of this assessment of personal rule to Jackson and Rosberg: 'the concept of governance as an activity of guiding the ship of state toward a specific destination – the assumption of modern rationalism and the policy sciences – fits poorly with much political experience in contemporary Black African countries. In African countries governance is more a matter of seamanship and less one of navigation – that is, staying afloat rather than going somewhere.'[14]

The search for legitimacy

Even in a neo-patrimonial state led by personal rule, however, legitimacy has to be generated. Political authority cannot rest on coercion alone. Bokassa, Amin and Macías Nguema came closest to attempting this, in the Central African Republic, Uganda and Equatorial Guinea respectively. They ruled by confiscation rather than conciliation, but even here the utility of violence had its limitations.[15] It was a case of diminishing returns. Violence is very effective in the short term, but over longer periods of time, coercion only stimulates opposition and counter-violence. Therefore the skilful personal ruler uses a combination of coercion *and* legitimacy in order to maintain government and social order.

Yet how is this legitimacy generated? Weber's pure sources of legitimacy only tell part of the story. Legal-rationalism is limited because of the neo-patrimonial nature of the state. Charisma is more of a factor, with Africans deferring to the 'Big Men' and the ideologies of nationalism they preached, but, again, this alone did not produce enough support. In the final analysis, it was material provision that contributed most to legitimising Africa's one-party states. Personal rulers relied on the distribution of state resources in order to 'buy' legitimacy for their regimes. As long as patrons could nourish their followers, through the manipulation of public goods and institutions, then they were safe. It was rewards for clients, therefore, distributed through the mechanism of *clientelism*, that became the key substitute for the legitimacy lost after Africa's independent liberal democratic institutions were dismantled, and personal rule was installed.

Clientelism

Christopher Clapham describes clientelism as 'a relation of exchange between unequals'.[16] It is a mutually beneficial association between the powerful and the weak. A patron extends public office (a salary and access to the state), security (something akin to the freedom from arbitrary violence), and resources (such as wells, roads and medical centres) to his or her clients. In return, the client offers support and deference that helps legitimise the patron's elevated position. In this respect, clientelism is a form of political contract.

Clientelism has permeated African societies from top to bottom. It is not just a case of presidential-monarchs exchanging patronage for support among their immediate lieutenants within the heart of the state. There is a whole chain of patron–client networks that spread out from this point. This web connects the president, through numerous links down the chain, to the lowly peasant. Each client uses the resources received from the patron above them to build their own patronage empire. Individuals therefore simultaneously act as a client of a superior, and as a patron to those below them. For example, the presidential-monarch is the patron to his or her lieutenants, but the lieutenants use a proportion of this patronage to recruit clients of their own, among middle-ranking bureaucrats. These middle-ranking state officials, in turn, have clients lower down the administrative hierarchy. The chain of clients and patrons extends all the way down to local patrons, who may have a particular village as their client base. In this respect, clientelist networks are 'vertical threads' binding whole societies together which, in turn, create political stability and order.[17]

Clientelism is particularly important in Africa as it provides political channels that are absent elsewhere in society. In an environment where personal rulers hold a monopoly on formal political activity, and all independent political associations are banned, client–patron networks do represent a limited form of political exchange. They help bring civil society back into the political arena to a small degree. These client–patron networks are tolerated by the elite, as the whole mechanism is reliant on the presidential-monarch providing the largest input of state resources. It is the ultimate 'trickle-down' system in this respect. The leader relies on the network to ensure that his patronage permeates through the whole of society. The more people who feel that they benefit from this political system, the more legitimacy and support the regime receives.

Legitimacy founded on patronage, however, is fragile. Although clientelism avoids violence, and is mutually beneficial to the two parties concerned, it is nevertheless an asymmetric contract. The whole relationship is forged on the recognition and acceptance that there is inequality between the two parties. Patrons will retain as much wealth as possible for themselves, only passing on the resources they consider necessary to keep clients loyal. In post-colonial Africa, resource distribution was usually kept to a minimum. This was because there was no alternative political market where clients could maximise their rewards by selling their loyalty to the highest bidder (as could happen under multi-party competition). One-party states rarely tolerated alternative opposition politicians who could have served as these competing patrons. As a result, most Africans in the first few decades of independence settled for trying to get what they could out of the existing patrons. The alternative path of contesting the *status quo* was too costly. Clients would risk losing out entirely if they challenged their existing patrons. Clientelism thus provided stability and legitimacy in post-colonial Africa. Yet this system of legitimacy relied too heavily on material provision. As will be seen in Chapter 10, once the patronage began to dry up due to economic difficulties in the 1980s and 1990s, so did the legitimacy supporting personal rule. Without the distribution of resources, presidential-monarchs could no longer offer African peasants any reason to support them, apart from the threat of violence.

State and civil society

In terms of this book's underlying theme, the process of centralisation clearly advantaged the state at the expense of civil society. Gone were the pluralist institutions left by the imperial powers at decolonisation. Power was drained from civil society and 'peripheral' institutions of the state, and amassed instead within the core executive. This would be the foundation on which presidential-monarchs would exercise their personal rule.

Africa's neo-patrimonial political structures did, however, maintain a modern state system after independence. Several countries did occasionally descend into periods of chaos and anarchy, but, on the whole, Africans lived under governments that offered a degree of stability and order. Indeed, in societies where national identities were fragile and resources scarce, it was argued that a highly centralised state was appropriate. Leaders reasoned 'alien' liberal democratic institutions would most likely only serve to tear apart the freedom and self-determination that Africans had won at independence. Under a centralised system, fragmented societies could be bound together, enabling all to enjoy the benefits of the modern state.

These benefits, however, failed to materialise. Civil society was particularly disadvantaged. Indeed, all alternative political mobilisation was promptly co-opted or brutally crushed. The patronage offered in lieu of this civil society representation was flawed. Clientelism did not work without the exploitation of clients by patrons. The political elite, in this respect, preyed on the vulnerability of their people. Patrons distributed some of their wealth into the network, but the priority was to serve their own personal needs first. The state bureaucracy prospered while civil society remained constrained. It was not a relationship of equal exchange.

The centralised state also failed to produce consistently strong government. Healthy states reflect the needs of their people, and seek advice and expertise from civil society. Conversely, centralised states *destroy* many of their links with society. Institutions that could have provided advice and feedback on policy, suggesting alternative approaches, as well as acting as a safety valve for dissent, were dismantled soon after independence. Instead, core executive institutions, and their leaders, relied on their own counsel and expertise. This is how the most powerful personnel at the heart of the African state often lost touch with their people. The gulf between state and civil society grew.

In states blessed with a sufficient resource base, such a gulf between the rulers and the ruled may not have been a problem. Resources could have been provided through client–patron networks to offset any misgivings Africans may have had about their governments. In a continent, however, where resources are limited, this lack of linkage between state and civil society often proved fatal. Inefficient and corrupt regimes that did not have the resources to 'buy off' civil society experienced regular crises of legitimacy. Coercion could be used to plug this 'legitimacy gap', but even with this violence, African governments were not always successful in hanging on to power. In this respect, witness the number of military coups on the continent.

By the end of the 1980s, the game was up. As a consequence of economic failure, there were no longer enough resources to maintain requisite levels of legitimacy in these neo-patrimonial African states. Patron–client networks shrank, and as a consequence some territories spiralled into state collapse. In others, presidential-monarchs attempted to liberalise their regimes. Multi-party competition was re-introduced in a last ditch effort to retain power (see Chapter 11). The era of the centralised state and personal rule, at least in its extreme form, was now at an end.

Case study: personal rule in Côte d'Ivoire

Côte d'Ivoire is home to some 14 million people in West Africa. Located on the Gulf of Guinea, its environment ranges from lagoons on the Atlantic coast and rainforest in the south, to plains in the north. After being formally colonised by the French in 1893, this territory gained its independence in 1960. The most striking feature of Côte d'Ivoire in the post-colonial period has been its economic growth. The country outstripped the performance of most of its neighbours, and was second on the continent only to South Africa in the per-capita income it raised. This Ivorian 'economic miracle', however, became somewhat tarnished in the 1980s and 1990s as a result of unstable cocoa and coffee prices.

Politically, the first three decades of independence in Côte d'Ivoire were dominated by one individual, Félix Houphouët-Boigny. He was the focus of all state activity, masterminding the centralisation of the state. Houphouët-Boigny exercised personal rule from the office of the president, gaining legitimacy for his regime through a complex patron–client network that cast his influence into all areas of Ivorian society.

Preparations for the one-party state started early. The *Parti Démocratique de la Côte d'Ivoire* (PDCI) purposefully went about absorbing significant opposition groups into its ranks between 1952 and 1957. Consequently, the PDCI became Côte d'Ivoire's ruling party when it won a large majority at the independence elections. It was helped by the fact that the electoral system involved only single (national) party lists. There were no regional constituencies which would have allowed smaller, ethnically mobilised parties to establish a regional power base. Instead, each party had to compete for electoral support nationally. The PDCI leadership also kept secret who had been selected as official candidates from among its ranks until just before polling day. This ensured that rejected nominees would not stand as independent candidates, or collectively organise as a separate opposition party.

The PDCI followed classic tactics of establishing a one-party state. It absorbed elements that could challenge its political monopoly, while, at the same time, eliminating lesser sources of opposition through electoral manipulation and intimidation. However, once the PDCI had successfully mobilised mass nationalist opposition against colonial rule, and had then seen off any residual opposition after independence (creating a *de facto* one-party state), Houphouët-Boigny let the PDCI atrophy. Elections for party posts became increasingly infrequent, while little effort was directed at maintaining the PDCI's links with the Ivorian people at a grass-roots level. Indeed, party structures degenerated into sources of patronage, rather than serving as a link between the governed and the governor. As the *Africa Contemporary Record* reported in the early 1970s, the PDCI acted as a kind of House of Lords, where the old party faithful could be retired with dignity and a source of income, but without extending them too much political power.[18] Indeed, of the PDCI's members, only the elite leadership within the Political Bureau retained any real power, and this bureau consisted of Houphouët-Boigny's trusted lieutenants who already occupied high office within the core executive. In this respect, the PDCI was following the path of many African nationalist movements after independence. The party was becoming, in Frantz Fanon's phrase, a 'skeleton of its former self'.[19]

Côte d'Ivoire displayed all the characteristics of a centralised state between 1960 and 1990. Any source of opposition was rapidly absorbed if possible, or suppressed if not. Houphouët-Boigny declared that 'competition is healthy for sport, but in politics, what must triumph is team spirit'.[20] In this respect, no independent source of political power was allowed to develop. Associations within civil society, for example, were either co-opted or dismantled by the state. Trade union leaders, for instance, were given positions in the government, but labour campaigners who continued to operate outside the state were imprisoned. Similarly, the PDCI's youth wing co-opted organisations of younger Ivorians, while traditional leaders were urged to join the *Syndicat des Chefs Coutumiers* (a state-sponsored talking shop with Houphouët-Boigny as its honorary president).[21] The banner used as a backdrop at the PDCI's first conference after independence summed up the Ivorian political environment well. It read, 'A single party, for a single people, with a single leader.'[22]

The legislative and judicial branches of government, as well as local government, also lost out to the core executive as a result of Houphouët-Boigny's centralisation of the state. Local councils fell into disuse, replaced by regional administrations directed from the centre. Similarly, the National Assembly became more a forum to legitimate Houphouët-Boigny's policy choices, rather than an institution willing to debate and resolve differences over public programmes. Following this pattern, the judiciary was also usurped, in this case by the establishment of special courts to hear political cases. The level of judicial independence that these courts observed can be judged by the fact that these trials took place in the president's own residence.

At the epicentre of this centralised political system was Félix Houphouët-Boigny himself. He did not relinquish this personal control over the PDCI, and his private monopoly over Côte d'Ivoire politics in general, until his death in 1993. Jackson and Rosberg described Houphouët-Boigny as an 'anti-politician'. This is because he was a ruler who attempted to remove politics from the public realm, while simultaneously holding a personal stranglehold on the political power that remained.[23] Any individuals occupying a position in the state below the president were merely Houphouët-Boigny's personal administrators and clients. As such, politicians or bureaucrats that sought high office in Côte d'Ivoire could only achieve this with Houphouët-Boigny's explicit approval. The president's lieutenants would be issued conditional licences to do his bidding. They used Houphouët-Boigny's patronage to build their own empires and client bases, but if they failed to serve the leader loyally, then they would soon lose their position and the wealth it generated.

Indeed, Houphouët-Boigny's court was a very tight-knit community. Many individuals held interlocking posts within the three key institutions of state: the PDCI's Political Bureau, the National Assembly, and the Economic and Social Council. Tessilimi Bakary has calculated that just 320 individuals held 1,040 positions within these institutions between 1957 and 1980.[24] As every young Ivorian knew, the chances of being adopted by the system, and maybe even reaching the higher echelons of the executive, was only possible if they conformed to the rules of the political game. Above all, loyalty had to be expressed at all times to the paramount patron, Houphouët-Boigny himself.

This is where Houphouët-Boigny gained his legitimacy. After all, the Ivorian state offered very little to civil society by way of legal-rational institutions. Democratic structures had been dismantled and public participation in the policy process curtailed. Instead, Houphouët-Boigny's system of personal rule relied on distributing rewards for continued political support. In this respect, the president believed that patronage, funded from economic growth, could be a substitute for political participation. Legitimacy would come from material provision. Hence, Houphouët-Boigny placed himself at the apex of a client–patron network that permeated deep into Ivorian society. The longevity of Houphouët-Boigny's regime (1960–93) can be largely explained by the presidential-monarch's ability to maintain these networks.

Perhaps the most obvious evidence of Houphouët-Boigny's patronage system can be seen at a local level. State resources were offered to local communities who supported the president. After a period of transient political dissent elsewhere, the town of Adjamé, for example, received a publicly funded marketplace in the mid-1960s. At the market's opening ceremony, Minister of State Auguste Denise thanked the local population, on behalf of 'our president, the government, and the political directors of the Party' for the loyalty they had shown during this wave of anti-government protests.[25] Similarly, the annual independence celebration, the Fête Nationale de l'Indépendance, was moved each year in order to reward, or seek favour from, a particular region.[26] Of course, for a local community to really benefit, they had to promote one of their number into the cabinet itself. Ministers of Construction and Town-Planning, for example, frequently awarded their home towns lucrative development schemes.[27] It was Houphouët-Boigny's own village of Yamoussoukro, however, that benefited the most. It became Côte d'Ivoire's capital, and the location for the president's own gift to his country, a multi-million franc basilica, which, when constructed, was the largest church in the world.

Towards the end of Houphouët-Boigny's life, however, more and more Ivorians began to demand representation from their state. Patronage could no longer buy off this more coherent challenge to personal rule. The people of Côte d'Ivoire joined civil societies elsewhere on the continent in demanding a return to multi-party democracy in the late 1980s and the 1990s. This was a direct consequence of poor economic performance, resulting in shrinking client–patron networks.

Houphouët-Boigny at first, as he had since 1960, argued that multi-party competition could not come to Côte d'Ivoire until the nation was fully united. In 1985, however, political liberalisation began. Open competition was allowed for PDCI National Assembly nominations. The campaign for multi-party democracy expanded, however, and by 1990, Houphouët-Boigny had been forced to compete in his first multi-party contest for the post of president (after holding this office for thirty years). Although he won this poll by a landslide margin, confirming his position as the paramount patron and presidential-monarch, the centralised state had been weakened and notions of legal-rational legitimacy advanced. Houphouët-Boigny's death in 1993 was itself symbolic, perhaps marking the beginning of the end for personal rule in Africa.

Côte d'Ivoire[28]

Territory:	322,465 sq km	Population:	15.3 million
Colonial power:	France	Independence:	1960
Major cities:	Abidjan	Ethnic groups:	Akan
	Bouaké		Volaïque
	Daloa		Mane Nord
Urban pop.:	45.3%		Krou
Languages:	French	Life expectancy:	50 years
	Baoule	Adult literacy:	40.1%
	Dioula	Exports:	Cocoa
	Bete		Timber
Currency:	CFA franc		Coffee
Infant mortality:	86 deaths/thousand births		Cotton
Religion:	Traditional	External debt:	US$19,713 million
	Christian	GDP per capita:	US$685

Glossary of key terms

Centralisation of the state	The process whereby power is drained from civil society and 'peripheral' institutions of the state, and concentrated instead within the core executive.
Clientelism	A largely instrumental political relationship between an individual of higher socio-economic status (the patron) who uses his own influence and resources to provide protection or benefits, or both, for a person of lower status (the client) who, for their part, reciprocates by offering general support and assistance to the patron.[29]
Client–patron network	The series of vertical links that bind patron and client, where the client of one patron often commands their own patronage network lower down the chain.
Legal-rational political order	Political authority built on impersonal state institutions which rule respecting acknowledged patterns of rules.
Legitimacy	A psychological relationship between the governed and their governors which engenders a belief that the state's leaders and

institutions have a right to exercise political authority over the rest of society.

Neo-patrimonial rule — Where patrimonial rule (see below) is exercised through the remnants of legal-rational institutions.

One-party state — Where formal political mobilisation is channelled through a single state-sponsored party.

Personal rule — A system of government where one individual, commanding the heights of state institutions and patron–client networks, enjoys a virtual monopoly on all formal political activity within a territory.

Patrimonial rule — Political authority based on an individual, where the state itself, and the affairs of state, are the personal interests of the ruler. All within this political system owe their position and loyalty to the one leader.

Questions raise by this chapter

1 Were African leaders justified in centralising their states and imposing one-party rule?

2 How democratic were the more open parliamentary elections found in states such as Kenya and Tanzania?

3 Why did local government and independent judiciaries not prosper in Africa's centralised states?

4 Was African personal rule an efficient form of government?

5 To what extent did clientelism legitimate personal rule in post-colonial Africa?

Further reading

Two books well worth reading on the centralisation of the African state and the move to one-party rule are Aristide Zolberg's *Creating Political Order* and James Coleman and Carl Rosberg's edited book. These two volumes, although slightly out of date now, give a flavour of events and the debate held at this time. For a more institutional and specialised look at government within the one-party state, Philip Mawhood's *Local Government in the Third World* is an interesting read.

The seminal volume on personal rule in Africa is Robert Jackson and Carl Rosberg's aptly named *Personal Rule in Black Africa*. Robert Fatton (Chapter 3) and Richard Sandbrook (Chapter 5) also make some useful points on this phenomenon in their more general books on African politics. In terms of a country study, the African one-party state and personal rule is analysed eloquently by Crawford Young and Thomas Turner's work on Zaire.

For those interested in the concepts of legitimacy and client–patron networks, Max Weber's work on legitimacy is still fascinating (pp.324–92), while a good starting point for further reading on clientelism is Christopher Clapham's edited book *Private Patronage and Public Power*.

Clapham, Christopher, ed. (1982) *Private patronage and public power*, London: Pinter.

Coleman, James S and Carl G Rosberg, eds (1970) *Political parties and national integration in Tropical Africa*, Berkeley: University of California Press.

Fatton, Robert (1992) *Predatory rule: state and civil society in Africa*, Boulder, CO: Lynne Rienner.

Jackson, Robert H and Carl G Rosberg (1982) *Personal rule in Black Africa: prince, autocrat, prophet, tyrant*, Berkeley: University of California Press.

Mawhood, Philip, ed. (1983) *Local government in the Third World: the experience of tropical Africa*, Chichester: John Wiley.

Sandbrook, Richard (1985) *The politics of Africa's economic stagnation*, Cambridge: Cambridge University Press.

Weber, Max [Talcott Parsons, ed.] (1964) *The theory of social and economic organization*, New York: Free Press.

Young, Crawford and Thomas Turner (1985) *The rise and decline of the Zairian state*, Madison: University of Wisconsin Press.

Zolberg, Aristide R (1966) *Creating political order: the party-states of West Africa*, Chicago: Rand McNally.

7 Coercion

Military intervention in African politics

A state's very existence rests on its authority. Where sufficient authority is present, citizens believe it is in their interests to respect state institutions and conform to their laws. The result is a stable political order where individuals defer to their government. Conversely, if a state loses its authority, confusion reigns, and established channels of conflict resolution decay. Groups take advantage of this situation, and compete with the failing elite, and with each other, in their attempts to mould a new political order. Indeed, such an environment often results in the political process being abandoned altogether, with violence as a substitute.

Political authority stems from two basic sources: legitimate authority, and the power of coercion. The previous chapter discussed the concept of legitimacy, where citizens *voluntarily* defer to the state. As Max Weber pointed out, they may do this as a result of tradition, charismatic leadership, or as a mark of respect for legal-rational institutions.[1] In addition, legitimacy can also be enhanced by the state's provision of material goods and services (in Africa's case largely through client–patron networks). In short, individuals are persuaded to support the state due to the positive benefits this form of social organisation brings them.

The other side of the authority coin, however, is coercion. An application of violence increases the possibility that states can still retain control over civil society even when they lack legitimacy. In other words, the state's agencies of coercion can be unleashed against citizens in order to force them, rather than persuade them, to accept a certain political order. As civil society can rarely match these coercive resources, state violence, or the threat of violence, will result in citizens obeying their political rulers for fear of what would happen if they did not. Coercion can therefore be defined as *the use or threat of violence to achieve a political or social purpose*.

The reality is that all states use a combination of these two basic sources of authority. In the West, legitimate authority is relied upon far more than coercion, but even here coercion is still utilised as a tool of government. Armies, police forces, courts and prisons, for example, will all be used to deter and punish law-breakers. The rule of law has to be maintained, and, at times, violence may be required to ensure this. Elsewhere in the world, state coercion is more widespread, often being used to secure group interests rather than the national interest. The fact remains, however, that, whether they serve the many or the few, all states need institutions of coercion in order to preserve their authority.

This reality has proved to be of particular significance in the evolution of post-colonial African politics. Coercive agencies may be a necessity of government, but it is essential that the military and police, as the custodians of state violence, remain subservient to political leaders. This has not been the case in Africa. On numerous occasions, the soldiers have used their access to violence in order to instigate military *coups d'état*. In effect, those who were employed to manage violence on behalf of the state chose to turn this violence on the state itself, to capture political power for themselves.

Given the frequency of these military coups, any book introducing the politics of post-colonial Africa has a duty to analyse this intervention in detail, and this is the task of the current chapter. Structurally, three vital questions are asked: why have so many coups occurred; what problems arise when military, rather than civilian, personnel take up the reins of government; and what have been the outcomes of military rule? The answers to these three questions provide a comprehensive assessment of the impact that coercive agencies have had on African politics since independence. It will be seen how the military had few political rivals on the continent that could match their power. Yet, toppling the old regime proved much easier than establishing an effective new government. The military soon found out that, despite their resources of coercion, government cannot be based solely on the capacity to inflict violence. Coercion may result in a population's acquiescence in the short term, but a more stable political order requires the state to generate legitimate authority as well. Most of Africa's military governments failed to do this. Consequently, yet more political instability followed.

African military *coups d'état*

The military is an integral part of any government. Yet if it is necessary for states to have security forces, it is also imperative, in a democratic society, that the military should only act in the public interest. As soon as this immense power is used to further private interests, of the military itself or those of a ruling elite, then democracy is lost. Democratic (legal-rational) rules demand that the military is politically neutral, and its institutions are subordinate to civilian government.

Despite this professional ethic of non-intervention, all security forces participate in the political process to some degree. Even in democracies, high ranking officers are involved in making defence policy, as well as in budgetary matters concerning the funding of their forces. Similarly, liberal democracies have also seen members of the military attain high office (examples include US president Dwight Eisenhower and French president Charles de Gaulle). The difference between professional soldiers with political ambitions in the West and their African counterparts, however, is the fact that officers such as de Gaulle and

Eisenhower, before they took office, first resigned their military command. They then went on to participate in the electoral process. In effect, they relinquished their access to the coercive powers of the state before competing for political power. African coup leaders, by contrast, became heads of state illegally. Usually, their sole credential for gaining political power was the threat of violence they still retained as active military officers.

A military *coup d'état* can be defined as *a sudden illegal displacement of government in which members of the security forces play a prominent role.* Coups can be reactionary or revolutionary, bloody or bloodless. They must, however, be sudden, lasting a matter of hours or days, rather than weeks.[2] Military coups, in this respect, differ from other types of political succession. They should not be confused with regime change instigated by democratic election, foreign invasion, more widespread internal rebellion, or any combinations of these.

There were 71 military *coups d'état* in Africa between 1952 and 1990. These resulted in the toppling of governments in 60 per cent of the continent's states (see Table 7.1). Some of these countries, such as Cape Verde or Equatorial Guinea, experienced just one coup; most were subjected to two or three; while other states, such as Benin, Burkina Faso, Ghana and Nigeria, were locked into a regular rhythm of coup and counter-coup. Exaggerating, to reflect the mood of this era when military rule became the norm instead of the exception, US diplomat George Ball wrote in his memoirs: 'During the years I was in the State Department, I was awakened once or twice a month by a telephone call in the middle of the night announcing a coup d'état in some distant capital with a name like a typographical error.'[3] Relief from these military takeovers only came in the 1990s. During this decade, the number of coups reduced significantly, with regime change now more likely to be prompted by mass rebellion or democratic elections instead.

The pattern was familiar in the 1960s, 1970s and 1980s. A faction of the military, usually led by middle-ranking or junior officers (occasionally non-commissioned officers), would seize government buildings and communication centres, and then detain the president and the cabinet. Once these symbols of the state had been captured, the coup plotters would then use the radio station to broadcast to the nation. They explained how civilian corruption and ineptitude had made it their duty to intervene, and promised to withdraw to barracks as soon as military rule had restored a just and disciplined society. In this respect, African military coups were relatively peaceful affairs. Casualties were usually confined to the small participating factions, while many were entirely bloodless. This was simply because few in society were prepared to defend the outgoing, usually illegitimate, administrations. Other forms of regime change in Africa, insurgency campaigns or civil war for example (and even democratic elections), have often prompted far more violence. By comparison the military *coup d'état* was quick and simple: 'Get the keys to the armoury; turn out the barracks; take the radio station, the post office and the airport; [and] arrest the person of the president...'[4]

Table 7.1 African miltary coups since independence

State	Independence	1950s/1960s	1970s	1980s	1990s	Total
Algeria	1962	1965			1992	2
Angola	1975					0
Benin (Dahomey)	1960	1963, 1965, 1965, 1967, 1969	1972			6
Botswana	1966					0
Burkina Faso (Upper Volta)	1960	1966	1974	1980, 1982, 1983, 1987		6
Burundi	1962	1966	1976	1987	1996	4
Cameroon	1960					0
Cape Verde	1975					0
Central African Republic	1960	1965	1979	1981		3
Chad	1960		1975			1
The Comoros	1975		1975, 1978	1989	1999	4
Congo, DRC (Kinshasa) (Zaire)	1960	1965				1
Congo, Rep. (Brazzaville)	1960	1963, 1968	1977, 1979			4
Côte d'Ivoire	1960				1999	1
Djibouti	1977					0
Egypt	1922	1952, 1954				2
Equatorial Guinea	1968		1979			1
Eritrea	1993					0
Ethiopia	–		1974			1
Gabon	1960	1964				1
The Gambia	1965				1994	1
Ghana	1957	1966	1972, 1978, 1979	1981		5
Guinea	1958			1984		1
Guinea-Bissau	1974			1980	1999	2
Kenya	1963					0
Lesotho	1966			1986	1991, 1994	3
Liberia	1847			1980		1
Libya	1951	1969				1
Madagascar	1960		1972			1
Malawi	1964					0
Mali	1960	1968			1991	2
Mauritania	1960		1978	1980, 1984		3

Mauritius	1968					0
Morocco	1956					0
Mozambique	1975					0
Namibia	1990					0
Niger	1960		1974		1996	2
Nigeria	1960	1966, 1966	1975	1983, 1985	1993	6
Rwanda	1962		1973			1
São Tomé and Principe	1975				1995	1
Senegal	1960					0
Seychelles	1976		1977			1
Sierra Leone	1961	1967, 1968			1992, 1996, 1997	5
Somalia	1960	1969				1
South Africa	1910					0
Sudan	1956	1958, 1964, 1969		1985, 1989		5
Swaziland	1968					0
Tanzania	1964					0
Togo	1960	1963, 1967, 1967				3
Tunisia	1956					0
Uganda	1962		1971, 1979	1980, 1985		4
Zambia	1964					0
Zimbabwe	1980					0
Totals		29	22	20	15	86

Given the impact that the military has had on post-colonial African politics, it is right that this book should investigate these *coups d'état* in detail. However, it should also be noted that such an analysis does tend to mislead, bolstering a 'continent of coups' stereotype. The military may be influential in Africa, but at no time have they enjoyed a total, continent-wide monopoly over the political process. Sixty per cent of African states experienced military rule at some point between independence and 1990, but this obviously means that 40 per cent did not. Morocco and Mauritius, for example, have remained under civilian control for the entire post-colonial period, as have Kenya and Tanzania and the majority of Southern African states. Even those countries that did succumb to military rule often enjoyed long periods of civilian government, either prior to the takeover, as a result of it, or after the army had returned to barracks. The Gambia, for example, maintained a multi-party democracy for 30 years before a coup in 1994. In short, it should be borne in mind when reading this chapter that not all African countries are, or have been, the domain of a uniformed dictator.

Why has Africa experienced so many military coups?

All coups involve a short-circuit of the 'normal' political process, creating an opportunity for violence to become the deciding factor. The military takes advantage of this opportunity, and captures the state for itself. Drawing accurate comparisons beyond this simple reality, however, proves to be difficult. This is because every military *coup d'état* is different. They affect all forms of government (democracies, personal regimes, and even existing military administrations); they are a consequence of different motives (altruistic nationalism, selfish desire, or ideological zeal); and they result in numerous types of rule (autocratic/democratic, liberal/socialist, conservative/revolutionary, and many that defy simple categorisation). Yet, since military coups have influenced so many political systems across the globe, political scientists have tried hard to isolate common factors that lead to these regime displacements.

One such typology of *coups d'état* involves three categories: the 'guardian coup', the 'veto coup' and the 'breakthrough coup'.[5] A guardian coup is where the military intervenes in order to rescue the state from civilian mismanagement. The men in uniform consider it their duty to replace their incompetent civilian predecessors. Under the military 'guardians', corruption and inefficiency are targeted, and politicians of the old regime are purged. In many cases, the military then (eventually) live up to their promise of returning to barracks, once they consider discipline has returned to the political process. Despite this political upheaval, the 'guardians' usually leave society and the economy largely unchanged. Nigeria could be considered to have experienced several guardian coups in the post-colonial period.

Veto coups, on the other hand, are prompted by social changes that directly threaten the interests of the military and their allies. The security forces calculate that they cannot stand idly by while a new group in society takes over the state. This type of coup has been more common in Central and South America, where the military has prevented leftist movements from capturing state power, but Africa has examples too. The 1992 takeover in Algeria, for instance, can be classed as a veto coup. Here, the secular military intervened because it feared the outcome of multi-party elections. An Islamist movement was poised to win, and to form the next government. The military, concerned about its position within such a regime, opted to reduce this risk, and took power itself.

The last of these three broad categories is the breakthrough coup. This is where the military ousts an outdated (authoritarian or traditional) regime, seeking to change society entirely. The *coup d'état* becomes a revolutionary break from the past. In effect, the army becomes the 'vanguard' of this revolution. Ethiopia experienced a breakthrough coup in 1974, where the military, allied to other social movements, established a socialist state in the wake of Emperor Haile Selassie's 44 years of 'traditional' rule.

This simple typology of coups, however, has to be built upon. Political scientists have dug deeper in an attempt to explain why military takeovers occur, and two major schools of thought have come to dominate. The first group of scholars emphasise the state's socio-political environment. These 'environmentalists', such as Samuel Huntington and S E Finer, argue that *coups d'état* are most likely to occur in states lacking institutionalised political cultures, and which also suffer economic hardship and social division.[6] The second school of thought concentrates more on the organisational ability and character of the military itself. Academics such as Morris Janowitz point to the patriotism, discipline, professionalism and cohesion found at the heart of military service. He argues that these factors eventually compel soldiers to intervene to rid their state of inept and corrupt civilian governments.[7]

It seems very artificial to separate these two contributing factors. Military coups occurred in Africa, first because the socio-political environment encouraged this, and second because there existed on the continent military establishments which were organised and motivated enough to take advantage of this situation. What is more, patriotism and professionalism were not the sole determining factors. Soldiers also rebelled to further their *own* corporate and personal interests.

Ultimately, the military intervenes in the political process because it *can*. In terms of coercive power, soldiers control the most puissant institutions of the state. They are, after all, the individuals who have direct access to instruments of state violence. Many coups may be bloodless, but this should not disguise the fact that the military has the organisational ability and technology to take on any other group within the state, or, indeed, within civil society. Consequently, if the military is willing to use violence to secure political goals, then few can stand in its way. Yet this fact alone does not explain why military coups have occurred so often in Africa. Globally, the vast majority of modern states maintain armies, but only a few of these have broken their professional ethic of non-intervention.

This is why Huntington and Finer argue that the military not only needs the ability, but also the right socio-political environment, before it is persuaded to intervene. Particularly relevant, in this respect, is the fact that most African economies throughout the post-colonial period failed to meet expectations of development. This often left Africans discontented, and damaged levels of legitimacy. Ruth First, for example, argues that Kwame Nkrumah's regime was brought down by the plummeting price of cocoa in the mid-1960s, just as much as it was by Ghana's army and police force.[8] Similarly, social division, especially the ethnic and class conflicts, discussed earlier in Chapters 3 and 4, will also act to destabilise many African governments.

Then there is the question of political culture. Due to their social and economic problems, African states need strong institutions to contain the political conflict found on the continent. However, as we saw in the Chapter 6, African regimes tend more towards personal rule rather than legal-rational structures. Consequently, most Africans are excluded from the political process. This puts the continent into Finer's categorisation of 'minimal political culture', compared to the 'mature political cultures' of the West.[9] As such, African regimes are left particularly vulnerable to crises of legitimacy.

In the West, such crises see politicians resort to legal-rational channels of political renewal (a general election or national coalition government, maybe), but in Africa, with no electoral mechanisms available to ensure a stable change of government, non-violent regime renewal is unlikely. And as soon as violence becomes the defining mechanism of regime change, then the military, with its superior access to the resources of coercion, becomes a key political player. As Huntington argued, in a state lacking authority, competing social groups employ

> means which reflect [their] peculiar nature and capabilities. The wealthy bribe; students riot; workers strike; mobs demonstrate; and the military coup. In the absence of accepted procedures, all these forms of direct action are found on the political scene. The techniques of military intervention are simply more dramatic and effective than the others because, as Hobbes put it, 'When nothing else is turned up, clubs are trumps.'[10]

This is where Huntington's and Finer's environmental causes of coups run into Janowitz's emphasis on the character and professional ethics of the military. With a crisis of legitimacy threatening the very existence of the nation-state, soldiers feel they have to act. The military is not only a strong institution within the state because of its capacity to invoke violence; armed forces are usually also highly organised, cohesive, loyal and hierarchical organisations. Their command structure, for example, ensures that a disciplined army can get things done. This is why the military holds failing civilian governments in contempt. In this respect, Janowitz talks of the army's 'ethos of public service' and 'national identity', which combines 'managerial ability with a heroic posture'.[11] The military is forced to intervene in the political process in the absence of other social groups with the ability to govern effectively. The patriotism and nationalism that keeps the military away from the machinery of political administration in Western states are the same characteristics that require officers to rebel in African countries. A body entrusted with the defence of the realm cannot sit idly by while civilians destroy the state as effectively as any invading army could. Under such circumstances, a 'guardian coup' ensues.

There is no doubt that the characteristics of the military can certainly encourage rebellion when a government's legitimacy is lost, but, again, this does not entirely explain why the military intervenes. Almost all African countries have experienced economic and social problems in the post-colonial period, yet not all of them have encountered military takeovers. Similarly, the 'guardian coup' is often too romantic a concept to explain actual events. The army does not always operate solely in the *national* interest. In the final analysis, a coup will only occur if members of the military feel it is in *their* interests to overthrow political leaders. Certainly they command the organisational ability and technology to do this, and need to be prompted by the right social environment, but, ultimately, military takeovers are a result of the military's own interests.

In this respect, despite its professional ethics, the military in Africa has to be regarded as just another faction of the ruling elite (indeed, Christopher Clapham describes it as the 'armed wing of the bureaucratic bourgeoisie'[12]). Due to the continent's lack of legal-rational institutions, the military has to compete to protect its own corporate interests among the day-to-day political manoeuvrings of other factions within the state. The military simply cannot afford to divorce itself from this political exchange, as nobody else will protect its interests within the political cauldron where all groups are seeking to maximise their share of state power. As a result, from time to time, the military may have to put pressure on civilian groups to recognise its demands. This pressure may turn into a full-scale military coup if the men in uniform feel that their interests are so threatened that the only way to protect them is actually to take over the state itself.

Typical threats to the military's welfare include cuts in the defence budget and a restriction of the army's organisational autonomy. The 1994 Gambian coup, for example, came in the wake of barrack food and accommodation problems, and pay not getting through to Gambian peace-keeping units serving in Liberia. The Gambian army's most pressing grievance, however, was the continued presence of seconded Nigerian personnel serving as commanding officers. Gambian soldiers wanted the opportunity to run their own military.[13] They achieved this goal when junior officers overthrew President Dawda Jawara's 29-year-old multi-party state in 1994. Earlier, the 1968 coup in Mali was prompted by President Modibo Keita's establishment of a separate special forces unit. Keita assembled this brigade as a personal presidential guard to specifically act as a counterweight to the regular army. As this move threatened dramatically to weaken the military's position within state structures, a *coup d'état* followed.

As a final note in this examination of why Africa has experienced so many military interventions, the foreign angle of these coups also has to be briefly explored. Although African *coups d'état* were largely a product of domestic politics, international agents also occasionally played a role. British troops, for example, helped quell army mutinies in East Africa during the early years of independence, while the US Central Intelligence Agency was also active on the continent (if not on the same scale as it was in Central and South America). It was France, however, that intervened most in African politics. Several coups were supported by Paris, while others were defeated by French influence. Gabon, for example, saw the French Foreign Legion restore the government of Léon M'ba after it had been ousted in a military *coup d'état* in 1964, while, conversely, the 1979 military overthrow of Emperor Bokassa of the Central African Republic resembled more a French invasion, rather than just a local military coup (this after previous governments in Paris had protected the Bokassa regime). Such evidence suggests that plotters are wise to first assess the likely reaction of key international agents before instigating a *coup d'état*. This theme of international intervention in the African political process is expanded in Chapter 8.

Problems facing military rulers

In many cases, few Africans missed their deposed governments once the military had struck. Indeed, with their apparent discipline and sense of national purpose, the men in uniform were often welcomed. Certainly, military regimes – with their simple hierarchical structures in which officials are expected to obey orders (rather than bargain over policies) – had a head start in tackling problems such as bureaucratic corruption and inefficiency. The notion that soldiers can bring their parade-ground precision to institutions of government, however, proved to be somewhat optimistic. In reality, the military introduced an additional set of problems to the administration of post-colonial African states.

The obvious predicament faced by all military regimes is the fact that a precedent has been set. Now, with the professional ethic of non-intervention violated, future generations of officers consider themselves to be quite within their rights to topple governments they judge to be acting against the national interest, or, indeed, against the military's own corporate interests. The threat of a counter-coup is very real. Officers leading the *junta*, therefore, have always to sate their colleagues left in barracks. Austerity drives initiated by the ruling army council, for example, usually do not include the military (for fear of how junior officers may react). Despite this accommodation, however, several African countries fell victim to a succession of coups and counter-coups during the post-colonial period. Once the military had taken the initial decision to intervene in the political process, it was very difficult to keep future generations of soldiers confined to barracks.

The second basic problem that the military had in ruling was that soldiers had little training for, or experience of, government, nor were their internal organisational structures sufficiently sophisticated to manage the entire state. Coup leaders soon realised that it was much easier to topple a government than it was to build its successor. To endure, military governments therefore had to learn the arts of political persuasion quickly, deploying these alongside their more familiar skills of coercion. The army's natural ally, in this respect, was the civilian bureaucracy. Although the African military usurped politicians, they nearly always retained the bureaucrats that served under the previous administration. After all, these individuals had experience of the day-to-day running of the country. Indeed, having purged *selected* politicians, coup leaders often invited opposition figures, or even individual former cabinet ministers, into their regime (ones representing a particular ethnic group, maybe). Ultimately, the army could not cope without these bureaucrats and politicians. They were required as a substitute for the military's own deficiencies in the practice of politics and public administration. This is why it is often misleading to talk of post-coup governments as strictly 'military regimes'. They were more often hybrids consisting of both civilian and army personnel.

The third key dilemma faced by the military when they took power was the problem of legitimacy. Like all leaders, these officers had to build and maintain links with civil society. Since those who seized power were usually few in number, their links to the rest of society were limited. As a result, they had to set about reviving or replacing the client–patron networks of the old regime (again, this often involved co-opting major patrons from the previous administration). Normally, new regimes were initially popular because they ousted the former corrupt elites, but once the honeymoon period was over, legitimising links to civil society became vital in ensuring the stability of government. Yet as soon as the military started dealing with established social groups within the country, or reviving the old clientelism, then the old inefficiencies of political bargaining returned.

Then there was the question of delivering promises. In their initial broadcasts to the nation, the military talked of curbing corruption and developing the economy. This was easier said than done. Effectively, a successful military administration had to produce more from the same hand of cards that had been held by the previous regime. Military coups occurred in the first place because of dire socio-economic conditions, and this situation did not change simply because soldiers were now in control. Inefficient government in Africa stemmed from ethnic balancing, the servicing of a bureaucratic bourgeoisie, and client–patron networks generally. Once they occupied the presidential palace, the military soon found out why the old regime tolerated these political relationships. Support from these social groups was required to maintain political order. Again, it is easier to overthrow a bad government than it is to create a good one.

The final key dilemma the military faced when it captured power related to what exactly the men in uniform were going to do in the future. Should they hold elections and return to barracks immediately? If they are to form a caretaker administration, in order to build the 'right environment' for a just society, how long should they stay in power? Should the leaders of the coup resign their commissions and carry out their political duties as civilians? Alternatively, they could use the army as a support base, but recruit from wider civil society, to create a new mass participatory one-party state. Many coups were instigated in Africa without their participants first devising a clear blueprint for the future. Once they took power, however, the army had to find answers to all the above questions rapidly.

The outcomes of military rule in Africa

Just as the reasons behind each military coup are different, so are the outcomes of these events. No one type of regime results. Soldiers preside over administrations as diverse, both in nature and in success, as their civilian counterparts. Sometimes the ideals behind the original takeover, especially in the case of guardian or breakthrough coups, result in governments distinct from those found on the rest of the continent. More often, however, with the military forced to forge close links with the bureaucracy and wider civil society, these regimes came to resemble their civilian predecessors (personal rulers and client–patron networks included). It was customary for post-coup African governments to revert to type.

One common outcome of this military rule was that, once in power, soldiers tended to increase public spending on themselves. Military budgets rose noticeably in post-coup Africa. Initially, the corporate interests that prompted the coup in the first place were addressed. Then, given that those in government had to look after their colleagues left in barracks (for fear of a counter-coup), pay, conditions and the equipment of the armed forces improved markedly. Ghana's defence spending, for example, increased by 22 per cent after 1966.

This was despite ongoing economic hardship that resulted in social services to the countryside being cut by 28 per cent in the same period.[14]

In terms of the simple typology introduced earlier, guardian coups occasionally follow a similar pattern. Immediately after taking power, the 'guardians' promise to return to barracks when an appropriate political order has been restored. A few have actually done this. Ghana, for example, demilitarised its government in 1969 and 1979. Nigeria, too, went through this handback process in 1979 and 1999. In effect, with its 'caretaker' regimes, the military appoints itself as a political referee. It becomes the institution that determines the rules of the game, drafting the new constitution for example. The military also reserves the right to re-take control (via another coup) if its civilian successors fail their probation. And most apparently do fail in the eyes of the soldiers. Several African states have been locked into a repetitive cycle of civilian and military regimes.

Elsewhere the military remains stubbornly on the political stage. Despite their 'guardian' pretensions, most post-colonial African military regimes have refused to hand back power voluntarily. Caretaker governments commonly evolve into more permanent institutions, resulting in the military–civilian hybrid regimes discussed later in this chapter.

Breakthrough coups often have slightly different outcomes. The regimes that result from them abandon the old political structures and create their own institutions for building links between the state and civil society. More often than not, a new (single) party is established. This becomes the tool to unite the army and the masses, and, apparently, to instil a new national spirit, one in which development will emerge from graft and discipline. People's militias and people's courts are also part of this process. The early years of Mariam Mengistu's Ethiopia are a good illustration of a military-led 'revolution'. Yet even breakthrough regimes fall foul of Africa's underlying political realities. The new mass party, for example, often atrophies like its civilian counterparts did before it. After all, Africa's single parties existed more to heighten a sense of participation for civil society, rather than to provide a mechanism to allow the masses to become involved in the making of public policy. Given these circumstances, it is easy for these 'radical breakthrough' governments to descend into the personal rule of one-party states, in which client–patron networks become the predominant mechanism of political exchange.

Post-colonial Africa saw the vast majority of its military coups (whether their pretensions were guardian, breakthrough or veto) result in a stalemate between civilian and military power. Armed forces felt no compulsion to keep out of the political process, yet they could not rule effectively without civilian support. The outcomes were hybrid governments. Military leaders were forced to 'civilianise' themselves to a degree, co-opting individuals from the old regime in order to maintain control, but, in Kunle Amuwo's words, as soon as the soldiers waded into the 'murky water of politics', they soon found themselves 'more or less submerged in the internal dynamics of civil society'.[15] Similarly, the restraints of the international economy were no less pressing simply because the president now wore a uniform. The average performance of Africa's post-colonial military regimes, in this respect, proved to be no more successful than had their civilian counterparts.

State and civil society

In terms of this book's central theme of analysing the relationship between state and civil society, military coups did little to alter the overall balance. On the state side of the equation, however, these *coups d'état* were dramatic. Military intervention helped 'speed the circulation of élites and the realignment of factions'.[16] In this respect, military coups were simply a reflection of the internal jockeying for power among the bureaucratic bourgeoisie discussed in Chapter 5. It was simply that, since soldiers had greater access to the violent resources of the state, it was the military, the 'armed wing' of this ruling elite, that usually came to dominate. However, once they had taken power, the ruling officers were usually forced to accommodate at least some of the factions active within the former civilian regime. It was only with the support of these powerful factions that the military government could retain power. Again, this illustrates the fact that, beyond the short term, the power of coercion alone cannot underpin government.

The vast majority of military coups did little to alleviate civil society's exploited position within post-colonial Africa. In most cases, the men in uniform, just like their civilian successors, failed to involve the masses in the political process. 'Breakthrough' administrations came closest to doing this, but even here it was largely a state elite who retained control. And, as long as political administrations remained under the control of a bureaucratic bour-geoisie, then personal rule and clientelism were substituted for more positive methods of generating legitimacy. Corruption and inefficiency were the consequence of this, leaving Africans under military governments no better off than those ruled by civilians. It was not until civil society itself, rather than the army, began to regulate regime change (in the 1990s, through multi-party elections) that African states became more responsive and accountable to their people.

Case study: Uganda's 1971 military coup

Uganda sits on a massive plateau in eastern Central Africa. It is a lush and fertile country, with large freshwater lakes and a number of towering mountains. More than most African states, Uganda has had difficulty in producing effective government in the independence period. Indeed to the outside world, one particular Ugandan regime, that of Idi Amin Dada, confirmed stereotypes of the perceived insta-bility and brutality of Africa's post-colonial politics. This case study investigates the 1971 military *coup d'état* that brought Amin to power, plotting both its origins and its outcomes.

Immediately prior to imperial rule, this part of East Africa was home to the polity of Buganda, along with a number of other smaller kingdoms. In 1891, the British East Africa Company signed a treaty with the *Kabaka* (king) of Buganda, bringing the territory under European administration. When the company collapsed due to financial problems, the British government itself took over, and Buganda became a formal British protectorate in 1894. Two years later, the neighbouring kingdoms of Bunyoro, Toro, Ankole and Bugosa also gained a similar status. All these territories would later be consolidated, with Buganda, to form the inclusive state of Uganda.

Unlike neighbouring Kenya, Uganda did not have a white settler problem to solve at independence. It did, however, have to tackle the issue of how Buganda would sit within the post-colonial Ugandan state. Bugandans saw their future as separate from the rest of Uganda. Indeed, the British exiled the Kabaka after he instigated a campaign demanding that Buganda be granted its independence as a distinct sovereign state. The removal of the Kabaka, however, did not quell the demand for Bugandan autonomy. Protests on this issue ensured that 95 per cent of Bugandans heeded the call to boycott Uganda's 1961 (pre-independence) national assembly elections.[17]

This boycott persuaded the British colonial authorities to end the Kabaka's exile, and to suggest that Buganda enjoy a semi-federal status after decolonisation. On his return, the Kabaka Yekka royalist party was established, and, in an alliance with the Uganda People's Congress (led by Milton Obote), it won a majority in the elections that paved the way to independence in 1962. This coalition formed Uganda's first post-colonial government, with the Kabaka as President and Obote serving as Prime Minister. This alliance, however, proved to be fragile.

Ugandan politics, in the nine-year period between independence and Amin's military coup, was marked by an ongoing power struggle within Uganda's political elite. Factional politics were the dominant feature. First, Obote wrestled power from the Kabaka, with the help of Amin and the military. Then the military itself asserted its power, finally toppling the Obote regime in January 1971.

Using the office of the Prime Minister as his power base, Milton Obote followed the well-worn path of post-colonial African politics by centralising the state. One-party rule was Obote's goal, with his own Uganda People's Congress (UPC) as the 'one party'. In this respect, the Kabaka and his Kabaka Yekka movement were rival sources of political power that had to be eliminated. And this is exactly what happened. By the mid-1960s, Obote had persuaded several Bugandan politicians to defect to the UPC with rewards of patronage. Remaining sources of opposition suffered state intimidation. Yet, in pushing through this centralisation programme, Obote alienated many in Uganda. In E A Brett's assessment, 'By the end of 1965 Obote was confronted by so much opposition that he would have certainly lost the next elections. He responded by building a base in the army and eliminating this opposition by force.'[18]

The power struggle between the Kabaka and Obote came to a head in 1966. Obote received intelligence that Shaban Opolot, a Kabaka loyalist and the commander of the Ugandan army, was moving units loyal to the Prime Minister away from Kampala. This was interpreted as paving the way for military action on behalf of the Kabaka. Obote acted quickly. He made himself President, cancelled the forthcoming elections, and sent Colonel Amin to arrest the Kabaka. The Kabaka's palace was overrun, which earned Amin promotion to the post of Obote's Chief of Staff.

As well as destroying the Kabaka's power base, this action also resulted in the political neutralisation of Opolot. Obote promoted him sideways into an advisory role, with Amin taking over the army's operational duties. A year later, constitutional amendments were added to Obote's political manoeuvrings. He used his majority in Parliament to revoke Buganda's semi-federal standing, creating a unitary state. With this act, Obote's consolidation of power was complete.

Obote's reliance on coercive force, however, proved to be his downfall. In his efforts to eliminate constitutional opposition, he had strengthened the hand of the state's agencies of violence. The military itself now became a prominent player in Ugandan politics. The result was yet another power struggle within Uganda's ruling elite, with Obote pitted against Amin's faction of the army. This struggle was settled in January 1971, when Amin led a *coup d'état*, taking advantage of Obote's absence at a Commonwealth conference in Singapore.

How, then, should Amin's coup be accounted for? Can the theoretical causes of African coups, outlined in the main text of this chapter (ability, environment, organisation and motivation), be identified in the specific case of Uganda?

The events of January 1971 certainly prove that the Ugandan army was capable of mounting a military coup. At independence, the small Ugandan army, with its origins in the British colonial King's African Rifles, gained symbolic importance as the defender of the state's newly won sovereignty. The Ugandan army's political significance, however, was more than just symbolic. As Obote was forced to rely heavily on the military to underpin his power, large sums of public money were invested in the army (10 per cent of the national budget, compared to 7 per cent in Kenya and 4 per cent in Tanzania). Uganda's military personnel grew in number, from 700 in 1962 to 7,000 by 1969.[19] By 1971 the Ugandan army clearly had the resources to take on other factions within Uganda's political elite – the first prerequisite for any potential military coup.

Military coups, however, as we saw above, are prompted by far more than just a well equipped army with organisational capabilities. They usually also require an appropriate economic, social and political environment. Uganda certainly experienced troubles in all three of these areas during the 1960s. As well as Buganda's demands for autonomy, for example, other ethnic groups also stressed their separate identities. Uganda, in this respect, fell far short of being a harmonious nation-state. This situation led to political unrest. Obote's clashes with the Kabaka, and his moves to centralise the state, left few channels open for constitutional opposition. Opportunities for institutionalised dissent, operating as a 'safety-valve', were thus effectively absent in Ugandan politics by the mid-1960s. Even the so-called 'Move to the Left' later in the decade, by which the president attempted to gain legitimacy for his regime by introducing populist and socialist reforms, failed to win Obote the people's respect.

The scene was set. The background requirements for a coup – the right economic, social and political environment, and a sufficiently resourced and organised army – were in place. All that was needed now was a motive for the military, or a faction of the military, to intervene. This motive came in the form of a personal threat to Amin's position within the state. The power struggle between Obote and his Chief of Staff reached a climax in January 1971. One of them had to go, and Amin struck first.

After Colonel Amin had become Obote's Chief of Staff, he sought to consolidate his status within the military, and the state in general. He promoted personnel from his own political stronghold of the north, court-martialling rivals from the south. Obote, however, acknowledging the power that his Chief of Staff had accumulated, tried to reduce his reliance on Amin's faction of the army. He sought to do this by expanding his own personal special forces units. This attempt to marginalise the army, combined with Obote's order to disband a military division loyal to Amin, created a flashpoint. Amin was also under suspicion of murdering Brigadier Okoya, an Obote loyalist and Amin's possible replacement as head of the army. The investigation of Amin for this murder, ordered by the president himself, and rumours of the Chief of Staff's imminent sacking, forced Amin's hand. He took advantage of Obote's absence and replaced him as Head of State. Having come so far, gaining high office and all the rewards that this brought, Amin was unwilling to submit to Obote's command, suffering demotion, imprisonment, exile or worse as a result. This personal motivation was the last element to fall into place, prompting the *coup d'état*.

Despite the initial popularity Amin gained from ridding Uganda of Obote's rule, and the fact that, in his first broadcast to the nation, he promised to hold democratic elections within five years, Amin's regime proved catastrophic for Uganda's political, social and economic development. Amin dealt with the key dilemma that all military regimes face by simply ignoring it. He made little attempt to build institutions or links with civil society in order to legitimise his government. Instead, he relied heavily on the state's powers of coercion. The national assembly was dissolved, with Amin ruling by decree; military tribunals replaced judicial hearings; and military personnel were employed as provincial governors. In one of his more absurd acts, Amin, seeking the 'Africanisation' of Uganda, simply exiled practically the whole of the country's economically significant Asian community (British economic interests in Uganda were also nationalised). Any opposition, or even any *potential* opposition, to the regime was brutally eliminated. Amin's personal 'Public Safety Unit' was kept busy perpetrating many of the hundreds of thousands of politically motivated murders committed between 1971 and 1979.

Only the army itself benefited from Amin's rule. As with most military governments, the army expanded dramatically after the coup. In 1971, there were 7,680 soldiers in Uganda; by 1974 this figure had risen to 20,000.[20] The military now enjoyed immense power within Ugandan society. It appropriated what it desired, and exercised summary justice when it saw fit. Half of the wealth left by the exiled Asian community, for example, found its way into military hands.[21] Yet being a soldier was not a particularly safe occupation during the Amin years. The military was repeatedly purged of potential opposition by its commanding officers, with many soldiers of Acholi or Langi ethnic backgrounds being massacred. Military factions competed for power, and there was intense distrust between senior and junior ranks. Indeed, towards the end of Amin's rule, the country came under the control of a number of army warlords.

Eventually the factional fighting became so intense that Amin had to manufacture an invasion of northern Tanzania in order to restore army unity. This proved to be a miscalculation. The Tanzanian army responded by repelling this invasion with ease, and then marched on Kampala itself. Fighting alongside Ugandan dissidents, the Tanzanian force finally succeeded in removing Amin in 1979. Although Amin's government was always weak, having never tried to legitimise its rule through linking state and civil society, its use of the state's powers of coercion had secured for the military the reins of power for eight brutal years.

Bringing Uganda's post-colonial history up to date, the 1980s was also a lost decade for Uganda in terms of economic and political development. Obote's UPC was returned to power in elections held after the Tanzanian army withdrew (despite widespread evidence of vote rigging). The UPC, however, once again failed to unite the country. Indeed, it is estimated that a further 100,000 Ugandans died in political violence between 1980 and a second military coup which took place in 1985.[22] This coup assisted Yoweri Museveni's insurgent National Resistance Army (NRA) to take Kampala a year later. The NRA has been in power since 1986, during which time economic stability has returned, as has a greater respect for human rights. Indeed, despite its commitment to 'no-party government', Museveni's regime has been held up as an example of good government on the African continent by both the World Bank and Western governments. It may be that Uganda now has a regime that will base its rule upon legitimacy more than on coercion.

Uganda[23]

Territory:	236,580 sq km	Population:	22.6 million
Colonial power:	Britain	Independence:	1962
Major cities:	Kampala (capital)	Ethnic groups:	Baganda
	Jinja/Njeru		Basoga
	Bugembe		Banyankole
Urban pop.:	13.4%	Life expectancy:	43 years
Languages:	English	Adult literacy:	61.8%
	Kiswahili	Exports:	Coffee
	Luganda		Gold
Currency:	Ugandan shilling		Fish
Infant mortality:	105 deaths/thousand births		Maize
Religion:	Traditional	External debt:	US$3,674 million
	Christian	GDP per capita:	US$305

Glossary of key terms

Breakthrough coup	Where the military acts in the vanguard of a revolution, replacing tradition political institutions with more radical structures of government.
Coercive power	The use or threat of violence to achieve a political or social purpose.
Coup d'état	A sudden illegal displacement of government in which members of the security forces play a prominent role.
Guardian coup	Where the military ousts a failing government, allegedly in the national interest.
Political authority	A psychological relationship, between the governed and their governors, which engenders a belief that state personnel and institutions should be obeyed.
Political culture	Commonly held political ideas, attitudes and behaviour that permeate a society.
Professional ethic of non-intervention	The acceptance that the military should remain under political control, and not use its capacity to inflict violence in an effort to influence the political process.
Veto coup	Where the military intervenes to arrest political transition, protecting its corporate interests.

Questions raised by this chapter

1 To what extent can African military coups be explained by environmental (socio-economic/political culture) factors?
2 Did the professional characteristics of the military force it to intervene in Africa's political process?
3 Can African military coups be accounted for by the personal interests of soldiers?
4 What problems do military governments face once they come to power?
5 How would you rate the performance of military regimes in post-colonial Africa?

Further reading

For those interested in the causes of military coups, Samuel Huntington (environmental), Morris Janowitz (organisational characteristics), and S E Finer (political culture) delimit the original debate on this issue. Samuel Decalo's, however, is a more up-to-date book on this subject, and confines itself to the African continent. Also worth reading are two articles: one by Arnold Hughes and Roy May, and the other by David Goldsworthy. They both take an inverted look at the military in Africa, asking why the army has *not* intervened in a large minority of African states. As to the problems military governments face once they have taken power, and the outcomes of this rule, a good starting point once again is Decalo's book, as well as Christopher Clapham and George Philip's edited book. For a case study, Amii Omara-Otunnu provides an excellent narrative of the role of the military in Ugandan politics.

Clapham, Christopher and George Philip, eds (1985) *The political dilemmas of military regimes*, London: Croom Helm.

Decalo, Samuel (1990) *Coups and army rule in Africa: motivations and constraints*, 2nd edn, New Haven, CT: Yale University Press.

Finer, S E (1962) *The man on horseback: the role of the military in politics*, London: Pall Mall.

Goldsworthy, David (1981) 'Civilian control of the military in Black Africa', *African Affairs* 80(318), 49–74.

Hughes, Arnold and Roy May (1988) 'The politics of succession in Black Africa', *Third World Quarterly* 10(1), 1–22.

Huntington, Samuel P (1968) *Political order in changing societies*, New Haven, CT: Yale University Press.

Janowitz, Morris (1977) *Military institutions and coercion in the developing nations*, Chicago: University of Chicago Press.

Omara-Otunnu, Amii (1987) *Politics and the military in Uganda, 1890–1985*, London: Macmillan.

8 Sovereignty

External influences on African politics

So far, this book has concentrated on the internal relationships between state and civil society in Africa. The competition and cooperation between these two protagonists have explained a great deal about the political process on the continent. Yet the introduction of this book identified *three* parties to be considered. Alongside those of the state and civil society, the influences of external interests also have to be taken into account when examining post-colonial African politics.

External interests have already come to the fore in previous chapters with the analysis of colonial rule, economic underdevelopment and the possible influence of an 'international bourgeoisie'. It is now time, however, to investigate this third party more systematically. The current chapter will do exactly this by assessing political influences on the continent's governments emanating from states outside Africa. It is no exaggeration to note that external intervention, in several states, dramatically changed the direction of these countries' modern political history.

Given this external intervention, sovereignty is the natural choice for this chapter's underlying theme. This is because the very concept of sovereignty, despite its flaws, lubricates the machinery of international relations.[1] Sovereignty, in this respect, can be defined as *the claim of supreme political authority within a territory*. It is about governments enjoying autonomy and freedom of constraint within their own borders.

The notion of sovereignty underpinned international politics throughout the twentieth century. It is a concept that gains respect from governments around the world because it is of mutual benefit. The recognition of state B's sovereignty by state A usually implies a reciprocal recognition of state A's own sovereign status. Consequently, an international system advocating 'non-interference' in the domestic jurisdiction of other states has developed. Each sovereign state is attributed unfettered power within its own territorial borders, being recognised as the sole political authority within these frontiers. This understanding of non-interference has the effect of reducing conflict between states, and has thus been enshrined in the charter of the United Nations.

Yet despite this international respect for sovereignty and non-interference, in reality no state enjoys total unconstrained power within its domestic jurisdiction.

The state's monopoly of power is challenged by two sources. There is internal opposition to this sovereignty (examined in Chapter 10), but more relevant to the present chapter are the external challenges. Like planets in a solar system, states in the international political arena all exert influence over one another. Small territories bordering larger states, for example, will often succumb to their neighbour's 'gravitational' pull. Similarly, the actions of the most powerful states within the system will have ramifications affecting the whole political universe. In this respect, governments can only hide behind their sovereignty to a certain degree. Even the United Kingdom, for example, a state that has enjoyed sovereign status for longer than most, has its domestic arena buffeted by external events. Take, for instance, the UK's gradual ceding of political sovereignty to the institutions of the European Union. Likewise, the British government has also yielded a degree of its economic sovereignty to foreign transnational corporations investing in this country.

African states know the strengths and limitations of the concept of sovereignty more than most within the international community. The vast majority of African states, after all, are direct creations of external intervention (via colonial partition). Although the continent now enjoys a degree of international respect and non-interference, having won its political sovereignty with decolonisation, economic and political fragility still result in vulnerability to outside intervention. In short, because of their relatively weak position, African governments find it difficult to resist the attentions of other states within the international political system. Consequently, as the following paragraphs show, although the continent has always been on the margins of 'Great Power' competition, global politics have had a considerable impact on the development of this part of the world. The chapter divides its investigation of this external impact between two time periods: the 'Cold War' era, followed by the subsequent 'New World Order'.

Inter-African international relations

The bulk of this chapter concentrates on political intervention from parties outside the African continent. This is in no way meant to imply that inter-African international relations are insignificant. As was shown in previous chapters, factors such as Somalia's irredentism, Libya's adventurism and South Africa's destabilisation have all had major ramifications on the continent. The search for a pan-Africanist, continent-wide solidarity among African states has proved elusive. Multi-lateral cooperation can be observed in institutions such as the Organization of African Unity (OAU), the Southern African Development Community (SADC) and the Economic Community of West African States (ECOWAS), but African governments, just like their counterparts in other regions of the world, have clashed from time to time. Both South Africa and Zaire (Congo-Kinshasa) intervened in Angola in 1975, for example: Tanzania invaded Uganda in 1979; and troops from Rwanda, Angola, Namibia, the Sudan, Chad and Zimbabwe were active in The Democratic Republic of the

Congo (DRC, Congo-Kinshasa) in the late 1990s. There have also been numerous cases of African governments assisting the continent's rebel forces.

Again, it should be noted that African countries have been remarkably successful in maintaining the continent's (colonial demarcated) borders, which, in turn, has brought a degree of harmony to inter-continental foreign relations. This does not imply, however, that there has been total respect for neighbours' sovereignty. Inter-African relations, though, both peaceful and violent, have been discussed elsewhere in the book: the task of the present chapter is to concentrate on extra-African intervention.

Superpowers, the Cold War and Africa

The vast majority of African countries gained their independence in the 20-year period between 1955 and 1975. This was a time when global politics were dominated by the Cold War. Newly sovereign African states were therefore thrust into an international political system where the capitalist West was engaged in ideological combat with the communist East.

At first glance, it would seem that Africa had no reason to be caught up in this conflict. The continent was too poor (with few resources to protect) and too peripheral (not within either superpower's immediate sphere of influence) to trouble these Cold War warriors. The Cold War, however, was truly global. With the United States and the Soviet Union locked in a nuclear stalemate in Europe, both these powers reasoned that strategic advantage could be gained elsewhere. Rivalries were therefore extended to the African continent, and, although these peripheral strategic policies may have been of only minor importance to officials in Washington DC and Moscow, their consequences had a dramatic impact within Africa itself.

The communist powers

The USSR portrayed itself as a natural ally for the newly sovereign states of Africa. This was because tsarist Russia had not involved itself in the colonisation of the continent, while the Soviet Union itself shared African nationalists' anti-imperialist sentiments. Indeed, many African leaders proclaimed their countries to be socialist after independence. With these shared ideological foundations, it was only natural that officials in Moscow sustained a generally sympathetic approach towards Africa. In particular, fraternal links were forged with the more radical governments of Ghana, Guinea and Mali, and later with the Marxist-Leninist states of Angola, Mozambique and Ethiopia.

Essentially, the Soviet Union sought to promote socialism in Africa. There was no question of the USSR overwhelming African governments, trying to establish a buffer zone (as it had in Eastern Europe). Instead, Moscow reasoned that any allies it could win through diplomacy and aid would help expand the communist world, denying opportunities to the West. The objective was therefore to reinforce the break between the ex-colonies and their ex-colonisers.

Soviet policy towards Africa in the 1950s and 1960s can be described as 'pragmatic'. Although the continent was never high on its list of priorities, Moscow was willing to intervene when opportunities emerged. For example, one of the first instances of Cold War tension on African soil was precipitated when the Soviet Union assisted Egypt in building the Aswan High Dam. This was after relations between Egypt and the West had become strained. The United States and Britain pulled out of the dam project after General Nasser's government had accepted an arms shipment from Czechoslovakia. This gave Moscow the opportunity to win friends in Africa, and in 1956 the USSR took over the Aswan construction programme itself. Similarly, the Soviet Union also built close ties with Guinea. Moscow became Guinea's patron after this country had defied France's wishes and opted for complete independence in 1958. Isolated from the West, Sékou Touré's government was grateful for any external assistance it could secure.

Later, in the 1970s, the Soviet Union took a more active role in African affairs. Officials in Moscow sought to profit from the political instability created by Portugal's withdrawal from Africa, as well as the removal of Emperor Haile Selassie in Ethiopia. They were also keen to assist liberation struggles against the white minority governments of Southern Africa. Consequently, Angola, Mozambique and Ethiopia received comparatively large amounts of aid, boosting the capacity of these new Marxist-Leninist regimes to defend themselves against 'counter-revolutionary' forces. Similarly, arms were also supplied to the liberation movements of the south (the ANC in South Africa, SWAPO in Namibia and ZAPU in Zimbabwe). It was hoped that these states would become Soviet allies once the insurgent nationalists had defeated the incumbent white minority governments.

The expansion of socialism was the long-term objective of Soviet foreign policy. In the shorter term, however, Moscow also sought to improve its strategic position in Africa. Over time, the USSR gained access to a network of airfields and seaports right across the continent. This advanced the Soviet Union's Cold War capabilities considerably. Flights out of Conakry in West Africa, for example, enabled Moscow to monitor Western shipping in the Atlantic, while defence facilities in Somalia, and then in Ethiopia, enhanced Soviet naval operations in the Indian Ocean. As will be seen later in the chapter, this superpower attention benefited African governments through the 'rent' that they could charge for granting such strategic access.

The Soviet Union's primary method of paying this rent was though the supply of arms. Millions of tons of military equipment were shipped to Africa. This was undertaken without charge (or very cheaply). By contrast, the West was in the business of selling more sophisticated arms at a considerably higher price. Although tanks, MiG aircraft and SAM missiles were reserved for prized clients (Angola and Ethiopia), Moscow was willing to sell arms to almost any country where it considered influence could be won. Just under half of the continent's governments took up this opportunity in the post-colonial period.

As a result, Soviet arm sales to Africa rose from US$150 million in the 1960s to US$2.5 billion in the 1970s.[2]

The Soviet Union, however, was not the only communist power involved in Africa. Cuba was also heavily committed to the defence of socialism on this continent. Cuba, as a Third World country, empathised with Africa's position. Consequently, African regimes were less suspicious of Havana's offers of assistance than they were of Moscow's overtures. This resulted in thousands of Cuban doctors, engineers, teachers and other technical advisors serving African governments. Perhaps more importantly, however, was the fact that Havana was willing to deploy combat troops. Up to 50,000 Cuban soldiers were despatched to Angola and Ethiopia from the mid-1970s onwards.[3] In Angola, for example, Cuban troops, fighting alongside government forces, saw active service against invading South African regiments, who had themselves intervened to support (US backed) UNITA rebels. Without this Cuban intervention, it is likely that the government in Luanda would have been defeated.

The People's Republic of China also involved itself in African affairs. Beijing, after its ideological rift with Moscow, attempted to export its own brand of socialism to the continent. As well as assisting African regimes, this intervention was also aimed at blunting rival Soviet expansionism. Again, Beijing stressed its Third World credentials (something Moscow had difficulty doing), and doctors, engineers and teachers were duly dispatched to the continent. The apogee of China's Africa policy, however, came with the building of the TAZARA railway, completed in 1975. This was a project that Western governments had earlier refused to undertake, considering it too difficult and too costly. This formidable piece of engineering laid 1,680km of railway track across Central Africa, linking Zambia to the Tanzanian port of Dar es Salaam (thus giving Zambia access to the sea, avoiding the need to transport goods through white-ruled Rhodesia and South Africa). However, China was not to repeat this scale of cooperation anywhere else on the continent. Indeed, Beijing's Africa policy remained somewhat discreet when compared to those of the Soviet Union or Cuba.

The Western powers

The global containment of communism was the primary foreign policy goal of the United States during the years of the Cold War. Not only did this involve the US shoring up democracies in Western Europe (with the provision of Marshall aid and the deployment of US troops), it also led Washington to seek out allies on other continents. Friendly governments in far off places, it was reasoned, could act as a bulwark against potential Soviet expansion.

Although, again, African states were only of minor importance to Cold War strategists in Washington, no area of the world could be neglected. It was feared that any state 'going communist' had the potential to tip the overall balance in this global confrontation. Therefore, despite the United States's limited economic and strategic interests on the continent, African governments were courted. Washington considered it imperative that the continent's nationalist and anti-imperial regimes should not be converted into Soviet satellites.

US administrations selected a number of states for special attention. These countries were seen as regionally important. At various times, for example, Zaire (Congo-Kinshasa), Morocco, Ethiopia, Somalia and Kenya could be identified as US clients. This resulted in economic aid flowing to these states, as well as diplomatic support when this was needed. Morocco, for example, received sympathy in Washington over its claims to the Western Sahara, while Zaire was aided in its border clashes with Angola.

The United States also sought to back 'moderate' groups, while disabling 'radical' factions, in the continent's disputed territories. In the 1960 Congo crisis, for example, which was precipitated by Katanga's secession, US power was directed against Prime Minister Patrice Lumumba. The CIA's local chief of station reported that he was unsure whether Lumumba was actually a 'Commie or just playing Commie', but 'there may be little time left in which to take the action to avoid another Cuba'.[4] Consequently, US activity contributed both to Lumumba's assassination and to the subsequent rise of General Mobutu Sese Seko. These actions eliminated any potential gains for the Soviet Union in this particular part of the world.

The Congo crisis, and other cases – such as Angola in the 1970s and 1980s – are dramatic examples of US intervention in Africa during the Cold War. The bulk of Washington's policy, however, revolved around the more mundane allocation of aid. Most African governments expressing pro-Western leanings could expect favourable attention. Indeed, it often seemed as if Washington was too eager to assist some of the continent's regimes. In several instances, the United States stood accused of supplying aid to governments that readily violated their own citizens' human rights. US strategic interests, in this respect, were being put ahead of humanitarian considerations. Although US support for Mobutu in Zaire, for example, clearly denied the Soviet Union opportunities, the military and monetary assistance offered to the General allowed him to sustain a brutal and corrupt dictatorship for several decades. Similarly, although the United States officially disapproved of white minority rule, no administration in Washington was prepared consistently to challenge South Africa over its policy of apartheid.[5] Throughout the Cold War period, US officials marginalised human rights concerns, hiding behind notions of state sovereignty and non-interference in domestic jurisdictions in order to capture the more coveted prize of global containment.

Moving on to look at other Western powers, Britain and France took very different approaches towards Africa after decolonisation. Britain, considerably less inclined to intervene than France, was content to operate a low-key Africa policy. Britain did help the newly independent governments of Kenya, Tanganyika and Uganda put down army mutinies in 1964, but these proved to be isolated incidents. Even when pushed by other Commonwealth countries to punish the white settler government of Ian Smith, when Rhodesia illegally declared unilateral independence in 1965, Britain refused to deploy troops.

Instead, London was more active in quietly pursuing its economic interests in the post-colonial era.

By contrast, inactivity is not a charge that could be levelled against France. Paris, after decolonisation, maintained a particularly close relationship with a number of African countries; much closer than the other ex-colonial powers or the newer Cold War patrons. Although Paris never managed to construct the *Communauté franco-africaine* envisaged by President Charles de Gaulle at independence (African nationalism was far too strong for this), France did remain the most influential foreign government on the continent. This was because France saw itself as having a particularly rich civilisation, with a duty to spread this culture overseas. Just as the *mission civilisatrice* (civilising mission) was at the centre of France's original colonial intervention in Africa, this remained ingrained in Franco-African relations throughout the Cold War period. Indeed, France's influence was so successful in Africa during the Cold War that several states from other colonial backgrounds, such as (Belgium's) Zaire, Rwanda and Burundi, also associated themselves with *la francophonie* (the French speaking cultural community/commonwealth). Underlining this point, more states were represented at the 1982 Franco-African summit in Kinshasa than attended a parallel meeting of the Organization of African Unity in Tripoli.[6]

Christopher Clapham attributes France's success in Africa to three factors: people, money and force.[7] In terms of people, diplomatic and financial ties between Paris and the continent's capitals were much more intimate than those offered by Britain, the United States or the Soviet Union. French relationships were underwritten by bonds of mutual trust and friendship. In this respect, several Africanists have likened the Franco-African international community to a family, with Paris acting as a paternal figure (tending to its children, especially when they become disobedient).[8] These personal links stretch back prior to independence. Most of France's colonies remained loyal to General de Gaulle and the Free French during the Second World War, for example, while several African nationalist leaders, such as Félix Houphouët-Boigny of Côte d'Ivoire, served as deputies in the French parliament and ministers in the national government before going on to rule their own countries.

Later, in the Cold War period, Paris continued to pay close attention to its ex-colonies. Africa policy was given the distinction of being coordinated by a dedicated department within the Elysée Palace itself. Regular Franco-African summits were held, reciprocal ministerial and head-of-state visits were undertaken, and several French nationals served as high-ranking civil servants within African governments. No other state, Western or communist, came close to matching the status and personal attention Paris accorded its Africa policy.

France also offered its African clients financial support. Throughout the Cold War period, Paris consistently gave twice as much aid as any other donor. In 1985, for example, France's contribution measured 70 per cent of Sub-Saharan Africa's total development assistance.[9] The French treasury also guaranteed the *Communauté Financière Africaine* (CFA) franc. This gave the member states of this common monetary zone a fully convertible currency tied to the value of the French franc. Although, in effect, members relinquished their financial sovereignty for this privilege, in return they received a degree of monetary stability absent elsewhere on the continent.

Then there was France's contribution of force. During the Cold War period, Paris negotiated military cooperation agreements with almost all the francophone African countries. These pacts brought a good deal of security to African governments. France, with some 13,000 troops stationed on African soil (with bases in Côte d'Ivoire, Gabon, Senegal, Togo, the Central African Republic and Djibouti), intervened militarily on numerous occasions.

In 1964, for example, French troops helped restore Léon M'ba to the presidency of Gabon in the wake of a military coup. The Foreign Legion arrived in Libreville, Gabon's capital, 24 hours *before* M'ba officially requested help. Similar examples of direct French military intervention include: Zaire, where incursions from Angola were thwarted; Chad, as a counter-measure to Libyan attentions; the Western Sahara, to help the Mauritanian government against POLISARIO rebels; and the Central African Republic, protecting President Jean-Bédel Bokassa's regime. This last case proves to be particularly interesting, as French troops also contributed to Bokassa's eventual overthrow in 1979. The self-proclaimed emperor's murderous regime had simply become too embarrassing for officials in Paris.

French patronage was an essential element in the politics of francophone Africa. Personal, economic or military support came to underwrite many of these regimes. Indeed, the French Foreign Legion is perhaps the best example of external interests influencing African politics. While the more powerful Cold War patrons concentrated their efforts in the Horn and Southern Africa, Paris enjoyed a *chasse gardée* (private hunting ground) elsewhere.

Other external interests

In terms of external states intervening in African politics, the countries analysed above are certainly those which created most impact during the Cold War period. This is not to say, however, that they were the only influences. Other ex-colonial powers still retained links with their former territories; bilateral trade strengthened contacts elsewhere (most notably with Germany and Japan); Scandinavian countries, after France, led the way in providing development and humanitarian aid; Arab states offered material assistance to the continent's Islamic countries; and, as will be seen in the next chapter, international financial institutions also played a major role in Africa's post-colonial political history. So far, however, this chapter has been concentrating on foreign policies *towards* Africa; the next section attempts to assess how African states pursued their own interests in this Cold War environment.

The impact of the Cold War on African politics

The diplomacy conducted with African regimes, and the military skirmishes acted out on this continent, rarely register more than a passing mention in most histories of the Cold War. Conflicts in Korea and Vietnam, and the Cuban missile crisis, draw far more attention. What was of little concern to Europeans and North Americans, however, had major ramifications in Africa itself. The Cold War brought both positive and negative challenges for regimes on this continent. With skilful manoeuvring, international patrons could be manipulated into providing much-needed external resources and security for African governments. This said, it was also possible for African countries to be drawn disastrously into the East–West conflict, notably through proxy wars.

Opportunities existed for African regimes in that the former colonial powers wished to retain their economic and strategic interests on the continent. Since they could no longer do this by the direct political subjugation of imperialism, Western powers now had to work through the new sovereign governments. Consequently an international patron–client relationship emerged. African governments, in return for access to economic markets or strategic sites, could demand concessions. If the material, diplomatic and military resources given were considered inadequate, then regimes could use their sovereign powers to play one patron off against another. Given that the Cold War protagonists were also now seeking access to the continent, even greater concessions could be secured. Zaire's President Mobutu Sese Seko, for example, was an expert at manipulating international patrons. During his thirty-year reign, Mobutu fostered contacts, first with the CIA, and then with Belgium, France, West Germany, Saudi Arabia and even China (not to mention additional negotiations with international financial institutions). Observing these, and other leaders' manoeuvrings, Tanzania's president, Julius Nyerere, considered there to be a 'second scramble for Africa' underway during the Cold War.[10]

African states welcomed the development aid, cheap loans, technical assistance and other benefits granted by international patrons. This material support made a considerable difference to the continent's regimes, given that there was often a scarcity of such resources produced within their own societies. There was also military support. Direct French and Cuban interventions have been noted above. In addition to this, the majority of African states also received arms shipments from the Cold War patrons. Between 1967 and 1978 alone, for example, the USSR supplied US$2.7 billion worth of weapons to Africa, while the United States contributed US$1.6 billion.[11] Numerous other suppliers, from France and West Germany through to Israel and Czechoslovakia, also found ready takers for their military hardware. In effect, with these weapons, external interests were underwriting the power of the state in Africa. Challenges to state sovereignty could now be countered by coercive agencies well armed with sophisticated weaponry.

Superpower patronage, however, did not always prove beneficial for African states. The danger was that if one side of the global divide paid an interest in a particular country, so might the other. On several occasions, rival domestic political camps came to be supported by clashing Cold War patrons. This happened in Angola, for example, where the MPLA government was favoured by the Soviet Union and the UNITA rebel movement was backed by the United States. Under such circumstances, internal conflicts become 'internationalised' and a proxy war may result. In other words, the Cold War becomes a hot war, and African lives are lost.

Conflicts in Africa that became 'internationalised' by Cold War intervention were particularly difficult to quell. Whereas before, the indigenous parties may have been able to come to some agreement based on local bargaining, now a resolution to the conflict also required superpower interests to be served. In the meantime, the fighting continued at an intensity that local resources could not have produced. With access to the armouries of the West or the Soviet Union, greater destruction and more deaths occurred. Indeed, external resources fuelled these wars, keeping them going where, with no external intervention, local resources would soon have been exhausted, and peace might have been sought. It is true that the Cold War may not have actually caused any conflicts in Africa; it did, however, exacerbate the intensity and duration of these confrontations. As President Olusegun Obasanjo of Nigeria observed, 'even the most innocuous of conflicts in Africa became intractable and protracted, often resulting in wars of attrition'.[12]

Africa and the New World Order

The early 1990s saw the Soviet Union lose its grip on its satellites in Eastern Europe. Soon after that, the Soviet Union itself disintegrated, abandoning socialism and splitting into a number of separate sovereign states. The Cold War was at an end. US President George Bush, accepting the responsibilities his country now had as the sole superpower, declared that a 'New World Order' had been born. This whole transitory period was symbolised in the West by the television pictures showing German citizens breaching the Berlin Wall. The end of the Cold War, however, did not just have ramifications for the people of Europe and North America; there were also major residual effects in Africa. Just as they had adapted to the demands of an international system dominated by the Cold War, African states now had to adjust to the New World Order.

The cessation of proxy wars

One of the more immediate effects of the Soviet Union's demise was the ending of proxy wars. In 1990, for example, Moscow ceased its supply of weapons to Ethiopia. This removed both external interests and external resources from this particular conflict. The incumbent Mengistu regime fell to an alliance of rebel forces a year later, something that would have taken much longer, or may not have happened at all, if Soviet backing had remained.

Similar patterns of events occurred in Southern Africa. The unwillingness of external patrons to continue funding proxy wars assisted a number of negotiated settlements in this region. With global strategic interests waning in Angola, for example, conflict resolution based on local realities now became possible. Previously, the MPLA government could rely on Soviet and Cuban support, while UNITA rebels received US and South African assistance. In a wider regional settlement, brokered by the US government and assisted by Moscow, South Africa agreed to withdraw its troops from both Angola and Namibia, in return for a simultaneous Cuban withdrawal. Now denied external backing, UNITA and the MPLA themselves sought a negotiated settlement. Although national reconciliation in Angola collapsed in 1992, the subsequent intermittent clashes between these two forces have not had the ferocity of those of the 1980s, because there is no longer access to superpower-supplied military hardware.

In South Africa itself, the end of the Cold War accelerated the arrival at the negotiating table of the incumbent National Party government and the rebel African National Congress (ANC). Having lost its weapons supply from Moscow, and with its rear bases under threat from improving relations between the Frontline States and Pretoria, the ANC was forced to put its negotiation strategy to the fore. Similarly, the South African government could no longer expect tacit support from the West. The days were numbered where Pretoria could rely on apologists in Western capitals advocating support on the grounds that South Africa was a bastion against communist encroachment. The threat of further sanctions was now very real. With external support fading, negotiations became the favoured option for both sides. An ANC-led government of national unity emerged in 1994, ending 350 years of white minority rule in this country.

Africa downgraded strategically

The end of the Cold War may have extinguished a number of proxy wars, it also, however, dramatically affected the flow of external resources to the continent's governments. With the strategic downgrading of the region, external powers were now more reluctant to provide material, diplomatic and military aid to African countries. In the New World Order, as Jeffery Lefebvre observed, 'The days of right-wing and left-wing dictatorial regimes being lavished with aid and excused for their internal excesses were over.'[13]

For a start, there was no longer the Soviet Union to act as a patron to countries expressing socialist solidarity. And without Soviet influence on the continent, Washington's attention also declined. Now the threat of communism was absent, the United States had few remaining interests in Africa. US economic investments on the whole continent, for example, measured considerably less than one-third of its exposure in the single country of Brazil.[14] Apart from a general desire to spread liberal democracy and capitalism across the globe, African affairs troubled few within Washington DC's circle of foreign policymakers. Consequently, consulates were closed, assistance programmes cut, and CIA agents packed their bags and sought more relevant hunting grounds elsewhere.

Tellingly, a number of former US clients lost power in the 1990s. Samuel Doe in Liberia, for example, Hissène Habré in Chad, Siad Barré in Somalia, and even Mobutu Sese Seko in Zaire, were all deposed. All these individuals would have stood a better chance of retaining power if the external-resource taps had been kept flowing. Washington, however, made it clear that ex-clients in Africa now had to deal with local realities largely on their own. They could no longer rely on superpower patrons to prop up their regimes.

Global economic trends also restricted the level to which African regimes could manipulate their former patrons. The development of the European Union (EU), for example, became much more of a priority for the ex-colonial powers than maintaining links with their former African possessions. Although Britain and France ensured that the EU gave a preferential trading status to their ex-colonies, through the Lomé Convention, this agreement, as a result of preparations for European monetary union, became less favourable to African countries in the 1990s.[15] Indeed, France actually devalued the CFA franc in 1995, reducing by half its fiscal subsidy of *la francophonie*. The funeral of Félix Houphouët-Boigny, President of the Côte d'Ivoire, symbolised this changing relationship between France and its former colonies. Although Houphouët-Boigny's funeral saw the attendance of three former French presidents, and six former Prime Ministers, it is unlikely that relations between Paris and current francophone African leaders will continue to be this intimate.

Political conditions tied to external aid

Western development aid did not dry up totally in the New World Order. Given that Africa is so dependent on external assistance, a humanitarian disaster would have occurred if aid had been severed completely. Aid, however, lost its geopolitical strategic function with the end of the Cold War. Consequently, assistance now came with political conditions attached. Whereas, before, domestic indiscretions were overlooked, African governments now had to do more for their money. As early as June 1990, Douglas Hurd, the British foreign minister, was talking about the need for 'good governance' in Africa. Similarly, French President François Mitterrand declared that French aid would not be forthcoming to 'regimes that have an authoritarian approach without accepting an evolution towards democracy'.[16] And the West was serious about this conditionality. Paris suspended development aid to Zaire in 1991, and to Togo in 1993. Both these countries' ruling elites fell foul of their international patrons because they had resisted pressures for democratic reform. It was Kenya, however, that came under most scrutiny during this new era of aid conditionality.

Kenya had taken a pro-capitalist, pro-Western stance throughout the years of the Cold War. In return, the West had given generously in terms of development and military assistance. The altered environment of the New World

Order, however, made many more demands on Daniel arap Moi's regime. By 1990, the Kenyan opposition had become more active, and organised demonstrations nationwide. Moi's government suppressed the pro-democracy protesters violently, calling them 'hooligans and drug addicts', who would be hunted down 'like rats'.[17] This kind of behaviour may have been overlooked previously, when the containment of communism, and not human rights, was the goal. In the 1990s, however, material assistance was now directly exchanged for 'good governance'. Consequently, Moi came under massive donor pressure to instigate reforms. International financial institutions, the United States, the EU, and Scandinavian countries, all of whom had previously helped sustain Moi's rule, now suspended their aid programmes to Kenya. Moi eventually succumbed to this donor pressure, amending the constitution to allow the registration of opposition parties. Further external (and internal) pressure brought a multi-party general election in 1992 (in which Moi managed to hold on to power).

Kenya was far from being alone in having to accept external political demands in return for aid. In the New World Order, the notion of non-interference in the domestic jurisdiction was now much less in vogue.

Continued French activity and failed US 'humanitarian intervention'

France, despite its more pressing European commitments, did not totally abandon its idea of a *chasse gardée* in Africa. Paris still reserved the right to intervene in order to maintain its influence and interests. Pressure may have been put on clients to hold multi-party elections, but this did not prevent Paris from helping a favoured candidate to victory. French aid to Cameroon, for instance, rose from US$159 million in 1990 to US$436 million in 1992. This increase in assistance can largely be explained by the fact that the incumbent, Paul Biya, fought a presidential election in 1992. These additional funds allowed Biya's government to expand public spending as part of its election campaign.[18]

Paris was also selective in its criticism of authoritarian behaviour. Former clients in Chad (1990) and Mali (1991) may have been left to their own fate when faced with opposition challenges, but there was little criticism when more favoured clients, in Côte d'Ivoire and Madagascar for example, suppressed rival political movements. Similarly, Algeria continued to receive preferential treatment from French policymakers (as it did from all Western governments), despite the military having annulled the 1991 national elections. The West was willing to overlook this annulment because the *Front Islamique du Salut* (FIS), an 'Islamist' party, had emerged as the poll's victor. External interests, in this case, were apparently only willing to promote multi-party competition if the result of this election suited their own interests.

France, however, reserved Central Africa as the theatre for its most obvious intervention in the New World Order. Paris was particularly concerned about losing its acquired influence in the former Belgian colonies. A chain reaction saw the Rwandan Patriotic Front (RPF) defeat the incumbent Kigali government (a French client) in 1994. The RPF then, in turn, assisted Zairian rebels to defeat Mobutu Sese Seko (another French client) in 1997. These events were seen as damaging to French interests. Accordingly, French troops mounted *Operation Turquoise* in Rwanda. This gained UN support as a humanitarian mission offering protection to civilians caught up in the Rwandan genocide. In reality, however, this operation seemed to be more interested in creating a safe haven in which defeated government forces could regroup. Similarly, France also tried unsuccessfully to arrange a 'humanitarian mission' to Zaire. Whatever assistance may have been given here, this military force would also have served to stall the Zairian rebels' advance on Kinshasa, possibly giving Mobutu time to negotiate a future for his regime.

Paris, with these manoeuvrings, may have failed comprehensively to retain clients in Central Africa, but with 10,000 French troops stationed on African soil, and another 800 military advisors serving the continent's governments, France still retains the capacity to intervene rapidly in this part of the world.[19]

US intervention in Africa during the New World Order proved to be brief. It was confined to Somalia in the early 1990s. The events of this 'humanitarian intervention' are discussed in more detail in the case study at the end of this chapter. It is enough to note, at this point, that the mission, despite successfully delivering emergency relief to many Somalis, ended in UN forces becoming embroiled in the country's civil war. When a number of US soldiers were killed attempting to arrest a militia leader, Washington withdrew its troops altogether, and the UN mission was scaled down dramatically. With this one incident, full-scale United States involvement in African humanitarian missions had ended. Not even genocide in Rwanda could persuade Washington to deploy ground troops. Indeed, US intervention in Africa for the rest of the 1990s was confined solely to the bombing of an alleged chemical weapons factory in the Sudan. This was in direct retribution for simultaneous Islamist-inspired terrorist attacks on US embassies in Tanzania and Kenya.

State, civil society and external interests

Relating the above evidence back to the book's central theme of the relationship between state and civil society in Africa, it can be seen that external interests had a major impact on the continent's post-colonial politics. It should also be noted that most of this support was channelled through sovereign governments. This automatically gave state elites an advantage over civil societies, which had little access to these external resources.

If sovereignty is defined as enjoying supreme political authority within a territory, then many African countries did not meet the theoretical requirements of statehood. They were simply not powerful enough. Not only was this because external interests violated this sovereignty relatively easily, but it was also because many African regimes struggled to assert their sovereignty internally (due to a lack of legitimacy within their own civil societies). In this sense, the African state often did not have the resources or penetrative power to command complete political control over its own territory. Given this failure to meet the empirical requirements of statehood, Robert Jackson regards such countries as 'quasi-states'.[20]

External interests, however, supporting the notion that international politics is conducted within a network of sovereign governments, are nevertheless willing to recognise these quasi-states. They accord these territories a level of sovereignty above that of empirical reality. This explains why micro-states incapable of supporting themselves, such as the Gambia and Lesotho, survive in a competitive world, and why regimes such as the MPLA in Angola are accorded international recognition, even when large tracts of their territory are held by rebel forces.

Given that many African countries fell into Jackson's category of quasi-statehood, such international recognition proved to be an invaluable asset for state elites during the post-colonial period. The trappings that accompanied this international sovereignty went a long way to secure the survival of these regimes. External resources, after all, flowed to those who 'represented' a particular state, and given that African countries produced relatively little internally, the controllers of these donated external resources gained considerable power. After elites had secured their own 'commission' on this wealth, they then used the remaining resources to bolster public services (to 'buy' legitimacy from society), or to expand the state's coercive capacity (in order to suppress opposition). The longest-surviving regimes of post-colonial Africa, such as Mobutu Sese Seko's Zaire and Houphouët-Boigny's Côte d'Ivoire, were those that could manipulate most from their international patrons. Indeed, in several cases, it was almost as if regime survival actually relied more on securing external backing than it did on building internal legitimacy.[21]

However, the end of the Cold War saw a change in the pattern of Africa's foreign assistance. No longer driven by ideological rivalry, external interests were now more precise in how they spent their money. Whereas, before, strategic imperatives had persuaded foreign donors to turn a blind eye to domestic excesses, now recipient state elites were made accountable for how they governed their domestic jurisdictions. Consequently, political conditions attached to aid programmes contributed to the pressures that produced political reform in the 1990s. Multi-party elections followed.

In effect, with the New World Order, civil society joined state elites in becoming a beneficiary of the attentions of external interests. Indeed, some aid projects specifically encouraged sub-state political activity in Africa. Foreign donors by-passed state elites, and engaged in assisting civil society directly. The United States, for example, funded an extensive programme of 'voter education' and 'voluntary sector management' in Ghana during the 1990s.[22]

Political conditionality, therefore, changed the nature of the political game in Africa. All the continent's governments remained reliant on external aid, yet to receive this aid they now had to serve their citizens', and not just their own, interests. 'Good governance' was the demand. There were certainly numerous deceptive practices adopted by rulers to ensure that the elite still benefited most from the distribution of this aid, but they could no longer hide behind Cold War interpretations of 'sovereignty' and 'non-interference in domestic jurisdictions'. Donors no longer blindly handed over resources to elites within African states, simply because they were the representatives of sovereign power. To conclude with Christopher Clapham's observation: 'African states, certainly, have continued in most cases to survive, and some of them have a remarkable capacity to reconstitute themselves from a condition of apparently terminal decay. If they are to sustain themselves, and to gain the capacity to carry out the functions for which no effective substitute for statehood has yet been devised, they will, however, have to do so on the basis of their relations with their own citizens, rather than the support of international convention.'[23]

Case study: Somalia's international relations

Occupying 3,000 kilometres of coastal territory where the Red Sea flows into the Indian Ocean, Somalia forms the 'horn' of East Africa. It is a country of arid plains which rise to mountains in the north. Traditionally, the Somali are a nomadic people whose subsistence relies on the herding of goats, cattle, sheep and camels. Arable cultivation, however, can be found in a fertile region located between the country's two permanent rivers, the Jubba and the Shebele.

Ethnically, Somalia is one of Africa's most homogenous countries. References to the Somali people go back as far as the fifteenth century. It was not until the arrival of colonialism, however, that these people were gathered into modern nation-states. Britain declared a protectorate over the north of this territory in 1887, while Italy completed the 'pacification' of the southern Somali people in 1927. Significantly, colonial boundaries left other Somalis outside these two main colonies. Many found themselves under French jurisdiction (in modern day Djibouti), others were stranded in northern Kenya, and yet more were left in the Ogaden region of the Ethiopian empire. This problem of a divided people was only partly solved by decolonisation.

In 1960, the former British and Italian territories merged, within days of independence, to form the Somali Democratic Republic. Nationalists of both north and south united behind the leadership of the Somali Youth League. Most Somalis, however, saw this unification as only the beginning. They desired a greater Somaliland which would include all their people. Consequently, the new government supplied arms to insurgent movements in both northern Kenya and the Ogaden region of Ethiopia. That the Republic also rejected the OAU's 1964 declaration on territorial boundaries clearly identified Somalia as an irredentist state.

The Somali Republic was dependent upon external actors at independence, and remained so throughout the post-colonial period. Decolonisation may have left Somalia with the political trappings of a modern state; it bequeathed it very little, however, by way of a modern economy. With a large proportion of the population engaged in subsistence herding, and no industrial base or mineral reserves to speak of, the government had to attract capital from abroad, both to develop the economy, and to enhance the capacity of the state itself. Somali leaders proved to be quite adept at this.

With respect to military assistance, for example, the government tapped into a number of external sources. Although wary of Somalia's irredentist ambitions, the superpowers jostled for influence in the Horn of Africa. Initially, for example, Western powers offered a small military programme amounting to US$10 million. The Soviet Union responded, however, by out-bidding this offer with a US$30 million package.[24] Ironically, Cold War competition resulted in a situation where the USSR supplied and trained the army during the 1960s, while the West did the same for the country's police force.

Economic assistance was also sought from equally diverse sources. Having very little domestic capital to invest itself, most of the costs of Somalia's development projects were met by foreign donors. Italy provided US$190 million of aid between 1953 and 1975, the Soviet Union US$152 million, China US$133 million, the United States US$75 million, and other Western countries a total of US$64 million.[25]

After 1969, however, the varied nature of these external patrons came to an end. This was prompted by a military coup led by Major-General Siad Barré. Seizing power, the military responded to the fragmented nature of Somali politics. Although Somalia can be described as an ethnically homogeneous state, its people are divided into five major clan-families, and can be further divided into numerous sub-clans after this. Between 1960 and 1969, Somalia resisted the trend elsewhere in Africa to form a one-party state. Consequently, pluralist competition mobilised along ethnic lines. In the 1969 election, for example, 1,002 candidates representing 62 parties competed for 123 seats in the national assembly.[26] Barré justified his *coup d'état* on the grounds that this inter-clan competition wasted scarce resources and bred corruption. Indeed, the military simply took advantage of the fact that it had become the most organised force in Somalia's fragmented society (external aid, after all, had made it the fourth biggest army on the African continent, next to those of Ethiopia, Nigeria and Ghana).

The range of external patrons shrank in post-coup Somalia because Barré's regime adopted scientific socialism as its ideological guide. Domestic and foreign businesses were nationalised, land became more strictly controlled by the state, political pluralism was suppressed, and a single Somali Revolutionary Socialist Party was established. Although the banana plantations (Somalia's biggest cash crop) remained in private hands, Barré's experiments in Marxism–Leninism won the backing of the Soviet Union. This alliance was confirmed with the signing of a Treaty of Friendship and Cooperation in 1974, and in return for external resources the USSR gained access to the Indian Ocean port of Berbera and several Somali airfields. Moscow considered its presence in the Horn of Africa as a vital counter-balance to the US arming of Emperor Haile Selassie's regime across the border in Ethiopia.

It was the army itself that benefited most from Soviet patronage. Military aid flowed into Somalia during the first half of the 1970s. The army, for example, increased in size from 12,000 soldiers in 1970 to 30,000 by 1977. These personnel had at their disposal Soviet-built tanks, as well as surface-to-air missiles, coastal patrol vessels and MiG aircraft. Similarly, there were over a thousand Soviet military advisors dispatched to Somalia during this period, while 2,400 Somalis travelled in the opposite direction to be trained in the USSR. Although Moscow concentrated on giving military aid to Somalia, as it did with most of its African clients, economic assistance was also forthcoming. Soviet aid helped build meat canning plants, irrigation systems and fisheries.[27]

Although Somalia now relied heavily on the Soviet Union as its primary patron, the government in Mogadishu was careful to keep its options open. External resources, after all, were invaluable whatever their ideological origin. For this reason, Barré made efforts to court fellow Islamic countries, joining the Arab League in 1974. Somalia also had profitable relations with China and North Korea.

In hindsight, it was a good job that these alternative diplomatic and aid channels remained open, because, by 1978, Soviet assistance had ceased. The break with Moscow came as a response to Somalia's invasion of Ethiopia. The border between these two states had never been precisely defined, and under colonial rule nomadic Somalis had retained grazing rights across the frontier. The irredentist government in Mogadishu had consequently always claimed the Ogaden to be an integral part of a greater Somaliland. In 1977, Barré, taking advantage of the political instability created by the Ethiopian revolution, decided to strike. The Somali regular army, trained and equipped by the Soviet Union, crossed the border in large numbers to fight alongside the insurgent (ethnic Somali) Western Somali Liberation Front.

These events posed something of a dilemma for officials in Moscow. The ousting of Haile Selassie by a Marxist-Leninist-oriented regime, led by Mariam Mengistu, had made Ethiopia a potentially valuable ally to the Soviet Union. In effect, Moscow was now forced to choose between Barré in Somalia (a country that the USSR had invested heavily in since 1969), and Mengistu in Ethiopia (a client state with more revolutionary potential). The USSR attempted to defuse the conflict by persuading all parties to abandon their nationalist claims and build, instead, a socialist federation in the Horn of Africa. Barré, however, refused Moscow's advances, and responded by unilaterally breaking the Treaty of Friendship and Cooperation, revoking the USSR's access to Berbera, and expelling all Soviet advisors from Somalia.

At first glance, Barré's decision to abandon the patronage of the Soviet Union seems odd. How could Somalia afford to lose these external resources? It would have seemed more prudent for Mogadishu to reel in its irredentist ambitions in favour of retaining Moscow's assistance. There was, however, a strategy behind Barré's actions.

Somalia was seeking to switch Cold War patrons. In April 1977, the United States had suspended its military aid to Ethiopia. Although Washington had continued to court the government in Addis Ababa after the revolution, US officials soon came up against ideological incompatibilities. This left the United States with no clients in this strategically important region. Barré's plan was to offer the services of Somalia in this role. If Washington accepted these advances, Somalia, he gambled, could both still receive external (now US) backing, and also be able to pursue its irredentist war in Ethiopia. This, however, proved to be one gamble too many.

Initially, it looked as if Barré had succeeded in his diplomatic *volte-face*. A deal involving US$460 million of US arms was negotiated between the two countries in June 1977 (with Saudi Arabia acting as mediator).[28] This was the breakthrough that prompted Barré's expulsion of the Soviet Union from Somalia. Yet, back in Washington, the administration of President Carter placed a good deal of emphasis on human rights in its foreign policy. As part of this arms deal, the United States insisted that Somalia should withdraw its army from the Ogaden. This, Barré refused to do. From having almost succeeded in manipulating historical events and Cold War competition to Somalia's advantage, Barré was now left with no major external backers. Consequently, although the Somali army had made impressive progress in its invasion of the Ogaden, it was now no match for Soviet-supplied Ethiopian forces, reinforced by Cuban combat troops. Somali forces, outnumbered and outgunned, finally withdrew from the Ogaden in March 1978.

Defeat in Ethiopia threatened the very future of Said Barré's regime. His government's overriding concern became the need to secure external patronage once more. Foreign assistance, in this respect, represented the regime's best hope of restoring legitimacy and prestige. Mogadishu sought help from Saudi Arabia, Iran, Egypt, China, France, the United Kingdom, West Germany, Italy, the United States, and Barré even made reconciliatory advances towards the Soviet Union.[29] Although economic assistance was forthcoming from some of these countries, none were prepared to re-arm the (potentially irredentist) Somali army. For Barré, however, military aid was essential. Arms were required not only to keep any idea of a greater Somaliland alive; they were also now desperately needed to maintain domestic order.

Barré eventually realised his main objective after two years in the wilderness. In 1980, Mogadishu came to an agreement with the United States whereby US forces gained access to the military facilities of Berbera in return for military aid. Washington was persuaded to extend this assistance in light of Cold War developments (where the US had lost a client state in Iran, and the Soviet Union had invaded Afghanistan). Barré's softer rhetoric, talking about creating a greater Somaliland only by peaceful means, clinched the deal. And once the United States was back in Somalia, other donors followed suit. Alongside Washington's US$51 million of military assistance and US$53 million of development aid, Italy gave US$9 million for irrigation and hydroelectric projects, while European Community institutions gave a further US$53 million.[30] In terms of external resources, the state of Somalia was now back in business.

Barré's regime, however, was never able to secure the levels of patronage it enjoyed in the 1970s. Western donors were too aware of the government's deteriorating human rights record, and the ever-present threat of irredentist adventurism. Eventually, with the Cold War waning, the United States suspended its aid to Mogadishu in

1988, and, in 1991, reacting to the collapse of the Somali state, despatched naval vessels to evacuate its citizens and diplomats. As T Frank Crigler, a former US ambassador to Somalia, put it, the United States 'turned out the lights, closed the door, and forgot about the place'.[31] With the imperatives of world politics having now changed, governments outside Africa were no longer particularly interested in Somalia's fate.

Without these external resources, the regime in Mogadishu could no longer assert its authority over the entire territory of Somalia. Since the Ogaden defeat, Barré had attempted to retain power by arming 'loyal' sub-clans, and encouraging them to 'pacify' other factions. Sources of opposition in rival clan lines were thus destroyed via harassment, exile, assassination and, towards the end, even the bombing of whole villages.[32] Barré's forces were pitted against the secessionist Somali National Movement in the north, the Majetein Somali Salvation Democratic Front in the north-east, the Somali Patriotic Movement in the south and west, and the United Somali Congress around Mogadishu. Essentially, as power in the centre faded, Somalia was carved up by local factions based on clan allegiances. Civil war was the result, and, defeated, Said Barré finally fled the country in 1991.

Somalia's former patrons had few remaining interests in this state, and had no wish to be embroiled in the civil war. Global strategic factors that previously may have fuelled a proxy war were now absent. As a result, clan warlords were left to fight among themselves.

This position did, however, briefly change in 1992. With non-government agencies (NGOs) reporting some 50,000 deaths in the fighting, and a further 4.5 million Somalis at risk through famine, the United Nations decided to act. UN emergency aid, and troops to protect it, were subsequently dispatched. Significantly, this operation coincided with the declaration of the 'New World Order' envisaged by US President George Bush. Wanting to show the potential for conflict resolution that this new international order offered, Bush agreed to bolster the UN operation with up to 30,000 US troops. The 'peace enforcement' of Operation Restore Hope commenced in December 1992.

Initially, this humanitarian intervention went well. Emergency aid reached the needy, ceasefires came into force among the clans, and there was even progress made at a conference of 'national reconciliation'. The United Nations, and the United States in particular, however, overstretched itself in terms of peace *enforcement*. Rather than mediating between factions, the UN operation suffered from 'mission creep', and began to dictate terms to the parties involved. US officials, for example, tried to marginalise a militia led by General Mohammed Farrah Aidid, who was seen as an obstacle to negotiations. When 23 Pakistani peace-keepers were killed trying to disarm Aidid's supporters, the UN sought to arrest the General. Months of raids against militia strongholds followed. US special forces, ferried by helicopter gunships across the skies of Mogadishu, exacted a high death toll on the city's population. The UN had lost its neutrality in the conflict.

Then, in October 1993, the tables were turned. During yet another raid against Aidid's militia, a US helicopter was shot down. In the ensuing firefight, 18 US Rangers were killed (alongside some 300 Somalis). The television pictures of dead US troops being paraded in the streets of Mogadishu proved too much for the American public. Washington DC's brief appetite for 'humanitarian' peace enforcement was at an end. By March 1994, US forces withdrew from Somalia, as did most of the UN mission.

Years later, Somalia still had no central authority. The state had collapsed. No government was able to generate legitimacy internally (among all Somalis), nor externally (benefiting from international patronage). Consequently, the country continued to be run by warlords, commanding clan militias. In effect, in the absence of the state, civil society ruled itself. Indeed, in the north, clan alliances sought to restore the state as a smaller secessionist Republic of Somalia (the territory of colonial British Somaliland). This new 'state', however, did not receive external recognition. The international community continued to recognise only the 'space-that-is-Somalia', despite its lack of leadership or functioning institutions.[33]

Somalia[34]

Territory:	630,000 sq km	Population:	9.7 million
Colonial power:	Britain/Italy	Independence:	1960
Major cities:	Mogadishu (capital)	Ethnic groups:	Somali
	Hargeysa	Life expectancy:	49 years
	Kismayu	Adult literacy:	25.1%
Urban pop.:	26.8%	Religion:	Islam
Languages:	Somali	Exports:	Bananas
	Italian		Livestock
	English		Hides
Currency:	Somali shilling	External debt:	US$2,561 million
Infant mortality:	113 deaths/thousand births	GDP per capita:	US$96

Glossary of key terms

Chasse gardée	A term (meaning 'private hunting-ground') used to convey the extent of France's diplomatic, economic and military activities within Francophone Africa.
Containment of communism	The primary goal of US foreign policy during the Cold War, which aimed to restrict opportunities for communist expansion globally.
Humanitarian intervention	Diplomatic and military activity more common in the 1990s, where state sovereignty may be violated in order to protect a population's human rights.
La francophonie	A reference to the French-speaking group of states or 'commonwealth'.
Non-interference in domestic jurisdictions	The respect of state sovereignty among countries, where it is agreed that no state has the right to interfere in the internal affairs of another.
Political conditionality	The demands of 'good governance' to which aid donors required recipient states to conform.
Proxy war	A local conflict which has been 'internationalised', effectively making the protagonists surrogates of competing 'superpowers'.
Quasi state	A state that is too weak to meet the empirical demands of a sovereign territory, but is still recognised as a full member of the international system of sovereign states.
Sovereignty	The claim of supreme political authority within a territory.

Questions raised by this chapter

1   Did African states benefit from the international political environment of the Cold War?

2   To what extent have external patrons differed in their policies towards African states?

3   Would you describe the 'New World Order' as a positive development for Africa?

4   Has the intervention of external interests merely served to underwrite the power of the Africa state in the post-colonial period?

5   Are external interests ever justified in violating a state's sovereignty?

Further reading

For a comprehensive overview of Africa's place in the global political system, Christopher Clapham's book is an excellent place to start. His focus on international relations from the African side of the fence is a welcome addition to the literature. After this, there have been a number of good books and articles concentrating more on the period following the Cold War. Gorm Olsen's articles on Europe, Guy Martin's on France specifically, F Ugboaja Ohaegbulam's on the United States, and Edmond Keller and Donald Rothchild's book which takes a more global look, are all well worth reading. In terms of case studies, although it was published in 1982 (before the end of the Cold War), Marina Ottaway's work on the Horn of Africa was invaluable to the writing of this chapter; while, for a more 'racy' read, John Stockwell's memoirs of being the CIA's task force leader in Angola is very revealing.

Clapham, Christopher (1996) *Africa and the international system: the politics of state survival*, Cambridge: Cambridge University Press.

Keller, Edmond J and Donald Rothchild, eds (1996) *Africa in the new international order: rethinking state sovereignty and regional security*, Colorado: Lynne Rienner.

Martin, Guy (1995) 'Continuity and change in Franco-African relations', *Journal of Modern African Studies* 33(1), 1–20.

Ohaegbulam, F Ugboaja (1992) 'The United States and Africa after the Cold War', *Africa Today* 4, 19–34.

Olsen, Gorm Rye (1997) 'Western Europe's relations with Africa since the end of the Cold War', *Journal of Modern African Studies* 35(2), 299–319.

Olsen, Gorm Rye (1998) 'Europe and the promotion of democracy in post Cold War Africa: how serious is Europe and for what reason?', *African Affairs* 97(388), 343–67.

Ottaway, Marina (1982) *Soviet and American influence in the Horn of Africa*, New York: Praeger.

Stockwell, John (1978) *In search of enemies: a CIA story*, London: Andre Deutsch.

9 Sovereignty again

Neo-colonialism, structural adjustment, and Africa's political economy

In terms of economics, there is no getting away from the fact that Africa is poor. The last two decades of the twentieth century saw many parts of the continent, particularly Africa south of the Sahara, come close to the point of financial collapse. In terms of Gross National Product (GNP), for example, the continent clearly produced less wealth for its people than other regions of the world (see Table 9.1). In 1995, Sub-Saharan Africa recorded a per capita GNP fifty-times smaller than that of the Western economies. This meant, for instance, that an average African economy, such as Mauritania, generated only US$460 for each of its citizens. The United States, by comparison, enjoyed US$26,980 per head. Mozambique, Africa's poorest country, was even more disadvantaged. It had to make do with a per-capita GNP of just US$80.[1]

Macro-economic indicators such as GNP, however, fail to get across what this poverty actually means for individuals in Africa. When a country fails to develop its economy faster than its population grows, hardship inevitably results. A quick survey of social statistics illustrates this point. Sub-Saharan Africans in the 1990s, for example, died, on average, in their early fifties. Europeans and North Americans, on the other hand, had a life expectancy well into their seventies. At the other end of life, babies in Africa had ten times more chance of dying before their first birthday than did those born in the West. Even in the field of Africa's post-colonial success stories, health and education, the comparisons are distressing. In 1995 over 40 per cent of Africans remained illiterate (with women particularly disadvantaged). In the West, literacy is almost taken for granted.[2]

These appalling statistics demand an explanation. How is it that, several decades after independence, Africa still finds itself in economic poverty?

The answer to this question involves factors both internal and external to the African continent. A neo-liberal school of thought tends to internalise the problem, largely blaming corrupt and inefficient African public policy. Others disagree. They claim that Africa's problems can be more accurately explained by the nature of the international economy. These scholars consider underdevelopment to have continued in the post-colonial era, with the West still exploiting African economies through mechanisms such as unfavourable 'terms of trade' and 'unequal exchange'.

Table 9.1 Comparative global economic and social indicators

	GNP per capita		Life expectancy at birth	Illiteracy
	US dollars 1995	Avg. annual growth (%) 1985–95	(years, 1995)	(percentage of adult population)
Sub-Saharan Africa	490	−1.1	52	d43
East Asia and Pacific	800	7.2	68	17
High Income Economies	24,930	1.9	77	<5
United Kingdom	18,700	1.4	77	<5
United States	26,980	1.3	77	<5
Algeria	1,600	−2.4	70	38
Angola	410	−6.1	47	58[a]
Benin	370	−0.3	50	63
Botswana	3,020	6.1	68	30
Burkina Faso	230	−0.2	49	81
Burundi	160	−1.3	49	65
Cameroon	650	−6.6	57	37
Cape Verde	960	–	65	28
Central African Republic	340	−2.4	48	40
Chad	180	0.6	48	52
The Comoros	470	−1.4	56	43
Congo, DRC (Kinshasa)	120	–	52[b]	23
Congo, Republic of (Brazzaville)	680	−3.2	51	25
Côte d'Ivoire	660	–	55	60
Djibouti	–	–	50	54
Egypt	790	1.1	63	49
Equatorial Guinea	380	–	49	22
Eritrea	608	–	48	–
Ethiopia	100	−0.3	49	65
Gabon	3,490	−8.2	55	37
The Gambia	320	–	46	61
Ghana	390	1.4	59	36
Guinea	550	1.4	44	72[c]
Guinea-Bissau	250	2.0	38	45
Kenya	280	0.1	58	22
Lesotho	770	1.2	61	29
Liberia	428	–	54	62

Lybia	5,650	–	65	24
Madagascar	230	−2.2	52	54
Malawi	170	−0.7	43	44
Mali	250	0.8	50	69
Mauritania	460	0.5	51	62
Mauritius	3,380	5.4	71	17
Morocco	1,110	0.9	65	56
Mozambique	80	3.6	47	60
Namibia	2,000	2.9	59	24
Niger	220	–	47	86
Nigeria	260	1.2	53	43
Rwanda	180	−5.4	46	40
São Tomé and Principe	350	−2.1	69	75[d]
Senegal	600	–	50	67
Seychelles	6,620	–	72	21
Sierra Leone	180	−3.6	40	69
Somalia	150[a]	–	49	76[a]
South Africa	3,160	−1.1	64	18
Sudan	400[a]	–	54	54
Swaziland	1,170	−1.4	58	23
Tanzania	120	1.0	51	32
Togo	310	−2.7	56	48
Tunisia	1,820	1.9	69	33
Uganda	240	2.7	42	38
Zambia	400	−0.8	46	22
Zimbabwe	540	−0.6	57	15

Sources: World Bank (1997) *World development report 1997*, Table 1 and Table 1a, Oxford: Oxford University Press; *Africa south of the Sahara, 1998*, 27, London: Europa; *The Middle East and North Africa, 1999*, 45, London: Europa.

Notes:
[a]=1990 figure
[b]=1990–5 figure
[c]=1993 figure
[d]=1991 figure

Both these schools make valid points in accounting for Africa's poverty. Consequently, both sides of the debate need to be explored. This chapter, however, focuses solely on the *external* factors hindering African development (as the *internal* constraints are discussed in the next chapter).

In this respect, structurally, the present chapter will first examine how under-development adapted itself to the post-colonial era. It will investigate how some charge that, after independence, the West merely substituted imperial rule with neo-colonial exploitation. Then, the chapter will take a closer look at the continent's debt crisis. Why do African states owe the West such colossal sums of capital? The final sections of the chapter bring the continent's post-colonial economic history up to date by exploring the phenomenon of 'structural adjustment'.

Structural adjustment, from the 1980s onwards, gave international financial institutions (IFIs) such as the World Bank and the International Monetary Fund considerable influence over the formulation of public policy within debtor states. In return for external loans, African countries were compelled to follow strict instructions on how to govern. Failure to comply to this external bidding would have resulted in bankruptcy. And this issue of conditional lending brings the book back to the same theme of sovereignty explored in the previous chapter. It is slightly different this time, given that the focus is on economic rather than political sovereignty, but, once again, external intervention helped determine the path of Africa's post-colonial political development. The chapter concludes by analysing how this loss of sovereignty affected the relationship between state and civil society on the continent.

Burdens of the international economy

The imperial inheritance, as documented in Chapter 2, left Africa somewhat disadvantaged in the modern international economy. During the colonial years, limited development based on the continent's primary sector had been undertaken (in agriculture and mining), and a basic infrastructure built to support this. Yet the actual level of economic growth produced in Africa was scant reward for this activity. Profits, on the whole, were exported to the West, rather than being invested locally. This left Africa, at independence, with highly specialised export economies, a minute manufacturing base, a lack of access to technology, and populations where few were trained in the ways of modern business, social services or public administration. In short, Europe had indeed underdeveloped Africa. As Walter Rodney put it, 'the vast majority of Africans went into colonialism with a hoe and came out with a hoe.'[3]

Exploitation of African economies did not end, however, with the flag-lowering ceremonies at independence. Decisions made in the West still continued to have a considerable influence over Africa's potential to develop. Indeed, Kwame Nkrumah, Ghana's first president, argued that colonialism had merely made way for a type of *neo*-colonialism. He explained: 'The essence of neo-colonialism is that the State which is subject to it is, in theory, independent and has all the trappings of international sovereignty. In reality its economic system and thus its political system is directed from outside.'[4] Hence, although formal political control had now ended, Africa still had to contend with the old colonial division of labour.

One of the major structural problems within this international economy, in African eyes, was 'unequal exchange'. Colonial rule left almost all African states with highly specialised 'monocrop' economies, usually producing just one, two or three commodities for export. The Rwandan economy, for example, was dominated by coffee, while Malawi concentrated almost exclusively on tobacco

Table 9.2 African export concentration, 1982–6 (countries where primary products account for over 75 per cent of a state's total export earnings)

One product (*15 countries*)

Algeria: *oil and gas*	Angola: *oil*	Botswana: *diamonds*
Burundi: *coffee*	Congo: *oil*	Gabon: *oil*
Guinea: *bauxite*	Libya: *oil*	Niger: *Uranium*
Nigeria: *oil*	Rwanda: *coffee*	São Tomé: *cocoa*
Somalia: *livestock*	Uganda: *coffee*	Zambia: *copper*

Two products (*14 countries*)

Cape Verde: *fish, fruit*	Chad: *cotton, livestock*	Comoros: *vanilla, cloves*
Congo-Kinshasa: *copper, coffee*	Egypt: *oil, cotton*	Equatorial Guinea: *cocoa, timber*
Ethiopia: *coffee, hides*	Ghana: *cocoa, bauxite*	Liberia: *iron ore, rubber*
Malawi: *tobacco, tea*	Mali: *livestock, cotton*	Mauritania: *iron ore, fish*
Réunion: *sugar, fish*	Seychelles: *oil, fish*	

Three products (*8 countries*)

Benin: *oil, coffee, cocoa*	Burkina Faso: *cotton, vegetable oil, livestock*
Cameroon: *oil, coffee, cocoa*	Central African Republic: *coffee, diamonds, timber*
Guinea-Bissau: *cashews, groundnuts, palm oil*	Kenya: *coffee, refined oil, tea*
Senegal: *fish, groundnuts, phosphates*	Sudan: *cotton, vegetable oil, livestock*

Four products (4 countries)

Côte d'Ivoire: *cocoa, coffee, refined oil, timber*	Madagascar: *coffee, cotton, cloves, fish*
Sierra Leone: *diamonds, cocoa, coffee, bauxite*	Togo: *phosphates, cocoa, cotton, coffee*

More diverse export economies (*11 countries*)

Djibouti, Gambia, Lesotho, Mauritius, Morocco, Mozambique, South Africa, Swaziland, Tanzania, Tunisia, Zimbabwe.

Source: Brown, Michael Barratt (1995) *Africa's choices: after thirty years of the World Bank*, London: Penguin; 28.

and tea (see Table 9.2). These countries had no other major sources of economic activity with which to generate additional income, or to act as a substitute should there be a bad harvest or a slump in that particular commodity market. What is more, given that there was little local demand for merchandise such as tea and coffee on the continent, all this produce had to be exported. Africa, as a result, was totally dependent on the West to buy its products.

This put Western buyers at a considerable advantage. They operated in so-called 'closed markets', and used this reality to depress prices. In 1988, for

Table 9.3 Index of international trade, 1960–95 (1980=100)

	1960	1970	1980	1990	1995
Volume of exports:					
Developed countries	24	54	100	155	191
S and SE Asia	46	51	100	276	523
Developing Africa	45	132	100	102	105
Unit value of exports:					
Developed countries	28	33	100	127	136
S and SE Asia	21	20	100	95	94
Developing Africa	12	10	100	81	84
Terms of trade:					
Developed countries	117	122	100	110	113
S and SE Asia	92	79	100	85	79
Developing Africa	49	36	100	70	64

Source: United Nations (1997) *Conference on Trade and Development. Handbook of international trade and development statistics, 1995*, New York: United Nations; tables 2.1, 2.3 and 2.5.

example, the French transnational corporation, SucDen, bought Côte d'Ivoire's entire cocoa harvest.[5] Given that the GNP of Côte d'Ivoire was almost totally dependent on this sale, and that there were few alternative companies to sell to, SucDen was always going to receive this produce at a bargain price. This helps to explain why the value of Africa's exports generally fell by 20 per cent between 1980 and 1995 (see Table 9.3 above) – a fact that only exacerbated Africa's problem of a lack of access to investment capital.

This structural inequity also meant that the continent had to buy expensive Western-manufactured goods with the income generated by the export of these cheap primary products. In effect, Africans had to buy back their own raw materials, in a manufactured form, at an inflated rate. A United Nations report, for example, estimated that 85 per cent of the value of manufactured goods was kept in the West. Only 15 per cent of this capital found its way back to the country that had provided the raw materials.[6] What is more, over time, prices paid for primary commodities fell, while the price of manufactured imports increased. Consequently, the West's terms of trade improved, while those of the developing world declined (see Table 9.3).

Until Africa is able to diversify its economies and process its own raw materials, it will be difficult for it to escape this trap of unequal exchange. It is not, however, an impossible task. The so-called 'Asian Tigers' have made considerable economic progress since independence. Starting, apparently, with similar imperial legacies, economic diversification has occurred to some degree, and wealth has been generated (compare, for example, the figures between Sub-Saharan Africa and East Asia in Table 9.3). This would seem to point to the importance of additional factors (both external and internal), beyond just unequal exchange, when explaining the African continent's poor economic performance in the post-colonial period.

The African debt crisis

African states were not passive victims of unequal exchange. Independence gave governments a degree of political autonomy with which they attempted to diversify their economies and break the continent's dependence on problematic primary exports. Each state drew up its own development plan, striving to build on what it could salvage from its colonial inheritance. Many adopted policies of import substitution, for example. They tried to establish local manufacturing plants to produce goods previously imported from the West. African states also invested heavily in infrastructure (roads and power generation, for example), as well as human resources (education and health).

Development requires investment capital, however, and since little economic surplus was generated within Africa, governments took the decision to borrow from the West in order to kick-start their economies.

By the 1990s, Africa was crippled by its debts. In the twenty years to 1994, Sub-Saharan Africa's total indebtedness had increased from the equivalent of 15 per cent to 90 per cent of its GNP. Just paying the interest on these loans had a debilitating effect on local economies. The service on the US$221 billion continent-wide debt cost Africa the equivalent of 21 per cent of its export income each year. With so much capital being drained from the continent, further development was almost impossible.[7]

But how did the continent get into such a precarious financial position? Why is Africa so indebted to the West? The answer to these questions lies in a combination of factors. Externally, it is a product of the continent's declining terms of trade; the massive increases in oil prices during the 1970s; and a rise of interest rates in the early 1980s.

Initially, African governments borrowed investment capital that they thought could be repaid through future sales of primary produce. In effect, they mortgaged prospective harvests and mining output for funds to launch Africa's development process. They did not, however, bank on the international price paid for these commodities declining as they did (see Table 9.3). Take the case of Ghana, for instance. Income from this country's 1981 cocoa exports measured just one quarter of their 1973/1974 value. A decade later, the price for cocoa had fallen by half again.[8] Given that Africa's monocrop economies had no alternative sources of income, declining commodity prices made it difficult for the governments to repay their loans.

Those African states that did not produce oil suffered even more. In 1973, and then again at the end of the 1970s, the Organisation of Petroleum Exporting Countries (OPEC) increased oil prices dramatically. Economic shockwaves hit the entire world. The West sank into recession, but Africa was pushed even further towards the brink. Where the continent had spent just 1 per cent of its GDP on fuel imports in 1970, ten years later this had risen to 6 per cent.[9] Put another way, in 1960, a ton of African sugar bought 6.3 tons of oil. By 1982, this same ton of sugar could be exchanged for only 0.7 tons of oil.[10] Consequently, the already declining terms of trade of these African states sank even further.

The OPEC oil-price hikes also had further repercussions. The newly enriched oil producing countries invested large amounts of their new-found wealth in the Western banking system. This gave the financial institutions a surplus of 'petrodollars', which they then offered to African countries in the form of cheap loans. Starved of foreign exchange by the very same oil price rises, African governments gladly accepted these loans. By the time these liabilities matured, however, they were no longer inexpensive debts. The second oil shock of 1979, combined with the reaction to a rising budget deficit in the United States, saw interest rates soar. What were initially attractive loans had now become impossible burdens on African economies. External factors not of Africa's making, then, had transformed the relatively responsible borrowing of the 1970s into the debt crisis of the 1980s and 1990s.

Zambia was one of the countries hit hardest by these economic trends.[11] After decolonisation in 1964, the country's economy was relatively prosperous. The first eight years of independence saw per-capita GNP grow annually at an average of 2.4 per cent. The government used this revenue to invest in human resources, building an impressive welfare state. Education and health improved rapidly, while poverty was alleviated through state food subsidies. A strategy of import substitution was also implemented, with relative success, and Zambia's manufacturing sector grew at 9.8 per cent per annum.

In 1973, however, Zambia, as a fuel importer, was hit by the OPEC oil rises. This was compounded by a fall in the price of copper on the international commodity markets.[12] Unfortunately, copper was Zambia's monocrop. Previously, copper (along with cobalt) had accounted for 97 per cent of Zambia's export income, and 58 per cent of government revenue. With no alternative economic activity to fall back on, Zambia was forced to seek loans from the West. The country's debt has spiralled upwards ever since. In 1994, Zambia owed US$5,207 million, the equivalent of 161 per cent of its GDP.[13] The drain of capital created by servicing this debt reduced a previously impressive public welfare service to almost nothing.

Susan George asks: 'What logic can there be for grinding down a whole continent...?'[14] Africa, in all probability, is never going to be able to repay its accumulated debts. Despite vast sums of capital leaving the continent in debt service, little impact is made on the total owed. The more the West demands its 'pound of flesh', the less chance Africa has of developing and generating income to clear these debts. In the meantime, people are dying. UNICEF, for example, calculates that the debt crisis kills half a million children in Africa annually.[15]

Africa could be given a fresh start. This could be done with little, or no, harm to Western economies. The actual amount owed by Africa is insignificant in global terms. What is more, over 80 per cent of this debt is owed to public institutions (Western governments, the World Bank and the IMF). Cancelling repayments, therefore, would not disadvantage any commercial company. As George comments: 'Africa's debt is modest as to be no threat to anyone except Africans. Even in the most unlikely event that all 43 Sub-Saharan countries suddenly stop servicing their debt, the world financial system would just keep trundling along, its computer screens scarcely registering a blip.'[16] Realising this fact, Western governments began to talk seriously about writing off African debts in the 1990s. International agreement to this end, however, is proving elusive. In the meantime, 'One can almost hear the sound of Africa sliding off the map.'[17]

The era of structural adjustment

With African economies imploding under the burden of debt, something had to give. The continent's governments were finding it increasingly difficult to raise new loans to service their previous borrowing. In most cases, the International Monetary Fund and the World Bank became the only sources of credit left. It was at this point that these IFIs introduced Structural Adjustment Programmes (SAPs).

SAPs are programmes of conditional lending. In return for further loans, recipients are obliged to make changes to their economic policy. IFIs require African countries to liberalise their economies, opening them to international and domestic private capital, while at the same time reducing the role of the state. African governments had very little choice but to go along with this structural adjustment, as there were no alternative sources of capital available.

Kenya, Malawi and Mauritius were the first states to introduce SAP reforms at the start of the 1980s, and by the mid-1990s almost all other African countries had followed suit. Even resisters, such as Zambia and Tanzania, which initially tried to continue socialist development strategies, had succumbed by this date. Despite there being no strong African constituency for structural adjustment, Western financial institutions were now dictating the basics of the continent's public policy.

After independence, African governments adopted statist development strategies. With only very small indigenous *private* sectors, governments decided that *public* institutions should be constructed to drive the development process forward. SAPs, however, were about dismantling these development states. IFI officials sought to introduce the discipline of the free market to Africa (mimicking the neo-liberal reforms of Western economic policy at this time). Placing the blame for Africa's previously poor performance on inefficient state-centred development strategies, IFIs decreed that the continent should change tack. Now the market, not the state, would determine the pattern of Africa's economic progress.

Each SAP was specifically tailored to the individual country concerned, but there were three universal pillars at the heart of all these programmes. Lending was conditional on: first, that development strategies should favour agricultural production; second, that governments operate more 'realistic' trade and exchange-rate policies; and third, that the public sector should be made more efficient.[18] Given the impact that these SAPs had on African politics during the 1980s and 1990s, it is well worth exploring these three conditions in more detail.

The key concern of the IFIs was that the continent's development policies prior to the 1980s had resulted in a significant urban bias. Despite rural areas being the most productive sector of the economy, and the vast majority of Africans relying on this sector to earn their living, it was urban districts that had benefited most from the state's allocation of public resources. Effectively, capital was being drained from the countryside to subsidise the activities of town and city life. The state, dominating the marketing of agricultural produce, for example, consciously paid farmers below market prices for their harvests. They then used the difference between this low price and the income they received for these crops, once they had been sold on the international market, to bolster urban interests. Import substitution industries, other state enterprises (known as parastatals) and bloated bureaucracies, all benefited from this state investment. An urban constituency of bureaucrats, industrial workers, business people, and the politicians themselves (in effect, all the most powerful social groups within African society), came to take this privileged position for granted.

The consequence of rural areas losing out in this manner, however, was that agricultural production performed badly in the post-colonial period. Farmers, given the low prices paid, had little incentive to increase their output. This situation eventually resulted in Africa having to import the majority of its food, rather than grow its own. It was this neglect of agricultural production, as well as the inefficient investment in urban areas, that structural adjustment sought to address.

SAPs demanded that farmers be paid the full market price for their crops. This rise in price would have the effect of encouraging greater agricultural output. This, in turn, would increase African export revenues, introducing surplus capital to economies. In effect, IFIs were directing African countries to concentrate their efforts on exporting agricultural goods, and to abandon their inefficient investments in state development enterprises such as import substitution (see below).

The second pillar of structural adjustment was the reform of trade and exchange-rate policies. A neo-liberal approach, for example, requires state restrictions on imports and exports to be lifted. The IFIs argued that administrative command over Africa's international trade proved costly. Not only was the system of issuing import and export licences too bureaucratic, it was also open to corruption.

Similarly, SAP directives also required governments to remove tariffs protecting the import substitution industries. The World Bank's 1981 Berg Report considered African manufacturers who had previously enjoyed this state protection to be, on the whole, inefficient. These state corporations were portrayed as parasitic, bleeding the economy of capital, rather than being able to pay their own way. IFIs reasoned that, if these organisations were not competitive, they should be liquidated, as Africans would benefit more from having access to cheaper foreign imports instead.[19]

The third, and final, SAP condition related to making the public sector more efficient. The Berg Report argued that previous African development strategies had resulted in too much state intervention. Instead, the IFIs required that state influence be 'rolled back', and economies opened up to more efficient private-sector investment.[20] A primary goal of the SAP reforms, therefore, was a significant reduction in government spending. Administrative budgets were to be cut, and services, where appropriate, handed over to the private sector. Again, it was a case of subjecting as much economic activity as possible to the discipline of the free market (rather than central planning). In short, African states had previously enjoyed a virtual monopoly over economic activity; structural adjustment was about eliminating this monopoly.

The economic, social and political ramifications of structural adjustment

Structural adjustment had widespread repercussions across the African continent, and these were not solely confined to the economic field. The West's requirement that African states change their economic policy had major knock-on effects on the continent's social and political processes as well.

The economic impact

Research on the economic results of structural adjustment has produced a variety of opinions. In 1994, the World Bank suggested that 'African countries have made great strides in improving policies and restoring growth'. Using six countries that had fully implemented their SAPs as case studies, the Bank showed how these states succeeded in transforming previous negative economic growth into positive growth (2 per cent annually over the 1987–91 period).[21] Other researchers are more sceptical. The United Nations Economic Commission on Africa, for example, considered the results of structural adjustment to be dubious, at best. Its 1989 report suggested that non-adjusting African economies had performed just as well, if not better, than their SAP counterparts.[22]

The reality of the situation is that some countries have shown modest improvements under the SAP regime, while others have continued their decline. No economy, so far, has experienced any outstanding improvement or degeneration as a result of structural adjustment. As the 1994 World Bank report itself concedes, of all the Sub-Saharan countries monitored, six have enjoyed obvious improvement, nine small improvements and eleven deterioration.[23] Even here, opinions are mixed. Is it true, for example, that decline continues in some countries because of the ill-conceived nature of the SAPs? Or has this merely resulted from poor implementation of these programmes by host governments? Similarly, could it be that, although economies continue to deteriorate, this would have been far worse without the implementation of structural adjustment? No clear pattern has emerged. What is certain, however, is that the continent remains uncomfortably close to the economic brink.

Even if, in time, the structural adjustment programmes do produce positive results, they can only provide minor relief. They are designed primarily to turn blighted economies around. This may build essential foundations for future growth, but SAPs by themselves will not stimulate sustained development. Work has to be undertaken elsewhere for this to happen, particularly in the area of debt relief. In 1990, for example, grants and loans to Africa (including the SAPs) exactly offset the debt service paid in that year.[24] In short, many African countries are still paying out more in interest than they receive in foreign capital. No money is left for development investment. As Edward Jaycox, of the World Bank's Africa Bureau, warned in 1990: 'For seventeen countries in Africa…the financial crisis is so deep, the debt burden so heavy, they will not make it.…[SAPs] will not, in fact, work unless there is an increase in the flow of resources from outside.'[25]

Structural adjustment's envisaged strategy for raising this foreign capital has also been questioned. The Berg Report clearly suggests that Africa should concentrate its efforts on increasing income from the export of primary produce. As the World Bank's 1995 report confirmed, SAPs are about 'putting exporters first'.[26] Yet the problem with pushing export-led growth is that this simply reproduces the disadvantages of unequal exchange experienced before. Also, even if African countries do succeed in increasing output, it may be that this will be offset by other SAP countries doing likewise. IFIs, after all, are encouraging a multitude of SAP countries worldwide to expand primary production. Once all these states have devalued their currencies and increased production, then there is little relative advantage to be gained. International markets will react to the increased availability of primary goods by lowering commodity prices. Consequently, increased production will not net greater income. Africa will be running in order to stand still. Percy Mistry, a former senior manager at the World Bank, has commented: 'To the extent that [Africa] continues to rely on primary commodities to generate further export earnings, it is cutting its own throat.'[27]

Future development, as the World Bank agrees, will emerge from the production of non-traditional primary produce and manufactured goods, both for the export and domestic markets. This, however, requires capital, most likely in the form of foreign investment. In this respect, SAPs were meant to attract external capital. This simply has not happened. Transnational corporations will not invest in fragile economies, whose governments, partly due to the impact of SAPs, cannot guarantee a stable currency, the maintenance of infrastructure, public order or administrative continuity. Transnational corporations (TNCs), in recent years, have been more attracted to Latin American and Asian operations.[28]

In terms of a development strategy, then, structural adjustment seems flawed. As the World Bank points out, 'development cannot proceed when inflation is high, the exchange rate overvalued, farmers overtaxed, vital imports in short supply, prices and productivity heavily regulated, key public services in disrepair, and basic financial services unavailable'.[29] SAPs, in this respect, have at least started to address constraints on growth, such as the urban bias and the inefficient bloated state. They have not, however, provided a strong enough foundation. Export-led growth through traditional primary products seems misguided, while there is little investment available to develop non-traditional economic activity (especially given the continued drain of debt service). It would therefore appear that Africa has received little that is positive, by way of long-term development, in return for its loss of economic sovereignty. This sad reality is all the more apparent when the social and political consequences of structural adjustment are considered.

The social impact of structural adjustment

If the economic impact of structural adjustment in Africa was somewhat uncertain, the social outcomes were very apparent. Reforms of the public sector resulted in widespread increases in unemployment and cuts in public services. In Zambia, for example, the reduction of state protection for the country's (import substitution) textile industry resulted in 8,500 workers losing their jobs. In Livingstone alone, 47 clothing manufacturers ceased producing. The remaining factories operated at between 15 and 20 per cent of capacity. Similarly, many of Zambia's loss-making parastatals were also liquidated under the SAP regime. Among the casualties were Zambia Airways, the United Bus Company of Zambia, the National Hotels Development Corporation, Manza Batteries, and the National Import and Export Corporation. Over 25,000 redundancies resulted. This, combined with 60,000 job losses in the civil service between 1991 and 1995, increased the country's already swollen ranks of unemployed.[30]

Structural adjustment also required government spending to be curtailed. Zimbabwe, for example, halved its budget deficit between 1989 and 1995. In order to do this, however, public services were hit hard. For instance, expenditure on medical staff and drugs was cut significantly. Similarly, education budgets were reduced. Fees for all secondary schools and urban primary schools were introduced, where previously education had been free.[31] This reduction of services brought the greatest disadvantage to the most vulnerable.

Perhaps the most contentious social consequence of structural adjustment, however, was the removal of state food subsidies. The urban poor, in particular, had come to rely on these subsidies simply in order to survive. They had few other sources of food (unlike their rural compatriots, who could grow their own). In Zambia during 1977, the maize subsidy amounted to 71 per cent of the market value for this staple. By 1983, Zambians were expected to pay the full price themselves.[32] Such subsidies were revoked right across the continent, making the SAP reforms deeply unpopular.

By the mid-1990s, even the World Bank was forced to admit: 'More could have been done, should have been done, to reduce poverty in the context of structural adjustment programs.'[33] When the extent of this suffering became apparent in the late 1980s, the IFIs began to build 'poverty alleviation programmes' into their SAPs. These were designed to combat the worst excesses that the switch towards neo-liberal economics brought. By this time, however, it was too late for many. Millions of Africans had experienced hardship. Consequently, the social impact of structural adjustment had already begun to have major repercussions on Africa's political process.

The political impact of structural adjustment

An IMF condition for an SAP loan to Sierra Leone in the mid-1980s demanded that the government cut its rice subsidies. President Siaka Stevens warned the IMF that it was asking his administration 'to commit political suicide'.[34] He felt his government's already strained legitimacy would collapse totally if it was forced to raise prices on this chief staple. In this respect, Stevens's comment highlights that what may be rational in terms of economic change is not necessarily rational politically. Most African governments had great difficulty building constituencies in favour of the SAP reforms among their people. Indeed, many failed miserably in this task, and the price of failure was removal from office.

The problem was that structural adjustment directly attacked Africa's political *status quo*. The political process on this continent, more so than other parts of the world, revolved around the state. Government institutions were recognised as the key providers of employment, services and resources. In effect, the state was the gatekeeper to opportunities of social mobility and welfare. This is how a political system based on client–patron relationships emerged in the post-colonial period (discussed in Chapter 6). Clients would offer their support to governments in return for benefits such as jobs in the public sector, administrative 'favours', new schools for their region, a well for their village, the metalling of a local road, and so on. It was this client–patron interdependence that provided the societal 'glue' that bound the whole political system together, thus generating a degree of stability. SAPs, however, consciously aimed to break these client–patron relationships, as they were judged to be economically (if not politically) inefficient.

A key element of structural adjustment, in this respect, was 'rolling back' the state. It aimed to keep the state's intervention in the economy to a minimum, promoting civil society activity instead. Consequently, government budgets were cut, parastatals liquidated or privatised, and public services reduced.

The political consequences of this 'roll back' were nothing short of traumatic. The shrunken state simply could not command the resources it had enjoyed previously. Patronage, as a consequence, also shrank. Clients lost their jobs in the liquidated parastatals and diminished civil services; 'favours' could no longer be given to importers and exporters, as international trade was now less controlled by state administrators; and governments did not have budgets from which they could offer new schools or wells to supporters. In short, SAP reforms resulted in the state elite being able to look after fewer of its existing clients, and having less flexibility to recruit new supporters. The result was declining government legitimacy, and growing political instability.

This instability was most apparent in the urban areas. It was here, after all, that most of the disaffected resided. These included unemployed industrial labourers, laid off when their import substitution factories closed; redundant civil servants and parastatal workers; students, protesting at reduced education funding; doctors, teachers and other professionals, hit by scaled-down public service provision; and most threatening, the urban poor, whose income had been dramatically affected by the removal of food subsidies. These urban groups operated in a confined area, which made mobilisation simpler, and in close proximity to the actual apparatus of government (parliament buildings and ministries). This made it all the easier for them to challenge their former patrons, calling for a change of government.

The consequences of this political instability were unique in each of the countries concerned. Common manifestations, however, included: sustained strikes by public sector workers; ethnic tensions, as states often did not now have the resources to commit to 'ethnic-arithmetic'; and, more violently, 'food riots', with the urban poor in particular registering their distress at the removal of state subsidies. In more extreme cases, SAPs contributed to an environment where the military or armed rebel groups were encouraged to topple the struggling incumbent governments (Sudan and Liberia, for example). Elsewhere, elites continued in their exploitative ways in a scaled-down state, risking complete state collapse (Zaire and Somalia – see Chapter 10). More frequently, however, this instability assisted campaigns which sought a transition to multiparty democracy (Zambia and Malawi – see Chapter 11). Whatever the outcome, this external intervention left state elites struggling to plug the gap left by declining legitimacy. IFIs had seriously undermined the old political *status quo* of centralised states based on clientelism.

State, civil society and external interests

The continent's debt crisis, and the structural adjustment that followed this, had a considerable impact on the three-way relationship between state, civil society and external interests in post-colonial Africa. The 1980s and 1990s saw external interests become more influential, civil society expand, while the state lost a significant amount of power.

The debt crisis allowed the West to poach a good deal of economic sovereignty from African states. With the continent's governments forced to accept conditional lending, IFIs succeeded in imposing their preferred neoliberal economic order on African economies. Consequently, African politicians lost considerable control over setting their own exchange rates, establishing price controls, organising budgets, and determining what services should be offered to citizens. Decisions of public policy now had to be made in consultation with IFI officials back in Washington DC.

Civil society was one of the main beneficiaries of this external intervention. Where once the state was truly a leviathan, now it no longer had the resources to maintain all the political space it once occupied. This enforced roll back of the state allowed civil society to expand. Rival sources of power, for example, emerged in the private sector, while local associations and non-governmental organisations took on some of the services formerly run by the state. Even in the political field, which was once so dominated by the apparatus of the one-party state, civil society once again became active. Sustained pro-democracy campaigns led to the holding of multi-party elections in most of the continent's territories during the 1990s.

As for the state elite itself, the last two decades of the twentieth century proved to be difficult times to navigate. The lack of economic development during this period always meant that resources available for political bargaining were scarce. The conditions imposed by the SAPs, however, severely compounded this problem. 'Empires' once commanded by state patrons were now under direct attack from the neo-liberal demands of the IFIs. Parastatals and civil services were 'downsized' (to use the parlance of the day), and budgets and public services cut. Patronage opportunities diminished as a result. To remain in power, elites had to adapt to these new conditions. Some managed this through manipulating the move towards multi-party competition, while others, such as Zaire and Somalia, lost control, and their states degenerated towards complete collapse.

It would be wrong to think, however, that SAPs always totally destroyed the power bases of the old elites. Even today, state institutions remain the best opportunity for social advancement on the African continent, and the state itself continues to be the main prize of political competition.

Given these facts, those in power did not give up their privileged position lightly. They sought, instead, to tame the intrusion of external interests into their domain. Perhaps the most obvious method that state elites deployed to defend their 'empires' was through the non-implementation of SAP conditions. On the whole, budgets were cut, trade liberalised and prices deregulated, but privatisation occurred at a much slower rate. Parastatals, after all, provided the most lucrative sources for state patronage. As the World Bank's 1994 report complained: 'The efforts to privatise state corporations and to improve their performance have yielded meagre results so far.'[35] Even where privatisation did eventually occur, elites still often managed to benefit from this arrangement. Ministers effectively sold state property to themselves or their associates at bargain prices.

Indeed, IFI intervention, in some cases, was even manipulated by state elites to provide additional sources of legitimacy. Personal rulers could now blame their economic and political failures on the 'imperialist' intervention of the IMF and the World Bank. They could wash their hands of responsibility, while pushing through economic and other reforms for which there was no local popular support. Indeed, it is was almost as if African states had become more accountable to the IFIs than they were to their own citizens. Keeping the World Bank, the IMF and Western governments happy, after all, ensured that loan and development aid continued to flow into the continent, and, for the state elite, this source of finance became their lifeblood. External capital was used to sustain remaining client–patron relationships, as a bid for survival. For the state elite, then, the 1980s and 1990s were about adaptation, evasion, stalling and collaboration. In this manner, a degree of sovereignty could be maintained, ensuring that many of their number, although by no means all, managed (partially) to ride out the attentions not only of the IFIs and their SAPs, but also of those within civil society as well.

Case study: Ghana's structural adjustment

Imperial rule ended in Ghana during 1957, when the former British Gold Coast Colony and British Togoland merged to form Sub-Saharan Africa's first independent 'black' state. As one of the wealthier colonial possessions, Ghana's economic future seemed secured. It was the largest producer of cocoa beans in the world, it had considerable reserves of minerals, vast timber supplies grew in its tropical forests, there was a relatively good transport infrastructure, and there existed the potential to generate hydro-electric power. Twenty-five years later, however, Ghana's economy had virtually collapsed. Food production had failed to keep pace with population growth, cocoa and timber output had fallen, a solid manufacturing sector was yet to emerge, and the country's health, education and transport services were in disarray.[36] This case study examines the reasons behind this economic decline, as well as the attempts to reverse this deterioration with structural adjustment reforms implemented from 1983 onwards.

Ghana's post-colonial political history mimics that of many other African countries. Once in power, the nationalist government centralised the state, and the political process became personalised around the chief executive (in this case President Kwame Nkrumah). Nkrumah was ousted from government in 1966 by a military coup, and during the next fifteen years Ghana underwent further coups and counter-coups, interspersed by transfers to civilian rule. A greater degree of stability entered Ghanaian politics, however, with the arrival of the military government of Flight-Lieutenant Jerry Rawlings. Coming to power in 1981, it was this regime that oversaw the country's structural adjustment. Rawlings went on to remain at the helm of the Ghanaian state at the end of the twentieth century, having successfully won multi-party elections in 1992 and 1996.

As ever, both external and internal factors conspired to limit Ghana's economic development prior to structural adjustment. Despite being one of Africa's wealthiest colonies, Ghana still inherited a monocrop economy distorted towards the export of primary produce. The country was locked into selling cocoa, timber and minerals to the West, and importing manufactured goods in return. As a result, regular economic crises arose when the cocoa harvest failed or international prices dropped. Even in good years, primary produce still had to be bartered for manufactured goods on the international market of 'unequal exchange'. With relatively little capital to invest in economic diversification, Ghana found it difficult to loosen this dependency on exports.

Ghana's decline, however, cannot be attributed solely to an exploitative international market. There were also internal constraints to development. Most of these arose from an 'urban bias' created by the government's chosen strategy of import substitution. Understandably, Ghana wished to rely less on the international market and more on domestic manufacturing. It therefore invested heavily in forging a fledgling manufacturing base, largely managed by parastatals and protected from outside competition by import tariffs. Foreign assets were also nationalised as part of this show of defiance against neo-colonialism.

State-led development, like all development, however, needs investment, and Ghana's only ready source of domestic capital was its cocoa crop and other primary produce. Profits were therefore squeezed from this sector of the economy in order to foot the bill for Ghana's welfare programmes, its import substitution investment, its food subsidies, its general administration, and indeed almost all state activity. Consequently, state marketing boards, who enjoyed a monopoly, paid cocoa producers below the market value for their harvests. The government then pocketed the difference between this low price and the higher international market price, once it had sold this produce on. This provided the bulk of government income. Effectively, rural producers were being forced to subsidise the state and its development strategy (as well as the elite's expansive and expensive client–patron networks).

Market forces, however, were not completely subdued by state intervention. Given the marketing boards' refusal to pay realistic prices, the incentive for rural Ghanaians actually to produce was minimal. In the case of cocoa, many farmers refused to sell to the state marketing boards, choosing illegal parallel markets (black markets) instead. Cocoa was smuggled across the border to Côte d'Ivoire, where higher prices could be obtained. Other farmers chose to cease production of cocoa altogether. In 1965, Ghana had exported 560,000 tonnes of cocoa; by 1981, the (official) yield was down to 150,000 tonnes.[37] Similar declines in output also occurred in the timber, diamond and bauxite industries.

In effect, the government had squeezed its only productive sector too hard, resulting in the entire economy collapsing. There was no incentive to produce when the state retained so much of the profit for itself. Yet, despite this reality of economic contraction, the state bureaucratically still attempted to expand. There were now over 235 parastatals, and the civil service was growing annually by 17 per cent.[38] The supply of capital from the rural areas may have been exhausted, but the state elite was still intent on building its patronage networks.

It was at this point (December 1981) that Jerry Rawlings intervened. 'Fellow citizens of Ghana, as you would have noticed we are not playing the National Anthem. In other words, this is not a coup. I ask nothing less than a revolution...'[39] This was the message of Rawlings's first radio broadcast. His Provisional National Defence Council (PNDC) aimed to build a people's democracy in Ghana.

In terms of economic policy, Rawlings, like his predecessors, initially blamed his country's poor position on external factors. His revolution therefore attempted to achieve 'total economic independence by ensuring a fundamental break from the existing neo-colonial relations'.[40] This meant trying to isolate Ghana from the influence of the international market. Under the threat of further nationalisation, for example, Rawlings negotiated more favourable contracts with transnational corporations operating in his country. Similarly, in an effort to stem inflation, the PNDC tightened its control of domestic prices. The cost of maize, for example, was reduced by 37 per cent, and cooking oil by 69 per cent. At the same time, while exhorting Ghanaians to produce more for the Revolution, Rawlings also cut the producer price of cocoa by half.[41]

These measures did little for the economy. Indeed, compounded by a drought and the return of hundreds of thousands of Ghanaians expelled from Nigeria, the situation worsened. Rawlings's lower producer prices resulted in few wanting to sell their produce in the formal market. Consequently, production declined further, while parallel markets and smuggling grew. Ironically, this slump in output occurred at the very time that cocoa prices reached an historic high. The government, however, could not take advantage of these increased commodity rates, as its own low producer prices had already chased too many farmers out of the formal, state controlled market. By the end of 1982, attempted coups against the Rawlings regime had become commonplace, foreign investors were threatening to disinvest, and the country had become dependent on food aid from Western relief agencies. Reading the signs, the PNDC changed tack. Rawlings now began to endorse a strategy of structural adjustment.

The PNDC, in its 1983 budget, introduced sweeping measures to liberalise Ghana's economy. It portrayed these reforms not as a U-turn, but as a continuation of its Revolution. Rawlings implored Ghanaians to produce for their country, and he promised that producers would be justly rewarded for their toil. It was a case of the PNDC embarking on a neo-liberal policy programme, with a populist spin.

Encouraged by World Bank advice, one of the first SAP measures to be implemented was a 67 per cent increase in producer prices paid for cocoa.[42] Cash incentives were also offered for the planting of new cocoa trees, and pesticides were made more readily available. Given that they were now being offered market rates in the formal economy, farmers were prepared to produce for the official market. Similar liberalisation reforms were applied to Ghana's trading sector and national currency. Price controls, for example, were abolished by the government on all but five products by mid-1985, while the Ghanaian cedi had devalued to just 2 per cent of its 1982 value by 1988.

Major changes also occurred in the public sector. Eighty parastatals were immediately earmarked for privatisation, and the government let it be known that it would consider bids from the private sector for all other state enterprises (apart from 18 deemed to be too strategic). By 1995, a total of 195 parastatals had been removed from the public sector.[43] Many had been sold to transnational corporations. Indeed, the Rawlings regime now actively encouraged TNC investment in its economy. Finance Secretary Kwesi Botchway went out of his way to assure a 1984 audience of international financiers that they would 'not be frustrated when the time comes to transfer their profits and dividends to their shareholders overseas'.[44]

The extent to which Ghana adopted these neo-liberal reforms made this country a flagship for the IFIs' programme of structural adjustment. Although the Rawlings regime initially dragged its feet a little with the proposed privatisation schedule (due to patronage concerns), the World Bank and the IMF regularly implored other African countries to follow Ghana's example. The result was that the PNDC enjoyed a good credit rating in the West, and development loans were forthcoming on a regular basis. The key question, however, is whether this structural adjustment has actually improved Ghana's economic position.

There is little doubt that SAP reforms did much to stabilise Ghana's economy, and pulling the country away from the financial nadir of 1982 was no mean feat. Responding to increased producer prices, the output of primary goods increased dramatically. The cocoa harvest, for example, increased by 65 per cent between 1983 and 1990. Timber, bauxite, manganese and diamond production saw similar improvements. Consequently, export earnings rose year on year throughout the SAP period, and Ghana's budget deficit benefited as a result (falling from 47 per cent of GDP in 1982 to 0.3 per cent in 1987, and recording several surpluses since).[45]

Yet it is arguable that structural adjustment did little beyond stabilising the economy. There was certainly no 'take-off' into sustained development. The country's economy was still dominated by cocoa, timber and minerals, and international commodity prices remained volatile. The price of cocoa, for example, fell during the SAP period (due to an increase in production and currency devaluations, not only in Ghana, but also in other adjusting countries around the world). Consequently, Ghana had to increase production each year merely to retain the same income. There were also concerns that this increase in primary produce for export was damaging the domestic food market. Should not farmers be concentrating on growing crops for home consumption? And, all the time, Ghana's debts grew. At current projection rates, it will take decades to bring the country's debt service commitments down to manageable levels.

One way to kick-start the economy, of course, would have been an influx of foreign direct investment. International capital, however, remained largely uninterested in the Ghanaian economy because of its continued fragility and lack of long-term growth prospects.[46] Not even the SAP reforms made Africa more attractive to the TNCs. In short, structural adjustment may have turned the Ghanaian economy around, but it had still to find a way to precipitate growth on these shaky foundations.

Structural adjustment also had a remarkable impact on Ghana's political system. The SAP reforms hit the PNDC's former clients hard. Forty per cent of the state cocoa board's employees, for example, were dismissed, as were 3,600 civil servants and numerous other public employees.[47] Industrial workers also fared badly as a result of import substitution investments being cut and the removal of tariff protection. Similarly, the professional and managerial classes (doctors, nurses, teachers and university staff, for example) had to cope with the state scaling down public services. Those who had previously benefited from these services also suffered. Numerous students, for example, could no longer afford higher education, while the introduction of user charges excluded many from schooling and basic health care. The removal of food and other subsidies added to the hardship. The belated Programme of Action to Mitigate the Social Costs of Adjustment (PAMSCAD) convinced few Ghanaians of the merits of the SAP reforms.

The PNDC faced considerable opposition from these disadvantaged groups. Former clients of the state elite, who before could be relied upon to support the government, now voiced their opposition. Initially, the state was able to contain these groups through suppression and harassment. Pressure for political change, however, continued to mount. The more organised opposition movements channelled this discontent into calls for multi-party democracy (in line with a continent-wide move towards pluralism). Eventually the Rawlings regime succumbed to this pressure, and contested open elections. The PNDC calculated that it could rely on its rural support, winning any poll, while at the same time this would defuse pressure emanating from the urban opposition. Rawlings was indeed victorious in 1992, capturing 58 per cent of the vote. With renewed legitimacy for the regime (and praise from the West for returning Ghana to democracy), the Flight-Lieutenant exchanged his airforce overalls for an immaculate civilian suit. Having secured re-election in 1996, Rawlings was set fair for another four years at Ghana's political helm.[48]

Ghana[49]

Territory:	238,305 sq km	Population:	18.5 million
Colonial power:	Britain	Independence:	1957
Major cities:	Accra (capital)	Ethnic groups:	Akan
	Kumasi		Ga
	Tamale		Ewe
Urban pop.:	37.8%		Guan
Languages:	English		Moshi-Dagomba
	Twi	Life expectancy:	58 years
	Fante	Adult literacy:	65%
	Ga	Exports:	Gold
	Ewe		Cocoa
Currency:	Cedi		Timber
Infant mortality:	64 deaths/thousand births		Electricity
Religion:	Traditional	External debt:	US$6,202 million
	Islam	GDP per capita:	US$379

Glossary of key terms

Debt service	Interest due on loans, over and above capital repayments.
Import substitution	An economic strategy that seeks to reduce a state's dependence on imported foreign goods, substituting these with domestically manufactured produce.
International financial institutions (IFIs)	Non-governmental bodies that help regulate the international economy, such as the International Monetary Fund and the World Bank.
Marketing boards	State institutions charged with buying goods from producers, and then selling these on to the international market.
Monocrop economy	Economies that rely heavily on a small number of (primary) exports for the bulk of their national income.
Neo-colonialism	Economic control and exploitation that Western powers still retain over the ex-colonies after independence.
Parastatal	Public sector companies or agencies, such as state marketing boards, state manufacturing industries, or state transport companies.
Primary sector	Economic activity other than secondary manufacturing industry or the service sector (e.g. mining and agriculture).
Producer prices	The price paid by state agencies to primary producers for their harvests/output.
Structural adjustment programme (SAP)	Neo-liberal economic reform strategies promoted by international financial institutions during the 1980s and 1990s.
Terms of trade	The ratio of a state's income from exports, measured against the cost of its imports.
Unequal exchange	A problem where the international economy purchases (Third World) primary produce relatively cheaply, compared to the expensive costs of (Western) manufactured products in the same market.
Urban bias	The result of state policies exploiting production, and revenues raised, from the rural sector, used to subsidise government and economic activities in urban regions.

User charges   Where citizens have to pay for public
                                   services at the point of use (prompted by
                                   SAP reforms).

Questions raised by this chapter

1   To what extent has the international economy hindered Africa's post-
    colonial economic development?
2   How did African states become so indebted to the West?
3   What are the key reforms associated with structural adjustment
    programmes?
4   Have structural adjustment programmes produced economic growth on the
    African continent?
5   What has been the political and social impact of structural adjustment?

Further reading

To understand why IFIs considered structural adjustment to be necessary in Africa,
the best place to start are two World Bank reports. Both of these are highly accessible. The 1981 Berg Report laid the framework for SAP policies on the continent,
while the 1994 report makes a preliminary assessment of this economic strategy. A
more critical look at structural adjustment can be gained by reading Michael Barratt
Brown's work on this subject. As for the political impact of the SAPs, two articles,
one by Jeffrey Herbst and the other by Christopher Clapham, raise some interesting
issues.

Brown, Michael Barratt (1995) *Africa's choices: after thirty years of the World Bank*,
    London: Penguin.
Clapham, Christopher (1996) 'Governmentality and economic policy in Sub-Saharan
    Africa', *Third World Quarterly* 17(4), 809–24.
Herbst, Jeffrey (1990) 'The structural adjustment of politics in Africa', *World Develop-
    ment* 18(7), 949–58.
World Bank [The Berg Report] (1981) *Accelerated development in Sub-Saharan Africa: an
    agenda for action*, Washington DC: World Bank.
World Bank (1994) *Adjustment in Africa: reforms, results and the road ahead*, New York:
    Oxford University Press.

10 Authority

The crises of accumulation, governance and state collapse

During the 1980s and 1990s several African countries experienced state collapse. Many others could be described as moribund. Security was not guaranteed, political institutions had decayed, and public services declined rapidly. In short, African governments were struggling to administer even the most basic functions of a modern state.

Previous chapters help explain why this point of crisis had been reached. The colonial inheritance had hindered governments since independence; the continent was disadvantaged by its position in the international economy; and the end of the Cold War restricted opportunities for foreign patronage. These external factors, however, only partly explain this evolving crisis of the post-colonial state. The current chapter will investigate additional *internal* contributions to Africa's malaise. It will concentrate on how state elites failed to oversee successful economic development, and also how governments neglected to represent society adequately.

These two crises, of accumulation and governance, prompted, in turn, a crisis of legitimacy. The second half of the chapter charts how this loss of legitimacy encouraged elements of civil society to 'disengage' from the state. Africans attempted to distance themselves from exploitative rulers, and the result of this disengagement was a decline of state capacity and control.

Given this situation, it makes sense to select political *authority* as the underlying theme of this chapter. State authority can be defined as *a psychological relationship, between the governed and their governors, which engenders a belief that state personnel and institutions should be obeyed.* Such authority, as was shown in previous chapters, can be generated from two sources: legitimacy and coercion. Legitimate authority is built by governors commanding the approval of their people through the provision of security, economic and social welfare, and good governance generally. Legitimate rulers are obeyed because citizens believe they receive reciprocal benefits for doing this. Coercive authority, on the other hand, is secured though the threat of violence. Citizens comply with state demands for fear of what may happen if they do not.

All governments around the world use a mixture of both persuasion and force (legitimacy and coercion) to maintain their authority over society. A combination of these two powers helps underwrite political stability. When the state's legitimacy declines, however, and rulers no longer command sufficient resources of coercion, authority is threatened. This is exactly what happened in many parts of Africa during the 1980s and 1990s.

The growing crisis of state legitimacy

During the last two decades of the twentieth century, declining legitimacy was a problem for most African leaders. At the same time, state coercive capacity also shrank. Consequently, governments experienced difficulty maintaining authority over both territory and people. Two major factors help to account for this state of affairs: a crisis of accumulation, and a crisis of governance. Africans no longer considered their leaders willing or capable of assisting their economic welfare, or of representing their political aspirations. As a result, individuals became less likely to respect the authority of the state. This first section examines the crises of accumulation and governance in turn.

The crisis of accumulation

Even a rudimentary glance at comparative economic figures shows Africa to be the poorest continent in the world.[1] Yet Africa is not short of natural resources. In terms of power generation, for example, the continent houses 40 per cent of the world's hydroelectric potential. It also has 12 per cent of global natural gas reserves, and 8 per cent of the world's petroleum operations. Similarly, Africa produces 70 per cent of the world's cocoa beans and 60 per cent of its coffee. Its earth is rich in minerals, and many regions have fertile soils.[2] Why, then, given these resources, did African economies perform so poorly in the post-colonial period? An answer to this question can be found in the continent's crisis of accumulation.[3]

To develop, all economies initially have to accumulate capital. This surplus capital is then invested back into the economy to produce further profits, which, in turn, can themselves be re-invested. The key to development, therefore, is the accumulation of surplus capital, followed by its productive investment. If this cycle of economic surplus and productive investment continues, then prosperity is generated.

Africa's economic problems stemmed from the fact that surpluses were scarce, and productive investments rare. Chapter 9 examined external factors that hindered this process of capital accumulation. Mono-crop export economies, unequal exchange and declining commodity prices, all hampered Africa's prospects for development. Yet disadvantage in the international economy cannot be offered as a comprehensive explanation of the continent's position. Even if Africa did not receive its 'fair' share of world profits, at least some income was generated from the cash crops and minerals sold, and these funds, together with loan capital, were invested in development projects. The problem was that much of this investment proved to be unproductive.

Capital was wasted because post-colonial state investments were largely founded on erroneous policy choices. In retrospect, two misguided development strategies stand out. First, many African governments concentrated too heavily on import substitution, and, second, they spent too much revenue on expanding institutions of the state. Fatally, this strategy of industrial and public sector investment came at the expense of developing agricultural production.

Import substitution became the centrepiece of most African development plans. The idea was to diversify economies away from existing primary production, expanding them into the secondary manufacturing sector. This would assist economic self-reliance, reducing the continent's dependence on imported manufactured goods. After all, had not the West itself developed by diversifying its agricultural economies into industrial production? Economists in both the developed and the developing worlds agreed that this was the most appropriate path to modernity.

The problem was that many of these import substitution projects were inefficient. They could only survive with state protection. Large, prestigious production units often became 'white elephants', not sustainable given the underdeveloped nature of their host economies. State-of-the-art assembly plants, for example, were of little use when Africans could not afford to buy the goods they produced. Indeed, ironically, most of the technology and materials needed for these import substitution operations had to be imported from the West, given that the local manufacturing base was unable to supply these needs. With little demand locally, and their goods uncompetitive in international markets, many of these import substitution industries became a burden on African economies rather than their saviours.

The capital invested in import substitution would have been more profitably invested in the agricultural sector. This, after all, was where most Africans earned their living. Diversifying farms away from export crops into the production of goods demanded locally (such as food) may have generated more wealth for a greater number of people. Instead, the agricultural sector was taxed heavily, bearing the brunt of the whole industrialisation project. State marketing boards, for example, who often enjoyed a monopoly over selling the country's cash crops, appropriated harvests from farmers at below market prices. They used the difference between the sum they paid the farmers and the income they raised on the international markets to underwrite the bulk of government expenditure (including the import substitution projects). Yet, with state marketing boards offering such low producer prices, farmers had little incentive to increase agricultural output. Consequently, in many parts of Africa, crop yields actually declined in the post-colonial period. State managers, in their desperation to accumulate capital for development, had over-burdened the agricultural sector. Year after year, they siphoned away too much of the farmers' profits, effectively strangling the most productive area of their domestic economies.

The agricultural sector, however, was not just squeezed to produce investment capital for import substitution. Rural capital was also used to expand the public sector. By the 1980s, African state institutions had clearly become 'over-developed'. Bureaucracies simply became too large to be supported by their own economies. In Congo-Brazzaville, for example, by 1985, the wages of the civil service alone accounted for 50 per cent of state expenditure.[4] Even in Kenya, which prided itself on private, as well as public, sector initiatives, the state extended its tentacles into almost all areas of economic activity. Richard Sandbrook, for example, found that 'In 1980, statutory boards and corporations operated all the conventional public utilities (telephones, electricity, water, ports, etc.) as well as transport services (for instance, Kenya Airways and Kenya Railway Corporation). Public corporations were also engaged in productive activities: agriculture (Kenya Meat Commission, Kenya Co-operative Creameries, National Cereals and Produce Board), finance (Agricultural Financial Corporation), commerce (Kenya National Trading Corporation) and industry (Industrial and Commercial Development Corporation).'[5] Parastatals (public corporations) came to dominate almost all large-scale economic activity across the continent. In doing this, they absorbed colossal amounts of public finance. This capital could most probably have been more productively invested elsewhere.

From an ideological point of view there is nothing necessarily wrong with public enterprise. Those on the Left argue that state-controlled economic activity can produce equity in the workplace, leading to greater social justice; while public services, rather than private enterprise, are better at targeting the needy within society. This was not entirely the case in Africa, however, where the public sector expanded more to meet *political* demands, rather than social or economic imperatives. Patronage was again the driving force.

As was seen in Chapters 5 and 6, access to state institutions became the main conduit of power and wealth in post-colonial African countries. Employment in the civil service, the military or parastatals was used by the state elite to reward clients. In effect, whole bureaucracies were built to service client–patron networks, rather than to manage and deliver public services. And with political considerations overriding administrative or economic needs in these neo-patrimonial institutions, efficiency suffered. Public servants were often employed because of their loyalty, faction or ethnic links, not for their skills, experience or ability to do the job. Indeed, the need to provide patronage often left these institutions considerably over-staffed. In this respect, African bureaucracies were far removed from the legal-rational institutions of Western civil services.

These over-developed bureaucracies may have represented a good *political* investment for ruling elites. They were the mainstay of the whole client–patron network that underpinned the state itself. Yet, in *economic* terms, the investment of scarce resources in this manner was clearly unproductive. These bureaucracies accounted for considerable sums of public finance, yet generated few profits. No capital was accumulated, and no surplus was available for re-investment. Instead, throughout Africa, bloated bureaucracies became serious burdens on fragile economies.

Max Weber's requirement of a legal-rational bureaucracy is that 'Public monies and equipment are divorced from the private property of the official.'[6] Again, this was not the case in Africa. Since the public sector had been 'patrimonialised', state offices were converted into patronage 'fiefdoms'. They were used by officials to generate material benefits, both for themselves and for their clients. In short, corruption was rife within the post-colonial state.

Corruption is a relative term. It occurs all over the world, and what may be regarded as corrupt in one society may be acceptable, and even expected, political behaviour in another. There can be little doubt, however, that corruption in Africa was endemic. Officials required bribes before they reached favourable decisions; public resources were misappropriated for private use; and individuals were employed and promoted on the basis of clientelism rather than merit. In many cases, ordinary people who used public services came to recognise only a minimal difference between bribes, gifts and official fees.[7] Chabal and Daloz, in this respect, talk of African corruption not being a case of 'a few "rotten apples" or of a venal "class",... On the contrary, it is a habitual part of everyday life, an expected element of every social transaction.'[8] After all, in the absence of a legal-rational order, it would have been irrational for individuals not to work the system like those around them.

Corruption could be found at all levels within state institutions. An investigation of the Rural Electricity Board of Nigeria, for example, revealed 'a whole range of malpractices'. Board officials 'acquired privileged access to electricity for their own private concerns. They extracted kickbacks from equipment suppliers. They consolidated their patron–client networks by the preferential allocation of electricity supplies to individuals, firms and communities who were political supporters. And some of the top officers channelled Board revenues to their own enterprises and acquisitions. Indeed, a popular state governor used illegally acquired funds from the Board to buy no fewer than 22 farms and several retail businesses.'[9]

Corruption could even be found at the pinnacle of the client–patron network. Kenya's president, Daniel arap Moi, for example, sought to purchase twelve jet fighters for his airforce in 1980. His first stop was British Aerospace. No deal could be struck here, however, because BAe refused to pay Moi's agent a 'personal fee' (they did, however, offer a £100,000 contribution to assist Kenya's anti-poaching campaign). Instead, the jets were bought from the French firm Marcel Dassault Pregue, even though the French aeroplanes would cost the Kenyan taxpayer considerably more money. More forthcoming, Dassault were prepared to offer Moi a free presidential jet as part of the deal.[10] Elsewhere, numerous state presidents spent years siphoning off public money into their own Swiss bank accounts. Perhaps the finest exponent of this 'creative accountancy' was Zaire's Mobutu Sese Seko (the subject of the case study at the end of the present chapter). It was common practice for leaders right across the continent to make self-authorised withdrawals of foreign exchange from their central banks. The impressive National Reserve building in Harare, Zimbabwe, for example, is locally known as Big Bob's Takeaway (referring to President Robert Mugabe's regular *personal* use of the bank).

Whether the source was a prestigious but loss-making import substitution industry, a bloated bureaucracy, or money wasted though the demands of patronage and corrupt public officials, there can be little doubt that Africa contributed considerably to its own economic problems in the post-colonial period. Added to the restraints of the international economy, the process of capital accumulation largely failed. With leaner bureaucracies, more appropriate development strategies, and fewer resources 'disappearing' into bureaucratic black holes, African economies would have fared better. And this is important in terms of the authority states commanded. With a healthy economy, the distributive powers of a government are improved. They can tap into the economy and offer citizens far more resources and services. This, in turn, generates legitimacy in the eyes of people, reinforcing state authority. An ailing economy, on the other hand, presents problems for those in power. They have fewer resources to convert into legitimacy. They also have fewer funds to invest in coercive actions, and with less legitimacy and less coercion, authority diminishes. The consequences of this loss of authority are explored in more detail later in the chapter.

The crisis of governance

'We have two problems: rats and the government.'[11] This comment, from a rural community leader in Lesotho, hints that there was not just a crisis of accumulation during the 1980s and 1990s. State authority was also being undermined by a crisis of governance. African elites were not representing their citizens adequately.

Chapter 6 explored the centralisation of the post-colonial African state. It was shown how, after independence, neo-patrimonialism led to the atrophy of legal-rational political institutions. Without this legal-rational order, African leaders came to rely instead on extensive client–patron networks to generate legitimacy. This was the main mechanism through which the political leadership represented their people.

The problem during the 1980s and 1990s, however, was that there were no longer enough resources to sustain these networks. Economic decline, and the changing nature of external support (due to structural adjustment and the loss of Cold War patronage), meant that governments now had little to pass down to their clients. Indeed, the shrinking distributive capacity of these states resulted in public services breaking down generally. Health centres experienced shortages of staff and drugs; textbooks were scarce in schools; trains did not run because of a lack of foreign exchange to buy spare parts; road systems fell into disrepair, as did electricity generating plants. Consequently, legitimacy declined.

This crisis of legitimacy became a crisis of governance because constitutional means of replacing these failing regimes were no longer available. During the earlier centralisation period, formal opposition organisations had been systematically neutralised, and political parties other than the one in power had been co-opted, harassed or banned. In many cases, representative local government, and independent parliaments, had also disappeared. Formal political activity was now confined to the core executive, or institutions that were closely controlled by the 'presidential-monarch'.

All governments, wherever they are in the world, will eventually lose the support of their citizens. In liberal democracies, however, this rarely precipitates a crisis of governance. This is because constitutional mechanisms exist which ensure that unpopular administrations can soon be removed from office. Elections are held, the ailing ruling party is exchanged for an opposition party, and legitimacy is renewed. Political succession occurs peacefully, with the authority of state institutions remaining intact. In post-colonial Africa, this was not the case. The centralisation of the state meant that incumbent governments could only be removed by force. Consequently, unless the military intervened with a *coup d'état*, or a mass rebellion occurred, the same party, and usually the same president, remained in power, however unpopular they became. This obstacle to political succession lay at the heart of the crisis of governance. Simply put, there was no constitutional method of re-legitimising governments through the removal of unpopular incumbents.

The pincer effect of these crises of governance and accumulation meant that Africans were effectively living in 'vampire states' (also known as 'kleptocratic states', 'predatory states' or 'pirate states'). Resources were 'sucked' out of society by the government, yet the government offered little in return. Neither economic improvement nor political representation were forthcoming. Indeed in many cases it seemed as if political elites were simply ignoring their duties of government. Many officials were too busy taking care of their own interests. Public money was being invested unproductively, with development projects designed to return political profits (for the elite themselves) rather than economic profits (for the wider national interest).

This is not to say, however, that civil society passively accepted the vampire state. After all, constitutional means are not the only channel though which citizens can challenge and remove their rulers. During the 1980s and 1990s, many Africans registered their discontent by effectively disengaged themselves from the state. And by removing many of their activities from government control, civil society seriously undermined the state's authority. Indeed, several states were so weakened by this disengagement that they approached a condition of complete collapse. In effect, civil society was taking its revenge on the vampire state.

The loss of state authority

In political environments where governments lacked legitimacy, and where powers of coercion were diminished, Africans did indeed begin to challenge the authority of their states. Given that formal channels of opposition had been destroyed by state centralisation, extra-constitutional political action was taken instead. In some cases, this resulted in outright rebellion. Urban riots and guerrilla campaigns became more common on the continent during the 1980s and

1990s (discussed below). Revolutions and insurgency wars, however, were only the more spectacular examples of civil society taking on the state. More frequently, collections of more insidious individual acts gained greater success in weakening a regime's political authority. Rather than being destroyed by one explosive act of violence, states were slowly ground into submission instead.[12] It is these less obvious, but still powerful, acts of disengagement that will be addressed first.

Disengagement and 'exit strategies'

In extreme cases, Africans evaded exploitative vampire states by disengaging totally, through emigration. There is no better way to escape the clutches of an abusive government than simply to leave its territory. In reality, however, only a small minority chose to exercise this ultimate form of disengagement. Ties to the local area proved strong, and obstacles to emigration were often significant. This is not to say, however, that those who chose to stay gave up exit strategies entirely.

Confronted by predatory states, Africans combined both engagement and disengagement. They tended to work with the state when it was in their interests to do this, but avoided it when it was not. Individuals, to use Eric Hobsbawm's phrase, were 'working the system…to their minimum disadvantage.'[13] Opportunities could certainly arise from interacting with state officials and institutions, but often this contact merely led to exploitation. The key, therefore, was carefully to control the level of engagement. If, for example, the government concentrated on extracting revenue from tobacco crops, farmers would switch production to less taxed commodities such as maize. If the state decided to tap into the revenue created by a city's bus companies, entrepreneurs moved into the taxi business instead. In the event of all commercial activity being prohibitively exploited, the extreme exit strategy was to revert to subsistence farming (only producing for the needs of the immediate family). It was about insulating oneself from the excesses of public policy, and removing economic activity to the margins of state control.

Declining state capacity also required civil society to increase its self-sufficiency. People could now rely even less on public services for their welfare than they did before. This self-sufficiency, too, should be seen as part of the disengagement process. Africans came to rely on family, kinship, village, community and professional relationships in place of state provision. As Naomi Chazan observed: 'The most noticeable changes took place at the local level, where the multiplication of communal associations was everywhere in evidence. Entrepreneurial, credit, banking, and barter groups were established alongside new welfare associations, mutual aid societies, educational initiatives, and self-defense groups.'[14] Where formal state institutions had decayed, civil society itself stepped into the breach. Communities built and ran their own schools, for example, and organised tax collection to pay for this.[15] They even formed their own militias to compensate for the state's declining ability to maintain law and order. Even in extreme cases of total state collapse, associational life continued. As Virginia Luling wrote of Somalia in the mid-1990s: 'The centre of Mogadishu may be bombed out, but the markets on the outskirts are busy; there may be no banks but there are plenty of money-changers; [and] with a well-functioning, privately run satellite service it is far easier to telephone Somalia than it was before the war.'[16] States are certainly the most efficient way of organising and administering a society, but civil societies can survive without them.

The above cases of switching markets, withdrawal from the formal economy, and establishing alternative public services within civil society, are all examples of 'legal' disengagement. None of these 'exit' or 'coping' strategies involve a direct challenge of state laws. Most Africans, however, also acted illegally in their efforts to survive the hostile political and economic environment of the 1980s and 1990s. They dealt with atrophy and exploitation by simply ignoring some of the state's regulations. After all, if African leaders were not subject to the rule of law, why should be the people they governed? The following paragraphs highlight some of the most popular illegal disengagement strategies found on the continent.

The most widespread challenges to state authority were 'parallel markets'. Instead of buying and selling produce in the formal (state controlled) economy, Africans took to operating in the informal sector instead (also termed the second economy, the shadow economy, parallel markets, black markets, and *magendo* in East Africa and *kalabule* in West Africa). Throughout the post-colonial period, governments had sought to manipulate economic production to their own ends. Producers, particularly those in rural areas, suffered accordingly. Consequently, many within civil society attempted to avoid the formal economy. Instead, farmers (illegally) sold their crops in the second economy, and not to the state marketing boards; street hawkers sold their wares without a government licence or reference to state regulations; landlords rented out property without government authorisation; and entrepreneurs, such as illicit brewers, operated largely in the informal sector.

By the 1980s, most African countries had considerable second economies. *Magendo*, for example, measured up to two-thirds of Uganda's GDP, while more than 90 per cent of Tanzania's grain production was sold through parallel markets.[17] Large-scale economic avoidance of the state reached equivalent levels in other areas of the continent. Smuggling, in particular, was a mainstay of this shadow economy.

African borders, given their artificial nature, had always been relatively porous. The (illegal) flow of people and goods across state boundaries, however, grew considerably in response to the crises of accumulation and governance. For example, instead of submitting to painfully low state-determined producer prices, farmers sought opportunities to sell their crops in neighbouring countries instead. Again, the figures are revealing. Two-thirds of Ghana's cocoa crop was smuggled out the country in 1982. Legally, the Ghanaian state was entitled to all the income from this harvest. Similarly, one-third of Guinea's coffee harvest was sold in parallel markets.[18]

The illegal sale of foreign exchange was another example of individuals undermining the authority of the state. Most African governments operated financial policies to keep the value of their national currency artificially high. This was a method of reducing the cost of imports. Parallel money markets developed, however, responding to this artificial price. Instead of exchanging their currency at official state-determined rates, Africans (and many tourists) conducted their business with street traders instead. In several cases, official currencies became virtually worthless, as states could no longer maintain their authority. US dollars often became the dominant means of exchange instead. In war-torn Angola, cans of beer were the preferred currency (with the value of these cans accurately reflecting the strength of the United States dollar).[19]

Other survival strategies included the resort to petty crime and banditry. Noting the state's declining coercive powers, criminal activity became more widespread. Again, it was a case of individuals taking matters into their own hands when the formal economy had failed them. In the worse cases, districts of cities, and even large tracts of rural areas, became virtual 'no-go' areas for the state's law enforcement agencies. Organised crime prospered in this environment. Consequently, whether it be Liberia, DRC or Somalia, today it pays to hire an armed guard when travelling by road from one part of the country to another.

A new wave of insurgency

With disengagement both contributing to, and compounding, a decline of state capacity in the 1980s and 1990s, central authority was severely weakened in many areas of the continent. Sometimes civil associations and parallel markets filled this institutional vacuum, bringing a degree of economic and political order. In other cases, Africans had to take their chances living in areas of insecurity and banditry. A third scenario developed during the 1990s in a smaller, but still significant, number of cases. This involved a new wave of insurgency campaigns.

Insurgency or guerrilla movements differ from bandit groups in that, although they operate outside the law, they are ideologically committed. They seek to overthrow the existing state, replacing it with a new political order. In this sense, although these rebels have disengaged from the state, they are actively attempting to build an alternative political authority.

Guerrilla armies had helped defeat colonialism in several countries on the continent (most notably in Kenya, Algeria, Guinea-Bissau and the Southern African states of Angola, Mozambique, Zimbabwe, Namibia and South Africa). Rebel groups had also challenged several ruling elites after independence. The governments of Angola, Mozambique, Chad, the Sudan, Uganda and Ethiopia, for example, all lost territory to rebel groups during this period. In the 1990s, however, guerrilla politics came to fore once more, this time continent-wide.

In Uganda, Yoweri Museveni's National Resistance Army started the trend by taking Kampala in 1986. The Ethiopian People's Revolutionary Democratic Front and the Eritrea People's Liberation Front followed suit in 1991, forming governments in Addis Ababa and Asmara respectively. Three years later the Rwanda Patriotic Front took Kigali, and three years after that an Alliance of Democratic Forces for the Liberation of Congo-Zaire ousted Mobutu from DRC. Added to these insurgency-induced regime transitions were the defeat of incumbent governments in Somalia, Liberia and Sierra Leone. Armed rebellion was back in fashion in Africa.

The reasons for this upsurge in insurgency, again, go back to the crises of accumulation and governance. Guerrilla warfare can only be conducted successfully in regions where incumbent governments have lost their authority. And given that the centralisation of the African state offered few constitutional channels of political regeneration, armed rebellion often prospered. Whether insurgents were separatist movements seeking independence for just one region, or they were attempting to capture the state as a whole, they stood more chance of succeeding in the 1990s than they had in previous decades.[20]

The road to state collapse

African states had survived in the post-colonial period because they were able to appropriate resources both domestically (minerals and cash crops) and internationally (trade and aid). These resources were then used to sustain institutions of the state, boost officials' private incomes, and also to 'buy' a degree of legitimacy through the provision of patronage and public services. By the 1980s, however, the crises of accumulation and governance had badly damaged African elites' abilities to appropriate these resources. Many African territories were on the road to state collapse.

Some post-colonial governments had experienced difficulty in controlling their territories prior to the 1980s. Angola won its independence from Portugal in 1975, yet, from day one, UNITA insurgents ensured that the MPLA government was never to enjoy total sovereignty within this country's borders. Similarly, northern (Muslim) administrations in the Sudan always failed to assert complete authority in the (Christian) south. The 1980s, however, saw a wider loss of state capacity across the continent. The government of Mozambique lacked control in rural areas when confronted by South African backed bandits/guerrillas; Ethiopia's leaders lost their authority over parts of Eritrea and Tigray; while the state collapsed completely in Uganda and Chad. Later in the 1990s, several more states withered away. Central authority disappeared in Liberia, Sierra Leone, Somalia, Rwanda and Zaire (DRC).

The phenomenon of state collapse occurs where national institutions of enforcement, execution and decision-making fail. As a result, basic functions of the state are no longer guaranteed. There is no rule of law; no security from external aggression; and few public services. What is more, power at the centre can no longer be projected into all the regions of a territory. Often, collapse occurs when opposition forces have been successful in ousting the incumbent elite, but in doing this have destroyed existing political institutions and the authority they previously ruled by. A problem arises if the victorious opposition then does not have the capacity and legitimacy themselves to reconstruct the state. Somalia is a case in point. Clans were united in bringing down Siad Barré's corrupt regime in 1991. After this, however, these disparate groups failed to reconstitute a national government in its place. Somalia, and the handful of other collapsed African states, acted as beacons to all other territories on the continent throughout the 1990s, warning them of the consequences of failing to address the crises of legitimacy and governance.

The state's own survival strategies

The end of the twentieth century saw a partial eclipse of state power in Africa. In a few cases, central authority collapsed completely. This was inevitable given the long list of problems facing incumbent regimes. Yet, to paraphrase Mark Twain, the death of the African state has been widely exaggerated.

Geographically, for example, maps of the continent still show the same number of states, in the same positions, that could be found in 1980 (with the exception of Eritrea). Territorially, all these states survived. There was no case of neighbours taking advantage of state collapse, moving in to annexe territory. The 'political-space-that-is-Somalia', for instance, still remains.[21]

Similarly, although several states did collapse in the 1980s and 1990s, many of these are now enjoying a successful afterlife. Central institutions that were destroyed by insurgent (and invading) forces in Uganda and Rwanda, for example, were subsequently replaced. Authority was generated by a new set of institutions, built from the rubble of the old state. Indeed, Yoweri Museveni's Uganda is now regarded as one of Africa's more successful countries by Western governments.

Elsewhere, central authority may have been undermined, but African leaders demonstrated considerable skill in maintaining their grip on state power. Just like civil society, state elites had their own survival strategies during these hard times. And the success of these strategies explains why there was a good deal of political continuity throughout these troubled years. States may have had to adapt, but few went the way of Somalia into total oblivion. The following paragraphs highlight the most common survival strategies employed by political elites.

Re-legitimisation of the state

In the long term, the most effective way to guarantee the state's survival was through the re-legitimisation of its institutions. If trust was restored, then authority would be regained. The holding of multi-party elections, as will be seen in Chapter 11, was the best way of achieving this. Indeed, by the end of the twentieth century, most African elites had taken this option.

Yet multi-party elections risked everything. Given the ongoing crises of accumulation and governance, it was very possible that incumbent elites would be defeated at these polls. Open political competition would result in the termination of these individuals' privileges that access to state institutions brought. Consequently, democracy was not the initial survival strategy to be enacted. In the short term, more exploitative behaviour was dominant.

State inversion

The first reaction of state elites to their predicament was to scale down operations. Like a balloon losing altitude, political leaders jettisoned parts of the state in an effort to keep the remaining structure airborne. It was a case of prioritising productive or strategic areas, and abandoning the rest. Consequently, scarce resources would now only be invested in the most important conduits of power (valuable economic activity, key clients, agencies of coercion, critical tracts of territory). Unproductive areas (weaker clients and poorer regions) were simply discarded. State managers could no longer afford to uphold the pretence that they controlled all the territory within their national boundaries. Neither did they try to serve all their citizens.

This scaling-down of the state came at the expense of wider civil society. For example, many public services were abandoned, and the whole economic development project was put on hold. Health care, welfare and education provision, in particular, suffered. As Azarya and Chazan point out, the aim was to reduce 'state responsibility' without relinquishing the 'benefits of state power'.[22] It was almost as if the state, to use Joshua Forest's term, had become 'inverted'.[23] Institutions turned in on themselves, supporting areas of the state that served elite interests yet abandoning everything else. A natural gas production plant, for example, would be maintained (as this generated considerable and scarce income for the elite). By contrast, demands for hospital funding would be ignored (as such an investment would bring no direct short-term benefits to the elite).

Tapping into foreign patronage

The scaling-down of their domestic operations also required elites to maximise resources and legitimacy that could be raised externally. In this respect, although diminished since the end of the Cold War, the international convention of state sovereignty was still an advantage. State managers continued to pose as 'representatives of their people', enabling them to win aid and preferential trade agreements from the outside world. These resources could then be used to shore up the remaining institutions of the state (and not necessarily for wider economic development, as the donors had intended). Given the even greater lack of resources now being produced locally, this international lifeline was essential for the survival of the elite and their state.

Exploiting parallel markets

Elites, however, could not just make do with consolidating their position within the state and the international community. Opportunities in both these areas had shrunk considerably. Now, hard-pressed officials had to find additional sources of power and wealth to exploit (if they were to maintain their privileged existence). The most obvious target for them to aim at was the most dynamic and productive area of their territory: the second economy.

Throughout the continent, public officials turned a blind eye to *magendo*. Indeed it is doubtful that the second economy could have survived without a degree of state collusion. The whole foundation of the informal sector, after all, was based on bribes, embezzlement, fraud and official theft. Consequently, state managers could maintain their incomes by facilitating these parallel markets. They received money when they chose not to prosecute illegal traders or smugglers; they could divert public goods (food aid, perhaps) into these parallel markets; and they could also issue official documents to illegitimate operations. Again, it was a case of holders of public office being able to extract rent by using their position in the state. Indeed, in many cases, it was actually the officers of the state who were leading these illegal entrepreneurial projects. Just as many KGB operatives moved in to run organised crime in Russia following the collapse of the Soviet Union, African holders of political office also found a home in the strategic niches of the criminal underworld. It is no coincidence that, in the 1990s, African countries such as Nigeria became prime staging posts for drugs smuggled into Western Europe and North America. Bayart, Ellis and Hibou refer to this development as the 'criminalisation of the African state'.[24]

The 'warlord state'

In some cases, these self-serving state survival strategies became the sole focus of a regime. Having lost, almost entirely, their bureaucratic power base through state collapse, leaders sought to convert their remaining influence into material gains through commercial activity. William Reno calls these extreme cases 'warlord states'.[25]

Warlord politics result in rulers abandoning the whole idea of administrating a state for the collective good. Instead, institutions now merely serve the elites' private interests. Opportunism replaces ideology, legal-rational motivations are even harder to find, and governments are no longer in the business of trying to generate legitimacy. In this respect, even client–patron networks are scaled down to a minimum. A warlord state is an inverted, predatory or vampire state – with knobs on.

Given that public responsibilities have vanished in warlord states, private syndicates tend to replace the previously more inclusive patronage networks.

Political leaders are also much more in touch with market opportunities, and do not just rely on rent raised from political office. For example, warlord governments often enter into partnerships with transnational corporations, concentrating their remaining authority on the most productive natural resource that their country has to offer. Loyal remnants of the national army, for example, will be deployed to guarantee the security of this particular region. They then grant concessions to TNCs to extract minerals or agricultural produce. Profits are shared between political leaders and the TNC, with little of this revenue filtering down into civil society.

Naturally enough, warlord states generate little legitimacy, and, as such, citizens have few incentives to support such governments (apart from the fear of any remaining coercive powers). Consequently, instability is a hallmark of this kind of state. Often, rebel or bandit groups wrestle vast tracts of territory away from central political control. Yet, the ruling elite is always careful to ensure that those parts of the country that do contain strategic resources remain in government hands. In several cases, elites have even hired mercenaries to guarantee this control (as they are no longer able to rely on their own military). The South African-based Executive Outcomes (EO), for example, helped the besieged government of Sierra Leone to protect its TNC partnerships based on diamond production. As William Reno observes, 'EO and its partners give politicians the option to jettison old, inefficient, but more inclusive patronage networks for efficient, powerful, and profitable commercial networks to boost their personal power.'[26] No longer able to rule the rest of the country, elites simply give up the pretence that they can serve all the citizens of this state.

In the 1990s, Zaire, Liberia and Sierra Leone came closest to meeting this notion of a warlord state. Central power all but evaporated in these countries, and rebel groups exercised alternative political authority in regions outside government control. Yet these states did retain enough power to look after the elite's private interests. Major cities remained in government hands, as did outlying economic installations (even if mercenaries had to be deployed). The elite was skilful enough in its survival strategies to ensure that political power continued to be converted to economic wealth. In these cases, the state was just as adept at disengaging from civil society as, seen above, civil society was at disengaging from the state.

State and civil society

This chapter has charted how the post-colonial African state reached something of a watershed in the 1980s. The crises of accumulation and governance had gnawed away at the capacity of central institutions to rule society. Legitimacy had declined, and since it is difficult for states to maintain their authority by coercion alone, the political environment was ripe for radical change.

The problem was that often no replacement was available for these ailing regimes. Due to shrinking client–patron networks, scope for circulating elites was limited. Similarly, few states harboured a strong enough opposition able to topple the political incumbents. Ruling elites therefore limped on, withdrawing into their inverted states. This resulted in citizens being more or less abandoned.

Civil society's response to this turn of events was to disengage. By taking their activities to the margins of state control, citizens avoided the worst excesses of the predatory bureaucratic elite. Parallel markets, smuggling and other illegal activities became well established during the 1980s and 1990s.

Some commentators regarded this disengagement as a positive phenomenon. Naomi Chazan, for example, considered that 'the centre of political gravity' had shifted on the continent. 'Viewed from above,' she continued, 'institutional mechanisms have been undergoing a process of contraction and disaggregation. But from below, social and economic niches have been carved out and are beginning to interact and adhere in new ways.... From this perspective, political rhythms may lack cohesion; they are not, however, incoherent.... As local arrangements come into play, political spaces are being reorganised and diverse links between government structures, specific social groups, and resource bases are being devised. A more diffuse and variegated, but perhaps more viable, pattern of political realignment is slowly taking shape.'[27] In other words, civil society was learning to look after itself, and potentially a new political order could be built on these foundations.

Yet disengagement was only *relatively* positive. It may have reduced citizens' exploitation, but in achieving this, civil society had to relinquish the benefits of the modern state. History has shown, after all, that legitimate states give individuals an advantage in realising security, economic gain and improved welfare generally. As Robert Fatton puts it, 'the phenomenon of exit should not evoke the utopian image of a brave new world of unalienated villagers discovering within African authenticity a miraculous cure for poverty, exploitation and tyranny'.[28] Life in such an environment may be better than that in a vampire state, but it is certainly no substitute for a well-managed society based on the rule of law, legal-rational institutions and participatory democracy. Disengaged civil societies could only, at best, provide their members with informal imitations of these political benefits.

And here lies the true crisis of the post-colonial African state. Civil society was adept at taking its revenge on the predatory state, helping destroy its capacity and legitimacy. Yet it was unable to replace this central authority. Consequently, weak (and still exploitative) state structures remained, 'ruling' disengaged civil societies. In the ebb and flow of political power, when the state gained the upper hand coercion increased. When civil society was in the ascendancy the state moved closer to disintegration and total collapse. Few gained any long-term benefits from this stalemate between state and civil society. It was costly both in terms of economic production and of public service provision. As such, the last two decades of the twentieth century proved to be difficult times for most Africans to live through.

The hope, however, is that widespread holding of multi-party elections in the 1990s will provide the foundation for a more productive relationship between state and civil society. As government becomes more accountable to the people, through these polls, it maybe that citizens will engage with the state more positively. This accountability will bolster the state's legitimacy, and thus restore some authority. Yet many of the 'state survival strategies' discussed above are still employed by state elites. A mature political culture of democracy is still to emerge. So, did these 1990s elections re-legitimise the state? This question is investigated fully in the next chapter, when the book turns to examine democracy in post-colonial Africa.

Case study: Zaire – Mobutu's vampire state

'Zaire under Mobutu has become almost a caricature of an African dictatorship', wrote Chris Simpson in 1990; it is 'autocratic to a fault' and 'its resources are shamelessly squandered'.[29] In his 32-year rule as president (1965–97), Mobutu Sese Seko oversaw a kleptocracy of the highest order. Once the ruling elite, and their TNC allies, had taken their cut of Zaire's mineral wealth, little of these profits found their way back into civil society. In Mobutu's pirate state, self-interested extraction became both an art form and an end in itself.

It did not have to be this way. Zaire, formerly the Belgian Congo, and renamed the Democratic Republic of the Congo (DRC) in 1997, is blessed with many natural resources. Straddling the equator in western Central Africa, DRC has an abundance of land, and agriculture should flourish given the good soils and plentiful rains. The country also has excellent mining and hydroelectric potential. Yet the twentieth century was not kind to the inhabitants of this part of Africa. Economic development was not only restricted by the vagaries of the international market, but it was also fatally hampered by the actions of domestic political leaders.

The new country got off to an inauspicious start in 1960. Within five days of independence the army, led by Colonel Joseph Désiré Mobutu, had mutinied, taking and holding power for a number of months. In the confusion, the mineral-rich province of Katanga seceded. It took a costly civil war, and the military intervention of the United Nations, to restore Congo-Kinshasa's territorial integrity. Political unity, however, was not restored. Constitutional deadlock was complete after the 1965 parliamentary elections, when the state president failed to secure a majority in the national assembly. Mobutu took this opportunity to intervene in the political process for a second time.

Initially, Mobutu's rule proved successful. With the state territorially re-united, and a military 'strong man' replacing the squabbling politicians, Congo-Kinshasa could get on with the business of economic development. Good relations with external powers, and the high price of copper on the international commodity markets, also helped. Yet within ten years Zaire (as it was renamed in 1971) had started its journey of state collapse. Like so many other African leaders, Mobutu's political decisions precipitated both a crisis of accumulation and a crisis of governance.

Zaire's crisis of accumulation, in classic fashion, was created by a combination of wrong policy choices and naked corruption. In terms of inappropriate public policy, for example, import substitution was pursued at the expense of developing agricultural production. A case in point was the Maluku steel mill (completed by Italian and German contractors in 1975). Unable to find foreign investors for this project, the US$250 million bill for this state-of-the-art factory was met entirely by government funds. Zaire, however, did not have enough capital to develop its own iron ore deposits to actually supply the smelting plant. Maluku therefore relied on imported scrap metal. This added to the production costs, resulting in the steel being uncompetitive on the international market. Indeed, even domestically, the steel produced in this mill cost eight times more than foreign imports. Consequently, Maluku never ran at more than 10 per cent of capacity. The whole project was an expensive and ill-conceived white elephant.[30]

Similar development mistakes were made throughout the Mobutu years. Take, for instance, the Inga–Shaba power scheme. The idea was to transport electricity, generated by the Inga hydroelectric plant, a distance of a 1,800 kilometres to Shaba province, where there was a concentration of mining activity. Despite the technical ingenuity displayed to achieve this, the reality was that it would have been cheaper for Shaba factories to generate their own electricity regionally. Other industrialisation measures also failed. Locally assembled cars and locally produced tyres and textiles, for example, cost between 20 and 40 per cent more than their imported equivalents.[31] Ultimately, since these projects generated little capital accumulation, the outcome was unproductive investment of public funds.

Agriculture was potentially Zaire's most profitable sector of the economy. Government policy, however, consistently squeezed the rural areas excessively. Marketing boards, year after year, bought farmers' harvests at below market prices. The result was a lack of incentive for these farmers to produce. Cotton yields, for example, fell from 60,000 tons of lint at independence to just 8,500 tons by 1976. Similarly, whereas the Belgian Congo had exported a small surplus of food, independent Zaire was forced to import its basic staples. Farmers were simply not prepared to supply the formal economy at the low prices set by the state. Since Zaire has such a conducive climate for agriculture, this was a criminal waste of resources.

Unproductive investment in ill-conceived development projects, and the misuse of the country's agricultural potential, however, pale into insignificance alongside the level of corruption found in Mobutu's Zaire. At times, it seemed there was no limit to the greed of this country's public servants.

At the pinnacle of government, and of the corruption therein, was Mobutu himself. He amassed between US$5 and US$8 billion worth of assets, much of it deposited in Swiss bank accounts.[32] It is difficult to see how Mobutu's 'legitimate' businesses could have generated so much wealth. Regular confusion between the President's public and private spending helps explain this discrepancy. Lower down the political hierarchy was General Eluki, secretary of state for national defence. His spouse was allegedly once stopped at a roadblock and found to be in possession of seventeen suitcases of money. A subsequent search of Eluki's home found US$2 million dollars stashed away. (Eluki was convicted of corruption, but his 20-year sentence was set aside and he returned as the military commander of Shaba province.[33])

Mobutu and Eluki, however, were just two of the more high-profile abusers of public office. From the state president down to the humblest government clerk, from generals through to privates operating road blocks, corruption was an everyday part of life in Zaire. It became a case of citizens having to buy public services through private negotiations with the official concerned.[34] As Archbishop Kabanga of Lubumbashi wrote in a 1976 pastoral letter, 'We bear daily witness to agonizing situations.... How many children and adults die without medical care because they are unable to bribe the medical personnel who are supposed to care for them? Why are there no medical supplies in the hospitals, while they are found in the marketplace? How did they get there? Why is it that in our courts justice can only be obtained by fat bribes to the judge?... Why do our government officers force people to come back day after day to obtain services to which they are entitled? If the clerks are not paid off, they will not be served. Why, at the opening of school, must parents go into debt to bribe the school principal? Children who are unable to pay will have no school... Whoever holds a morsel of authority, or means of pressure, profits from it to impose on people and exploit them...'[35]

As well as ruling over a state that failed to accumulate, Mobutu's Zaire also suffered from a crisis of governance.

Zaire followed a familiar path to other African countries in the post-colonial period, with Mobutu overseeing the centralisation of the state and a personalisation of power. Spurred on by the failure of political parties to stabilise the country in the First Republic, the President abandoned multi-party democracy. This was replaced by a one-party structure, and Mobutu himself came to dominate the legislative and judicial, as well as the executive, roles of the state. Sources of opposition were systematically eliminated by co-option, harassment, imprisonment, exile and assassination. It was also made plain to those members of the ruling party itself that they owed their position specifically to Mobutu's patronage. As one reporter commented, the number of significant political players in Zaire was kept to just 80 or so individuals. Among these, at any one time, '20 of them are ministers, 20 are exiles, 20 are in jail and 20 ambassadors. Every three months, the music stops and Mobutu forces everyone to change chairs.'[36] No one, friend or foe, was left in any doubt about who held supreme power in Zaire. To challenge Mobutu was to risk losing everything, including one's life.

Whereas the political elite enjoyed the wealth that its access to state institutions brought, most individuals within Zaire gained little from their government. Members of civil society were the victims of a declining economy, public services were shrinking, and they were often on the wrong end of demanding corrupt officials. Yet there was no constitutional way of ridding Zaire of this kleptocratic elite. No opposition parties existed, and any political challenge that Mobutu perceived to threaten his regime was brutally crushed. Mobutu, until the final resource-diminished days of this regime, maintained agencies of violence that were more than a match for civil society. Lacking the ability to change the incumbent government directly, then, Zairians opted for the next best option. They sought to distance themselves as far as possible from the state.

The scale of this disengagement is perhaps best illustrated by the growth of Zaire's parallel economy during the 1980s and 1990s. By this time, official statistics showed Mobutu's economy to be a disaster. There was a massive trade deficit, production was declining in all sectors, annual inflation stood at over 1,000 per cent, the national debt was colossal, and wages were at starvation levels. In short, in terms of economics, nothing worked as it should.[37] Yet 35 million Zairians did get on with their lives. It may be true that the formal economy could no longer meet even the most basic needs of the Zairian people, but

this was *just* the formal economy. Indeed, by the late 1980s, it is estimated that the second economy sector measured up to three times that
of Zaire's official GDP.[38]

A few statistics serve to show the extent of this economic disengagement. From the 1970s onwards, up to 60 per cent of Zaire's coffee
crop annually by-passed state marketing boards and was smuggled into
neighbouring countries.[39] By 1985, farmers could sell their coffee to
smugglers for 42 cents per kilogram, while the state only offered 7
cents.[40] Similarly, the second economy set about supplying what the
official economy could not. Low state-determined prices and transport
problems (due to the collapsing infrastructure) saw few willing to
supply the official market with even the most basic of commodities.
Yet in parallel markets, where higher prices could be charged, it was
profitable to trade in staple goods.[41]

Disengagement, however, did not bring down the Zairian state
immediately. Mobutu's regime limped on until the mid-1990s. Indeed,
those members of the elite who were able to adapt to the shrinking
state were still able to prosper. It was almost as if these individuals
welcomed the disengagement of civil society. The growing gulf
between the governed and their governors allowed state managers
greater political space to operate their own personal survival strategies
(free now from even the notional responsibility of government).
Among these survival strategies were the scaling down of patronage
networks, the nurturing of foreign rather than domestic resources, and
tapping into the productive activity within the second economy. Each
of these is looked at in turn in this study.

The crisis of accumulation began to bite during the late 1970s, grew
considerably throughout the 1980s, and then reached a critical mass in
the early 1990s. Reacting to this developing crisis, the state elite scaled
down its patronage networks accordingly. Naturally enough, to maintain their privileged position certain stronger clients still had to be
placated. State managers, however, no longer had resources to
distribute to weaker citizens. Consequently, public services such as
health care, education and security virtually disappeared. Education
provision, for example, slumped from 17.5 per cent of the national
budget in 1972 to just 2.1 per cent in 1990. Similarly, rural communities were also abandoned. Agriculture's share of the budget fell from
29.3 per cent to just 4 per cent over the same period. Investment in
infrastructure was another casualty. Only 15 per cent of roads inherited
from the colonial authorities still remained passable by the mid-1980s.
Even in the cities, the Mobutu regime was only offering minimal

government. Kinshasa itself had only intermittent water and electricity supplies, and even the sickest people refused to attend its hospitals. All this was because state patronage had dwindled to a bare minimum.[41]

The disintegration of these client–patron networks, of course, had major ramifications for the government's legitimacy. The state now served fewer people, and those former clients who had been jettisoned were naturally aggrieved. Yet Mobutu and his lieutenants were very careful to retain those that they needed for their own personal survival. For example, whereas much of the army had been abandoned to its own devices by 1990, Mobutu made sure that his own 5,000-strong presidential guard still continued to be paid regularly. The president could lose legitimacy in the eyes of his people, but he could not afford to lose the support of his most reliable agency of coercion.

Once the Zairian state abandoned its welfare and infrastructure responsibilities, as well as much of its rural territory, it was almost if Kinshasa was content to rule only strategic enclaves within the country. The regime sought to maintain its authority in major cities, important trading centres and sites of extraction (such as mines and plantations) – all the key areas that could still produce a profit for the benefit of state managers. It did not matter too much that the government's authority could rarely now be found elsewhere (in the non-profitable regions of the country). Mobutu's regime certainly did not conform to Weber's idea that it should be able to exercise sovereignty over all its territory.

Ironically, however, one of the regime's most successful survival strategies relied directly on this Weberian notion of sovereignty. It required that other governments and TNCs still recognised Mobutu as Zaire's head of state, and thus the chief representative of his people. If this was the case, the General could still gain access to international resources. And this is exactly what happened. There was still an external demand for Zaire's minerals and coffee. Mobutu granted foreign TNCs concessions to extract these commodities, in return for a share of the profits. Even in 1991, when state collapse was imminent and the Mobutu government exercised authority over only the most strategic enclaves within the country, these exports earned the regime US$2.1 billion. International aid brought in another US$494 million.[43] Given that the government was now spending very little on public services, these sums went a considerable way to allowing the state elite to maintain its privileged position. It was able to shore up its profitable enclave operations, and run (albeit reduced) agencies of coercion. And there was also enough money left for Mobutu to employ foreign mercenaries to bolster his own presidential guard.

Nor was the international community the only source of wealth into which the state elite could tap. With public-sector wages falling behind inflation (and many instances of employees not being paid at all), officials could not now rely solely on the formal economy to secure their living. They, too, came to rely on the second economy. For example, state employees used their positions of political power to extract rent from parallel markets. Their largest source of income, in this respect, was the bribes received for turning a blind eye to illegal operations. Customs officers at Zaire's border with Zambia, for instance, regularly agreed only to charge excise duty on part of a lorry driver's cargo. The official and the driver would then share the remaining unpaid duty between them. And as they were now travelling with false documents, drivers would have to bribe personnel at subsequent military and police roadblocks between the border and the destination.[44]

Benefits, however, were not confined merely to an indirect association with the second economy. Many of the elite also played a more central role in these informal activities. With their *bureaucratic* power base disintegrating, state managers had been forced to switch to additional *economic* entrepreneurial projects in order to maintain their social position.

Jean-François Bayart gives a good illustration of how one arm of the state, the Zairian air force (FAZA), adapted to the conditions of a collapsing state. No longer enjoying regular pay, FAZA cargo pilots turned the airforce into an unofficial transport company during the 1980s. Taking advantage of Zaire's ailing road network, they were able to take goods into the interior and sell them at a profit. FAZA ground crews, however, were angered that they did not share these profits. Consequently they took less care in maintaining the cargo planes, which resulted in a number of crashes. This persuaded the cargo pilots, now that they had started an additional unofficial passenger service, to bring the ground crews into their operations. Not to be left out, fighter pilots also began using their position within the state to supplement their wages. They stole aircraft parts to sell in parallel markets. Eventually, the whole airforce was grounded due to a lack of spare parts. Undeterred, FAZA personnel then went on to sell the airforce's remaining fuel. By the 1990s, Zaire had an airforce in name only.

The demise of FAZA represents, in microcosm, the wider collapse of the Zairian state. By the mid-1990s, the game was up for the whole Mobutu regime. The state had exhausted its power and the economy had totally collapsed, as had the regime's bureaucratic structures. As a result, TNCs were now reluctant to risk investing in Zaire, while IFIs and foreign governments (especially now that the Cold War was over) were no longer prepared to stomach Mobutu's excesses and the country's massive external debt.

Mobutu attempted to cling to power, despite the growing strength of opposition groups. Forced to liberalise the constitution, he still managed to stall his opponents with a series of manoeuvres, including constitutional conventions, the postponement of multi-party elections, the funding of numerous bogus opposition parties, and by simply buying off opposition leaders. In the end, the country was left in constitutional deadlock, just as it had been at the start of Mobutu's 32-year reign. The president refused to relinquish control of what remained of the executive and the army, while opposition leaders in parliament failed to command the political strength to remove him.

Eventually, Mobutu would be ousted by force of arms. This came in the form of the *Alliance des Forces Démocratiques pour la Libération du Congo-Zaire* (AFDL) led by Laurent Désiré Kabila. The rebellion was precipitated by the influx of two million refugees into eastern Zaire after the Rwandan genocide of 1994. When the forces of the former Rwandan government began using these refugee camps as a base from which to attack ethnic Tutsis in Zaire itself, these communities retaliated. They then, with the new Rwandan government's support, began to march on Kinshasa to topple Mobutu himself. The AFDL reached Kinshasa in May 1997, and Kabila took on the presidency of the renamed Democratic Republic of the Congo. Mobutu's own death from cancer a few months later symbolised the demise of one of the most predatory states Africa has ever known.

Democratic Republic of the Congo (DRC)[45]

Territory:	2,345,410 sq km	Population:	46.6 million
Colonial power:	Belgium	Independence:	1960
Major cities:	Kinshasa (capital)	Ethnic groups:	Over 200 ethnic
	Lubumbashi		groups
	Mbuji-Mayi	Life expectancy:	52 years
Urban pop.:	30.1%	Adult literacy:	77%
Languages:	French	Exports:	Diamonds
	Kiswahili		Gold
	Tshiluba		Copper
Currency:	Congolese franc	External debt:	US$12,826 million
Infant mortality:	89 deaths/thousand births	GDP per capita:	US$93
Religion:	Traditional		
	Christian		

Glossary of key terms

Authority	A psychological relationship, between the governed and their governors, which engenders a belief that state personnel and institutions should be obeyed.
Corruption	The abandonment of legal-rational practices by officials in order to secure personal gain.
Crisis of accumulation	The failure to create wealth through the productive investment of surplus capital.
Crisis of governance	The failure of states to provide political structures able to represent civil society.
Disengagement, or exit, coping and survival strategies	The act of distancing civil society activities from the state, by-passing state authority (for instance by the use of parallel markets).
Insurgency	An 'ideological' challenge to state authority from within civil society, using violence.
Kleptocratic state	A state that exploits, rather than serves, civil society (also termed a vampire, pirate or predatory state).
Over-developed or bloated bureaucracies	Bureaucracies and parastatals that are too large to be supported by their host economies, and are dominated by imperatives of patronage.
Parallel markets	Alternative illegal economic markets, which seek to avoid exploitation by formal state regulations (also termed the second economy or the shadow economy).
Parastatal	Public-sector companies or agencies, such as state marketing boards, state manufacturing industries, or state transport companies.
State collapse	Where formal central state institutions no longer command authority.
State inversion	Where officials, pressed by a lack of resources, prune state activity to perform only specific (self-interested) functions, rather than the previous wider public services.
Unproductive investment	Economic activity that fails to produce a profit or a surplus of capital.
Warlord state	A state, usually unstable, that seeks to serve the private interests of its leaders, and does not seek to generate legitimacy among its 'citizens' or provide public service.

Questions raised by this chapter

1 Why had the post-colonial African state reached a point of crisis by the 1980s?
2 How successful was civil society in countering the power of the vampire state?
3 To what extent did African states collapse in the last two decades of the twentieth century?
4 Who prospered most in the 1980s and 1990s, state elites or members of civil society?
5 Assess the performance of the state's own survival strategies.

Further reading

There are several excellent books that cover the issues raised in this chapter. Robert Bates's work is informative for those who wish to read more about how the African developmental states failed the agricultural sector; Saahr Kpundeh's, likewise, is revealing on corruption; and I William Zartman's edited volume investigates the phenomenon of state collapse. Much has been written about civil society's disengagement from the state. Victor Azarya and Naomi Chazan's article is the pick of the crop, while Michael Bratton's review article gives a flavour of additional research in this area. Janet MacGaffey's book on Zaire's second economy is also well worth investigating. Those interested in state survival strategies should refer to Patrick Chabal and Jean-Pascal Daloz's volume, as well as William Reno's book.

Azarya, Victor and Naomi Chazan (1987) 'Disengagement from the state in Africa: reflections on the experience of Ghana and Guinea', *Comparative Studies in Society and History* 19(1), 106–31.
Bates, Robert H (1981) *Markets and states in Tropical Africa: the political basis of agricultural policies*, Berkeley: University of California Press.
Bratton, Michael (1989) 'Beyond the state: civil society and associational life in Africa', *World Politics* 41(3), 407–30.
Kpundeh, Sahr John (1995) *Politics and corruption in Africa: a case study of Sierra Leone*, Lanham, MD: University Press of America.
MacGaffey, Janet, ed. (1991) *The real economy of Zaire: the contribution of smuggling and other unofficial activities to national wealth*, London: James Currey.
Reno, William (1998) *Warlord politics and African states*, Boulder, CO: Lynne Rienner.
Zartman, I William, ed. (1995) *Collapsed states: the disintegration and restoration of legitimate authority*, Boulder, CO: Lynne Rienner.

11 Democracy

Re-legitimising the African state?

The last decade of the twentieth century brought dramatic political changes to Africa. The whole continent was swept by a wave of democratisation. From Tunisia to Mozambique, from Mauritania to Madagascar, government after government was forced to compete in multi-party elections against new or revitalised opposition movements. To use South African President Thabo Mbeki's words, the continent was experiencing a political 'renaissance'.[1]

Prior to 1990, opposition parties had been outlawed in most African countries. As Chapter 6 highlighted, the political norm was for a highly personalised executive to govern through tightly controlled one-party structures. There was little room for dissent or (legal) challenge to this ruling elite, as the multi-party systems inherited from the departing colonial administrations had been abandoned soon after independence. Only in Botswana (since 1966) and Zimbabwe (since 1980) has political pluralism been maintained throughout the post-colonial period (the Gambia, Senegal and Mauritius sustained multi-party competition for significant lengths of time, but not for this entire period). Elsewhere, the democratic picture was bleak. Africa had become a continent where governments were removed by force, not by elections.

By contrast, competitive democracy bloomed in the 1990s. As late as 1988, one-party states and military governments had still been dominant (see Table 11.1), and Africa was still in an era of 'one leader, one ideology, and one political party'.[2] Reasonably free and fair elections did occasionally occur in these countries (when the military returned to barracks, for example – Nigeria and Ghana being good cases in point), but these elections never amounted to an on-going commitment to democracy. Follow-up elections were rarely held. Yet by 1999, the number of multi-party constitutions on the continent had risen from 9 to 45. Granted, several of these 'multi-party democracies' amounted to paper exercises only, but many more proved to be fruitful. Momentous occasions such as that when Kenneth Kaunda, President of Zambia for 27 years, respectfully bowed to the will of the people in 1991, or Nelson Mandela's 1994 victory in South Africa's first non-racial elections, demonstrated that multi-party democracy had gained a foothold, however precariously, on the African continent. This is why it is appropriate that the final theme of this book should indeed be 'democracy'.

Table 11.1 Comparative African political systems, 1988 and 1999

1988

One-party systems (number = 29)
Algeria, Angola, Benin, Burundi, Cameroon, Cape Verde, Central African Republic, Comoros, Congo-Brazzaville, Côte d'Ivoire, Djibouti, Equatorial Guinea, Ethiopia, Gabon, Guinea-Bissau, Kenya, Madagascar, Malawi, Mali, Mozambique, Rwanda, São Tomé and Principe, Seychelles, Sierra Leone, Somalia, Tanzania, Togo, Zaire, Zambia

Military oligarchies (number = 10)
Burkina Faso, Chad, Ghana, Guinea, Lesotho, Libya, Mauritania, Niger, Nigeria, Uganda

Multi-party constitutions (number = 9)
Botswana, Egypt, The Gambia, Liberia, Mauritius, Senegal, Sudan, Tunisia, Zimbabwe

Monarchies (number = 2)
Morocco, Swaziland

Racial oligarchies (number = 2)
Namibia, South Africa

1999

Multi-party constitutions (number = 45)
Algeria, Angola, Benin, Botswana, Burkina Faso, Cameroon, Cape Verde, Central African Republic, Chad, Comoros, Congo-Brazzaville, Côte d'Ivoire, Djibouti, Egypt, Equatorial Guinea, Ethiopia, Gabon, The Gambia, Ghana, Guinea, Guinea-Bissau, Kenya, Lesotho, Liberia, Madagascar, Malawi, Mali, Mauritania, Mauritius, Mozambique, Namibia, Niger, Nigeria, Rwanda, São Tomé and Principe, Senegal, Seychelles, Sierra Leone, South Africa, Sudan, Tanzania, Togo, Tunisia, Zambia, Zimbabwe

Military oligarchies (number = 3)
Burundi, Libya, Zaire

Monarchies (number = 2)
Morocco, Swaziland

No central government (number = 1)
Somalia

'No party' government (number = 1)
Uganda

One-party systems (number = 1)
Eritrea

Democracy

Democracy literally means 'rule by the people'. It is the idea of popular sovereignty, where each individual participates in their society's government. At its most efficient, this will involve the whole community meeting regularly to make decisions, with each citizen's vote having an equal weighting. The citytates of ancient Greece are the most frequently used examples of this *direct* orm of democracy. Yet the democracy enjoyed in the Western world today liffers considerably from that of classical Greece: it is largely a twentieth-entury invention, and it is *representative* democracy.

The institutions of modern states are far too complex to be governed directly by the people. Citizens, on average, are too busy living their own lives to ecome involved with the minutiae of government. This is why they empower oliticians to rule on their behalf. In any form of democracy, however, the overnors must remain accountable to the governed, and in the case of repre-entative democracy this is principally achieved through regular elections. Each itizen should have an equal opportunity to vote for the candidate they feel will est serve their interests. What is more, laws should be in place, and adhered to, llowing free competition between individuals to win these votes. Freedom of peech, association and assembly are of paramount importance, as is the right to tand for office, a free press, and a secret ballot. With these guarantees, citizens an collectively select representatives of their choice, and – perhaps more mportantly – have the opportunity to remove those officials that have disap-ointed. Abraham Lincoln's ideal of 'government of the people, by the people, or the people' sums up the concept of representative democracy well.[3]

In the West, multi-party competition has become the accepted mechanism or delivering this type of democracy. Parties assist the aggregation of differing iews and interests found within society, and they also offer the electorate alter-ative public policy choices. Should the incumbent ruling party be perceived as ot serving the people's interests, then they can be voted out of office and eplaced by a more popular opposition party. Historically, it has been this multi-arty competition that has fostered the most productive examples of open, epresentative and accountable government.

The emphasis on multi-party competition, however, is not universally ccepted as the most appropriate method of representing the people. Marxists, or example, argue that there can be no true democracy without social justice. he equal political rights found in these liberal or bourgeois democracies do not quate to equal economic rights. Indeed, Marxists regard access by the masses to nulti-party competition as merely creating a false consciousness. Citizens are luped into supporting political structures that only serve to perpetuate the egemony of the bourgeoisie and economic exploitation.

Liberal democracy was also largely rejected in Africa in the first three lecades of independence. As Chapter 6 demonstrated, the continent's political eaders considered pluralist competition to be destructive. They favoured more nified and centralised mechanisms of government. The argument ran that nulti-party politics would only serve to deepen ethnic divisions, as well as leflecting the new states from their primary tasks of nation-building and conomic development. Consequently, one-party states became the most ommon form of political representation.

Some of these ruling parties, such as TANU in Nyerere's Tanzania and ANU in Kenyatta's Kenya, did manage, to a degree, to link the governed and the governors. It was more common, however, for African parties to atrophy, isolating presidential-monarchs from their people. The absence of a legal opposition left the continent's political systems too open to abuse by these ruling elites. Nor could Africa's leaders claim their governments were benign 'developmental dictatorships', where economic benefits were provided as a replacement for absent political rights. Economic advancement did not materialise. Consequently, by the mid-1980s, even Nyerere conceded that the one-party experiment had failed Africa. Always a sincere believer in democracy, Nyerere called upon his party to open up Tanzania to multi-party competition.[4]

And Tanzania was not alone. After 1990, the whole of Africa was immersed in political reform. The pattern was familiar. First, isolated demonstrations would break out in urban areas, with protesters targeting structural adjustment austerity measures. These would then become more sustained and organised, with demands moving from the economic sphere to more general political reform. Before long, full-scale multi-party democracy became the rallying cry of these protesters.

Eventually, the ruling elite grudgingly conceded to this political pressure. Constitutional changes were made to permit the registration of opposition groups, and this opened the flood gates for further political concessions. Governments were soon drafting plans for a return to full pluralist competition. In most of francophone Africa, for example, this involved constitutional conferences, followed by referenda of the people. By 1995, most countries on the continent had met the initial demand of multi-party democracy: the holding of reasonably free and fair competitive elections.

There can be no doubt that these momentous events spectacularly changed Africa's political environment. Africanists were left reeling at the speed of this democratisation process, and much of what happened needs explanation. What this chapter seeks to do is tackle three fundamental issues related to this political watershed. Initially, an examination of what prompted this return to multi-party democracy will be undertaken. The chapter will then assess the chances of political pluralism being consolidated on the continent. Conclusions can then be drawn about the impact of these events on Africa's relationship between state and civil society.

Explaining the emergence of multi-party democracy

Simply put, Africa's embrace of multi-party democracy in the 1990s can be explained by an agreement among all the parties involved. State elites, who for so long were ideologically committed to more authoritarian forms of government, were now converted to pluralism. Similarly, civil society expanded its campaign for the same goal. It was also a period where the international community backed these political trends.

This agreement between state, civil society and international agencies, however, seems remarkable given their divergent interests just a few years earlier. Why were all three now citing multi-party democracy as the way

orward? What had changed? An explanation can be formulated via four inter-
nked phenomena: the state's loss of authority, a new international political
nvironment, the rejuvenation of civil society, and precedent. Each of these
ictors is considered in turn.

he state's loss of authority

by the 1990s, Africa's political environment was ripe for change. The previous
hapter highlighted the problems now faced by state institutions. Starved of
esources due to the crisis of accumulation, and lacking legitimacy due to the
risis of governance, state authority was in terminal decline. The old governing
ormulas where presidential-monarchs could skilfully combine a mixture of
ccommodation and coercion were no longer effective. Elements of civil society
vere in a process of disengagement, or, in some cases, actually violently
ebelling against the ruling elite. For many African countries the prospect of
otal state collapse was a serious possibility.

Several ruling elites chose to ignore, as best they could, this crisis of
uthority. Their states became more and more inverted, with governments
bandoning their public obligations. These polities were well on the way to
ecoming warlord states (Liberia and Zaire/DRC being good cases in point). By
ontrast, however, other African leaders heeded the warning signs, and
ttempted to steer their regimes out of danger.

The game was up. Faced by anti-government protests, the only thing the
residential-monarchs could now do was to 'utter pious, self-serving calls to
liscipline and order'.[5] In previous years, the full weight of the state would have
een directed at these malcontents, and the protests crushed. Now, the state
iad few replies. Its powers of coercion were diminished, and its abilities of co-
ption starved by a lack of resources. Previous state survival strategies were no
onger enough to ensure the regime would endure, and a different, more effec-
ive, set of tactics had to be employed.

The re-invention of multi-party democracy in Africa can therefore be seen as
. reaction to this crisis of authority. State elites considered the dissolution of
heir monopoly over political activity to be the only survival strategy left. After
ll, what better antidote to a crisis of authority is there than a 're-legitimisation'
of the state through multi-party elections?

It was not that presidential-monarchs had suddenly been converted to
luralism. This was a concession forced upon them, and given grudgingly. It was
i case of leaders weighing up the impossible costs of delaying these reforms,
igainst the short-term benefits that could be gained.[6] Indeed, many ruling
iarties thought they could control the pace of this reform, remaining in power
ndefinitely. When the incumbent National Party, for example, decided to
ngage the African National Congress of South Africa (ANC) in negotiations,
ew of its members would have envisaged full multi-party democracy arriving
ust five years later. Similarly, when the presidents of most francophone coun-
ries established constitutional conferences, many . thought they could

manipulate proceedings, steering these towards their own interests. Few expected the far-reaching reforms that actually emerged from these political assemblies.

To some extent, the gambles undertaken by ruling elites with this ultimate survival strategy paid off. As we shall see, a considerable number of incumbents managed to stay in power, even after free and fair elections took place. There can be no doubt, however, that these state elites' search for legitimacy, and subsequent (partial) abandonment of authoritarian structures lay at the very heart of Africa's conversion to multi-party democracy in the 1990s.

The changing international political arena

Embattled leaders were not only experiencing internal pressures for reform. The international environment also now favoured a move towards political pluralism. Whereas before, state elites had come to rely on external patronage to prop up their regimes (even when internal legitimacy was lacking), in the 1990s this source of support had largely dried up.

A change of emphasis in how foreign governments and IFIs gave aid to Africa came with the end of the Cold War. As we saw in Chapter 8, state managers had previously been able to market their countries in terms of ideological allegiance and strategic importance. The United States supported its allies in Africa as an investment against communist encroachment (backing such governments as Kenya, Morocco and Zaire), while the Soviet Union assisted states with socialist leanings (Ethiopia and Angola). Concentrating on their Cold War priorities, neither Washington nor Moscow seemed too concerned that these countries were largely autocratic and had poor human rights records.

The collapse of the Soviet Union, however, had massive implications for African state elites. The writing, as Bratton and van de Walle put it, was on the Berlin Wall.[7] Soviet clients now had no external patron to turn to, while allies of the United States received less unconditional support because Washington's strategic interests on the continent had diminished dramatically. 'The winds from the East', as President Omar Bongo of Gabon lyrically stated, were truly 'shaking the coconut trees.'[8]

Indeed, those international agencies still interested in providing aid to Africa only did so with significant conditions attached. In terms of economics, for example, aid recipients were required to undertake structural adjustment reforms (see Chapter 9). It was these reforms that provided the catalyst for embryonic pro-democracy movements. Political conditions were also attached to aid packages. Assistance would be suspended or resumed as a direct consequence of a regime's human rights record and its commitment to democratic reforms. For example, international aid to Kenya was suspended in 1991, when President Daniel arap Moi halted his country's transition to pluralism. Hastings Banda, in Malawi, came under identical donor pressure in 1993. Talking for all the continent's leaders, President André Kolingba of the Central African

Republic stated: 'We have to accept the fact that those who lend us money for development want us to provide a choice of political parties.'[9] And given that state managers still relied heavily on the patronage of the international community, the West eventually got what it wanted.

A rejuvenated civil society

The most significant pressure for democratic reform, however, came from African civil society itself. Churches, trade unions, ethnic associations, women's organisations, professional bodies, farming cooperatives, community groups, and eventually political parties, had all at some time played a key role in the fight against colonial rule. These same associational organisations would also contribute significantly to Africa's 'second liberation' of the late 1980s and early 1990s.

Once political space had been created by the decline of state authority, opposition forces took their chances and began to challenge the state elite. There was a feeling that anything was now possible. The façade of government was visibly crumbling, and the 'emperor' was 'indeed naked'.[10]

The transition process was initiated by the reaction to structural adjustment's austerity measures. Thousands of urban Africans took to the streets. Such 'bread riots' had always been a feature of the post-colonial period. These were usually short-lived, quickly put down by the state's coercive agencies, and a conciliatory adjustment to public policy made. This time, however, the state was less able to quell the demonstrations, and the protests became more sustained. Before long, these gatherings took on a more political nature. Zairian protesters, for example, were now openly chanting '*Mobutu, voleur!*' ('Mobutu, thief!').[11]

It was at this point that the leading institutions of civil society took on the organisation of this popular protest. New groups formed specifically to campaign for multi-party democracy, while older associations, previously co-opted by the state, began to de-link themselves from the ruling elite. Politicians, sensing the changing political mood, similarly entered the battle. Those in exile attempted to return to their countries, others came out of retirement, and yet more defected from the ruling party to join the growing opposition.

Churches were often a significant force within the anti-authoritarian campaign. Difficult to ban, and very probably more legitimate than the government itself, religious organisations offered national opportunities for people to assemble. Consequently, church pulpits were used to hold governments to account. Archbishop Desmond Tutu, for example, with black opposition parties having been outlawed in South Africa, proved to be one of the most effective advocates against apartheid, both nationally and internationally. And in Malawi, nobody had dared criticise the rule of Hastings Banda for decades, yet in March 1992, Archbishop James Chiona and the country's Catholic bishops did just this. Banda's own denomination, the Church of Scotland, called upon its congregation to 'pray for this profoundly lonely man who is locked in the prison house of power'. After these brave opening salvos, others within Malawian civil society amplified these calls for multi-party democracy.[12]

Trade unions also played a major role in the transition to pluralist elections. In Niger, for instance, the largest labour federation, the *Union des Syndicats des Travailleurs du Niger* (USTN), put immense pressure on the ruling elite to concede democratic reforms. Previously this organisation had largely been controlled by state co-option. By the late 1980s, however, the USTN was at the heart of the opposition movement, coordinating strikes in support of protests elsewhere. This action successfully brought Niger's formal economy to a stand-still, and multi-party elections followed in 1993.[13]

Zambia, however, is perhaps the best example of trade union activity securing pluralist democracy. Frederick Chiluba, as the leader of the Zambian Congress of Trade Unions (ZCTU), had for a long time been an irritant to Kenneth Kaunda's UNIP one-party state. The government tried on numerous occasions to co-opt the Congress, without success. When UNIP's tolerance ran out, Chiluba was briefly imprisoned. This changed little, however, as, on his release, he again rejected a place on UNIP's central committee. Thus, when the opportunity arose in 1990 to challenge Kaunda's political monopoly, ZCTU proved to be an ideal popular and organisational base for the Movement for Multi-Party Democracy (MMD). The MMD subsequently defeated UNIP in elections in 1991, and Chiluba himself became the new president of Zambia.[14]

Church groups and trade unions, along with other associations involving human rights activists, students, legal professionals, medical practitioners and academics, provided leadership for a rejuvenated civil society. Through this leadership, mass discontent was channelled into a call for multi-party democracy. It proved to be a political demand that enfeebled state managers found difficult to resist.

Precedent

In accounting for Africa's democratic transition, the issue of precedent should also be considered. African leaders, within both state and civil society institutions, were well aware of what was happening not only in Eastern Europe but also on their own continent. Nelson Mandela's release from gaol in 1989, and the subsequent dismantling of apartheid, for example, demonstrated to all that even the most powerful state elites were vulnerable to pressure from below. With one-party states toppling like dominoes, the way forward seemed inevitable to most. It would take a brave, or a foolhardy, leader to try to stem this tide of history. Most eventually committed themselves to try to ride this wave of democratisation.

The obstacles to democratic consolidation

By 1999, most African states had constitutions in place that encouraged political pluralism. Reflecting this, more than 150 multi-party elections were held in the last decade of the twentieth century (compared to less than 70 competitive polls held in the three decades prior to this – see the Appendix). Some of these elections were flawed, but others represented a reasonable reflection of voters' wishes. Given these facts, there can be little doubt that post-colonial African politics had reached a critical juncture.

The holding of elections, however, is not the sole prerequisite for democracy. A mature democratic order requires that the new rules of the political game endure between elections, and, indeed, compel incumbent governments to hold further polls within a constitutionally defined period of time. Similarly, continued accountability and representation are far more important than the simple mechanics of holding elections. In this sense, the danger is that the wave of pluralism is simply a 'one-off response to a particular set of political circumstances'. It may be that, just like the multi-party polls at independence, or those following the military's return to barracks, these 1990s events were isolated elections, merely serving (temporarily) to 're-legitimise' the state. It could be, to use Christopher Clapham's words, a case of 'one man, one vote, once'.[15] Richard Sandbrook highlights exactly this point when he states: 'Africa's hostile conditions encumber not so much *transitions* to democracy as the *consolidation* of enduring democracies.'[16]

Despite post-colonial Africa's poor democratic record, however, the large number of multi-party elections held at the end of the twentieth century have generated a glimmer of hope. Amid the fall of presidential-monarchs and, in several cases, near state collapse, pluralist competition could represent a way forward. Consolidation, however, is by no means guaranteed. Several major obstacles will need to be overcome before Africa can even start to contemplate a prosperous political future.

The need for a credible opposition

To state the obvious, multi-party democracies need multiple parties. If the electorate is unhappy with its government's policies or conduct, it needs an alternative political force which it can vote into power. Credible opposition choices, however, are not always guaranteed. The 1995 General Election in Zimbabwe, for example, was remarkably free from instances of intimidation and malpractice. Yet, as Liisa Laakso writes: 'Unfortunately, the progress in the practical arrangements of the polling [were] accompanied by a lack of any alternatives or even counterforces to the ruling party.'[17] Robert Mugabe's regime was unpopular, procedural democracy was in place, yet ZANU-PF faced no serious opposition. This had also been the case in the General Elections of 1985 and 1990.

Elsewhere in Africa the converse has been the problem: too many parties. Political reforms have led to hundreds, maybe thousands, of parties mobilising across the continent. When Chad moved to pluralist competition, for example, over 60 movements registered with the state authorities.[18] Democracy, however, cannot be measured by the quantity of competitors alone. The quality of these parties is also important. Above all, they should be able to offer alternative policy choices and leadership options to the electorate.

Yet John Wiseman describes many of the recently emerged organisations as merely 'vanity parties'.[19] They served more as a vehicle for party bosses than as an aggregation of ideological or policy demands. Often these movements consist of just one charismatic leader, with only a handful of acolytes. Even the larger parties, with wider support, often revolve around a 'big man'. Election campaigns therefore became competitions between personalities rather than ideas. Wiseman, pointing to this absence of issue-driven politics, notes that opposition platforms are usually based on 'support for multi-party democracy, a defence of human rights, criticisms of government corruption, and an attack on statist approaches to economic policy. None of these elements are negligible or unworthy but they hardly add up to an ideological masterplan for reconstructing society.'[20]

The concentration on the politics of personality has led to factionalism within Africa's opposition movements. This partly explains why such a remarkable number of incumbent leaders and their parties survived the transition to multi-party politics (see the Appendix). Where pro-democracy forces remained coherent, successful campaigns against the presidential-monarchs were mounted. The united MMD in Zambia, for example, defeated Kaunda; the Alliance pour la Democratic au Mali helped oust Traoré; and the Alliance for Democracy in Malawi saw off Banda.

Divided oppositions, however, fared less well. Often, various factions ended up competing more with each other than they did against the incumbent. Côte d'Ivoire proves to be a case in point. Here, 26 parties registered after the constitution was amended. Of these, 17 fielded candidates in the 1990 elections. Only the *Front Populaire Ivoirien* (FPI) could make any impression on Houphouët-Boigny's status and his incumbent party's well-oiled electoral machine. Even the FPI, however, led by history professor Laurent Gbagbo, had little appeal beyond the educated urban classes.[21] Consequently, Houphouët-Boigny won by a landslide.

Kenyan politics also suffered from a divided opposition. Moi, detested in many areas of the country, still won two presidential polls during the 1990s. On both occasions he emerged victorious, despite winning less than 40 per cent of the vote. More coherence and cooperation among the opposition parties would almost certainly have defeated this autocratic president and brought a new lease of life to Kenyan politics.

This brief examination of opposition groups indicates that the consolidation of multi-party democracy is still a long way off in Africa. Until the electorate can be offered a genuine choice between competing policy programmes, rather than only between ambitious political cliques, then 'true' representation remains a distant goal.

The need for a strong civil society

A second prerequisite for democratic consolidation is a strong civil society. Healthy associational activity can act as a powerful independent counter-force to prevent the state monopolising the political process. In a multi-party democracy it is essential that civil society is present both to cooperate with, and to challenge, the government. This helps ensure the pubic interest is always paramount, and that governments continue to respect the rules of the democratic game.

In the past, African civil societies have defeated imperialism and brought post-colonial predatory states to their knees through disengagement. The question now, however, is whether contemporary associational life is strong enough on the continent to help preserve newly won multi-party democracies.

This preservation will require the growth of Africa's middle classes. After all, you cannot have liberal, or bourgeois, democracy without a bourgeoisie.[22] It is the middle classes that have the wealth, the time and the education to organise groups that can monitor and influence the state. Professionals can provide an intellectual challenge to the ruling party; church, mosque and human rights groups can provide a moral challenge; women's associations can keep issues of gender to the fore; and an independent media can challenge the government's dissemination of information, should this be needed. Without this independent associational activity there is a grave danger that the state will become too dominant and abuse its power.

Yet, as we saw in Chapter 5, few African countries have a powerful and independent middle class. The state itself has been the focus of class formation. In this respect, it could be that multi-party elections, rather than opening up the political process to all Africans, have instead simply initiated new personnel into the state elite. Indeed, there is no guarantee that former civil society leaders will act in the wider interests of the population. Just like state elites, it could be that they are more content to pursue just their own, or their narrow constituency's, interests.

The key is whether this new (or amended) political elite is more committed to the ideal of democracy and representation than was its predecessors. The sincerity of many who campaigned for pluralism cannot be doubted. It is possible, however, that the commitment of others to multi-party democracy was only instrumental. Now that they are in power, their belief in pluralism may diminish. Only a civil society continuing its independence from the state will be able to check these new ruling elites.

The need for stronger economies

The maintenance of multi-party democracy also relies on governments looking after the economic and social welfare of their citizens. Should a ruling party fail to provide what the electorate expects, then they will soon be voted out of office. Accountable governments have therefore to meet many demands. As well as a sound economic environment in which one can prosper, health care, education, social provision and transport infrastructure are just a few of the basic services that are expected by citizens. This is why, in western Europe, multi-party democracy developed alongside the construction of the welfare state.

Resources in Africa, however, remain scarce. It may be that newly elected governments will have trouble meeting the demands of their citizens. However representative these regimes may be, many simply do not have the means to service the politics of the 'pork barrel' that democratic systems often demand. Consequently, severe economic problems could lead to a loss of legitimacy, and even to the collapse of pluralism itself. In Nazi Germany, for example, citizens were willing to give up liberal democracy altogether in favour of national socialism. Nationalist socialism, it was considered, would be a more efficient form of rule, given that Germany's existing political and economic institutions were perceived to be failing the people. In light of this example from history, political leaders should always heed Afrifa Gitonga's advice: 'democracy is founded on full bellies and peaceful minds'.[23] In Africa, only an improved economic performance can guarantee this.

The need to separate the state and the ruling party

Multi-party democracy also needs a neutral state whose institutions provide the 'level playing-field' on which political parties can compete. By winning an election, a party has the right to rule through these institutions, in the national interest. Political leaders should not, however, use the power and resources of the state to specifically bolster the position of their own party. This would give it an unfair advantage at the next election. Democratic consolidation thus needs a new political environment in Africa in which there is a clear distinction between state institutions and those of the ruling party.

This clear distinction is yet to emerge in many African countries. Although multiple parties are now allowed to compete, opposition groups often do so at a clear disadvantage. In the more serious cases, for example, electoral registers may 'inadvertently' be incomplete in opposition areas of the country; constituency boundaries will be gerrymandered; ballot boxes will be 'lost', while others will be stuffed with pre-prepared voting slips; and, if all these methods fail, then the state's electoral commission could always simply declare a fictitious result.

Zambia provides a good example of how electoral rules can be manipulated, in a more subtle manner, by the ruling party. Chiluba's MMD defeated Kaunda's UNIP in 1991, marking one of the first cases of transition to a democratic regime in Africa. Yet UNIP, as a political force, was not totally defeated. It took its place as the loyal opposition in parliament, and successfully rebuilt support among the electorate. Fearing UNIP's revival as the 1996 elections approached, Chiluba moved to defeat Kaunda's presidential campaign by using the power of the state (rather than through winning more votes in an open election). The MMD majority in parliament was used to amend the constitution to prevent 'first generation' Zambians from running for president. All concerned knew that Kaunda's parents were born in present-day Malawi, and with Kaunda out of the race, Chiluba successfully secured his second term of office.

Ruling parties will not just use the state's power to improve their chances of re-election, they will also appropriate public resources. With access to the national treasury, for example, incumbent parties can mount extensive and elaborate election campaigns. Opposition groups, starved of funds, cannot compete with this 'public' spending. Kenya's president, Daniel arap Moi, for example, took full advantage of his position in the 1997 campaign. Government spending was increased by US$100 million prior to the elections, increasing the country's money circulation by 35 per cent.[24] Moi effectively bought the votes he needed for victory.

Other resources that incumbents readily utilise are the state-owned media and the security forces. Almost all state newspapers, radio and television on the continent provide a pro-government outlook in their reporting. By contrast, opposition groups find it hard to get their views and policies expressed through these media. Agencies of coercion are also at the ruling party's disposal. The police and the army can be used to disrupt anti-government rallies and harass opposition leaders. This may be of particular advantage during election campaigns. Voters at one polling station in Equatorial Guinea, for instance, were apparently told that any person wanting to vote for an opposition candidate could do so in a separate ballot box to be found behind the building. A soldier would show them the way.[25]

All the above cases are extreme examples of the way governments use state institutions to manipulate elections. Most of the multi-party polls held in the 1990s, however, were declared *reasonably* free and fair. Yet the fact remains that incumbent parties have a major advantage over their rivals. Until there is a clear separation between state and ruling party institutions, there will not be a 'level playing-field', and democracy will not be consolidated. A shadow is cast over the whole multi-party experiment when many incumbent leaders still share the views of President Pascal Lissouba of Congo-Brazzaville. He reasoned: 'You don't arrange elections if you are going to lose them.'[26]

The unleashing of ethnic mobilisation?

A fifth potential problem that democratic consolidation will have to overcome is the perennial issue of ethnicity. The fact remains that imposed colonial borders have caged different ethnic groups within a single state. Competition between these groups was previously restricted by the one-party state and centralised structures. Multi-party democracy, however, opens up the possibility of full-scale ethnic mobilisation. After all, as Claude Ake points out, 'Liberal democracy assumes individualism, but there is little individualism in Africa.'[27] Africans interact on a more communal basis. In this respect, there is a possibility that African political parties will come to mirror the ethno-regional divisions within their societies. The recent revival of ethnic tensions in Congo-Brazzaville, Kenya, Malawi and Zambia, among other countries, certainly suggests this.

The danger with competition based on ethno-regional identities is that a victory for one group may be seen as a total defeat for another. One 'tribe' is to rule over the rest. Under these circumstances, it may be difficult for the losing ethnic group to accept the election results. Indeed, if an ethnic group feels that its interests will not be served within a nation ruled by its rival, then outright secession may be sought. And the consequence of this could be dismemberment of the state, just as occurred in the fledgling democracies of Yugoslavia and Czechoslovakia, and within the former Soviet Union.

Yet, so far, secession has not been a popular demand on the continent. Most Africans are still committed to the project of nation-building and accommodation within inherited nation-state structures. Indeed, ethnicity may be a positive contribution to democratic behaviour, offering an aggregation of demands. Pluralism, after all, revolves around the competition of interests. It is a way of resolving such conflicts peacefully. As long as all respect the rules of the game, then democracy will survive. Harvey Glickman's conclusion seems to be sound: 'while democratization trends provide opportunities for expansion of ethnic conflict, they also allow opportunities for controlling such conflict through institutional mechanisms'.[28]

The threat of the military

Along with the need for a strong opposition, civil society and economy, the requirement that state institutions and the ruling party be separated, and that ethnic conflict be successfully managed, the behaviour of the military will also be critical in this period of democratic consolidation.

Chapter 7 has already examined how the coercive agencies of the state have previously intervened in African politics. Time after time, the military usurped civilian politicians. However, for democracy to survive, the men in uniform will now have to take an apolitical role, leaving issues of regime change to the electorate.

A universal end to military intervention in African politics will not materialise immediately. The 1990s saw several instances in which security forces vetoed election results, installing their own governments instead (Algeria, Nigeria, Burundi, Congo-Brazzaville, the Central African Republic). Even when some of these countries subsequently returned to multi-party competition, there was often a tacit understanding that candidates must first have the approval of the army. In Nigeria's case, the 1999 return to pluralist competition saw Olusegun Obasanjo elected as president. Earlier, General Obasanjo had previously run Nigeria's 1976-79 military government. Did this hand-back to civilian rule represent the army endorsing the electorate's choice, or was it the people endorsing the military's nominee? Electoral victories for several (military-approved) Algerian presidential candidates throughout the 1990s beg the same question.

It is a sobering thought that even the Gambia suffered a military coup in this last decade of the twentieth century. This brought to an end 29 years of multi-party democracy. Going by this evidence, consolidation will take several generations to complete.

Political culture

All the above considerations can be drawn into the idea of political culture; political culture being *the shared political ideas, attitudes and beliefs that underlie a society*. Naturally enough, all individuals have their own views and interests, but more stable societies usually have some general political principles held in common. Ideas of liberal democracy, for example, permeate the whole of society in Britain and the United States. Individuals, whether they are politicians or lay persons, respect and defend the rules of the political game. Consequently, democracy as a method of conflict resolution is valued in institutions throughout both the state (parliaments, cabinets) and civil society (board rooms, trade union conferences, club meetings). African states have to replicate this political culture if multi-party democracy is to survive.

Normally, one would look to political leaders to be at the forefront of defending their society's political culture. It could be argued, however, that many of the political elites in Africa, both incumbents and opposition, are only using multi-party democracy instrumentally. In other words, they support pluralism because it is a method of retaining or gaining power, not because they inherently believe in its moral value. Take Zaire's politicians Etienne Tshisekedi and Nguza Karl-i-Bond, for example. Both formed political parties attempting to benefit from the new era of multi-party competition. They also made late bids to join Laurent Kabila's rebellion against Mobutu Sese Seko. Earlier, however, they had both been quite happy to serve Mobutu. Such political chameleons (or political entrepreneurs) cannot be trusted as the guardians of democracy. As Robert Fatton observes: 'When the old guard, the "dinosaurs", abruptly discover that they are after all good democrats, a country's release from authoritarianism may be facilitated, but its future as a democratic society can only be endangered.'[29] A drift back into personal rule and neo-patrimonialism is highly likely unless other political forces can check the elite's authoritarian tendencies.

The 'masses' could be one obvious source to keep notions of representation and accountability foremost in politicians' minds. Yet there is no real evidence to suggest that multi-party political culture is ingrained in the African 'masses' either. Botswana, for example, has enjoyed pluralist competition since independence in 1966, but, despite this, an opinion poll conducted in the 1980s found that only 47 per cent of a representative sample considered multi-party democracy essential. The study concluded that, 'among those with less than a secondary school education there is not yet a significant majority in favour of the idea that the public should have a voice in who should rule and for what purpose'.[30] The majority of Batswana were content for the political elite to rule on their behalf, and expected only minimally to participate in the political process. If this is the case in Botswana, then it would not be unreasonable to expect there to be even more deference to politicians in other African countries, and deference is not an effective check against potential authoritarianism.

Pluralism also requires a political culture where democrats wear victory or defeat gracefully. An indication of Africa's weak democratic culture, however, is the fact that fewer parties have accepted the results of multi-party elections than have been willing to participate in them. Certainly, there *have* been numerous cases of grace in defeat, but there have also been a worrying number of ignored results. In Angola, for example, multi-party elections were held in 1992 after 17 years of civil war. The MPLA government defeated UNITA in free and fair elections, yet UNITA's response was not to form a loyal opposition, but to return to the bush and carry on its insurgency campaign. Elsewhere there have also been many cases of defeated parties refusing to take up their seats in parliament. When the losing party's first reaction to defeat is to boycott or take up arms, then democratic consolidation is still a long way off.

The need for regime change?

Samuel Huntington considers that free and fair elections have to result in two turnovers of government before a state can be classified as a democracy. This, he argues, is the only proof that pluralism is truly working.[31] It shows that both incumbents and oppositions are committed to the rules of the political game, and, above all, that they are willing to concede defeat if that is the people's wish. In Africa, only Mauritius, Benin and Madagascar meet Huntington's double turnover criterion.

This fact, however, should not hide the reality that the continent made remarkable strides towards multi-party democracy during the 1990s. This is reflected both in the sheer volume of pluralist elections held, and in the number of occasions that peaceful regime changes came as a result (see the Appendix). Most of the elections were reasonably free and fair, and even where the incumbents clung onto power, this was usually more to do with genuine popular support than simple electoral manipulation.

This has left African countries at various stages of democratic transition (see Table 11.2). A few countries never started the reform process (where incumbents were able to resist the pressures for liberalisation); others have stumbled along the way (with authoritarian practices resuming, military intervention occurring, or a descent into state collapse); more have made hesitant progress (involving a limited liberalisation of the political arena, but the incumbent elite remaining very much in control); while a good number have displayed more positive signs of a democratic culture. It should be recognised, however, that none of this last category is free from the danger of retrogression. Newly won democratic concessions are easily reversed, and several more countries are bound to fall back into old habits. Conversely, no state on the continent is incapable of making further progress. Even those that have collapsed completely may wish to start the re-building process with multi-party elections. Consequently, after an amazing period of change in Africa, the continent's political future is still very uncertain.

Table 11.2 African democratic transitions, 1990–9

Precluded transitions	Blocked transitions	Flawed transitions	Democratic transitions
Liberia	Algeria	Burkina Faso	Benin
Sudan	Angola	Cameroon	Cape Verde
	Burundi	Comoros	Central African
	Chad	Côte d'Ivoire	Republic
	Ethiopia	Djibouti	Congo
	Guinea	Equatorial Guinea	Guinea-Bissau
	Rwanda	Gabon	Lesotho
	Sierra Leone	Ghana	Madagascar
	Somalia	Kenya	Malawi
	Tanzania	Mauritania	Mali
	Uganda	Nigeria	Mozambique
	Zaire	Swaziland	Namibia
		Togo	Niger
			São Tomé and
			Principe
			Seychelles
			South Africa
			Zambia

Source: After Bratton, Michael and Nicolas van de Walle (1997) *Democratic experiments in Africa: regime transitions in comparative perspective*, Cambridge: Cambridge University Press, 120.

State and civil society

Both state and civil society have benefited from the move to multi-party democracy. In terms of the state, for example, the previous chapter saw most African governments in a pincer movement between the crisis of accumulation and the crisis of governance. Legitimacy was declining rapidly, states were inverting, and, for many, a complete collapse beckoned.

In this respect, the transition to multi-party constitutions from 1989 onwards has to be seen as the deployment of yet another state survival strategy. The presidential-monarchs set about mounting a tactical retreat through the offer of democratic reforms. It was their last hope to re-legitimise the state, and thus to retain a degree of power for themselves and their clients.

The price paid for using this particular survival strategy was the liberalisation of African political systems. Political space that previously was deliberately restricted by the elite, became liberated. Civil society could now openly and legally challenge the ruling party on several fronts. To survive, incumbents had first to win elections and then to cope with official oppositions within state legislatures. Indeed, many of the old guard failed in their attempts to do just this. They did not possess the skills of manipulation, resources or public support to survive the transition to the new system. Others did make it into the new era, however, and although these politicians may well still possess their old authoritarian reflexes, they are all aware that they now have new responsibilities towards the electorate. Both democracy and the state can only be strengthened by this recognition.

Civil society, or at least parts of it, was also strengthened by the transition to multi-party competition. Churches, trade unions, human rights groups and professional associations have all gained confidence and experience with respect to participating in the political process. Having forced the old regimes to concede democratic reforms, they are now in a position to help ensure that pluralist competition survives.

The depth to which this democratic culture has permeated civil society, however, has to be questioned. Leaders within these social institutions may be fully committed to the new era of pluralism, but to what extent has the peasantry in Africa been converted? Does this form of politics offer them anything but an occasional chance to vote?

Indeed, it may be that multi-party democracy has only served to expand the political class on the continent (with circulating elites now encompassing the higher echelons of both the state and civil society). Government, under these circumstances, would only be accountable and representative to these higher echelons of society. If this is the case, the vast majority of Africans will still be left with few benefits from government. The links between the governors and the governed remain weak. Only a consolidated democracy together with economic development will produce a political system that is truly relevant to these people. In this respect, more successful democracies 'arise from popular demands for a share in a going concern'. They are less effective if they emerge as a 'last gasp attempt' to hold together a concern that is 'on its way down'.[32]

There is no doubt that the political environment in Africa improved greatly in the 1990s. There is a possibility that these reforms mark the start of a positive political journey that will benefit many over the coming decades. It would be remiss, however, to be over-optimistic about Africa's political future. This would be relying too heavily on hope, and ignoring the hard evidence presented above – for it is painfully plain to see that the consolidation of widespread multi-party democracy in Africa is possible, but by no means guaranteed.

Case study: the search for democracy in Algeria

Most of Algeria's population inhabits a narrow strip of territory just inland from the country's Mediterranean coastline. To the south of this fertile plain lie the Atlas Mountains, and beyond these can be found the massive expanses of the Sahara desert. Historically, Algeria's indigenous Berber communities interacted with the Phoenician, Carthaginian and Roman empires. A more permanent influence, however, was the 'Arabisation' of this part of the world from the seventh century onwards. France, by contrast, was a comparative latecomer: its forces occupied parts of Algeria in 1830, and completed its colonisation by 1902. French imperial rule, however, only lasted a further 60 years, and by 1962 Algerians had won their own sovereign state.

Independence was not a peaceful process for Algeria. The French had colonised this country extensively, and were extremely reluctant to leave. Indeed, Paris regarded Algeria as an integral part of France itself. The consequence was perhaps Africa's most brutal and destructive war of liberation. In a bitter conflict between the *Front Libération Nationale* (FLN) and the colonial authorities, over one million people lost their lives – one in ten of Algeria's population.[33]

When it finally came, however, the act of independence was swift. France, unable to defeat the FLN, and reeling from the domestic political consequences of this conflict, organised a referendum of Algerians who duly voted overwhelmingly for decolonisation. Paris granted formal independence just two days later, and after a brief power struggle among factions of the FLN, Ahmed Ben Bella emerged as independent Algeria's first president. National elections, which attracted a much lower turnout than the earlier referendum, legitimised the new government and the powers it had granted itself.

Ben Bella's rule mirrored the options taken by most governments, right across post-colonial Africa. Constitutionally, the executive became dominant, the FLN was to be the sole political party of the land, and sources of opposition were either systematically repressed or co-opted. As elsewhere, socialism was to be the guiding ideology, with the state at the heart of any economic planning.

Having taken similar options to countries in other parts of Africa, Algeria also replicated many of these regimes' fate. Ben Bella became a casualty of a military *coup d'état*, with Colonel Houari Boumédienne taking over the reins of power in 1965. Boumédienne, as head of the Council of the Revolution, declared that he would attempt to build 'authentic' socialism, unlike the previously corrupt personalist Ben Bella regime. In reality, however, the new government displayed most of the authoritarian tendencies of its predecessor. The army and the FLN monopolised state institutions, and there was never an attempt to secure a popular mandate via competitive democratic elections. Later, following the death of Boumédienne in 1978, Colonel Chadli Benjedid became president.

Within ten years of Chadli's accession to head of state, however, the FLN/military state was in trouble. Protesters were seriously threatening the government's authority, and Chadli's legitimacy was shrinking. The size and frequency of demonstrations steadily grew from the mid-1980s onwards. By 1988 they had become difficult to contain. The joint strategy of repression and co-option was no longer working. In October 1988, for example, discontent boiled over. Rioting spread from the capital, Algiers, to include all of Algeria's major towns and cities. Up to 500 people were killed by the army in its efforts to quell these disturbances.[34] The crises of accumulation and governance had begun to bite.

Up to this point, the protests had been relatively spontaneous. Unemployed youths (joined occasionally by students) were taking to the streets to express their frustration at the government's inability, and lack of will, to do something about their plight. Algeria's failing economy had treated this section of the urban community particularly harshly. As government authority began to waver, however, civil society organisations stepped into the political space that opened. They began to channel these spontaneous protests into a more organised campaign advocating multi-party democracy. Foremost among these associational organisations were Islamist groups (groups that wanted the Algerian state institutions to take more notice of Islam's laws and traditions).

These civil society Islamist groups began to offer what the FLN state could not. Azzedine Layachi observed: 'As political disputes, strikes, and inefficiency caused ever greater hardship for the people, numerous Islamic networks grew to match, surpass, and even replace state action. In 1989, for example, when an earthquake hit Tipaza, west of Algiers, they performed the disaster relief work. Islamists also opened "Islamic souks" (markets), where prices were well below those of regular distribution circuits. They also established popular courts, settling disputes with more justice, speed, and efficiency than did the state system; established neighbourhood militia groups; and directed traffic when no policeman was in sight.'[35] Just as a trade union had offered the organisation and rallying point for pro-democracy protests in Zambia, and Christian churches had done the same in Malawi, many of Algeria's anti-government protesters took up the Islamist cause.

But why had the street protests reached such an intensity by 1988? Why were relatively disorganised groups of youths able to challenge the state so effectively? The answers to these questions can, once again, be found in a crisis of accumulation and a crisis of governance.

In terms of economics, at least in the short term, Boumédienne's one-party state had been relatively successful. A programme of state industrialisation, bolstered significantly by oil and natural gas revenue, had provided Algeria with an average annual economic growth rate of

8.6 per cent between 1967 and 1978.[36] This produced increasing levels of employment throughout the country, and created income to pay for welfare services such as health and education. Algerians, for example, enjoyed free education provision, free medical care and subsidised food. Boumédienne's development programme, however, had longer-term implications. It produced a bloated bureaucracy, agricultural stagnation, occasional food scarcity, and high inflation. Above all, it was over-reliant on oil and gas revenues (hydrocarbons representing 97 per cent of Algeria's foreign earnings). Realising this, President Chadli attempted to liberalise the economy during the 1980s. Following structural adjustment policies, but never formally submitting to the IMF or World Bank, Chadli attempted to cut the size and costs of the public sector, while increasing its efficiency. He also reduced welfare services and subsidies, and increased producer prices to farmers.

The social costs of this structural adjustment were high. Unemployment increased rapidly, and this was in a country where many, especially young people, were already out of work. Algeria's debt exposure also reached alarming levels. Then the whole situation was dramatically exacerbated by a devastating fall in the price of oil in 1986. Disagreement among OPEC members over quotas saw prices fall from US$32 to US$8 a barrel. Algeria's main source of income had been drastically cut at a time of already-existing economic hardship. The result was that the state could no longer continue to act as 'development agent and welfare provider'.[37]

Economic hardship brought on by this crisis of accumulation also highlighted the crisis of governance. With patronage networks being scaled back dramatically due to dwindling state resources, Algerians began more readily to compare their situation to that of the state elite. In the eyes of the people, not only were these state managers incompetent, unable to run the economy, but they were also corrupt and unfit for public office. Many Algerians were now too young to remember the great independence war in which these FLN leaders fought, and did not hold the symbolic attachment to the FLN that many of the older generation still had. The government's legitimacy, consequently, declined rapidly. Under these circumstances, Algerians were now prepared to take to the streets and demand a change of government.

Civil unrest, particularly the events of October 1988, quickly convinced Chadli that he had to re-legitimise the state. As Martin Stone puts it: 'For the first time, not only did the state repression fail to silence the opposition; it empowered it instead. Opposition groups of all hues – students, trade unionists, communists and Islamists – exploited the unrest to demand substantial political reform and the dismantling of the state apparatus which had allowed a tiny élite and the military to abuse Algeria in the name of the people. The regime was shaken, and in the next nine months rapidly set about reforming the apparatus on which it had depended for two decades.'[38] In the first instance, Chadli proposed constitutional changes that would allow independent (non-party) candidates to stand against FLN members at forthcoming legislative elections. By 1989, however, as would happen in most African countries, pressure from civil society had forced Chadli to concede full multi-party competition. What is more, the army also agreed formally to withdraw from the political arena, leaving the FLN to rule as a civilian party. One-party rule was at an end, and a new era of political pluralism beckoned.

Algeria's democratisation process was to be held in two stages. Local elections would come first in June 1990, followed by national elections for the legislature. The national elections would consist of two rounds, in December 1991 and January 1992. Over 60 political parties registered with the state authorities between 1989 and 1991. Most of these were small organisations, often consisting of just a leader and a few followers. Three, however, developed national support, and would be the main players in the 1991 campaign. They were: the FLN, attempting to hold on to power via outmanoeuvring its rivals in the new pluralist environment; the *Front des Forces Socialistes* (FFS), a social democratic party; and the *Front Islamique de Salut* (FIS), mobilising on an Islamist platform.

The local elections in June 1990 proved to be something of a shock to the state elite. Rather than succeeding in outflanking its new opposition, the FLN (with 32 per cent of the vote) was soundly beaten into second place by the FIS (with 55 per cent). The FFS had boycotted the poll, on the ground that the opposition had not been given enough time to prepare.

From this point on, the FIS started to behave like a government in waiting. It organised mass demonstrations against the government, called a general strike when the FLN attempted to push through electoral rules designed to favour its own party, and took an increasingly violent stance towards the security forces. The state responded with a State of Emergency and detained a number of FIS members. This confrontational atmosphere leading up to the national elections in December was certainly not conducive to orderly pluralist politics.

When the first round of the national assembly elections finally came, the FIS repeated its June 1990 victory, winning 47 per cent of the vote. The FLN took 23 per cent, and the FFS 7 per cent. The FIS was on the verge of becoming the world's first democratically elected Islamist government. It was at this point, however, that the military intervened. First, they annulled the elections and put pressure on President Chadli to dissolve the existing national assembly, and then forced Chadli himself to resign from office. Fearing what would happen under a FIS regime, the army had simply vetoed Algeria's democratic process. The second round of elections was never held. Instead, the military established a provisional ruling council, the *Haut Comité d'Etat* (HCE), to govern in place of the formal institutions that it had usurped.

With the benefit of hindsight, the military coup should have shocked the followers of Algerian affairs less than it actually did. The military, after all, had always been a hegemonic force in this country's politics. At independence, for example, Ben Bella only gained power through the assistance of Colonel Boumédienne's faction of the army. Boumédienne himself then directly took power in 1965, running the country through a military/civilian hybrid government for 13 years. It was also the military, again, that chose Boumédienne's successor, Chadli, from its own ranks in 1978. In this light, the army's decision to remove Chadli from office and to cancel the January 1992 second ballot should be seen as just one of many occasions on which the military assumed command of the political process.

One of the ruling HCE's first acts was to declare a State of Emergency. Under this, the FIS was banned, its offices closed, and many of its leaders and supporters interned. The local councils that the FIS had won in the June elections were also dissolved, being replaced by state administrators. Reports of the security forces harassing and torturing Islamist sympathisers were widespread.

Many FIS supporters, for their part, turned to an armed struggle. The FIS-led *Armée Islamique du Salut* (AIS) targeted state structures and personnel, insisting that the violence would continue until the FIS was re-admitted to the political process. The more radical *Groupes Islamique Armées* (GIA) was less selective in its targets, and had as its goal the complete overthrow of the secular state and its replacement by an Islamic republic. The GIA had, among its number, the 'Afghans'. These were militants who had previously served as volunteers with the *Mujahideen* in Afghanistan. Assassinations, car bombs, massacres, ambushes and gun battles became daily events in Algeria. Some 100,000 people had lost their lives by July 1997 in this second civil war, and the violence continued into the next millennium.[39]

On the political front, the military realised that it had once again somehow to re-legitimise the state. For the next few years the HCE attempted to co-opt secular politicians, and indeed some of the more moderate Islamists, into a national 'transitionary' government. Many of the minor parties readily accepted this 'national conference' plan. The more powerful FLN and the FFS, however, refused to enter negotiations without the re-legalisation of the FIS. The FFS leadership, for example, considered such a conference undemocratic, and merely 'a vital necessity for the regime...they can avoid the perils of direct management [but still] keep [their] political hegemony and privileges of power'.[40] This forced the HCE unilaterally to appoint its own president, Liamine Zéroual, to head a three-year government of transition.

President Zéroual pressed ahead with a re-legitimisation strategy. His plan involved three stages. First, presidential elections would be held, to legitimise his own position. Second, a referendum would then be organised to back a constitution (which would permit pluralist competition among non-religious and non-ethnic political parties). The third stage would involve holding multi-party legislative elections.

Zéroual, initiating this three-stage strategy in November 1995, picked up 61 per cent of the presidential vote, against 25 per cent for his moderate Islamist opponent, Mahfoud Nahnah. This bolstered his position as head of state (despite the continued ban on the FIS, electoral irregularities, and a boycott by the FLN and FFS). Following this, Zéroual's constitution was accepted by referendum, and then, in June 1997, the FLN and the FFS agreed to take part in multi-party elections.

The 1997 legislative election can be seen as a major victory for Zéroual and his state backers. He marshalled his supporters into an alliance of parties, the *Ressemblement National Démocratique* (RND); this organisation received 33 per cent of the vote (compared to the FLN's 14 per cent and the FFS's 5 per cent). The largest poll for an Islamist party was the *Mouvement de la Société pour la Paix* with 14 per cent. The turnout of 65 per cent, was a figure comparable with the earlier 1991 vote. Inevitably, the RND, being the pro-Zéroual party, had received considerable and exclusive access to state resources, such as the media. The result itself, however, was relatively free and fair (despite a continued ban on the FIS). It would seem that Zéroual and his army backers had manufactured the semi-democratic conditions they desired. There was enough democracy to legitimise (at least partially) the government, but not enough actually to endanger their control over the political process.

Despite the willingness of the state to hold multi-party elections (excluding only the FIS), this resumption of pluralism in the later 1990s should not be interpreted as the consolidation of liberal democracy in Algeria. Operating in the background, the military has consistently held a veto over this country's political process. The 1999 presidential elections, for example, bore all the hallmarks of army manipulation. Abdelaziz Bouteflika won a poll that all six of his opponents had decided to boycott. They collectively withdrew the day before, complaining of electoral irregularities. Unopposed, the military's preferred choice was victorious once again. Yet the other candidates' boycott meant very little in terms of a stand against authoritarianism. As one resident of Algiers commented on election day, these politicians were 'all part of the same old corrupt cliche. Imagine if one of them had [himself] been chosen by the army, would he have complained about fraud? No way.'[41] Multi-party democracy will not be consolidated in Algeria until the people themselves, without the army's intervention, are able to select candidates for election.

Algeria[42]

Territory:	2,381,745 sq km	Population:	29.8 million
Colonial power:	France	Independence:	1962
Major cities:	Algiers (capital)	Ethnic groups:	Arabs
	Oran		Berbers
	Constantine		European settlers
	Annaba	Life expectancy:	69 years
Urban pop.:	57.7%	Adult literacy:	61.6%
Languages:	Arabic	Religion:	Islam
	Berber dialects	Exports:	Oil
	French		Gas
Currency:	Algerian dinar	External debt:	US$1,838
Infant mortality:	41 deaths/thousand births	GDP per capita:	US$33,259 million

Glossary of key terms

Consolidation of democracy   Ensuring that the democratic process endures beyond the first multi-party election. This will be assisted by a favourable political

	culture, a strong civil society and a supportive economy.
Democracy	A form of government where sovereignty rests with the people.
Double turnover criteria	The view that the democratic process has not been proven until elections have removed two regimes fairly and peacefully from office (S Huntington).
Military veto	Where the military instigates a *coup d'état* in order to block the civilian political process.
Political culture	The shared political ideas, attitudes and beliefs that underlie a society.
Rejuvenation of civil society	A reference to the re-vitalisation of African associational life in the 1980s and 1990s, caused by organisations de-linking themselves from government co-option and by civil society moving into political space vacated by the state.
Re-legitimising the state	State efforts to forge new links with civil society in the wake of the crises of legitimacy and governance.
Vanity party	A political party acting more as a vehicle for the personal interests of its leader, rather than genuinely aggregating demands emanating from society (J Wiseman).

Questions raised by this chapter

1   Why were so many multi-party elections contested in Africa during the 1990s?
2   Will multi-party democracy be consolidated on the African continent?
3   Are Africa's political cultures a suitable host for multi-party democracy?
4   To what extent did the move to multi-party democracy alter the relationship between state and civil society in Africa?
5   Did the 1990s democratisation process re-legitimise the African state?

Further reading

Those interested in learning more about multi-party democracy in Africa during the 1990s could start with John Wiseman's own book (1996), and then go on to his edited collection (1995) for some detailed case studies. Michael Bratton and Nicolas van de Walle's volume is also worth a look, as they offer a comprehensive, more statistical, approach to the subject. In terms of journal articles, three papers stand out: Patrick Molutsi and John Holm provide a fascinating study of Botswana, where democracy has been in place since 1966; Claude Ake looks at how traditional democratic values have been incorporated into modern African states; and Christopher Clapham puts the recent wave of democratisation into its historical context, and offers hopes and fears for the future.

Ake, Claude (1993) 'The unique case of African democracy', *International Affairs* 69(2), 239–44.

Bratton, Michael and Nicolas van de Walle (1997) *Democratic experiments in Africa: regime transitions in comparative perspective*, Cambridge: Cambridge University Press.

Clapham, Christopher (1993) 'Democratisation in Africa: obstacles and prospects', *Third World Quarterly* 14(3), 423–38.

Molutsi, Patrick P and John D Holm (1990) 'Developing democracy when civil society is weak: the case of Botswana', *African Affairs* 89(356), 323–40.

Wiseman, John A, ed. (1995) *Democracy and political change in Sub-Saharan Africa*, London: Routledge.

Wiseman, John A (1996) *The new struggle for democracy in Africa*, Aldershot: Avebury.

12 Conclusions

State and civil society in post-colonial Africa

As this book has shown, the relationship between state and civil society should be of considerable interest to all political scientists. A lot can be learned. It is an approach that helps to place basic political events into some kind of historical and social context. Isolated political incidents gain greater meaning, and political outcomes are easier to explain. Indeed, for Africanists, this technique is invaluable as it allows a sense of order to be imposed on the multitude of (potentially confusing) individual episodes that seem to flow from the continent on an almost daily basis. Thankfully, as a conceptual tool it proves to be equally as useful for those studying the politics of just one country, as it is for those seeking to understand a whole continent.

Africa, throughout the post-colonial period, had to endure an uneasy relationship between state and civil society. Each party clearly needed the other, but there was considerable inefficacy in their engagement. It was a case of states trying to dominate civil society, yet failing to command enough power to complete their hegemonic ambitions. Civil society, for its part, mastered various techniques of distancing itself from state exploitation, but it was never in a position to rid itself entirely of these predatory regimes. As the balance of power ebbed and flowed between state and civil society, it became clear that, in the long term, few Africans would actually benefit from this political stalemate. The continent, quite rightly, may not have wanted simply to mimic the systems of government found in Europe and North America. The political institutions that did emerge after independence, however, comprehensively failed to maximise the continent's economic welfare and political freedom. Africans were left somewhat enviously considering their own position compared to the material wealth and liberty being generated in the West. It is no coincidence that these more prosperous countries enjoyed a generally positive (though by no means perfect) relationship between state and civil society.

At the start of the post-colonial period, African civil societies were in the ascendant. Indeed, they were much more vibrant than their partner states. Ethnic ties, for example, were perhaps the strongest social bonds to be found on the continent. These had become more coherent during the colonial era, and would be powerful conduits of political mobilisation throughout the independence years. Similarly, it had been civil society that had actually overthrown the colonial state. Associational activity among ethno-regional groups, trades unions, professional societies and community organisations had all combined to make the nationalist movements the powerful forces that they were. Decolonisation was largely a case of Africans acting collectively to topple the mighty European empires that had ruled over them for the previous 70 years or so.

African states, by contrast, were relatively weak at independence. Most obviously, the colonial inheritance had left them with arbitrary boundaries. Ruler-straight borders, reflecting European rather than African interests, divided some traditional communities between different nation-states, while others found themselves caged together with potential domestic rivals. Virtually nothing had been done previously by the imperial authorities to build a collective consciousness among these people, so now, after independence, it was up to the new governments to build nations within these artificial state territories.

Similarly, the nationalist governments also had to develop their economies rapidly. Colonial policy had resulted in underdevelopment. This produced an urgency to increase these countries' productive capabilities, for only in this manner could investment capital be raised, enabling diverse modern economies to be created. Without economic success, African states would be unable to command the resources needed to provide the social welfare that civil society now demanded. After all, a significant element of political legitimacy is the ability of governors to supply adequate public services to the governed.

Yet, African political managers had not been left with suitable state capacity, or established institutional tools, to do this job. This made the provision of effective government problematic. The departing colonial powers may have bequeathed to their successors liberal democratic constitutions, but these hastily erected pluralist institutions had been built on woefully weak political foundations. European imperial rule had usually consisted of seven or eight decades of bureaucratic authoritarianism. No political culture of democracy had been nurtured, and no tradition of political pluralism established. The inherited mechanisms of power were as unfamiliar to the new state leaders as they were to members of civil society.

In hindsight, then, it is not surprising that African countries abandoned liberal democracy soon after independence. Faced by complex, economically disadvantaged and divided civil societies, as well as by untested and weak governmental structures, the continent's political leaders chose to rule though more centralised institutions instead. This, it was argued, would help states create both unity among their people and strategies to produce economic development. As a result, Africa entered the age of the one-party state.

In this era of centralised rule, political pluralism was curtailed, with any formal representation now being channelled through one-party structures; remaining civil society institutions were co-opted, harassed or banned; local government became local administration directed from the centre; economic activity was discouraged in the private sector, while public corporations dominated; and parliaments and the judicial functions of government were usurped by the executive. Indeed, with even the 'one-parties' soon experiencing atrophy,

African core executives now had a monopoly over formal political activity within their territories. At the apex of this highly centralised state there usually resided a 'presidential-monarch' enjoying the power of 'personal rule'.

These autocrats had little to fear by way of formal political challenges to their leadership. No constitutional mechanisms remained to unseat them. Civil society, after all, had virtually been excluded from the political process. Indeed, political competition within post-colonial Africa was now limited to the in-fighting found within the state elite itself. In this environment, factional politics dominated, with various 'wings' of the bureaucratic bourgeoisie manoeuvring in their attempts to either consolidate or to increase power. Often it was the military who benefited most from this internecine conflict. Using its access to the resources of violence to stage *coups d'état*, on numerous occasions, the army captured the state for itself. Civil society, now largely detached from the formal political arena, stood on the sidelines and was forced to accept the leadership of whichever faction of the state elite was in the ascendant.

Skilful manipulation of his (rarely her) lieutenants, however, often resulted in presidential-monarchs being able lift themselves above this factional in-fighting. Indeed, they could use internal competition to their advantage. Presidents made sure that potential challengers were too busy fending off their own rivals, and thus too distracted to mount any threat to the president himself. Consequently, political leadership was often remarkably stable in post-colonial Africa. 'Big men', such as Mobutu, Gaddafy, Kaunda, Moi and Houphouët-Boigny, for example, became almost permanent features on this continent's political landscape.

All of these leaders, however, had to deal with the central paradox of the African state. The continent's post-colonial regimes were 'lame leviathans'.[1] Despite having accumulated a monopoly of (formal) political activity within the country, these states still did not have enough power to project their authority into all areas of the territory. Similarly, states were 'overdeveloped'. Although they had appropriated many functions of society, becoming bloated as they absorbed (too many) resources from civil society, they still did not command enough resources to secure their legitimacy. In short, African states had accumulated virtually all the formal economic and political functions of a society, draining civil society of considerable potential in order to maintain this hegemonic position. Yet, even with these massive powers, states still failed to deliver. Africans were left with little by way of welfare services and political representation.

State elites had, however, to offer civil society something. They could not survive by coercion alone. And since centralisation had seriously undermined the state's legal-rational credentials, other sources of legitimacy had to be found.

It was therefore client–patron networks that formed the main links between state and civil society for most of the post-colonial period. These patronage chains allowed presidential-monarchs to 'buy' legitimacy from their people, in return for distributing goods and services. The president looked after his lieu-tenants, those individuals attended to their own clients, and intermediaries could be found right the way down to the local patrons operating at village level. In this manner, (unequal) exchange took place between the governed and the governors, and a degree of legitimacy was generated.

State elites, however, could not rely solely on these domestic networks to secure their position. There were rarely enough resources generated internally to keep such patronage mechanisms 'oiled' and functioning at the required level. This is why Africa's international links were of major importance in the post-colonial period. The concept of international sovereignty ensured that state elites gained access to resources available from the external environment. As 'representatives' of their people, government officials could appropriate capital from foreign trade and aid. During the Cold War, when foreign powers were not especially concerned about their African clients' human rights records, these external resources proved to be a massive asset to elite power. It was almost as if the continent's rulers gained greater rewards for servicing the inter-ests of the international community than they did for representing their own people.

The end of the Cold War, however, saw a withering of indiscriminate inter-national aid. In the 'New World Order' and the era of structural adjustment, donors now gave funds for specific purposes, with stringent conditions attached. At the same time, domestic economic problems reduced the availability of the already limited internal resources. Client–patron networks were consequently starved and began to contract. Africa had reached a political watershed. State legitimacy began to fail, and with no constitutional mechanisms present enabling a re-legitimisation of political systems, something had to give.

In a few cases, the state's agencies of coercion were still strong enough to mount a *coup d'état*. Elsewhere, state authority was so diminished that elements of civil society could mount a direct and violent challenge to government authority (usually via insurgency campaigns). In most cases, however, there was a further period of stalemate. Although states were now critically weak, and had difficulty controlling both citizens and territory, civil society itself still did not possess enough power to overthrow the ruling elite. Under these conditions, Africans opted for a less dramatic challenge to state authority. This came in the form of disengagement.

Through withdrawing from formal markets and operating instead in the second economy, Africans slowly undermined their rulers. In most cases, this prompted inverted states (that scaled down their public services); in other instances, warlord states emerged (where no pretence of legitimacy was main-tained); and on a few extreme occasions, total state collapse occurred.

Most regimes, however, managed to steer their countries away from this extreme fate of total collapse. Africa's state managers of the 1990s attempted to re-legitimise their rule by submitting their governments to multi-party competi-tion. Leaders were willing to take the risk of losing control of this democratisation process, and consequently being ousted from power, because many considered this to be their only remaining chance of securing a political future. The last decade of the twentieth century, therefore, brought a tidal wave of multi-party elections to the continent. Some of the 'Big Men' perished in this exercise, but many more survived (either by consolidating genuine popularity among the voters, or by manipulating the electoral process itself). Although a considerable number of these political contests were far from free and fair, many more were true reflections of the people's wishes. Consequently these polls did indeed go a long way to re-legitimise the African state. Civil society had been brought back into the constitutional political process. Whether these events mark the beginning of a long-term consolidation of democracy on the continent, however, remains to be seen. There are still many obstacles to be overcome before this is the case.

Is it fair to say, then, that Africans have rid themselves of their centralised 'vampire' states? Have the predatory governments that so dominated the post-colonial period now been defeated, just like their colonial predecessors?

Indeed, this could be the case. The continent is now left at a critical juncture. The states that have emerged from the political upheaval of the 1990s certainly retain many authoritarian reflexes from the past, yet governments today are now more accountable to their people. A resort to exclusive personal rule has been discouraged by the (partial) restoration of legal-rational institutions. Similarly, civil society is once again permitted to participate, and is more engaged, in the political process. This improved relationship between state and civil society will not guarantee, but dramatically increases, the possibility of bringing a brighter political future to the continent.

Imperial rule, however, robbed Africa of much. Governments were always going to struggle with their respective colonial inheritances. Inappropriate public policy choices, damaging styles of personal rule and the burdens of international markets then compounded these problems by encouraging centralised states, disengaged civil societies and unproductive economies. Consequently, too many Africans were left in unacceptable poverty during the post-colonial years, with little political representation to help them overcome this state of affairs. By the 1980s, the euphoria and expectations of independence had become little more than distant memories. Failure in the past, however, is not necessarily a prelude to failure in the future. It may be that the multi-party elections of the 1990s have provided Africans with the foundations, and the confidence, to build new, more productive, political systems. Such political reform will hopefully benefit all the continent's inhabitants in the new millennium. It is a sombre reality, however, that these new democracies cannot start with a clean slate. They first have to secure all that Africans were denied by the political events of the twentieth century.

Appendix

Multi-party legislative and presidential elections in Africa, independence to 1999

State	Multi-party elections	Victory to:		Comments
		Incumbents	Opposition	
Algeria	1991 leg			One-party state to 1989.
	1995 pre	X		1991 election nullified by military.
	1997 leg	X		Military dominates weak multi-
	1999 pre	X		party system through 1995, 1997
				and 1999 elections.
Angola	1992 leg	X		One-party state to 1992.
	1992 pre	X		Opposition returns to waging civil
				war after losing 1992 multi-party
				elections.
Benin	1991 leg		X	Pluralism at independence soon
	1991 pre		X	becomes one-party/military rule,
	1995 leg		X	until 1990.
	1996 pre		X	Incumbent president loses initial
	1999 leg		X	multi-party election, followed by
				an exchange of power after this.
Botswana	1969 leg	X		Botswana Democratic Party has
	1974 leg	X		held power since independence,
	1979 leg	X		gaining a mandate through regular
	1984 leg	X		multi-party elections.
	1989 leg	X		
	1994 leg	X		
	1999 leg	X		
Burkina Faso	1970 leg	X		Pluralism at independence soon
	1978 leg	X		becomes one-party/military rule,
	1978 pre	X		until 1989.
	1991 pre	X		1970 and 1978 multi-party elections
	1992 leg	X		break in this cycle, prompted by
	1997 leg	X		the military returning to barracks.
	1998 pre	X		1991 presidential election
				boycotted by all opposition.
				Incumbents continue to rule
				despite charges of electoral
				irregularity since.

State	Multi-party elections	Victory to:		Comments
		Incumbents	Opposition	
Burundi	1965 leg 1993 leg 1993 pre	X	X X	Multi-party state to 1966. One-party state/military rule 1966–92. Military coup in 1996: political parties remain legal, but no further multi-party elections held.
Cameroon	1964 leg 1992 leg 1992 pre 1997 leg 1997 pre	X X X X X		Multi-party state to 1966. One-party state 1966–92. Incumbents mandated by multi-party elections since 1992, but serious electoral disruption and boycotts throughout the 1990s.
Cape Verde	1991 leg 1991 pre 1995 leg 1996 pre	X X	X X	One-party state to 1991. Opposition wins initial multi-party elections in 1991, and then confirms mandate with later polls.
Central African Republic	1981 pre 1993 leg 1993 pre 1998 leg 1999 pre	X X	X X	One-party state/military rule to 1981. Brief experiment with multi-party elections 1981. Military coup and return to one-party state 1981–93. Opposition wins 1993 elections, and confirms mandate in subsequent poll (among internal unrest).
Chad	1996 pre 1997 leg	X X		Pluralism at independence soon becomes one-party/military rule, until 1996. Incumbents continue to rule, confirmed by multi-party polls since 1996.
The Comoros	1990 pre 1992 leg 1993 leg 1996 pre 1996 leg	X X X	X X	Pluralism at independence soon becomes one-party/military rule, until 1990. Incumbents continues to rule, confirmed by subsequent (boycotted) multi-party polls. 1996 multi-party elections held after military intervention, opposition wins (parties boycott).
Congo, Rep. (Brazzaville)	1992 leg 1992 pre 1993 leg	X	X X	Pluralism at independence soon becomes one-party/military rule, until 1992. Opposition wins first multi-party elections, but destabilised by factional competition. Military coup in 1997 after internal unrest.

State	Multi-party elections	Victory to:		Comments
		Incumbents	Opposition	
Congo, DRC (Kinshasa)	1965 leg			1960–64 civil war. Relatively inconclusive 1965 multi-party elections. Military coup 1965, and presidential rule since.
Côte d'Ivoire	1990 leg 1990 pre 1995 leg 1995 pre	X X X X		One-party state to 1990. Incumbents continue to rule, confirmed by multi-party polls until military coup 1999.
Djibouti	1992 leg 1993 pre 1997 leg 1999 pre	X X X X		One-party state to 1992. Incumbents continue to rule, despite discredited multi-party elections.
Egypt	1950 leg 1976 leg 1979 leg 1984 leg 1987 leg 1990 leg 1995 leg	X X X X X X		1922–50 power shared between monarch, nationalists and British authorities. 1950 multi-party elections held. 1952–76 one-party/military rule. Since 1976 mixture of semi-, and full, multi-party elections (amid boycotts and political violence), in which incumbents remain in power.
Equatorial Guinea	1993 leg 1996 pre 1999 leg	X X X		Pluralism at independence soon becomes one-party/military rule, until 1993. Since 1993 nominal multi-party system, but accompanied by gross electoral irregularities, that ensures incumbents continue rule.
Eritrea				Since Eritrea's creation in 1993, no legislative or presidential elections have been held.
Ethiopia	1995 leg	X		Indigenous imperial rule to 1974. One-party/military rule 1974/91. Power-shared between EPRDF alliance since 1991, mandated by (opposition boycotted) 1995 legislative multi-party elections.
Gabon	1990 leg 1993 pre 1996 leg 1998 pre	X X X X		Pluralism at independence soon becomes one-party/military rule, until 1990. Incumbents continue to rule confirmed by multi-party elections since 1990.

State	Multi-party elections	Victory to:		Comments
		Incumbents	Opposition	
The Gambia	1966 leg	X		The People's Progressive Party held power 1966–94, mandated by regular multi-party elections. In 1994, Gambia's constitution was suspended by a military coup. The military incumbents subsequently mandated their rule, through multi-party elections since 1996.
	1972 leg	X		
	1977 leg	X		
	1982 leg	X		
	1982 pre	X		
	1987 leg	X		
	1987 pre	X		
	1992 leg	X		
	1992 pre	X		
	1996 pre	X		
	1997 leg	X		
Ghana	1969 leg			Pluralism at independence soon becomes one-party/military rule until 1992 (with the exceptions of the 1969 and 1979 multi-party elections held on the occasion of the military's return to barracks). Incumbents continue to rule, confirmed by multi-party elections since 1992.
	1979 leg			
	1979 pre			
	1992 leg	X		
	1992 pre	X		
	1996 leg	X		
	1996 pre	X		
Guinea	1993 pre	X		One-party/military rule to 1992. Incumbents continue to rule, confirmed by multi-party elections since 1993.
	1995 leg	X		
	1998 pre	X		
Guinea-Bissau	1994 leg	X		One-party/military rule to 1991. Incumbents win initial multi-party poll, but lose power in 1999.
	1994 pre	X		
	1999 leg		X	
	1999 pre		X	
Kenya	1963 leg	X		Multi-party competition to 1969. One-party rule 1969–92. Incumbents win initial multi-party poll, but lose power in 1999.
	1966 leg	X		
	1992 leg	X		
	1992 pre	X		
	1997 leg	X		
	1997 pre	X		
Lesotho	1993 leg		X	Incumbent refuses to accept 1970 multi-party election result, and rules by decree until 1986. Military rule 1986–93. Opposition win 1993 elections, followed by a splinter of this party winning the 1998 poll.
	1998 leg		X	
Liberia	1985 leg	X		1878–1980 True Whig Party rules, occasionally mandated by multi-party elections. Military rule 1980–85. Incumbents confirmed by 'one-off' multi-party poll in 1985, ruling until civil war (commencing 1989). Multi-party elections held in 1997 as part of peace agreement.
	1985 pre	X		
	1997 leg		X	
	1997 pre		X	

State	Multi-party elections	Victory to:		Comments
		Incumbents	Opposition	
Libya				Monarchy dominated weak multi-party system to 1969. Military/presidential rule since 1969.
Madagascar	1960 leg 1965 leg 1970 leg 1977 leg 1982 pre 1983 leg 1989 leg 1989 pre 1993 leg 1993 pre 1996 pre 1998 leg	X X X X X X X	X X X X	Semi-competitive elections to 1993, manipulated by incumbents. Leader of opposition wins 1993 presidential poll, but later impeached and defeated by former 1975–93 president (Didier Ratsiraka) in 1996 free and fair poll. Ratsiraka's party win 1998 legislative elections.
Malawi	1994 leg 1994 pre 1999 leg 1999 pre	X X	X X	Pluralism at independence soon becomes one-party rule, until 1993. Opposition wins multi-party elections in 1994, and confirmed in competitive polls since.
Mali	1992 leg 1992 pre 1997 leg 1997 pre	X X	X X	Pluralism at independence soon becomes one-party/military rule, until 1992. Opposition wins 1992 multi-party elections, and confirmed in competitive polls since (although the 1997 legislative elections boycotted).
Mauritania	1992 leg 1992 pre 1996 leg 1997 pre	X X X X		One-party/military rule to 1991. Incumbents continue to rule, confirmed by multi-party elections since 1992.
Mauritius	1976 leg 1982 leg 1983 leg 1987 leg 1991 leg 1995 leg	X X X	X X X	Multi-party elections since independence (interrupted by State of Emergency 1971–76). Several turnovers of government have resulted.
Morocco				Monarch dominates political activity since independence. Although multi-party elections have been held regularly since decolonisation, the monarch has an effective veto over the legislature's decisions.

State	Multi-party elections	Victory to: Incumbents	Victory to: Opposition	Comments
Mozambique	1994 leg 1994 pre 1999 leg 1999 pre	X X X X		One-party rule to 1994. Incumbents continue to rule, confirmed by multi-party elections since 1994.
Namibia	1994 leg 1994 pre 1999 leg 1999 pre	X X X X		Main liberation movement (SWAPO) wins free and fair poll for constituent assembly prompted by end of South African occupation. Incumbents confirm position as ruling party in subsequent multi-party elections.
Niger	1993 leg 1993 pre 1995 leg 1996 leg 1996 pre 1999 leg 1999 pre	 X X	X X X X X	Pluralism at independence soon becomes one-party/military rule, until 1992. Opposition coalition wins multi-party elections in 1993, only to splinter and allow former ruling party control of the legislature after 1995 poll. Military intervenes in 1996 to break institutional deadlock. Military leader and allied parties win mandate in (flawed) 1996 elections, and then restore multi-party elections in 1999.
Nigeria	1964 leg 1979 leg 1979 pre 1983 leg 1983 pre 1992 leg 1993 pre 1999 leg 1999 pre	 X X	X	Multi-party rule to 1966. Military rule 1966–79. Military return to barracks and multi-party elections held in 1979, incumbents then confirmed in 1983 multi-party poll. Military rule 1983–99, having vetoed attempted return to multi-party rule in 1992–93. Multi-party elections held in 1999 on military's return to barracks.
Rwanda				Pluralism at independence soon becomes one-party/military rule, until 1991. Move to multi-party elections halted by civil war. RPF victorious in 1994, but no elections yet held.
São Tomé and Principe	1991 leg 1991 pre 1994 leg 1996 pre 1998 leg	 X X	X X X	One-party rule to 1990. Opposition wins initial multi-party elections in 1991, and president confirmed in subsequent poll, but old ruling party regain control of the legislature in 1994 and 1998.

State	Multi-party elections	Victory to:		Comments
		Incumbents	Opposition	
Senegal	1963 leg	X		Multi-party system to 1966. One-party rule 1966–76. Incumbents confirmed by restricted, and then full, multi-party elections since 1978 (a number of these polls have been disputed by the opposition).
	1978 leg	X		
	1978 pre	X		
	1983 leg	X		
	1983 pre	X		
	1988 leg	X		
	1988 pre	X		
	1993 leg	X		
	1993 pre	X		
	1998 leg	X		
Seychelles	1993 leg	X		Pluralism at independence soon becomes one-party/military rule, until 1993. Incumbents confirmed by multi-party elections since 1993.
	1993 pre	X		
	1998 leg	X		
	1998 pre	X		
Sierra Leone	1962 leg	X		Multi-party rule to 1967. Military/one-party rule 1967–91, with brief interlude when opposition competed in 1977 poll. Multi-party elections delayed by military intervention and civil war 1992–96. Military makes way for multi-party rule in 1996. Democratic incumbents restored to power (through external intervention) after military coup in 1997.
	1967 leg		X	
	1977 leg	X		
	1996 leg			
	1996 pre			
Somalia	1964 leg	X		Multi-party rule to 1969. Military/one-party rule 1969. Central government collapses with Barré's fall in 1991.
	1969 leg	X		
South Africa	1994 leg		X	Whites-only multi-party rule to 1994. Non-racial multi-party elections since 1994, with opposition winning initial poll and confirming mandate in polls since.
	1994 pre		X	
	1999 leg	X		
	1999 pre	X		
Sudan	1958 leg		X	Multi-party rule to 1958. Military rule 1958–64. Return to multi-party competition attempted 1965–69, but cut short by military intervention. Military and one-party rule 1969–86. Multi-party rule 1986–89. Military rule 1989–96. Competitive (non-party and boycotted) presidential poll held in 1996, where incumbent won.
	1965 leg			
	1968 leg		X	
	1986 leg			

State	Multi-party elections	Victory to: Incumbents	Victory to: Opposition	Comments
Swaziland	1972 leg	X		Politics dominated by Swazi monarchy. Opposition campaigned in 1972 multi-party poll, but monarch dissolved parliament soon afterwards. Non-party competitive legislative elections permitted in 1993 and 1998.
Tanzania	1995 leg 1995 pre	X X		One-party rule to 1995. Incumbents confirmed by 1995 multi-party elections.
Togo	1993 pre 1994 leg 1998 pre 1999 leg	X X X X		Uncompetitive/military rule to 1993. Incumbents confirmed in (illegally manipulated and boycotted) multi-party elections since 1993.
Tunisia	1981 leg 1989 leg 1994 leg 1994 pre 1999 leg 1999 pre	X X X X X X		Pluralism at independence soon becomes one-party rule, until 1981. Incumbents confirmed in multi-party elections in 1981, although opposition failed to gain any seats in the legislature until 1994.
Uganda	1980 leg			Pluralism at independence soon becomes one-party/military rule, until 1980. Flawed multi-party elections held in 1980 after Amin deposed, UPC wins. Museveni's rebel movement helps depose UPC in 1985, and forms government. Non-party competitive elections held since 1989.
Zambia	1968 leg 1968 pre 1991 leg 1991 pre 1996 leg 1996 pre	X X X X	 X X 	Pluralism at independence soon becomes one-party rule, until 1991. Opposition wins initial multi-party elections in 1991, and is confirmed in subsequent multi-party polls.
Zimbabwe	1985 leg 1990 leg 1990 pre 1995 leg 1996 pre	X X X X X		Multi-party rule since 1980. Incumbents confirmed by regular multi-party elections (faced by ineffective opposition).

Sources: *Africa south of the Sahara*, various issues, London: Europa; Nohlen, Dieter, Michael Krennerich and Bernhard Thibaut, eds (1999) *Elections in Africa: a data handbook*, Oxford: Oxford University Press.

Notes: National elections: leg = legislative; pre = presidential

Notes

Chapter 1: Introduction

Alagiah, George. 'New light on the dark continent'. *Guardian* (London); Media section 4–5.

Weber, Max (1994) 'The profession and vocation of politics', in Max Weber [Peter Lassman and Ronald Speirs, eds], *Weber: political writings*, Cambridge: Cambridge University Press; 310–11.

Chapter 2: History

See, for example, Robinson, Ronald and John Gallagher (with Alice Denny) (1981) *Africa and the Victorians: the official mind of imperialism*, Basingstoke: Macmillan.

See Nugent, Paul and A.I. Asiwaju (1996) 'Introduction: The paradox of African boundaries', in Paul Nugent and A.I. Asiwaju, eds, *African boundaries: barriers, conduits and opportunities*, London: Pinter; 1–14.

See Wilson, Henry S. (1977) *The imperial experience in Sub-Saharan Africa since 1870*, Minneapolis: University of Minnesota Press; 95.

Griffiths, Ieuan Ll. (1995) *The African inheritance*, London: Routledge; 91.

Ibid.; 84–98.

Young, Crawford (1988) 'The African colonial state and its political legacy', in Donald Rothchild and Naomi Chazan, eds. *The precarious balance: state and society in Africa*, Boulder, CO: Westview; 37.

Hodder-Williams, Richard (1984) *An introduction to the politics of Tropical Africa*, London: George Allen and Unwin: 32.

Mamdani, Mahmood (1976) *Politics and class formation in Uganda*, New York: Monthly Review Press; 208.

Warren, Bill (1980) *Imperialism: the pioneer of capitalism*, London: Verso.

10 The Portuguese territories of Angola, Mozambique and Guinea-Bissau were exceptions to this relatively peaceful transfer of power, as were the white settler states of Algeria, Southern Rhodesia (Zimbabwe), South West Africa (Namibia) and South Africa. Guerrilla war was required to force independence in each of these cases. Kenya, with its Mau Mau uprising, could be added to this list, but the intensity of this guerrilla war was not as widespread as in the other settler states listed. See the case study at the end of the chapter.

11 Berman, Bruce and John Lonsdale (1992) *Unhappy Valley: conflict in Kenya and Africa*, London: James Currey; 19–20.

12 Griffiths. *The African inheritance*; 91.

13 See Ogot, B.A. (1995) 'The decisive years 1956–63', in: B.A. Ogot and W.R. Ochieng', eds, *Decolonization and independence in Kenya, 1940–93*, London: James Currey; 54–7.

14 1995–97 statistics taken from *The world economic factbook 1998/99*, London: Euromonitor; and *Africa south of the Sahara 1998*, London: Europa; 27.

Chapter 3: Ideology

1 Putnam, Robert D. (1973) *The beliefs of politicians*, New Haven, CT: Yale University Press.
2 Anderson, Benedict (1991) *Imagined communities*, London: Verso; 6.
3 See Gellner, Ernest (1983) *Nations and nationalism*, Oxford: Blackwell; 1–2.
4 Vail, Leroy and Landeg White (1989) 'Tribalism in the political history of Malawi', in Leroy Vail, ed., *The creation of tribalism in Southern Africa*, London: James Currey; 151.
5 Cited in Mamdani, Mahmood (1996) *Citizen and subject: contemporary Africa and the legacy of late colonialism*, Princeton: Princeton University Press; 135.
6 Nyerere, Julius K. (1961) *Spearhead*. Reprinted in Paul E. Sigmund, ed., (1963) *The ideologies of the developing nations*, New York: Praeger; 199. Original emphasis.
7 Jowitt, Kenneth (1979) 'Scientific socialist regimes in Africa: political differentiation, avoidance, and unawareness', in Carl G. Rosberg and Thomas M. Callaghy eds, *Socialism in Sub-Saharan Africa: a new assessment*, Berkeley: Institute of International Studies, University of California; 148.
8 Zolberg, Aristide R. (1964) 'The Daka colloquium: the search for a doctrine', in William H. Freidland and Carl G. Rosberg, eds, *African socialism*, Stanford, CA: Stanford University Press; 118–19.
9 Touré, Ahmed Sékou, *The doctrine and methods of the Democratic Party of Guinea*, II 24. Cited in Ottaway, Marina and David Ottaway (1986) *Afro-communism*, New York: Africana; 15.
10 Senghor, Léopold Sédar, *Afrique Nouvelle*, 11. Cited in Ottaway and Ottaway, *Afro-communism*; 91.
11 Senghor, Léopold Sédar (1959) *On African socialism*, New York: American Society for African Culture; 32.
12 Barré, Mohamed Siad (1976) 'Revolutionary resolve', *World Marxist Review* 19(5) 26.
13 See Clapham, Christopher (1987) Revolutionary socialist development in Ethiopia', *African Affairs* 86(343), 151–65.
14 Cited in Ottaway and Ottaway *Afro-communism*; 9.
15 Jowitt, in: Rosberg, *Socialism in Sub-Saharan Africa*; 133.
16 Munslow, Barry, ed. (1986) *Africa: problems in the transition to socialism*, London: Zed; 1.
17 See Yeebo, Zaya (1985) 'Ghana: defence committees and the class struggle', *Review of African Political Economy* 32, 66.
18 Robinson, Pearl T. (1992) *Grassroots legitimisation of military governance in Burkina Faso and Niger: the core contradictions*, in Goran Hyden and Michael Bratton, eds, *Governance and politics in Africa*, Boulder, CO: Lynne Rienner; 163.
19 Young, Crawford (1982) *Ideology and development in Africa*, New Haven, CT: Yale University Press; 184 and 188.
20 Quoted in Neuberger, Benyamin (1991) 'Irredentism and politics in Africa', in Naomi Chazan, ed., *Irredentism and international politics*, Boulder, CO: Lynne Rienner; 97.
21 For an example of this argument, see Stone, John (1983) 'Ethnicity versus the state: the dual claims of state coherence and ethnic self-determination', in Donald Rothchild and Victor A. Olorunsola, eds, *State versus ethnic claims: African policy dilemmas*, Boulder, CO: Westview; 85.
22 See Neuberger, 'Irredentism', in Chazan, *Irredentism and international politics*; 104–6.
23 Clapham, Christopher (1985) *Third World Politics: an introduction*, London: Routledge; 62.

4 Cabral, Amílcar (1969) *Palavras de ordem gerais*, Conakary: PAIGC; 23. Cited in Chabal, Patrick (1986) 'Revolutionary democracy in Africa: the case of Guinea-Bissau', in Patrick Chabal, ed., *Political domination in Africa: reflections on the limits of power*, Cambridge: Cambridge University Press; 84.

5 Nyerere, Julius K. (1969) *Nyerere on socialism*, Dar es Salaam: Oxford University Press; 30; and Nyerere, Julius K. (1966) *Freedom and unity: a selection from writings and speeches 1952–1965*, Dar es Salaam: Oxford University Press; 164.

6 Nyerere, *Nyerere on socialism*; 41 and 42.

7 Nyerere, *Freedom and unity*; 170.

8 Nyerere, Julius K. (1960) 'Africa's place in the world', in *Symposium on Africa*, Wellesley; 157; and Nyerere, *Freedom and unity*; 164.

9 Nyerere, *Nyerere on socialism*; 44.

0 Sindima, Harvey J (1995) *Africa's agenda: the legacy of liberalism and colonialism in the crisis of African values*, Westport, CT: Greenwood; 103.

1 Kaiser, Paul (1996) 'Structural adjustment and the fragile nation: the demise of social unity in Tanzania', *Journal of Modern African Studies* 34(2), 229.

2 Hyden, Goran (1980) *Beyond Ujamaa in Tanzania: underdevelopment and an uncaptured peasantry*, London: Heinemann; *passim*.

3 *Ibid.*; 115.

4 *Ibid.*; 114.

5 Nyerere, Julius K. (1977) 'The Arusha Declaration ten years after', *Africa Review* 7(2), 13.

6 1995–97 statistics taken from *The world economic factbook 1998/99*, London: Euromonitor; and *Africa south of the Sahara 1998* 27, London: Europa.

Chapter 4: Ethnicity

Calhoun, Craig (1997) *Nationalism*, Buckingham: Open University Press; 40.

Prunier, Gérard (1995) *The Rwanda crisis: history of a genocide*, London: Hurst; 265 and xi–xii.

Ibid.; xii.

Southall, Aidan W. (1970) 'The illusion of tribe', *Journal of Asian and African Studies* 5(1), 36.

Young, Crawford (1994) *The African colonial state in comparative perspective*, New Haven, CT: Yale University Press; 232.

See Kofele-Kale, Ndiva (1987) 'Class status, and power in postreunification Cameroon: the rise of an Anglophone bourgeoisie, 1961–1980', in Irving Leonard Markovitz, ed., *Studies in power and class in Africa*, New York: Oxford University Press; 138.

Bates, Robert H. (1983) 'Modernization, ethnic competition, and the rationality of politics in contemporary Africa', in Donald Rothchild and Victor A. Olorunsola, eds, *State versus ethnic claims: African policy dilemmas*, Boulder, CO: Westview; 164.

Rothchild, Donald (1985) 'State–ethnic relations in middle Africa', in Gwendolen M. Carter and Patrick O'Meara, eds, *African independence: the first twenty-five years*, Bloomington: Indiana University Press; 72–3.

Obote, A. Milton (1970) *Proposals for new methods of election of representatives of people to parliament*, Kampala: Milton Obote Foundation; 6–7. Cited in Rothchild, in Carter and O'Meara, *Africa independence*; 94.

10 Jinadu, L. Adele (1985) 'Federalism, the consociational state, and ethnic conflict in Nigeria'. *Publius* 15; 77.

11 Law, Robin (1996) 'Local amateur scholarship in the construction of Yoruba ethnicity, 1880–1914', in Louise de la Gorgendière, Kenneth King and Sarah

Vaughan, eds, *Ethnicity in Africa: roots, meanings and implications*, Edinburgh: Centre of African Studies, University of Edinburgh; 65–87.
12 1995–97 statistics taken from *The world economic factbook 1998/99*, London: Euromonitor; and *Africa south of the Sahara 1998* 27, London: Europa.

Chapter 5: Social class

1   Marx, Karl and Friedrich Engels (1967) *The communist manifesto*, Harmondsworth: Penguin; 79.
2   Engels, Friedrich (1972) *The origin of family, private property and the state*, London: Lawrence and Wishart; 71.
3   Marx and Engels, *The communist manifesto*; 82.
4   *Ibid.*; 80.
5   *Ibid.*; 94
6   Mboya, Tom (1965) 'African socialism and its application to planning in Kenya', Sessional Paper No.10. Cited in Katz, Stephen (1980) *Marxism, Africa and social class: a critique of relevant theories*, Montreal: Centre for Developing Area Studies, McGill University; 9.
7   Marx, Karl (1970) *A contribution to the critique of political economy*, Moscow: Progress Publishers; 21
8   Shanin, Teodor, ed. (1988) *Peasants and peasant societies: selected readings*, London: Penguin; 4.
9   Leys, Colin (1976) 'Political implications of the development of peasant society in Kenya', in Peter C.W. Gutkind and Peter Waterman, eds, *African social studies*, London: Heinemann; 356.
10 Magubane, Bernard 'The evolution of class structure in Africa', in Peter C.W. Gutkind and Immanuel Wallerstein, *The political economy of contemporary Africa*, Beverly Hills: Sage; 183.
11 Parsons, Jack (1984) 'The peasantariat and politics: migration, wage labour and agriculture in Botswana', *Africa Today* 31(4), 5–25.
12 Cited in Young, Crawford and Thomas Turner (1985) *The rise and decline of the Zairian state*, Madison: University of Wisconsin Press; 108.
13 Weber, Max [Edited by H.H. Gerth and C. Wright Mills] (1948) *From Max Weber: Essays in Society*, London: Routledge and Kegan Paul; 180.
14 Poulantzas, Nicos (1969) 'The problem of the capitalist state', *New Left Review*, Nov–Dec, 67–78.
15 Ossowski, Stanislaw (1963) *Class structure in the social consciousness*, London: Routledge and Kegan Paul; 185
16 Sklar, Richard (1979) 'The nature of class domination in Africa', *Journal of Modern African Studies* 17(4), 531–52.
17 Cited in Young and Turner, *Rise and decline of the Zairian state*; 110.
18 Kofele-Kale, Ndiva (1987) 'Class status, and power in postreunification Cameroon: the rise of an Anglophone bourgeoisie, 1961–1980', in Irving Leonard Markovitz, ed., *Studies in power and class in Africa*, New York: Oxford University Press; 156.
19 Marx, Karl (1976) *Capital*, I, London: Penguin; 797.
20 Coquery-Vidrovitch, Catherine (1997) *African women: a modern history*, Boulder, CO: Westview; 75–82.
21 *Comprador* is the Portuguese word for 'purchaser'.
22 See, for example, chapter 13 of Chabal, Patrick (1992) *Power in Africa: an essay in political interpretation*, Basingstoke: Macmillan.
23 Bayart, Jean-François (1993) *The state in Africa: the politics of the belly*, London: Longman; 218–27.

24 *Ibid.*; 94.
25 Price, Robert (1974) 'Politics and culture in contemporary Ghana: the big-man small-boy syndrome', *Journal of African Studies* 1(2), 173–204.
26 Parson, Jack (1984) 'The trajectory of class and state in dependent development: the consequences of new wealth for Botswana', in Nelson Kasfir, ed., *State and class in Africa*, London: Frank Cass; 44.
27 Molutsi, Patrick P. (1993) 'International influences on Botswana's democracy', in Stephen John Stedman, ed., *Botswana: the political economy of democratic development*, Boulder, CO: Lynne Rienner; 59.
28 See Good, Kenneth (1994) 'Corruption and mismanagement in Botswana: a best-case example?', *Journal of Modern African Studies* 32(3), 506–9.
29 Parson, Jack (1993) 'Liberal democracy, the liberal state, and the 1989 General Elections in Botswana', in Stedman *Botswana*; 84.
30 *Ibid.*; 86.
31 1995–97 statistics taken from *The world economic factbook 1998/99*, London: Euromonitor; and *Africa south of the Sahara 1998* 27, London: Europa.

Chapter 6: Legitimacy

1   Weber, Max [Edited by Talcott Parsons] (1964) *The theory of social and economic organization*, New York: Free Press; 324–92.
2   Cited in Bayart, Jean-François (1993) *The state in Africa: the politics of the belly*, London: Longman; 188.
3   George Washington's Farewell Address, 1796; and Nyerere, Julius K (1961) *Spearhead*. Reprinted in Sigmund, Paul E., ed., (1963) *The ideologies of the developing nations*, New York: Praeger; 201.
4   Hyden, Goran and Colin Leys (1972) 'Elections and politics in single-party systems: the case of Kenya and Tanzania', *British Journal of Political Science* 2(4), 396.
5   *Ibid.*, 400.
6   Sylvester, Christine (1995) 'Whither opposition in Zimbabwe?', *Journal of Modern African Studies* 33(3), 421.
7   See Weber, *Theory of social and economic organization*.
8   See *ibid.*; 346–54; and Medard, Jean-François, (1982) 'The underdeveloped state in Tropical Africa: political clientelism or neo-patrimonialism', in Christopher Clapham, ed., *Private patronage and public power*, London: Pinter; 178; and also Young, Crawford and Thomas Turner (1985) *The rise and decline of the Zairian state*, Madison: University of Wisconsin Press; 165.
9   Clapham, Christopher (1985) *Third World politics: an introduction*, London: Routledge; 48.
10 Jackson, Robert H. and Carl G. Rosberg (1982) *Personal rule in Black Africa: prince, autocrat, prophet, tyrant*, Berkeley: University of California Press.
11 Weber, Max (1978) *Economy and society*, Berkeley: University of California Press; 1084.
12 Jackson and Rosberg, *Personal rule in Black Africa*; 12.
13 Sandbrook, Richard, with Judith Barker (1985) *The politics of Africa's economic stagnation*, Cambridge: Cambridge University Press; 92.
14 Jackson and Rosberg, *Personal rule in Black Africa*; 18.
15 Bayart, *State in Africa*; 174.
16 Clapham, Christopher, 'Clientelism and the state', in: Clapham, *Private patronage*; 4.
17 *Ibid.*; 31.
18 Legum, Colin, ed. (1973) *Africa contemporary record: annual survey and documents 1972–73*, London: Rex Collings; B628.

19 Fanon, Frantz (1967) *The wretched of the earth*, Harmondsworth: Penguin; 137.
20 Cited in Rondos, Alex (1980) 'The team spirit in Ivory Coast', *West Africa* 3274, 694.
21 See Aristide R. Zolberg, 'Ivory Coast', in James S. Coleman and Carl G. Rosberg, eds (1970) *Political parties and national integration in Tropical Africa*, Berkeley: University of California Press; 83.
22 Zolberg, Aristide R. (1966) *Creating political order: the party-states of West Africa*, Chicago: Rand McNally; 100.
23 Jackson and Rosberg, *Personal rule in Black Africa*; 145.
24 Bakary, Tessilimi (1984) 'Elite transformation and political succession', in I.W. Zartman and C. Delgardo, eds, *Political economy of the Ivory Coast*, New York: Praeger; 24.
25 Cohen, Michael A. (1974) *Urban policy and political conflict in Africa: a study of the Ivory Coast*, Chicago: University of Chicago Press; 89–90.
26 Cohen, Michael A. (1973) 'The myth of the expanding centre: politics in the Ivory Coast', *Journal of Modern African Studies* 11(2), 231–45.
27 Cohen, *Urban policy*; 90–1.
28 1995–97 statistics taken from *The world economic factbook 1998/99*, London: Euromonitor; and *Africa south of the Sahara 1998*, 27, London: Europa.
29 Here I am paraphrasing Scott, J.C. (1977) 'Patron–client politics and political change in Southeast Asia', in S.W. Schmidt, J.C. Scott, C. Lande and L. Guasti, eds, *Friends, followers and factions: a reader in political clientelism*, Berkeley: University of California Press.

Chapter 7: Coercion

1   Weber, Max [Edited by Talcott Parsons] (1964) *The theory of social and economic organization*, New York: Free Press; 324–91.
2   McGowan, Pat and Thomas H. Johnson (1984) 'African military coup d'état and underdevelopment: a quantitative historical analysis', *Journal of Modern African Studies* 22(4), 634.
3   Ball, George W. (1968) *The discipline of power*. Cited in First, Ruth (1970) *The barrel of a gun: political power in Africa and the coup d'état*, London: Allen Lane The Penguin Press; 1.
4   First, *The barrel of a gun*; 4.
5   See Huntington, Samuel P. (1968) *Political order in changing societies*, New Haven: Yale University Press; 192–263; and Clapham, Christopher (1985) *Third world politics: an introduction*, London: Routledge; 140–9.
6   Huntington, *Political order*; and Finer, S.E. (1962) *The man on horseback: the role of the military in politics*, London: Pall Mall.
7   Janowitz, Morris (1977) *Military institutions and coercion in the developing nations*, Chicago: University of Chicago Press.
8   First, *The barrel of a gun*; 17.
9   Finer, *The man on horseback*.
10 Huntington, *Political order*; 196.
11 Janowitz, *Military institutions*; 104.
12 Clapham, *Third world politics*; 143.
13 See, Wiseman, John A. (1996) 'Military rule in the Gambia: an interim assessment', *Third World Quarterly* 17(5), 917–40.
14 Decalo, Samuel (1990) *Coups and army rule in Africa: motivations and constraints*, New Haven, CT: Yale University Press; 18.

15 Amuwo, Kunle (1986) Military-inspired anti-bureaucratic corruption campaigns: an appraisal of Niger's experience', *Journal of Modern African Studies* 24(2), 299.
16 Luckham, R. (1991) 'Militarism: force, class and international conflict', in Richard Little and M. Smith, eds, *Perspectives on world politics*, London: Routledge; 386.
17 Grace, John and John Laffin (1991) *Fontana dictionary of Africa since 1960: events, movements, personalities*, London: Fontana; 363.
18 Brett, E.A. (1995) Neutralising the use of force in Uganda', *Journal of Modern African Studies* 33(1), 135.
19 *Ibid.*; 135–6.
20 *Africa South of the Sahara 1992*, 21, London: Europa, 1991; 1054.
21 *Ibid.*
22 *Africa south of the Sahara 1998*, 27. London: Europa, 1997; 1080.
23 1995–97 statistics taken from *The world economic factbook 1998/99*, London: Euromonitor; and *Africa south of the Sahara 1998*, 27, London: Europa.

Chapter 8: Sovereignty

1 See Hoffman, John (1998) *Sovereignty*, Buckingham: Open University Press.
2 See Clapham, Christopher (1996) *Africa and the international system: the politics of state survival*, Cambridge: Cambridge University Press; 153; and Grey, Robert D. (1984) 'The Soviet presence in Africa: an analysis of goals', *Journal of Modern African Studies* 22(3), 518.
3 Sarris, Louis George (1985) 'Soviet military policy and arms activities in Sub-Saharan Africa', in William J. Foltz and Henry S. Bienen, eds, *Arms and the African: military influences on Africa's international relations*, New Haven, CT: Yale University Press; 35.
4 Gavshon, Arthur (1981) *Crisis in Africa: battleground of East and West*, Harmondsworth: Penguin; 70.
5 See, for example, Thomson, Alex (1996) *Incomplete engagement: US foreign policy towards South Africa*, Aldershot: Avebury.
6 Young, Crawford (1985) 'African relations with the major powers', in Gwendolen M. Carter and Patrick O'Meara, eds, *African independence: the first twenty-five years*, Bloomington: Indiana University Press; 221.
7 Clapham, *Africa and the international system*; 88.
8 See, for example, Golan, Tamar (1981) 'A certain mystery: how can France do everything that it does in Africa – and get away with it?', *African Affairs* 80(318), 3–11.
9 Clapham, *Africa and the international system*; 95; and Martin, Guy (1995) 'Continuity and change in Franco–African relations', *Journal of Modern African Studies* 33(1), 11.
10 Cited in Campbell, Kurt M. (1987) *Southern Africa in Soviet foreign policy* [Adelphi Paper 227], London: International Institute for Strategic Studies; 8.
11 Gavshon, *Crisis in Africa*; 79.
12 Obasanjo, Olusegun (1996) 'A balance sheet of the African region and the Cold War', in Edmond J. Keller and Donald Rothchild, eds, *Africa in the new international order: rethinking state sovereignty and regional security*, Boulder, CO: Lynne Rienner; 16–17.
13 Lefebvre, Jeffery A., 'Moscow's Cold War and Post-Cold War policies in Africa', in Keller and Rothchild, *Africa in the new international order*; 215.
14 United States Department of Commerce, Bureau of the Census (1997) *Statistical abstract of the United States: 1997*, Washington DC: Hoover's Business Press; Table 1302.

15 Olsen, Gorm Rye (1997) 'Western Europe's relations with Africa since the end of the Cold War', *Journal of Modern African Studies* 35(2), 299–319.
16 *Ibid.*; 306.
17 Volman, Daniel (1993) 'Africa and the New World Order', *Journal of Modern African Studies* 31(1), 16.
18 Schraeder, Peter J. (1997) 'France and the great game in Africa', *Current History*, 96(610), 207.
19 Cumming, Gordon (1995) 'French development assistance to Africa: towards a new agenda?', *African Affairs* 94(376), 392.
20 Jackson, Robert H. (1990) *Quasi-states: sovereignty, international relations and the Third World*, Cambridge: Cambridge University Press.
21 This section draws on Christopher Clapham's work *Africa and the international system*.
22 See Hearn, Julie (forthcoming) 'The US democratic experiment in Ghana', in edited collection by Diane Frost, Alex Thomson and Alfred Zack-Williams, London: Pluto.
23 Clapham, *Africa and the international system*; 272.
24 Ottaway, Marina (1982) *Soviet and American influence in the Horn of Africa*, New York: Praeger; 25.
25 Yohannes, Okbazghi (1997) *The United States and the Horn of Africa: an analytical study of pattern and process*, Boulder, CO: Westview; 225.
26 Simons, Anna (1998) 'Somalia: the structure of dissolution', in: Leonardo A. Villalón and Phillip A. Huxtable, eds, *The African state at a critical juncture: between disintegration and reconfiguration*, Boulder, CO: Lynne Rienner; 59.
27 Marina Ottaway, *Soviet and American influence*; 67; and Gavshon, *Crisis in Africa*; 267.
28 Yohannes, *The United States and the Horn of Africa*; 241–2.
29 Marina Ottaway, *Soviet and American influence*; 124.
30 *Ibid.*; 126; and Yohannes, *The United States and the Horn of Africa*; 244.
31 Cited in Volman, *Africa and the New World Order*; 7.
32 Adam, Hussein (1995) 'Somalia', in William I. Zartman, ed. (1995) *Collapsed states: the disintegration and restoration of legitimate authority*, Boulder, CO: Lynne Rienner; 74.
33 Simons, in: Villalón and Huxtable, *African state at a critical juncture*; 70.
34 1995–97 statistics taken from *The world economic factbook 1998/99*, London: Euromonitor; and *Africa south of the Sahara 1998*, 27, London: Europa.

Chapter 9: Sovereignty again

1 World Bank (1997) *World Development Report 1997*, Oxford: Oxford University Press; Table 1.
2 United Nations, Department for Economic and Social Information and Policy Analysis, Statistical Division (1996) *Statistical yearbook 1994*, 41, New York: United Nations; 74–88.
3 Rodney, Walter (1972) *How Europe underdeveloped Africa*, Nairobi: East African Educational Publishers; 239.
4 Nkrumah, Kwame (1965) *Neo-colonialism: the last stage of imperialism*, London: Panaf; ix.
5 Brown, Michael Barratt and Pauline Tiffin (1992) *Short changed: Africa and world trade*, London: Pluto; 100.
6 *Ibid.*; 97–8.
7 United Nations, Conference on Trade and Development (1995) *Handbook of international trade and development statistics, 1994*, New York: United Nations; Table 5.7;

and United Nations, Conference on Trade and Development (1997) *Handbook of international trade and development statistics, 1995*, New York: United Nations; Table 5.7.

8   Haynes, Jeff, Trevor W. Parfitt and Stephen Riley (1987) 'Debt in Sub-Saharan Africa: the local politics of stabilisation', *African Affairs* 86(344), 352; and United Nations, *Handbook of international trade and development statistics, 1994*; Table 2.7.

9   World Bank (1981) *Accelerated development in Sub-Saharan Africa: an agenda for action* (The Berg Report), Washington DC: World Bank; 18.

10 Cheru, Fantu (1989) *The silent revolution in Africa: debt, development and democracy*, Harare: Anvil; 28.

11 The data on Zambia has been drawn from Jones, Stephen (1994) 'Structural adjustment in Zambia', in: Willem van der Geest, ed., *Negotiating structural adjustment in Africa*, London: James Currey.

12 Makgelta, Neva Seidman (1986) 'Theoretical and practical implications of I.M.F. conditionality in Zambia', *Journal of Modern African Studies* 24(3), 396.

13 United Nations, *Handbook of international trade and development statistics, 1995*; Table 5.7.

14 George, Susan (1993) 'Uses and abuses of African debt', in Adebayo Adedeji, ed., *Africa within the world: beyond dispossession and dependence*, London: Zed; 60.

15 Cited in Susan George's foreword to Brown and Tiffin, *Short changed*; xvi.

16 George, in Adedeji, ed., *Africa within the world*; 61.

17 *Ibid.*; 68.

18 World Bank, *Accelerated development* (The Berg Report); 1.

19 *Ibid.*; 27.

20 *Ibid.*; 99.

21 World Bank (1994) *Adjustment in Africa: reforms, results and the road ahead*, New York: Oxford University Press; 3 and 1.

22 United Nations, Economic Commission on Africa (1989) *African alternative framework to structural adjustment programmes for socio-economic recovery and transformation*, Addis Ababa: UNCEA; 9–10.

23 World Bank, *Adjustment in Africa*; 3.

24 Brown, Michael Barratt (1995) *Africa's choices: after thirty years of the World Bank*, London: Penguin; 85.

25 Cited in *Ibid.*; 84.

26 World Bank, *Adjustment in Africa*; 11.

27 Mistry, Percy (1988) *The present role of the World Bank in Africa*. Cited in Brown and Tiffin, *Short changed*; 25.

28 United Nations, *Handbook of international trade and development statistics, 1995*; Table 5.3.

29 World Bank, *Adjustment in Africa*; 2.

30 Simutanyi, Neo (1996) 'The politics of structural adjustment in Zambia', *Third World Quarterly* 17(4), 831–7.

31 Tevera, Dan (1995) 'The medicine that might kill the patient: structural adjustment and urban poverty in Zimbabwe', in David Simon, Wim Van Spengen, Chris Dixon and Anders Närman, eds, *Structurally adjusted Africa*, London: Pluto; 79–90.

32 Jones, Stephen, 'Structural adjustment in Zambia', in Geest, *Negotiating structural adjustment*; 46.

33 World Bank, *Adjustment in Africa*; 14.

34 Stevens, Siaka (1985) 'The people will decide', *West Africa* 3523, 404.

35 World Bank, *Adjustment in Africa*; 12

36 See Price, Robert (1984) 'Neo-colonialism and Ghana's economic decline: a critical assessment', *Canadian Journal of African Studies* 18(1), 163–93.

37 *Africa South of the Sahara 1997*, 26, London: Europa, 1996; 449.

38 Gyimah-Boadi, E. (1995) 'Ghana: adjustment, state rehabilitation and democratisation', in Thandika Mkandawire and Adebayo Olukoshi, eds, *Between liberalisation and oppression: the politics of structural adjustment in Africa*, Dakar: CODESRIA; 218.
39 Jerry Rawlings's radio broadcast of 31 January 1981. Quoted in Nugent, Paul (1995) *Big men, small boys and politics in Ghana*, London: Pinter; 15.
40 PNDC policy statement. Quoted in Ahiakpor, James C.W. (1985) 'The success and failure of dependency theory: the experience of Ghana', *International Organisation* 39(3), 542.
41 Ahiakpor, 'The success and failure of dependency theory'; 546.
42 *Africa south of the Sahara 1997*, 26, London: Europa, 1996; 451.
43 *Ibid.*; 449.
44 Eshun, Isaac (1984) 'Investment priorities', *West Africa* 3485, 1155.
45 Gyimah-Boadi, in Mkandawire and Olukoshi, *Between liberalisation and oppression*; 220.
46 *Ibid.*
47 *Ibid.*; 223.
48 Nugent, *Big men, small boys*; 268.
49 1995–97 statistics taken from *The world economic factbook 1998/99*, London: Euromonitor; and *Africa south of the Sahara 1998*, 27, London: Europa.

Chapter 10: Authority

1   World Bank (1997) *World development report 1997*, New York: Oxford University Press; Table 1.
2   Ayittey, George B.N. (1993) *Africa betrayed*, New York: St. Martin's Press; 2–3.
3   Chabal, Patrick (1992) *Power in Africa: an essay in political interpretation*, Basingstoke: Macmillan; 150.
4   Decalo, Samuel (1990) *Coups and army rule in Africa: motivations and constraints*, New Haven: Yale University Press; 49–50.
5   Sandbrook, Richard, with Judith Barker (1985) *The politics of Africa's economic stagnation*, Cambridge: Cambridge University Press; 124.
6   Weber, Max [Gerth, H.H. and C. Wright Mills, eds], (1948) *From Max Weber: essays in sociology*, London: Routledge and Kegan Paul; 197.
7   Kpundeh, Sahr John (1995) *Politics and corruption in Africa: a case study of Sierra Leone*, Lanham, MD: University Press of America; 44.
8   Chabal, Patrick and Jean-Pascal Daloz (1999) *Africa works: disorder as political instrument*, Oxford: James Currey; 99.
9   Sandbrook, *The politics of Africa's economic stagnation*; 126–7.
10 Ayittey, *Africa betrayed*; 245.
11 Cited in *Ibid.*; 306.
12 Monga, Célestin (1998) *The anthropology of anger: civil society and democracy in Africa*, Boulder, CO: Lynne Rienner; 6.
13 Cited in *Ibid.*; 6–7.
14 Chazan, Naomi (1994) 'Engaging the state: associational life in Sub-Saharan Africa', in Joel S. Migdal, Atul Kohli and Vivienne Shue, eds, *State power and social forces: domination and transformation in the Third World*, Cambridge: Cambridge University Press; 269.
15 Rothchild, Donald and Letitia Lawson (1994) 'The interactions between state and civil society in Africa: from deadlock to new routines', in John W. Harbeson, Donald Rothchild and Naomi Chazan, eds, *Civil society and the state in Africa*, Boulder, CO: Lynne Rienner; 270.

16 Luling, Virginia (1997) 'Come back Somalia? Questioning a collapsed state', *Third World Quarterly* 18(2), 288.
17 Cited in Lofchie, Michael F. (1989) *The policy factor: agricultural performance in Kenya and Tanzania*, Boulder, CO: Lynne Rienner; 113.
18 Azarya, Victor and Naomi Chazan (1987) 'Disengagement from the state in Africa: reflections on the experience of Ghana and Guinea', *Comparative Studies in Society and History* 19(1), 121. The situation was the same elsewhere: in 1985, more than half of Senegal's groundnut harvest was smuggled over borders, while US$60 million worth of goods escaped formal state scrutiny when they passed from Nigeria to Benin in the same year.
19 Birmingham, David (1998) 'Images and themes in the nineties', in David Birmingham and Phillis M. Martin, eds, *History of Central Africa: the contemporary years*, London: Longman; 270.
20 See Clapham, Christopher, ed. (1998) *African guerrillas*, Oxford: James Currey.
21 Simons, Anna (1998) 'Somalia: the structure of dissolution', in Leonardo A. Villalón and Phillip A. Huxtable, eds, *The African state at a critical juncture: between disintegration and reconfiguration*, Boulder: Lynne Rienner; 70.
22 Azarya and Chazan, 'Disengagement from the state in Africa'; 130.
23 Forrest, Joshua Bernard (1998) 'State inversion and nonstate politics', in Villalón and Huxtable, *The African state at a critical juncture*; 45.
24 Bayart, Jean-François, Stephen Ellis and Béatrice Hibou (1999) *The criminalization of the state in Africa*, Oxford: James Currey; 48.
25 Reno, William (1998) *Warlord politics and African states*, Boulder: Lynne Rienner.
26 Reno, William (1997) 'Privatizing war in Sierra Leone', *Current History* 96(610), 230.
27 Chazan, Naomi (1988) 'State and society in Africa: images and challenges', in Donald Rothchild and Naomi Chazan, eds, *The precarious balance: state and society in Africa*, Boulder, CO: Westview; 337.
28 Fatton, Robert (1992) *Predatory rule: state and civil society in Africa*, Boulder: Lynne Rienner; 80.
29 Simpson, Chris (1990) 'Africa's absolutist', *West Africa* 3793, 752.
30 Young, Crawford and Thomas Turner (1985) *The rise and decline of the Zairian state*, Madison: University of Wisconsin Press; 296–9.
31 *Ibid.*; 300 and 305.
32 Clark, John F. (1998) 'Zaire: the bankruptcy of the extractive state', in Villalón and Huxtable, *The African state at a critical juncture*; 118.
33 Ayittey, *Africa betrayed*; 253 and 152.
34 Clark, in Villalón and Huxtable, *The African state at a critical juncture*; 119.
35 Cited in Young and Turner, *Rise and decline of the Zairian state*; 73.
36 Cited in Askin, Steve (1990) 'Zaire's den of thieves', *New Internationalist* 208, 18.
37 MacGaffey, Janet (1991) 'Issues and methods in the study of African economics', in Janet MacGaffey, ed., *The real economy of Zaire: the contribution of smuggling and other unofficial activities to national wealth*, London: James Currey; 7.
38 *Ibid.*; 11.
39 *Ibid.*; 18.
40 Reno, *Warlord politics*; 153.
41 Mukohya, Vwakyanakazi (1991) 'Import and export in the second economy in north Kivu', in MacGaffey, *The real economy of Zaire*; 57.
42 Reno, *Warlord politics*; 153–4.
43 *Ibid.*; 156.
44 Nkera, Rukarangira Wa and Brooke Grundfest Schoepf (1991) 'Unrecorded trade in Southeast Shaba', in MacGaffey, *The real economy of Zaire*; 82–3.

45 1995–97 statistics taken from *The world economic factbook 1998/99*, London: Euromonitor; and *Africa south of the Sahara 1998*, 27, London: Europa.

Chapter 11: Democracy

1   Thabo Mbeki's address to the Corporate Council on Africa, April 1997, Chantilly, Virginia, USA.
2   Hyden, Goran and Michael Bratton, eds (1992) *Governance and politics in Africa*, Boulder, CO: Lynne Rienner; ix.
3   Abraham Lincoln's Gettysburg Address, 1863.
4   See Kweka, A.N. (1995) 'One party democracy and the multi-party state', in Colin Legum and Geoffrey Mmari, eds, *Mwalimu: the influence of Nyerere*, London: James Currey; 74.
5   Fatton, Robert (1992) *Predatory rule: state and civil society in Africa*, Boulder, CO: Lynne Rienner; 107.
6   See Sandbrook, Richard (1993) *The politics of Africa's economic recovery*, Cambridge: Cambridge University Press; 88.
7   Bratton, Michael and Nicolas van de Walle (1997) *Democratic experiments in Africa: regime transitions in comparative perspective*, Cambridge: Cambridge University Press; 182.
8   Cited in Wiseman, John A. (1996) *The new struggle for democracy in Africa*, Aldershot: Avebury; 70.
9   Cited in Toulabor, Comi (1995) '"Paristroika" and the one-party system', in Anthony Kirk-Greene and Daniel Bach, eds, *State and society in Francophone Africa since independence*, Basingstoke: Macmillan; 115.
10 Fatton, *Predatory rule*; 107.
11 Bratton and van de Walle, *Democratic experiments in Africa* 105.
12 Wiseman, *New struggle for democracy*; 38–40.
13 *Ibid.*; 46.
14 *Ibid.*; 44–5.
15 Clapham, Christopher (1993) 'Democratisation in Africa: obstacles and prospects'. *Third World Quarterly* 14(3), 425.
16 Sandbrook, *Politics of Africa's economic recovery*; 91. Original emphasis.
17 Laakso, Liisa (1996) 'The relationship between state and civil society in the Zimbabwean elections of 1995', *Journal of Commonwealth and Comparative Politics* 34(3), 218.
18 Buijtenhuijs, Robert (1998) 'Chad in the age of the warlords', in David Birmingham and Phillis M. Martin, eds, *History of Central Africa: the contemporary years*, London: Longman; 36.
19 Wiseman, *New struggle for democracy*; 107.
20 *Ibid.*; 111.
21 Bratton and van de Walle, *Democratic experiments in Africa*; 200.
22 Beckman, Björn (1989) 'Whose democracy? Bourgeois versus popular democracy', *Review of African Political Economy* 45/46, 84.
23 Gitonga, Afrifa K. (1988) 'The meaning and foundations of democracy', in Walter O. Oyugi, E.S. Atieno Odhiambo, Michael Chege and Afrifa K. Gitonga, eds, *Democratic theory and practice in Africa*, Portsmouth, NH: Heinemann; 19.
24 Bratton and van de Walle, *Democratic experiments in Africa*; 204.
25 McGreal, Chris (1999) 'Tourist deaths cap a loss', The *Guardian*, 6 March, 4.
26 *Ibid.*

27 Ake, Claude (1993) 'The unique case of African democracy', *International Affairs* 69(2), 243.
28 Glickman, Harvey (with Peter Furia) (1995) 'Issues in the analysis of ethnic conflict and the democratization processes in Africa today', in Harvey Glickman, ed., *Ethnic conflict and democratization in Africa*, Atlanta: African Studies Association Press; 4.
29 Fatton, *Predatory rule*; 110.
30 Molutsi, Patrick P. and John D. Holm (1990) 'Developing democracy when civil society is weak: the case of Botswana', *African Affairs* 89(356), 330.
31 Huntington, Samuel P. (1991) *The third wave: democratization in the late twentieth century*, Norman: University of Oklahoma Press; 267.
32 Clapham, 'Democratisation in Africa'; 434 and 435.
33 Grace, John and John Laffin (1991) *Dictionary of Africa since 1960: events, movements, personalities*, London: Fontana; 13.
34 Stone, Martin (1997) *The agony of Algeria*, London: Hurst; 64.
35 Layachi, Azzedine (1995) 'Algeria: reinstating the state or instating a civil society?', in William I. Zartman, ed., *Collapsed states: the disintegration and restoration of legitimate authority*, Boulder, CO: Lynne Rienner; 182.
36 *Ibid.*; 174.
37 *Ibid.*; 181 and 176.
38 Stone, *Agony of Algeria*, 65.
39 *Ibid.*; 178.
40 Tahi, Mohand Salah (1995) 'Algeria's democratisation process: a frustrated hope', *Third World Quarterly* 16(2), 211.
41 De Gier, Jaqueline (1999) 'Algerians drift to polls in one-man elections', *Guardian* (London), 16 April, 14.
42 1995–97 statistics taken from *The world economic factbook 1998/99*. London: Euromonitor; and *Africa south of the Sahara 1998*, 27, London: Europa.

Chapter 12: Conclusions

1 Callaghy, Thomas M. (1986) 'Politics and vision in Africa: the interplay of equality and liberty', in Patrick Chabal, ed., *Political domination in Africa*, Cambridge: Cambridge University Press; 36.

Index

Abiola, Moshood 70
accumulation, crisis of 190–4, 197, 199, 203, 219, 231
AFDL (Alliance des Forces Démocratiques pour la Liberation du Congo-Zaire) 199, 212
AFRC (Armed Forces Ruling Council) 70
Africa: diversity 2–3; map (at the outbreak of First World War) 11; obstacles that needed to be overcome after independence 20; pre-colonial inheritance 7–9; western views of and preconceptions 1–2
Africa Contemporary Record 115
African National Congress *see* ANC
African socialism *see* socialism, African
agriculture: decline in crop yields 191; and SAPs 173–5
aid 148; decline of at end of Cold War 151, 155, 245; from France 147; from United States 146; political conditions tied to external 152–3, 155–6, 220–1, 245; and structural adjustment programmes *see* SAPs
Aidid, General Mohammed Farrah 161–2
AIS (*Armée Islamique du Salut*) 237
Ake, Claude 227
Alagiah, George 1–2
Algeria 10, 18, 228, 232–9; crisis of accumulation and governance 234–5; democratisation process 236–7; demonstrations and rioting against Chadli's government 233–4, 235–6; economy 234–5; elections (1997) 238–9; and France 153, 232–3; growth of Islamist groups 234; independence 31, 233; military coup (1965) 233; military coup (1992) 126–7, 237; multi-party elections (1990–1) 236–7;

re-legitimisation strategy by military regime 238; second civil war 237–8; war of independence with France 31, 233
Alliance for Democracy (Malawi) 224
Alliance des Forces Démocratiques pour a Liberation du Congo-Zaire *see* AFDL
Alliance pour la Democratic au Mali 224
Amin, Colonel Idi 106, 110; military coup and regime of 106, 135, 136–7; removal of 45, 137–8
Amuwo, Kunle 132
ANC (African National Congress of South Africa) 144, 151, 219
Anderson, Benedict 33
Angola 10, 38, 142, 155, 198; and Cabinda 12; clashes between UNITA and MPLA 151, 199; and Cuba 145, 151; independence 31, 199; multi-party elections (1992) 230; and Soviet Union 143, 144, 150, 151
Arab League 158
Arab states 148
Armed Forces Ruling Council (AFRC) 70
Armée Islamique du Salut (AIS) 237
arms: selling of by Soviet Union to Africa 144–5; shipments of during Cold War to Africa 149
Arusha Declaration (1967) 50–1
Ashanti 8, 101
'Asian Tigers' 19, 171
Aswan High Dam 144
authoritarianism: as characteristic of personal rule 108
Azarya, Victor and Chazan, Naomi 201

Babangida, Major-General Ibrahim 70
Bakary, Tessilimi 116
Balkans 57

Ball, George 123
Banda, President Hastings 35, 109, 220, 221, 224
banditry 198
Bantu 21–2
Barré, President Mohamed Siad 38, 159, 160, 200; deposing of 152, 161; military coup led by 157–8
Bates, Robert 61, 66
Bayart, Jean-François 90, 91, 202, 211
BDP (Botswana Democratic Party) 93, 96
Bechuanaland 94
Belgian Congo 10, 81, 207
Ben Bella, Ahmed 233, 237
Benin 8, 38, 123, 230
Berg Report (1981) 175, 176
Berlin Conference (1884–5) 9–10
Biafra 68
Biya, Paul 153
black market *see* parallel markets
Bokassa, Emperor Jean-Bédel 106, 109, 110, 129, 148
Bongo, President Omar 220
Botchway, Kwesi 184
Botswana 3, 92–6, 215; achievements 92; economic growth 92; inequality in 95–6; political stability 92; ruling elite 92–3, 94–5; and Seretse Khama 93–4; view of public on multi-party democracy 229–30
Botswana Democratic Party *see* BDP
Boumédienne, Colonel Houari 233, 234, 235, 237
boundaries, colonial 46, 243; acceptance of by most African states 46, 47; creation of and consequences of 11–13, 19t, 20, 34; endurance of 44; illegal flow of people and goods across 197–8; and Kenya 23; OAU's agreement on (1964) 44–5, 46, 157
bourgeoisie 75, 76, 88–9t, 90; bureaucratic 83–5, 88t 90–1, 104, 133; commercial 82–3, 86, 88t, 91; international 86–7, 89t
Bourguiba 109
Bouteflika, Abdelaziz 239
Bratton and van de Walle 220
breakthrough coups 126, 131, 132
Britain 142; colonisation of Africa 10; and decolonisation 31, 32t; relations with Africa 146–7; and Somalia 156
British Aerospace 193
British East Africa Company 133–4
Buganda 8, 133–4, 135, 136

Buhari, Major-General Muhammadu 70
bureaucratic bourgeoisie 83–5, 88t, 90–1, 104, 133; in Botswana 93, 95
Burkina Faso 13, 41, 123
Burundi 13
Bush, President George 150, 161

Cabinda 12
Cabral, Amílcar 47–8
Cameroon 10, 42; and bureaucratic bourgeoisie 84; French aid to 153; and Fulbe 60–1
Cape Town 9
Cape Verde 123
capitalism 16, 36, 42, 44t, 77, 78
Caprivi, Count von 12
Carter, President Jimmy 159
Central African Republic 106, 109; and France 148; military coup (1979) 129
centralised state 100–7, 199, 243–4; banning of opposition 101, 194, 195; and civil society–state relationship 112–13; ending of 113; features 100–1; and Ghana 101–2, 181; and one-party state 102–4, 243; subordination of 'peripheral' state institutions to the core executive 104, 105–7
Ceuta 31
CFA (Communauté Financiére Africaine) franc 147, 152
Chabal, Patrick and Daloz, Jean-Pascal 193
Chad 152; collapse of state 199; conflict with Libya over Aouzou Strip 45; and France 148, 153; opposition movements 223
Chadli Benjedid, President 233–4, 235, 236, 237
charisma 111
Chazan, Naomi 196, 204
chiefs 14–15, 61, 85
Chiluba, Frederick 222, 226
China: relations with Africa 145; and Somalia 157, 158
Chiona, Archbishop James 221–2
Christianity: spread of 9
churches 232; force within anti-authoritarian campaign 221–2
CIA (Central Intelligence Agency) 129
civil society 4–5; definition 4; increase in self-sufficiency 196–7; need for a strong as a prerequisite for consolidation of democracy 224–5; rejuvenation of 221–2

civil society–state relationship 14, 203–5,
242–6; and centralised state 112–13;
and democracy 231–2; and external
influences 154–6, 179–81; and
historical inheritance 20–1; impact of
ideology on 44–8; and social class 91–2
Clapham, Christopher 108, 111, 128, 147,
156, 223
class, social 74–98, 225; Botswana case
study 92–6; Marx on 74–6, 78, 79, 86;
and modes of production 77–9, 83, 89;
problems with Marx's interpretation of
in Africa 76–7; and relationship
between state and civil society 91–2;
social groups within society 79–89;
value of analysis of in explaining
African politics 89–91
clientelism 107, 111–12, 113, 121, 133,
178, 192, 193, 194, 244–5
coercion 111, 113, 121–39, 189
Cold War 144, 147; decline of aid at end
of 151, 155, 245; effect of end of
150–1, 189; impact of on African
politics 143, 145, 149–50; strategic
downgrading of Africa at end of 151–2
colonialism 2, 7, 9–20, 189, 246;
advantages of 18; and bureaucratic
authoritarianism 20, 21, 26; creation of
elites 14–15, 19t, 84; and economy
15–19, 76, 168, 243; and emergence of
tribes 60–1; establishment of European
rule 9–10; formation of states 10;
impact 10; imposition of arbitrary
boundaries 11–13, 19t, 20, 34; and
nationalism 34–5; rule through
domination and coercion 13–14, 20;
underdevelopment during 16–18, 19,
24; and weak political institutions 19t,
20; weakness of links between state and
society 13–14, 19t; *see also*
decolonisation
commercial bourgeoisie 82–3, 85, 86, 88t,
91
Communist Manifesto (Marx and Engels)
74
communist powers 143–5
Comoros Islands 31
comprador class 87, 89t, 94
Congo crisis (1960) 146
Congo-Brazzaville 192
Congo-Kinshasa 3, 46, 82, 205–6 *see also*
DRC; Zaire
Convention People's Party (Ghana) *see*
CPP

corruption 2, 84, 104, 133, 193
Côte d'Ivoire 18, 42, 63, 114–18, 125,
153, 170; centralised state and personal
rule 102, 114–18; economic growth
114; election (1990) 224;
independence 114; judiciary 115–16;
return to multi-party system 117–18
coups *see* military coups
CPP (Convention People's Party) 101–2
Crigler, T. Frank 161
crime 198
Cuba: relations with Africa 145, 151

de Gaulle, Charles 122–3, 147
DeBeers 94
debt crisis 167, 171–3, 176, 179
decolonisation 31–3, 106, 243
democracy 215–40; abandoning of
pluralism after independence 100, 217,
243; Algerian case study 232–9; and
civil society–state relationship 231–2;
development of in 1990s 215; meaning
and features 216–17; and multi-party
elections *see* multi-party elections;
need for credible opposition 223–4;
obstacles to consolidation of 222–31;
reasons for emergence of multi-party
218–22; representative 217; strides
towards multi-party 230; transitions
231t
Democratic Republic of the Congo *see*
DRC
Denise, Auguste 117
dependency theorists 86–7, 94
disengagement: from the state 196–8, 219,
225, 242, 245
Djibouti 31
Doe, Samuel 152
DRC (Democratic Republic of the Congo)
12, 46, 47, 85, 142–3, 205
Dumont 84

Economic Community of West African
States (ECOWAS) 142
economy 127, 165; burdens of the
international 168–71; colonial
inheritance 15–19, 76, 168, 243; crisis
of accumulation 190–4, 197, 199, 203,
219, 231; debt crisis 167, 170–3, 176,
179; GNP 165, 166–7t; impact of SAPs
175–7; lack of growth after
independence 15–16; need for strong as
prerequisite for consolidation of

democracy 225–6; poverty and reasons for 165, 167, 190; underdevelopment of during colonial rule 16–18, 19, 24
Egypt 8, 144
Eisenhower, Dwight 122–3
elites, state 38, 44, 79–80, 244; and ethnic groups 62; formation of under colonialism 14–15, 19t, 84; and international recognition 155; links between 90–1; and nationalism 64–5; and SAPs 180–1; survival strategies 200–3
Eluki, General 207
emigration: disengagement through 196
Engels, Friedrich 74
entrepreneurs, informal sector 85–6, 88t, 89
EPLF (Eritrean People's Liberation Front) 45, 199
Equatorial Guinea 106, 123, 227
Eritrea 10; border clash with Ethiopia 47; secession from Ethiopia 44, 46
Eritrean People's Liberation Front *see* EPLF
Ethiopia 3, 132, 143; border clash with Eritrea 47; and Christianity 9; deposition of Selassie 38; Eritrea's secession from 44, 46; escapes colonisation 10; and feudalism 77–8; and Marxist-Leninist regime 39; military coup (1974) 126; and Soviet Union 144, 150, 157, 158, 159, 160; war with Somalia 13, 45, 158–9, 160
Ethiopian People's Revolutionary Democratic Front 199
ethnicity 57–72, 110, 242; agent of political mobilisation 59, 62–4; and creation of colonial boundaries 13; creation of 'tribes' 58–62; definition 58; Kenya case study 65–71; and multi-party democracy 227–8; and state and civil society 64–5
European Union (EU) 57, 142, 152
Executive Outcomes (EO) 203
exit strategies *see* disengagement
external influences 5, 141–64; and civil society–state relationship 154–6, 179–81; communist powers 143–5; impact of Cold War on African politics 143, 145, 149–50; and New World Order 150–4; western powers 145–8; *see also* international relations

famine: Sudan (1988) 2

Fanon, Frantz 115
Fatton, Robert 204, 229
FAZA (Zairian air force) 211
feudalism 77–8
FFS (*Front des Forces Socialistes*) 236, 237, 238
Finer, S.E. 127
First, Ruth 127
FIS (*Front Islamique de Salut*) 153, 236, 237, 238
FLN (*Front Libération Nationale*) 233, 235, 236, 237, 238
food riots 179, 221
food subsidies: removal of state 177, 179
foreign exchange: illegal sale of 198
foreign investment 42, 176
Forrest, Joshua 201
FPI (*Front Populaire Ivoirien*) 224
France: and Algeria 31, 153, 232–3; and colonisation of Africa 10; and decolonisation 31, 32t; relations with Africa 129, 146, 147–8, 152, 153–4
Franco-African summit (1982) 147
French Foreign Legion 148
Front des Forces Socialistes (Algeria) *see* FFS
Front Islamique du Salut (Algeria) *see* FIS
Front Libération Nationale (Algeria) *see* FLN
Front Populaire Ivoirien see FPI
Fulani-Hausa 67, 68
Fulbe 60–1

Gabon 42, 129, 148
Gaddafi, Colonel Muammar 41
Gambia 2, 12, 155, 215; military coup (1994) 125, 129, 228–9
Gbagbo, Laurent 224
George, Susan 172
Germany 10, 34, 226
Ghana 8, 82, 127, 143, 155, 181–6; cocoa production 17, 171, 181, 182, 185; debt crisis 185; defence spending 131–2; demilitarisation of 132; economic decline and reasons for 181–4; formation 181; independence 31; military coups 123, 181; and Peoples' Defence Committees (PDCs) 41; Rawlings regime 41, 183–4; and SAP 184–6; smuggling of cocoa crop out of 197–8; and state centralisation 101–2, 181
GIA (*Groupes Islamique Armées*) 237
Gitonga, Afrifa 226

Glickman, Harvey 228
GNP (Gross National Product) 165, 166–7t
governance, crisis of 194–5, 199, 203, 219, 231
Great Lakes region 46
Groupes Islamique Armées (GIA) 237
guardian coups 126, 128, 131, 132
guerrilla movements 195–6, 198–9
Guinea: independence 31; and one-party state 102; selling of coffee in parallel markets 198; and Soviet Union 143, 144
Guinea-Bissau 10, 18, 31, 47–8

Habré, Hissène 152
Hausa-Fulani 66
health: improvement under colonialism 18
hegemonial exchange model 62–4, 70, 99
Hobbes, Thomas 107, 128
Hobsbawm, Eric 196
Horowitz, Donald 45
Houphouët-Boigny, Félix 63, 102, 109, 114–15, 116–18, 147, 152, 224
Huntington, Samuel 127, 128, 230
Hurd, Douglas 152
Hutus 59
Hyden, Goran 52, 53
Hyden, Goran and Leys, Colin 105

Ibo 66, 67, 68
IFIs *see* international financial institutions
illiteracy 165, 166–7t
IMF (International Monetary Fund) 40, 168, 173
imperialism *see* colonialism
import substitution 191
industrialisation 82
infant mortality 18, 165
Inga-Shaba power scheme 206
institutions: weak inheritance from colonial rule 20, 243
insurgency campaigns 198–9, 245
interest rates, rise in 172
international bourgeoisie 86–7, 89t
international financial institutions (IFIs) 40, 42, 54, 86, 148, 168, 220, *see also* IMF; World Bank
International Labour Organisation 95
International Monetary Fund *see* IMF
international relations 5, 220, 245; China 145; Cuba 145, 151; inter-African 142–3; Somalian case study 156–62;

Soviet Union 143–5; United States 145–6, 154; and the West 145–8
inverted states 201, 245
irredentism 13, 20, 45
Islam, spread of 9
Italy 10; formation of 34; and Somalia 23, 156, 157, 160

Jackson, Robert 155
Jackson, Robert and Rosberg, Carl 108, 109, 110, 116
Janowitz, Morris 127, 128
Jawara, President Dawda 129
Jaycox, Edward 176
Jowitt, Kenneth 39–40
judiciary 106–7

Kabaka Yekka movement 134
Kabaka, the 134, 135, 136
Kabanga, Archbishop 207
Kabila, Laurent Désiré 212, 229
Kaiser, Paul 52
KANU (Kenya African National Union) 26, 105, 217
Kariuki, J.M. 105–6
Karl-i-Bond, Nguza 229
Katanga 46, 205
Kaunda, Kenneth 36, 109, 215, 222, 224, 226, 227
Keita, President Modibo 129
Kenya 10, 21–7, 42, 63, 125, 146; aid and suspension of 152–3, 220; British rule 22–3; colonial boundaries 23; constitution 25; divided opposition 224; economy 24; general election (1969) 105; historical inheritance 21–7; independence 25; industry 24; and Kariuki's death 106; Mau Mau uprisings 24–5; migrations into 21–2; as one-party state 26, 105, 106; parliament 105; pre-colonial 22; relationship with Somalia 23–4, 45; SAP reforms 173; state intervention in economy 192
Kenya African National Union *see* KANU
Kenya People's Union 26
Kenyatta, President Jomo 25, 26, 63, 106, 109
Kérékou, Lieutenant-Colonel Mathieu 38
Khama III 93
Khama, President Seretse 93–4
Kikuyu 24, 25
Kinshasa 210

kinship 8
Kirdi 60–1
Kisangani 82
Kofele-Kale, Ndiva 84
Kolingba, President André 220–1

Laakso, Liisa 223
labour 81; exploitation of by West 16–17, 19; organised 82
Lamb, David 18
language 35–6
Layachi, Azzedine 234
leaders 108–10; traditional 85, 89t
League of Nations 10
Lefebvre, Jeffery 151
legal-rational states 99–100, 106, 107, 108, 109, 111, 121, 194
legitimacy 99–119, 121, 199; and centralisation of the state *see* centralised state; and clientelism 107, 111–12, 113, 121, 133, 178, 192, 193, 194, 244–5; Côte d'Ivoire case study 114–18; decline and crisis of 64, 189, 190–5, 231, 245; definition 99; and legal-rational authority 99–100; and military regimes 130–1; and neo-patrimonialisation 100; and personal rule 100, 107–10; re-legitimisation of state 200–1; search for 110–11; sources of 99–100
Léopold of Belgium, King 10, 12
Lesotho 2–3, 13, 155
Leys, Colin 80
liberal democracy 30, 229; abandoning of after independence 100, 217, 243
Liberia 10, 152, 203
Libya 10, 142; conflict with Chad over Aouzou Strip 45; independence 31; populist regime 41
life expectancy 18, 165, 166–7t
Lincoln, Abraham 217
lineage 8–9, 34, 59, 78
Lissouba, President Pascal 227
local government 106
Lomé Convention 152
Luling, Virginia 197
Lumumba, Patrice 146

Masai 22
Machel, President Samora 35, 39
Machiavelli 107
Madagascar 38, 153, 230

Majetein Somali Salvation Democratic Front 161
Malawi 35, 42, 220, 224, 234; economy 168; force of church within 221–2; and SAP 173
Mali 8, 143, 153, 224; coup (1966) 129
Mandela, Nelson 85, 215, 222
Marcel Dassault Preguet 193
Marx, Karl 50, 83; on feudalism 77–8; problems with using class analysis in Africa 76–7; on social class 74–6, 78, 79, 86
Marxism-Leninism 38–9, 40
Mau Mau uprisings 24–5
Mauritania 165
Mauritius 125, 173, 215, 230
M'ba, Léon 129, 148
Mbeki, President Thabo 215
Mboya, Tom 76–7
Melilla 31
Mengistu, Colonel Haile Mariam 39, 46, 132, 150, 159
middle classes 225
military 128; threat of to consolidation of democracy 228–9
military coups 2, 38, 40, 90, 104, 110, 113, 122–9, 131, 136, 244, 245; categories 126; and civil society–state relationship 133, 138; and counter-coups 130; definition 123; list of since independence 124–5t; number of in Africa (1952–1990) 123; pattern of 123; reasons for 125–9; Uganda case study 133–8
military regimes 40; outcomes of 131–3; problems facing rulers 129–31
missionaries 9, 67
Mistry, Percy 176
Mitterrand, François 152
MMD (Movement for Multi-Party Democracy) 222, 224, 226–7
Mobutu Sese Seko, President Joseph Désiré 85, 109, 146, 229; corruption 207; and 'creative accountancy' 193; death 212; downfall and ousting of 152, 154, 199, 211–12; fostering of international relations 146, 149; regime of 110, 205–12
Moi, Daniel arap 109, 224; donor pressure to institute reforms 153, 220; and (1997) election campaign 227; purchasing of jet fighters 193; regime of 26–7, 106
Montesquieu 107

Morocco 10, 42, 44; independence 31; occupation of Western Sahara 45; relations with United States 146
Mouvement de la Société pour la Paix (Algeria) 238
Movement for Multi-Party Democracy (Zambia) *see* MMD
Mozambique 10, 35, 38, 80, 143, 199; GNP 165; independence 31; introduction of forced labour during colonial era 81; and Soviet Union 144
MPLA 150, 151, 155, 199, 230
Mugabe, President Robert 109, 193, 223
multi-party elections 21, 200–1, 204–5, 218, 245–6; ignoring of results 230; increase in number 215, 222–3; manipulation at 226; and state accountability 100; table of 247–54
multi-party system: comparison between (1988) and (1999) 215, 216t; reasons for not adopting 102–3; return to 104, 113; and the West 217
Munslow, Barry 40
Museveni, Yoweri 41, 138, 199, 200

Nahnah, Mafoud 238
Namibia 12, 31
Nasser, General Abdel 144
nation: definition 33
National Party (South Africa) 219
National Party of Nigeria (NPN) 69
National Resistance Army (Uganda) *see* NRA
nationalism, African 15, 33–6; and African socialism 36–8; challenging of imperial rule 34–5; characteristics and examples table 43; definition and features 33–4; domination of 30, 35, 36; internal conflict caused by 44, 48; objectives of national unity and economic development 35–6, 37–8; origins 34; and populism 40–1; and scientific socialism 38–40; and separatism 45–6; and state capitalism 42, 44t; and state elites 64–5
neo-colonialism 5, 167, 168
neo-patrimonialisation 100, 194
New World Order 150–5, 161, 245
Ngeuema, Macías 106, 110
Ngouabi, Marien 38
Niger 13, 222
Nigeria 42, 46, 65–71, 202, 228; Babangida regime 70; civil war 68, 69; corruption in Rural Electricity Board

193; demilitarisation of government 132; development of 'tribes' 66–7; economic problems 69–70; ethnic groups 65–6; ethno-regional constitution 67–8; execution of Saro-Wiwa 101; military coups 68, 69, 70, 123,126; military rule 68–9; population 2
Nkrumah, President Kwame 101, 102, 127, 168, 181
NPN (National Party of Nigeria) 69
NRA (National Resistance Army) 138, 199
Nyerere, President Julius 36, 77, 102, 103, 149, 218; and nationalism 35; and *ujamaa* 49–50, 51, 53, 54

OAU (Organisation of African Unity) 142, 147; agreement on boundaries 44–5, 46, 157
Obasanjo, President Olusegun 69, 71, 150, 228
Obote, President Milton 64, 134–5, 136
oil: fall in price 235; impact of increase in prices 171–2
Okoya, Brigadier 136
one-party state 101, 105, 111, 215, 217, 243; and centralised state 102–4, 243; failure of 104, 218; justifications for 102–4; in (1988) and (1999) 216t; problems with 104
OPEC (Organisation of Petroleum Exporting Countries) 172, 235
Operation Turquoise 154
Opolot, Shaban 135
opposition parties 101, 227; need for credible for consolidation of democracy 223–4
Organisation of African Unity *see* OAU
Organisation of Petroleum Exporting Countries *see* OPEC
Ossowski, Stanislaw 83

parallel markets 197–8, 202, 204
parastatals (public corporations) 178, 180, 192
parliaments: loss of power to executives 105–6
Parson, Jack 96
Parti Démocratique de la Côte d'Ivoire see PDCI
patrimonialism 107–8
patron–client relationship *see* clientelism

patronage 100, 108, 110, 111, 112, 116, 178, 192, 199, 244–5; in Côte d'Ivoire 116–17; diminishing of with SAPs 180; foreign 220; tapping into foreign 201–2; *see also* clientelism

PDCI (*Parti Démocratique de la Côte d'Ivoire*) 114–15, 116, 117

peasantry 38, 80–2, 86, 88t, 94, 232

Peoples' Defence Committees (PDCs) 41

personal rule 100, 107–10, 112, 113, 127, 132, 133, 244; in Côte d'Ivoire 114–18

pluralism 47, 219, 225, 228, 230

PNDC (Provisional National Defence Council) 183, 184, 186

political culture 229–30

political parties 223–4

political systems: table of comparative 216

population 2–3

populism 40–1, 44t

Portugal: colonisation of Africa 9, 10; and decolonisation of Africa 31

Poulantzas, Nicos 83

poverty 190, 246; reasons for 165, 167; and SAPs 177

privatisation 180

Programme of Action to Mitigate the Social Costs of Adjustment (PAMSCAD) 186

proletariat 75, 76, 82, 88t

Provisional National Defence Council (Ghana) *see* PNDC

proxy wars 149; ending of 150–1

Prunier, Gérard 59

public policy: and ethnicity 63–4

public sector 192, 193

Putnam, Robert D. 30

'quasi-states' 155

Rawlings, Flight-Lieutenant Jerry 41, 181, 183–4, 186

religion 9

Reno, William 202, 203

representative democracy 217

Ressemblement National Démocratique (RND) 238

Rhodesia 146 *see also* Zimbabwe

riots, urban 195–6

Robinson, Pearl 41

Rodney, Walter 168

Rothchild, Donald 62, 63, 69

ruling class 75, 83–4

Rural Electricity Board of Nigeria 193

Russia: organised crime 202

Rwanda 13; economy 168; genocide 46–7, 59, 154, 212

Rwandan Patriotic Front (RPF) 154, 199

Salisbury, Lord 12

Sandbrook, Richard 110, 192, 223

Sankara, Captain Thomas 41

SAPs (Structural Adjustment Programmes) 40, 173–5, 220, 221, 245; and agriculture 173–4; conditions for lending 173–5; economic impact 175–7; political impact 178–9; and poverty 177; primary goal 174–5; social impact 177; and state elite 180–1

Saro-Wiwa, Ken 101

Scandinavian countries 148

scientific socialism 38–40, 43t

'Scramble for Africa' 9–10

second economy *see* parallel markets

Selassie, Emperor Haile 38, 126, 144, 159

Senegal 215

Senghor, President Léopold 36, 37, 77, 103

Seychelles 31

shadow economy *see* parallel markets

Shagari, President Alhaji 69

Shanin, Teodor 80

Sierra Leone 178, 203

Simpson, Chris 205

Sklar, Richard 83

slave trade 16

Smith, Ian 31, 146

smuggling 197, 204

social class *see* class, social

socialism 143; Marx on 75–6; scientific 38–40, 43t

socialism, African 36–8, 38–9, 47, 50

Somali National Movement 161

Somali Patriotic Movement 161

Somali Revolutionary Socialist Party 158

Somali Salvation Democratic Front 161

Somali Youth League 156

Somalia 10, 144, 152, 156–62, 180, 197, 200; Barré's regime 158; and China 157, 158; civil war 161; and decolonisation 157; foreign aid 157; joins Arab League 158; military coup 157–8; pursual of irredentism 45, 142; refusal to agree to OAU principle of inviolable boundaries 44, 45; relationship with Kenya 23–4, 45; relationship with Soviet Union 144, 150, 157, 159, 160; relationship with

United States 154, 157, 159–60, 160–2; and scientific socialism 38; and United Nations 161–2; war with Ethiopia 13, 45, 158–9, 160
Somaliland 23
Somalis 156; in Kenya 23, 24; scattering of by imperial partition 13, 23, 45
South Africa 3, 10, 82–3, 94; and Angola 142; and apartheid 45, 146; elections (1994) 215; and majority rule 31, 151, 215; and proletariat 82
Southall, Aidan 59
Southern African Development Community (SADC) 142
sovereignty 141–2, 154–5, 167–8
Soviet Union 36, 38, 39, 40; collapse of 150, 220; relations with Africa 143–5; and Somali–Ethiopia dispute 158, 159; and Somalia 144, 150, 157, 158, 159, 160; supply of arms to Africa 144–5, 149; and United States 143
state(s): and African socialism 37; centralisation *see* centralised state; and crisis in legitimacy 64, 189, 190–5, 231, 245; definition 4; civil society's disengagement from 196–8, 219, 225, 242, 245; evolvement of in pre-colonial times 8; formation of as a result of colonialism 10; inversion of 201, 245; loss of authority and collapse 189, 195–200, 219–20, 245; need for separation from ruling party as prerequisite for consolidation of democracy 226–7; one-party *see* one-party state; paradox of African 244; relationship with civil society *see* civil society–state relationship; relationship with ethnicity 62–4; road to collapse 199–200; survival strategies 200–3, 231; warlord 202–3, 219, 245; *see also* elites, state
state marketing boards 191
Stevens, President Siaka 178
Stone, Martin 235–6
street traders 86
Structural Adjustment Programmes *see* SAPs
SucDen 170
Sudan 199; bombing of chemical weapons factory by United States 154; famine (1998) 2; independence 31
SWAPO 144
Swaziland 13, 85

Syndicat des Chefs Coutumiers (Côte d'Ivoire) 115

Tanganyika 35, 44, 48, 146 *see also* Tanzania
TANU 217–18
Tanzania 48–54, 103, 125, 197; and Arusha Declaration 50–1; desire to build national unity and foster economic development 48–9; economy 54; ethnic groups within 13, 48; invasion of Uganda (1979) 45, 137, 142; and multi-party competition 218; and one-party state 102; rural development and 'villagisation' programme 51–4; and SAP 54, 173; socialism and *ujamaa* 49–54
TAZARA railway 145
TNCs (transnational corporations) 94, 95, 176, 185, 203, 210
Togo: suspension of French development aid 152
Touré, Ahmed Sékou 36, 77, 102, 144, 224
trade 18, 169, 170t; and SAPs 174
trade unions 222, 232
traditional leaders 85, 89t
transnational corporations *see* TNCs
tribalism 35, 47, 58, 59, 62
tribes 58–62; conflict between 58–9; development of in Nigeria 66–7; emergence during colonial era and reasons for 60–1; increase in importance 59; as instrumental social constructions 61
'tribute', notion of 78
Tshisekedi, Etienne 229
Tunisia 31
Tutsis 59, 212
Tutu, Archbishop Desmond 221
Twain, Mark 200

Uganda 41, 133–8, 146, 200; Amin's rule 106, 136–7, 138; and Buganda 134, 135, 136; centralisation programme under Obote 134–5, 136; collapse of state 199; formation of 134; guerrilla movements in 199; invasion of by Tanzania (1979) 45, 137, 142; military coup (1971) 133–8; military coup (1985) 138; second economy *see* parallel markets

Uganda National Congress 15
Uganda People's Congress *see* UPC
ujamaa 49–53
underdevelopment 16–18, 19, 24, 165,
   167, 168, 243
unemployment 179
UNICEF 173
Union des Syndicats des Travailleurs du Niger
   see USTN
UNIP (Zambia) 222, 226
UNITA (Angola) 150, 151, 199, 230
United Nations 141, 170; Economic
   Commission on Africa 175; and
   Somalia 161–2
United Somali Congress 161
United States 31, 220; aid to Africa 146,
   155; arms shipments to Africa during
   Cold War 149; decline in interest in
   Africa 151–2; and ethnicity 57, 58;
   relations with Africa 145–6, 154; and
   Somalia 154, 157, 159–60, 160–2; and
   Soviet Union 143
UPC (Uganda People's Congress) 134,
   138
USSR *see* Soviet Union
USTN (*Union des Syndicats des Travailleurs
   du Niger*) 222

veto coup 126
Victoria, Queen 23

warlord states 202–3, 219, 245
Warren, Bill 18
Washington, George 103
Weber, Max 4, 79, 83, 99, 107, 109, 111,
   121, 192–3
West: relations with Africa 145–8
Western Sahara 45, 148
Western Somali Liberation Front 159
Wilhelm II, Kaiser 23

Wiseman, John 223
Worker's Banner (Ghana) 41
Workers' Party of Ethiopia 39
World Bank 40, 168, 173, 177; Berg
   Report (1981) 174, 176; (1994) report
   175, 180; (1995) report on SAPs 176

Young, Crawford 14, 42, 60
Yoruba 66–7, 68

Zaire 180, 205–12, 229; agriculture 206–7,
   209; and Angola 142; collapse of state
   211–12; corruption 207; crisis of
   accumulation 206, 209; crisis of
   governance 208; disengagement from
   state by citizens 208–9; and FAZA 211;
   and France 148, 154; Mobutu's rule *see*
   Mobutu Sese Seko; natural resources
   205; relations with United States 146;
   survival strategies of state elite 209–11;
   suspension of French development aid
   152; as warlord state 203; *see also*
   Congo-Kinshasa; DRC
Zairian air force *see* FAZA
Zambia 224, 234; copper extraction 17;
   debt crisis 172; manipulation of
   electoral rules 226–7; and organised
   labour 82; removal of maize subsidy
   177; and SAP 173; and trade unions
   222; unemployment 177
Zambian Congress of Trade Unions
   (ZCTU) 222
ZANU-PF (Zimbabwe) 223
Zanzibar 44, 48; *see also* Tanzania
ZAPU (Zimbabwe) 144
Zéroual, President Liamine 238–9
Zimbabwe (was Rhodesia) 18, 80, 82–3,
   215; election (1995) 223; halving of
   budget deficit 177; independence 31
Zolberg, Aristide 36